THE RELATIONSHIP ADVANTAGE

The Relationship Advantage

Information Technologies, Sourcing, and Management

THOMAS KERN

and

LESLIE P. WILLCOCKS

OXFORD

UNIVERSITY PRESS

OXFORD

UNIVERSITY PRESS

Great Clarendon Street, Oxford OX2 6DP

Oxford University Press is a department of the University of Oxford.
It furthers the University's objective of excellence in research, scholarship,
and education by publishing worldwide in

Oxford New York

Athens Auckland Bangkok Bogotá Buenos Aires Cape Town
Chennai Dar es Salaam Delhi Florence Hong Kong Istanbul Karachi
Kolkata Kuala Lumpur Madrid Melbourne Mexico City Mumbai Nairobi
Paris São Paulo Shanghai Singapore Taipei Tokyo Toronto Warsaw

with associated companies in Berlin Ibadan

Oxford is a registered trade mark of Oxford University Press
in the UK and in certain other countries

Published in the United States
by Oxford University Press Inc., New York

© T. Kern and L. Willcocks, 2001

The moral rights of the authors have been asserted
Database right Oxford University Press (maker)

First published 2001

British Library Cataloguing in Publication Data
Data available

Library of Congress Cataloging in Publication Data
Data available

ISBN 0–19–924192–9

1 3 5 7 9 10 8 6 4 2

Typeset by Florence Production Ltd., Stoodleigh, Devon
Printed in Great Britain
on acid-free paper by
Biddles Ltd., *www.biddles.co.uk*

Acknowledgements

In the course of writing this book many people contributed directly and indirectly, and it is here that we take the opportunity to heartily thank all of them for their kind help, insights, suggestions, and comments.

A special thank you goes to all the interviewees who so kindly spared their time, and shared their views and experience with us over an often extended period. In particular, we thank all the interviewees from Xerox, Inland Revenue, ESSO/EXXON, British Aerospace, British Petroleum, ITNet, EDS, CSC, SEMA, BT Syncordia, SAIC, and other information technology service providers, who so kindly participated in the research and in many ways shaped this book. Thanks also to the many students and practitioners over the years who patiently listened to our presentations and ideas and invariably offered us further insights.

Crucial to undertaking such a long-term study is of course the financial support, and in this matter we wish to express our sincere gratitude to the Trustees, Mrs Linda Harper (Assistant Secretary), Mr Michael Parry (Secretary), and Sir Peter Miller (Chairman of the Board) of the Lloyd's of London Tercentenary Foundation in the UK.

We would also like to thank our many colleagues at Templeton College, Oxford, Christchurch Oxford, and at Erasmus Universiteit Rotterdam for their support, good humour, and understanding. A special thanks to Clara Finkelman for the stimulating work environment. Finally, the most testing part of undertaking the research and writing the manuscript has been on family and loved ones. The value of their emotional strength, patience, and help over several years has been immense, and it is to them that we dedicate this book.

T.K.
L.P.W.

Contents

List of Figures

List of Tables

About the Authors

THOMAS KERN is assistant professor for information management at the Rotterdam School of Management, Erasmus University Rotterdam. He has an international reputation for his work on Information Systems Outsourcing, Application Service Provision, Relationship Management, and Electronic Commerce. He is also a research affiliate with the Oxford Institute of Information Management at Templeton College, University of Oxford, and the European Editor of the Journal of Information Technology.

He received his M.Sc. (Econ.) from the London School of Economics and Political Science in 1995 and his D.Phil. in Management Information Systems from the Said Business School, University of Oxford in 1999. He was the 1996–1998 Lloyds of London Tercentenary Foundation Business Scholar. Beforehand, he was partner and director of InSync Limited, Strategic Management Consultancy in the UK. He has consulted and advised numerous international companies such as IBM, EXXON, CMG, Xerox, KPN, WorldSpace Corp., and BP Amoco. He is currently Executive Director of KERN AG in Germany.

His track record of publications spans numerous book chapters, conference papers at European and International Conference on Information Systems, Academy of Management Conference, International Marketing and Purchasing Conference, International Strategic Partnering Conference, and numerous journal articles in the *European Journal of Information Systems, European Journal of Management, Journal of Information Systems, Journal of Global Information Management, Journal of Strategic Information Systems, Journal of Information Technology*, and *Journal of Management Information Systems*.

LESLIE P. WILLCOCKS has an international reputation for his work on Information Management, IT evaluation, and Information Systems Outsourcing. He is Andersen Professor of Information Management and E-Business at Warwick Business School, UK. He is also Associate Fellow at Templeton College, Oxford, Visiting Professor in Information Systems at Erasmus University Rotterdam, Professorial Associate at the University of Melbourne, and Distinguished Visitor at the Australian Graduate School of Management. He holds a doctorate in information systems from the University of Cambridge, and has been for the last twelve years Editor-in-Chief of the *Journal of Information Technology*.

He worked for twelve years in accounting and management consultancy, for Touche Ross and several smaller firms, before heading a Research Centre at City University Business School, London. He moved to Oxford University in 1992 where he was until 2001 Fellow and University Reader at Templeton

College. He is co-author of nineteen books, including *Global IT Outsourcing: In Search of Business Advantage* (Wiley, 2000), *Moving to E-Business* (Random House, 2000), *Building the E-Business Infrastructure* (Business Intelligence, 2001), *Managing IT as a Strategic Resource* (McGraw Hill, 1997*)*, *Strategic Sourcing of Information Systems* (Wiley, 1998), *A Business Guide to IT Outsourcing* (Business Intelligence, 1994), and *Beyond the IT Productivity Paradox* (Wiley, 1999). He has published over 130 papers in journals such as *Harvard Business Review, Sloan Management Review, MIS Quarterly, Journal of Management Studies, Communications of the ACM*, and *Journal of Strategic Information Systems*.

He is a regular keynote speaker at international practitioner and academic conferences, has extensive consulting experience, and is regularly retained as adviser by major corporations and government institutions. Recent clients have included Transco, Thames Water, IBM, Lend Lease Corporation, ANZ Bank, NatWest Bank, Royal Sun Alliance, Norwich Union, Ericsson, WH Smith, Eli Lilley, RailTrack, and several government institutions in the UK and Australia. In 1998 he served as expert witness on information management issues to the US Congressional Committee on Restructuring the Internal Revenue Service.

He is also chief adviser to an LA-based high-tech service provider Mainpass Technologies.

1

The IT Outsourcing Phenomenon: Trends, Practices, Challenges

INTRODUCTION

Following intensive research on the subject throughout the 1990s, a great deal is now known about Information Technology (IT) outsourcing, here defined as the handing over to a third party of the management and operation of an organization's IT assets and activities. It is not the only way of using the market for external IT services. For example, buying in resources to run under in-house management control—sometimes called insourcing—is also widely practised. An organization may also choose to give suppliers long-term, preferred choice status, or buy IT services more competitively, typically involving more short-term relationships. In this chapter, we seek to summarize this growing understanding of reasons for success and disappointment, and of how best to use the IT outsourcing market. We draw upon our own work, as well as that of colleagues, practitioners, and a range of other researchers. However, it will become clear that two areas in particular—risk mitigation and the relationship dimension—have received all too little attention, and these will be the primary focus of the second chapter, as well as of the rest of the book.

In this chapter, we draw primarily upon several sources. The first is a case history research database held at Oxford Institute of Information Management of over 250 organizations assembled and studied across the 1990–2001 period. We also draw upon three European and US IT outsourcing surveys carried out in 1994, 1997, and 2000 (Currie and Willcocks 1998a; Lacity and Willcocks 2000a; Willcocks and Fitzgerald 1994); and additional case work carried out as part of separate research projects (Currie and Willcocks 1998b; Kern 1999; Kern and Blois 2000; Kern, Willcocks, and van Heck 2000; Kern and Willcocks 2000a; Lacity and Willcocks 1996, 1998, 2000b; Willcocks and Currie 1997; Willcocks and Kern 1998; Willcocks, Lacity and Kern 2000). This ongoing research base, built as it is on assessment of successes and failures, enables us to pinpoint the circumstances in which different IT sourcing practices can be effective, or can contribute to disappointed expectations. In this chapter we first provide an overview of the research findings on past, current, and emerging IT outsourcing practices. We then focus in detail on proven practices across the life-cycle of a typical IT outsourcing arrangement. Using illustrative case material and survey findings we investigate how effective IT sourcing decisions can be made using decision matrices that pinpoint the key business, economic, market capability, and technical factors. Next, the processes of assessing vendor bids and then arriving at a suitable contract and system of measurement are considered. Finally, we detail the key in-house capabilities needed to make any IT outsourcing arrangement work. The chapter acts as a sounding board for the more detailed investigation into practices in the case studies in Chapters 3 through to 7.

TOWARDS A GLOBAL PHENOMENON

In the early 1990s, many company boards and government departments world-wide increasingly asked: 'Why not outsource IT?' Much of this was a questioning of escalating IT costs and a reaction to increased competitive and recessionary pressures. Vendors were seen as being able to provide the same or superior service cheaper, offer access to technical expertise in short supply, change fixed to variable costs, and/or through headcount reduction and purchase of IT assets, improve the financial position of a client organization. IT outsourcing has also been portrayed as an opportunity to apply a core-periphery model to managing and organizing. On this argument, an organization should focus on its key tasks and capabilities, and outsource the rest to world-class providers. On this analysis, all IT is sometimes mistakenly characterized as an undifferentiated, albeit occasionally 'strategic', commodity that can largely be outsourced.

A further reason for outsourcing IT is all too familiar. Faced with rising IT costs and little demonstrable business value, senior managers have often given up on the internal IT function, and contracted out to third party management some or most IT assets and activities. Finally, we are finding in most recent work that speed and access to scarce IT skills are becoming much more important influences on IT sourcing decisions generally, and not just for e-business activities (Lacity and Willcocks 2000*a*; Seddon, Rouse, et al. 2000). By 2001 how has all this turned out? What practices have actually been adopted, and with what results? Are there proven sound practices in IT outsourcing, and what are the future prospects globally?

IT outsourcing has outlived the five-year period typical of a management fad. Global market revenues have grown from $US 9 billion in 1990 to a projected $US 121 billion by year 2001, and $150 billion by 2004. The underlying compound annual growth rate has been 15–20 per cent in the 1992–2000 period, with the leading markets of USA and UK showing sometimes dramatic rises in a particular year when a number of mega-deals have been signed. Another leading market is Australia which has shown rapid growth—$AUS 2.2 billion in 1998, and an IDC estimated $AUS 3.87 billion in 2002 with a 24 per cent annual growth rate from 1997 to 2002. Regionally, other predictions of annual growth for the 1997–2002 period are: Japan 6 per cent, Asia Pacific 16 per cent, Latin America 20 per cent, Canada 14 per cent, Western Europe 9 per cent, USA 10 per cent and rest of the world 26 per cent. As we shall see, this buoyancy is likely to be maintained by further developments in areas such as e-commerce, applications service provision, business process outsourcing, managed network services, and supply chain management.

From an initial main focus on cost reduction, IT outsourcing is fast moving to becoming a complementary or alternative, routine mode of managing IT. On our own estimates, on average 30–5 per cent of most large organizations' IT budget will be managed by outsourcing arrangements by 2003 (Lacity and Willcocks 2000*a*). The question 'why not outsource IT?' is no longer, if it ever was, an adequate base from which to make and manage outsourcing decisions. The real question now has to be: 'How do we exploit the ever maturing external IT services market to achieve significant business leverage?'

The high profile mega-deals, for example those at Xerox, McDonnell Douglas, and Continental Bank in the USA, Commmonwealth Bank, Lend Lease Corporation, and South Australia government in Australia, and British Aerospace, British Petroleum, and Inland Revenue in the UK, are often referred to as 'strategic alliances' or 'strategic partnerships'. One could be forgiven for believing this type of total outsourcing to be the dominant trend, but globally, this is the reverse of the case. In fact a rich picture emerges of organizations taking one of three main paths to IT sourcing (see Figure 1.1).

Our 2000 survey (Lacity and Willcocks 2000*a*) found that by far the dominant mode is selective sourcing, especially in the USA (82 per cent of organizations) and UK (75 per cent). A mixed portfolio, 'best-source' approach typically sees 15–25 per cent of the IT budget under third party management,

	In-house Commitment	*Selective Sourcing*	*Total Outsourcing*	*Total Outsourcing*
ATTITUDE	Core Strategic Asset	Mixed Portfolio	Non-Core Necessary Cost	World Class Provision
PROVIDERS	IT Employees Loyal To The Business	Horses for Courses	Vendor	'Strategic Partner'
EMPHASIS	'Value Focus'	'Value For Money'	'Money'	'Added Value?'
DANGERS	High Cost Insular Unresponsive	Management Overhead	Exploitation By Suppliers	Unbalanced Risk/Reward/ Innovation

Fig. 1.1. *IT sourcing: main approaches*

with other IT needs met through buying in resources under in-house management (insourcing), and through internal IT staffing. Many organizations (USA
10 per cent, UK 23 per cent) have no significant IT outsourcing contracts. Here
IT is perceived as a core strategic asset, with IT employees loyal to the business
and striving to achieve business value in a way in which external providers are
deemed not to be able to do (Willcocks, Feeny and Islei 1997). Total outsourcing (80 per cent or more of the IT budget under third party management of a
single or multiple supplier(s)) is a distinctly minority pursuit. In the USA some
8 per cent of organizations take this route, in the UK about 2 per cent; worldwide we found there are just over 140 such deals.

Figure 1.1 shows that all arrangements have inherent risks. A mainly in-
house function needs to be continually assessed against the market if it is not
to grow unresponsive and cost-inefficient. One common underestimated factor
is the management overhead cost of IT outsourcing. From reviewing more than
250 case histories we estimate that this is falling typically between 4 and 8 per
cent of total outsourcing costs, even before the effectiveness of the consequent
management arrangements is assessed.

We have found that total outsourcing deals focusing primarily on cost reduction can achieve these, but often at the expense of IT operational service, and
business strategic inflexibilities. Alternatively, incomplete contracts, or negligible profit margins through over-tight contracts, can, and have, promoted
hidden costs or opportunistic vendor behaviour. Finally 'strategic partnerships'
are often high risk. Many have experienced significant restructuring of the deal
18 months to 24 months in. Contracts are often found to need more detail, and
more service performance measures. Sometimes the innovation expected from
the vendor is not forthcoming. In others, the risk-reward element is too marginal to the overall deal to affect behaviours, and a more traditional fee-for-
service arrangement becomes the basis of practice on the ground. These issues
will be investigated in more detail in the total outsourcing deals analysed in
Chapters 3, 4, and 7.

THE TRACK RECORD: COMPLEX

Too much of the discussion of the IT outsourcing track record is based on the
opinions of interested parties, often arrived at before the ink on contracts is
dry, or on research conducted without rigorous outcome metrics against which
to assess the efficacy of IT sourcing arrangements. Here we present two sources
of evidence, that consider actual practices adopted against outcomes.

First, our 1999/2000 survey of USA and Europe (see Lacity and Willcocks
2000*a*) found 56 per cent of organizations rating supplier performance as 'good'
or better. Many respondents were realizing benefits, primarily some mix of cost
reduction (52%), refocusing of in-house IT staff (45%), improved IT flexibility
(42%), access to scarce IT resources (42%), better quality service (41%) and

improved use of IT resource (39%). The majority of respondents characterized problems/issues as 'minor', but some customers were having severe/difficult problems in some areas. Some qualifications are necessary, however. It is important to recognize that these results are positively conditioned by three characteristics of respondent practice: the vast majority pursue the *selective IT outsourcing* option; most use *multiple suppliers*, most have *short-term contracts* (four years or less in length) and respondents generally targeted *infrastructure activities*, mainly mainframe operations, PC support, helpdesk, network management, mid-range operations, disaster recovery. The *least* commonly outsourced IT activities involved IT management and applications—in particular IT strategy, procurement, systems architecture, project management. An example of this overall approach to outsourcing is provided by the ESSO case in Chapter 6.

The 79 per cent of organizations using multiple suppliers pointed to several main advantages—the use of 'best of breed' providers, risk mediation, and vendor motivation through competition. They also pointed to higher transaction costs, and hidden post-contract management overhead in terms of time, effort, and expense. In parallel research we have found much 'disguised' multi-supplier outsourcing in the form of subcontracting. In some large-scale contracts we have found up to 30–5 per cent of the work actually subcontracted to other suppliers, especially in the areas of technical consulting, desktop hardware and installation, network specialists and software specialists (Lacity and Willcocks 2000*b*).

There was evidence of lack of contract completeness, with only 30 per cent of respondents including all ten major clauses cited by us as vital to any outsourcing contract (Kern and Willcocks 2000*b*). There was a noticeable negative gap between anticipated and actual benefits. In most cases organizations were getting benefits but invariably less than they had expected. Only 16 per cent reported significant cost reduction, while another 37 per cent reported 'some' cost reduction. Other main benefits, each reported by between 33 per cent and 44 per cent of respondents, included: refocus in-house IT staff, improved IT flexibility, better quality service, improved use of IT resource, and access to scarce IT skills.

More worryingly, a number of organizations encountered 'severe/difficult' problems in six areas as a consequence of outsourcing IT. These were:

- *Strategic*—supplier does not understand our business (37%); corporate strategy and IT no longer aligned (35%); poor strategic IT planning (24%)
- *Cost*—costs for additional services (38%); cost escalation due to loopholes (31%); cost monitoring/control (27%)
- *Managerial*—poor supplier staffing (43%); managerial skills shortage (28%); in-house staff resistance (26%)
- *Operational*—defining service levels (41%); lack of supplier responsiveness (38%); getting suppliers to work together (35%)

- *Contractual/Legal*—too loose (41%), contract monitoring (41%), inadequate SLAs (35%)
- *Technical*—suppliers' IT skills shortage (33%); outsourcing led to systems duplication (20%); failure to upgrade IT (17%).

These outcomes provide a fairly detailed 'worry list' and pre-emptive agenda for action for any senior managers contemplating IT outsourcing.

The second source of evidence is provided by Lacity and Willcocks (2000*b*). Here we established the outcomes from 116 IT sourcing case histories across the 1991–2000 period. The metrics used were: organizational objectives against results, cost reductions achieved against anticipated, and satisfaction levels established by the organization by for example user satisfaction questionnaires, level of disputes, invoking of penalty clauses. The results are shown in Table 1.1.

Selective IT outsourcing emerges as the most effective practice, closely followed by the in-house route. Underlining the survey results above, we found successful selective outsourcers embracing several distinctive practices. They had more limited and realistic expectations, signed short (2–4 year) contracts for which the business and technical requirements remained relatively stable, kept in-house resource and knowledge to fall back on resulting in less power asymmetry developing in favour of the vendor and lower potential switching costs, often leveraged competition through using multiple suppliers, and found ways in the contract to give the supplier an incentive and to build in flexibility.

The track record of total in-house IT sourcing has improved from that before 1996 (Lacity and Willcocks 1998). At that time, one-third were found to be unsuccessful due to an amalgam of in-house complacency, little sense of crisis,

Table 1.1. *IT Sourcing Decisions and Outcomes 1991–2000*

DECISION	Success	Failure	Mixed	Unable to determine/ too early to tell	TOTAL
Total outsourcing	11 (38%)	10 (35%)	8 (27%)	4	33
Total in-house sourcing	13 (76%)	4 (24%)	0 (0%)	2	19
Selective outsourcing	43 (77%)	11 (20%)	2 (3%)	8	64
TOTAL	67	25	10	14	116

Source: Lacity and Willcocks 2000*b*

lack of external benchmarking, and lack of threat from an external vendor outsourcing bid. The evidence suggests that in-house functions have been actively responding to market-place developments in the last three years, and have been seeking to improve IT management, replicate vendor practices in-house, compete with potential vendor bids, and benchmark performance against market developments.

Total outsourcing emerges as a distinctly high-risk practice, a reason why, on our evidence, most organizations have not been going down that route. As Table 1.1 shows, we have looked at outcomes from 29 of the 120 plus biggest IT outsourcing deals in the world, and they show a 35 per cent failure rate. It should be said that this is a significantly better result than we were getting from a number of early 1990s total outsourcing deals. Those unsuccessful deals shared certain characteristics. Virtually all sought primarily cost reduction. The organizations were in financial trouble, and saw total IT outsourcing as a financial package to improve their company's position, rather than as a way of leveraging IT for business value, and keeping control of their IT destiny (see also Strassmann 1997). All were 10–12 year single supplier deals, initiated by the company board with little IT management input. The unsuccessful client organizations saw IT as an undifferentiated commodity, contracted incompletely and failed to keep enough requisite in-house management capability. They incurred significant hidden costs, degradation of service, power asymmetries developing in favour of vendors, and loss of control over their IT destiny. They did little to build and sustain client–vendor relationships, yet were reluctant to change vendor because of the high switching costs.

Most of the failing total outsourcing deals shown in Table 1.1 were still following this pattern. The interesting group is that with 'mixed' results. Typically these are experiencing some success in one part of the deal, but little in other major parts. Thus one aerospace company signed a $US 3 billion long-term contract, received a cash influx of $US 300 million, and transferred 1,500 IT employees to the vendor. The infrastructure part of the contract was well managed, but some other sections had to be cancelled after the first year. Subsequently, the vendor was found to lack idiosyncratic business knowledge needed for designing and running engineering-based systems. Serious service and cost issues continued to plague parts of vendor performance.

Success in total IT outsourcing has taken a variety of routes. On the evidence, it requires a lot of management maturity and experience of IT outsourcing, as exemplified by BP Exploration in the early 1990s (see Chapter 5). It needs complete and creative contracting; a less long-term focus in the contracting arrangements, but a more long-term one in the relationship dimension, and very active and fully staffed post-contract management along the lines suggested by Feeny and Willcocks (1998). Among the successes shown in Table 1.1, several were total outsourcing, long-term deals for IT infrastructure/mainframe operations. One involved a strategic alliance, where the company spun off its entire IT function in a shared risk reward and joint ownership venture with a software and services supplier. One involved a short-term contract to wind down a public sector agency about to be privatized. Several went down the multiple supplier 5–7 year contract route, while several were single supplier deals that took on board the above prescriptions, had detailed contracts and were also high profile, with the vendors wary of adverse publicity in specific countries or markets. These issues will be explored in depth in Chapters 3, 4, and 7 of this book.

EMERGING PRACTICES AND PROSPECTS

From 1996, we have seen some organizations responding to the growing experience base and the undoubted risks inherent in IT outsourcing by focusing more on certain practices or adopting new ones. Some preliminary judgements can be passed on the efficacy of eight practices we will highlight in the following, and which look set to continue. The three most effective emerging practices have been:

Transitional outsourcing—outsourcing legacy systems to enable in-house focus on building the new IT world. Thus in 1996 NASDAQ stock exchange outsourced legacy systems to Tate Consulting Services, while the in-house IT staff continued to develop client/server systems.

Smarter contracting—some companies include a customer-written contract with the Request for Proposal, for example Elf Alochem who signed a four-year, $US 4.3 million contract with Keane for accounting systems management. ICI did something similar in eventually signing a five-year contract with Origin in the UK. Others have built in competitive bidding for services beyond the contract, though competition does not always protect the customer from sitting suppliers who are reluctant to support contracts with other vendors. Various flexible pricing mechanisms are being adopted successfully, to alter prices within one contract. Other practices include negotiating shares in their suppliers' savings, adopting 'open book' accounting on suppliers' costs, using third party benchmarks and market rates to test supplier prices annually, or seeking the best prices in line with what suppliers offer to their most favoured customers. We shall see examples of several of these practices in the case chapters of this book.

Offshore outsourcing—taking advantage of programming and software development expertise and lower prices emerging in countries such as India, Ireland, Israel, Malaysia, and Mexico. Thus Sainsbury, the UK retailer, budgeted £30 million to deal with the year 2000 problem, with the work being done entirely in India via satellite link. Subsequently, Sainsbury was so satisfied with the results that it has expanded the work outsourced in this way. There is evidence that the cost advantage is eroding for some types of work, and control is always an issue. As we found in a case study of Holiday Inns, distance needs detailed contracts and clear definitions of responsibilities and IT requirements (Kumar and Willcocks 1999). One response has been 'nearshore outsourcing'. Thus, with its proximity to the USA and with potentially fewer control, cost and time-zone problems, Mexico can compete successfully against a country like India, the market leader.

Five other practices have been growing, some are successful in some respects, but all raise questions:

Value-added outsourcing—combining client and vendor strengths in order to market IT products and services. As one example, Mutual Life Insurance of New York and CSC planned to market software and services to the insurance industry. To be successful, the partners must truly add value by offering products/services demanded by customers in the market. Too often the added value service part of the contract is marginal to the major client–vendor focus. It is also rendered less attractive when participants discover that it requires up to nine times the initial development cost to transform a home-grown application into a commercial one. The issue is pursued in the EDS-Xerox case in Chapter 3.

Equity holdings—taking ownership in each other's companies. Examples include the 1996 Perot Systems–Swiss Bank deal (25 per cent share in Perot posited, while Perot took shares in software company Systor AG—owned by the bank), Lend Lease (35% holding in ISSC), Commonwealth Bank (35% stake in EDS Australia) and Telstra (26% stake in joint venture with IBM). However, it is not clear that the incentive of joint ownership is strong enough to influence behaviour at the operational level, and there are instances of suppliers becoming complacent on service to the partner, while focusing attention and resources on pursuing new contracts elsewhere. With their investment in the supplier, the customer's Board is also likely to support such expansion, but could face dilemmas in doing so. Interestingly, Swiss Bank (now UBS) signalled the end of the 'strategic alliance' with Perot in January 2000 when it bought back Perot's 40 per cent stake in Systor. UBS remained Perot's biggest customer, accounting for more than 25 per cent of its revenues, but the focus was only to be on the management of legacy and computer operations (see also Chapter 2).

'*Co-sourcing*'—performance-based contracts by which the vendor seeks to achieve and get rewarded on improving the client's business performance, not just delivering on its IT goals. Such deals work well, when the supplier core capabilities are contractually structured to complement customer needs. However, despite claims, not all vendors have the necessary business know-how in what is a client's rather than the vendor's core business. Moreover, many suppliers are not really geared up to deliver this type of arrangement, as opposed to fee-for-service contracts. We have also witnessed problems experienced in delivering improved business performance. There are many factors that influence business performance and suppliers do not always have overall control of these. This can be frustrating when the supplier has taken the risk of being paid mainly out of business improvements, has put in the necessary effort, but, because of other parties, is not making the standard, and thus does not get rewarded appropriately.

Multiple suppliers—this approach pursues the logic of hiring the 'best-of-breed' supplier for specific IT activities. Thus in 1993, British Petroleum Exploration (BPX) arranged five-year contracts with SEMA, Syncordia, and SAIC (see Chapter 5). In 1996 JP Morgan signed a seven-year $US 2.1 billion contract with four major suppliers. With this approach the risks of going with a single supplier are mitigated, but there are problems and costs in managing and organizing suppliers. As we shall see in Chapter 5, from 1998, BPX gave up on getting suppliers to manage each other and has moved back to a more traditional, direct relationship with each supplier. Chapter 6 also focuses in detail on the issues inherent in managing multiple suppliers.

Spin-offs—creating a separate company out of an effective IT function. In practice companies like Mellon Bank, Sears Roebuck, and Boeing have had limited success with their spin-off companies. They need a core IT competence to attract external customers. Too often the empowered IT function has too few marketing and customer service skills, is too dependent on the former company for business, and has difficulties in getting new business, without a strong track record in an increasingly competitive IT services market place. Two success stories are Origin and EDS. Origin was formed originally from Dutch software house BSO and NV Philips software and development staff. In the early 1990s Philips also transferred its communications and processing staff to form Origin, which has developed into a competitive IT services company. EDS was initially sold to General Motors in 1984, but, following a buyout, became its own company in 1996. Clearly EDS has been able to attract many external customers, being now amongst the largest IT services providers worldwide.

By 2001 six other developments have been taking off, though it is too early to make a full judgement about their likely impact and levels of success:

Application service providers. Firms such as Oracle, SAP, Microsoft and others are offering remotely hosted software spanning the complete enterprise, while Compaq, for example, offers to install and run a firm's new systems. By mid-2000 some 400 firms fitted the ASP definition—provision of 'pay-as-you-use' access to centrally managed applications distributed over the Internet and other networks. The market size has been predicted by Gartner and IDC to rise from $US150 million in 1999 to anything between US$11.3 billion and $21 billion in 2003. Early adopters have been primarily small to medium-sized firms. Amongst the advantages cited are: reduced total cost of ownership, improved efficiency of internal IT staff, access to latest technology/applications and skills, accelerated application deployment, and transfer of ownership risk. Our own studies show some major concerns around: security of proprietary information, availability, scalability, adaptability of software, degree of customization possible, bandwidth capacity, and contract lock-in (see Kern and Kreijger 2001; Kern, Lacity, and Willcocks 2001).

Business process outsourcing. This has been reckoned to be the fastest growing market with revenues moving from $US6.1 billion in 1997 to an estimated $US16 billion in 2002. As one example in early 2000 BP Amoco (subsequently BP) announced the outsourcing of its human resource function, including its IT components on a $US600 million five-year deal with Exult, based in Irvine, California. BP outsourced the administrative and IT burden, reserving for itself only 'the things that require judgement and policy'. The risks inherent in such a large IT project are considerable, of course, and we will discuss such risks in the next chapter. On the other hand, BP estimated there would be a $US 2 billion reduction in operational costs as a result of this type of outsourcing.

Backsourcing. Over several years a few organizations have cancelled contracts and brought IT back largely in-house—for example East Midlands Electricity in 1999 cancelled its 1992 twelve-year total outsourcing deal with Perot Systems, five years early. By 1995 East Midlands had redefined the importance of IT to the business and began rebuilding its in-house skills. In 1999 it terminated the contract, taking advantage of a clause permitting this in the event of a merger (East Midlands merged with Powergen in 1998—see also Chapter 2). More often we have seen a steady creep back of some previously outsourced IT activities, due to changing requirements and contexts, or from the realization that the activity was in fact better positioned in-house all along. Partial backsourcing was also evident in Xerox's deal with EDS, although the consequences caused considerable contractual turmoil (see Chapter 3).

Shared services. As an example seven oil companies share Accentuic accounting services in Aberdeen, Scotland. Participant companies include Elf, Talisman, BP, and Saga Petroleum. In practice these companies have defined accounting services as a non-competitive area, and have outsourced these in order to reduce costs. The development of shared e-procurement exchanges throughout many sectors from early 2000 onward carries a similar logic, with these typically being run by a technology provider such as Commerce One or Oracle (Willcocks and Sauer 2000).

New joint ventures. As an example, FI Group and the Royal Bank of Scotland established in 1999 an independent entity—First Banking Systems—to develop commercial software and manage IT systems planning and architecture. Some 310 bank staff and 120 FI staff were transferred to First Banking Systems, and given a budget of £150 million over five years. FBS is jointly owned—51 per cent by Bank of Scotland, and 49 per cent by FI.

Complex Internet hosting/eCommerce projects. This was a major growth area in 2000. On some estimates it will generate for IT service providers global revenues of $US18 billion by 2002. Elsewhere, we have pointed to the importance of keeping business responsibility and control for e-business projects in-house, and to the dangers of ceding too much management control to the IT function or IT service providers (Willcocks and Sauer 2000).

This provides an overview of the main trends and practices. A more detailed assessment of these and other developments appears in Lacity and Willcocks

(2000*b*). In the remainder of this chapter we will focus on what we know about how to manage IT sourcing across the life of an outsourcing contract. We look at three main areas: how to make IT sourcing decisions; evaluation practice to contract and beyond; and the minimum, core, in-house IT capabilities needed to manage any IT sourcing arrangement, before addressing relationship management in detail in Chapter 2.

MANAGING IT SOURCING: (1) MAKING DECISIONS

An important point to make at this stage is that outsourcing IT is similar to outsourcing other activities and resources in many ways, but is also different on at least five counts. Although many senior executives approach IT outsourcing like any other make or buy decision, this can turn out to be a mistake. Unlike other functions—such as mailrooms, cafeterias, legal departments, manufacturing, distribution, and advertising—IT cannot be easily handed over to a vendor. According to Willcocks, Feeny, and Islei (1997), IT is different in the following ways:

- Information technology is not a homogeneous function, but comprises a wide variety of IT activities.
- IT capabilities continue to evolve at a dizzying pace; thus, predicting IT needs past a three-year horizon is wrought with uncertainty.
- There is no simple basis for gauging the economics of IT activity.
- Economic efficiency has more to do with IT practices than inherent economies of scale.
- Most distinctively of all, large switching costs are associated with IT sourcing decisions.

Based upon our research, successful organizations carefully select which IT activities to outsource, rigorously evaluate vendors, tailor the terms of the contract, and carefully manage the vendor. From the rich variety of case experiences studied we have been able to build a set of frameworks for thinking through sourcing decisions for IT, application services, and e-business (Kern and Kreijger 2001; Lacity, Willcocks, and Feeny 1996; Plant and Willcocks 2000). These frameworks embody a logic of first clarifying the sourcing options, then considering the critical business, cost, market capability, and technical factors influencing the effectiveness of sourcing decisions.

There are four distinct ways of using the external IT market:

Buy-in—companies buy and manage vendor resources to meet a temporary resource need, such as the need for programmers in the latter stages of a new development project. In these cases, companies are often unsure of the exact hours needed to complete the coding, so they sign contracts that specify the skills required and per day cost per person.

Contract-out—the vendor becomes responsible for managing, and delivering the results of, IT activities. This strategy is most successful when the companies can clearly define their needs in a detailed contract.

Preferred supplier—a company develops close relationships with a vendor in order to access their resources for ongoing IT activities. The relationship is managed with an incentive-based contract that defines complementary goals. For example, one company engaged a preferred supplier to provide contract programmers whenever they were needed. The contract ensured complementary goals—the participant received a volume discount in exchange for not going out to tender when programmers were needed. The vendor was motivated to perform because they relied on a steady stream of revenue.

Preferred contractor—companies intend to engage in a long-term relationship with a vendor to help mediate risk. The vendor is responsible for the management and delivery of IT activities. To ensure vendor performance, the company tries to construct an incentive-based contract that ensures shared goals.

There remains the *in-house* arrangement. We found this option having a critical role to play even when organizations were spending over 80 per cent of the IT budget on contracting out or on preferred contractors. As we shall see in the next chapter and in the case histories, all forms of contract run larger risks if certain capabilities are not retained in-house.

Business Imperatives

Selecting which IT activities to outsource and which to retain in-house requires treating IT as a portfolio. Successful sourcing begins with an analysis of the business contribution of various IT activities. Conventional wisdom has it that 'commodity' IT functions, such as payroll or data centre operations, are potential outsourcing fodder, while 'strategic' functions, such as on-line reservation systems, should be retained in-house (McFarlan and Nolan 1995). This delineation is too simplistic. Companies that consistently succeed in their selection of what can be outsourced to advantage use a richer vocabulary. They distinguish between two ideas—the contribution that an IT activity can make to business operations, and its impact on competitive positioning. The business factors matrix shown in Figure 1.2 helps managers to determine how these two business factors drive sourcing decisions. Four categories of potential outsourcing candidates emerge:

'Critical Differentiators'—IT activities which are not only critical to business operations, but also help to distinguish the business from its competitors. For example, a European ferry company considers its reservation and check-in systems to be 'critical differentiators' and 'order winners' (see Figure 1.2). The company has ships similar to those of its main rival, and operated them from the same major ports across the Channel between Britain and France. Its competitive strategy is to differentiate through improved services, including the

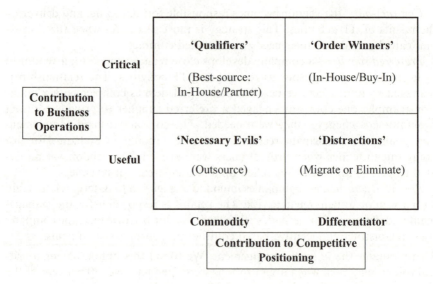

Fig. 1.2. *Strategic IT sourcing analysis:* (a) *By business considerations*

speed and ease with which passengers and their cars complete the boarding process. It is constantly making innovations in this respect, and the systems are instrumental in achieving this. While the company outsources a number of its IT activities, the reservation and check-in systems are retained in-house, though the company is prepared to buy-in expertise in short supply to support the in-house operation. This protects their ideas, expertise, and continuing ability to innovate rapidly.

'Critical Commodities'—IT activities that are critical to business operations but fail to distinguish the business from its competitors. A major British airline views its IT systems that support aircraft maintenance as critical commodities (while its yield management system for seat reservations is deemed a critical differentiator). Like its rivals, the airline must obviously maintain its fleet to specification or face very serious consequences. However, the maintenance activity and supporting systems respond to the mandated requirements of the manufacturers and regulatory authorities. The IT activities are 'qualifiers'—minimum entry requirements to compete in the sector, but no benefits accrue from over-performance. Although the airline has not yet outsourced these systems, it is in principle prepared to do so. Because of the risks involved for the business, such a decision would be based on clear evidence that an external vendor could meet stringent requirements for quality and responsiveness, as well as offer a low price. The policy is 'best source', not 'cheapest source'.

'Useful Commodities'—the myriad IT activities that provide incremental benefits to the business, but fail to distinguish it from its competitors. In our experience,

payroll, benefit, and accounting systems are the first examples of useful commodities volunteered by most businesses. But sweeping generalizations cannot be made, even within industries, as we have noted with a security guard firm. Useful commodities are the prime candidates for outsourcing. One CIO we talked to called them 'necessary evils'. Examples include personal computer support at a US chemical manufacturer, accounting services at a UK oil company, and mainframe operations at a US bank (Lacity and Willcocks 2000*b*). External suppliers are likely to have achieved low costs and prices through standardization. The business makes further gains if it can free up internal management time to focus on more critical activities. But the expectation of outsourcing must be validated through analysis of economic, market, and technical considerations.

'Useful Differentiators'—IT activities that differentiate the business from its competitors, but in a way that is not critical to business success. Useful differentiators should not exist, but Kern (1999) and Lacity and Willcocks (2000*b*) found that they frequently do. One reason is that the IT function is sometimes relatively isolated from the business and subsequently pursues its own agenda. For example, the IT department at a European paint manufacturer created a system that precisely matched a paint formulation to a customer's colour sample. IT managers envisioned that the system would create competitive advantage by meeting customers' wishes that paint should match their home furnishings. However, senior management had established the company's strategy as colour innovation. They failed to market the system because it ran counter to their strategy, and the system became an expensive and ineffective distraction. The system was eventually eliminated.

A more common reason for the creation of useful differentiators is that a potential commodity has been extensively reworked to reflect 'how we are different' or to incorporate the 'nice-to-haves'. This was an extensive phenomenon at a Dutch electronics company, resulting in very problematic and high-cost software maintenance. The CIO of the company has now implemented a policy requiring that all needs for useful systems be met through standard software packages, with strict limits to customization. Useful differentiators are 'distractions' (see Figure 1.2) and need to be eliminated from or migrated within an IT portfolio, but never outsourced merely to reduce their costs.

In addition to business contribution, cost considerations, which are often prematurely assumed to favour the vendor, are an important consideration in confirming the viability of IT outsourcing candidates.

Cost, Market Capability, and Technical Considerations

Cost Issues
Many senior executives assume that a vendor can reduce their IT costs because vendors possess inherent economies of scale that elude internal IT departments.

But a distinctive feature of IT is that economies of scale occur at a size achievable by many medium to large organizations. If this is true, how can a vendor underbid current IT costs? Often, the answer is that vendors implement efficient managerial practices that may be replicated by internal IT departments if empowered to do so. Suppliers may also claim economic advantages from experience curve effects, but in-house managements are not precluded from learning to operate more efficiently over time either. Two economic considerations—in-house economies of scale and adoption of leading practices—guide senior executives through these issues (see Figure 1.3).

If the internal IT department has reached critical mass and has adopted leading management practices, it is unlikely a vendor will be able to reduce costs further because vendors have to earn a 15 to 20 per cent profit, whereas internal IT departments merely need to cover costs. If the in-house IT department possesses theoretical economies of scale but has failed to implement efficient managerial practices, Lacity, Willcocks, and Feeny (1995) recommend that senior executives allow internal IT managers to compete against vendor bids. The competition serves to empower IT managers to overcome user resistance to the idea of reducing costs. If the internal IT department is of subcritical mass but has adopted efficient practices, it is quite possible that a vendor's size advantage may be negated by its need to generate a profit. 'Best-source' is recommended in these cases. That is, test the market to determine the economic validity of outsourcing. Finally, if the internal IT department is

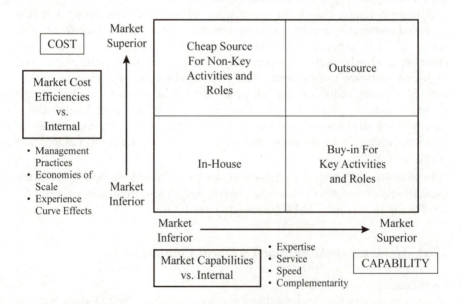

Fig. 1.3. *Strategic IT sourcing analysis* (b) *By market comparison*

of subcritical mass and has failed to adopt efficient practices, there is a strong economic justification for outsourcing (see Figure 1.3). But even companies that fall in this quadrant may wish to empower IT to implement what practices they can before outsourcing to avoid giving the vendor the large share of easy savings.

But what happens when external vendor bids beat internal bids? Prudent managers question where and how the vendor proposes to earn a profit while still meeting the bid. In the most desirable scenario, vendors clearly outbid internal IT departments based on a number of valid reasons—superior management practices which could not be replicated by the internal staff, inherent economies of scale, or superior technical expertise. But in many cases, vendor bids may be based on 'voodoo' economics i.e. customers are offered long-term, fixed prices which are attractive in year one but will be out of step with price/performance improvements a few years into the contract (see Kern, Willcocks, and van Heck 2000). Or the vendor may be trying to buy market share in a fiercely competitive market. Once the contract is signed, the vendor may recoup losses by charging exorbitant high fees for any change, realizing that customers are captive. Vendor bids may also contain hidden costs of the kind detailed in Lacity and Willcocks (1996).

Market Capability Issues
Another set of reasons that make outsourcing attractive relates to supplier capability relative to an in-house IT function. Especially with moves to e-business we are finding that organizations regularly experience a shortage of certain IT skills, difficulties in retaining staff, and difficulties in obtaining levels of service and expertise rapidly enough to deliver on fast-moving business requirements (Willcocks and Sauer 2000). In such circumstances organizations regularly turn to the IT services market to check out the available capability there. Where the market has superior capability, and offers a matching or cheaper price compared to the in-house option, outsourcing is an obvious decision, remembering, however, that all outsourcing decisions also need to be checked against the business considerations described in Figure 1.2. But even where price may not be an attractive reason for outsourcing, it is often the case that an IT activity or skill is so critical—in terms of speed it is required and its importance to business performance—and so unavailable in-house that a buy-in strategy will be suitable (Figure 1.3). On the other hand some organizations cheap-source. Having identified an IT activity/skills as non-critical, and wanting to reduce IT costs, they are prepared to make a cost-service trade-off, willing to potentially lower service and performance by outsourcing to an IT service provider who will do it cheaper and probably less well (see Figure 1.3). On the other hand, in-house is an obvious preferred option if the IT function can perform both cheaper and better than the market, and we have found many organizations continuing to perform 'useful-commodity' IT activities in-house for these reasons.

Technical Issues

Finally, the degree of technology maturity and the degree of technology integration are two key technical considerations that influence the effectiveness of IT sourcing decisions.

The degree of technical maturity determines a company's ability to precisely define its requirements to a vendor. Feeny, Earl, and Edwards (1997) describe an IT activity as having low technology maturity when the technology itself is new and unstable, when the business has little experience with a technology that may be better established elsewhere, and/or when the business is embarked on a radically new use of a familiar technology. Examples include an organization's first venture into imaging or client-server technologies, or the development of a major network to support a new business direction of globalization.

Outsourcing technically immature activities engenders significant risk. Ironically, these are precisely the IT activities many senior executives wish to outsource. Outsourcing technically mature activities provides less risk to organizations because they can precisely define their requirements. For example, a US commercial bank outsourced its mainframe operations to a vendor. The CIO was able to negotiate an airtight contract because of her experience and understanding of the requirements and costs of her mainframe operations. In the contract, she fully specified the service levels required, such as response time and availability, service level measures, cash penalties for non-performance, and adjustments to changes in business volumes. After three years into the contract, she achieved the anticipated savings of 10 per cent.

A second important technical consideration is the degree of integration with other business processes. In cases where technical integration with other business processes is high, the risks from outsourcing increase. For example, when a UK food manufacturer outsourced the development of factory automation, managers soon realized that the new system had profound implications for almost every business unit in the company. Although the vendor was an expert in factory automation software, it lacked an understanding of business interfaces. The system took four years to develop instead of two.

In contrast, one financial services company successfully outsourced the development of a highly integrated system using a preferred supplier model. This company invested in imaging technology to replace paper records (such as customer letters) with an electronic file. The company first explored the technology through a discrete R&D project. Senior executives reached a point at which they were convinced of the benefits of large-scale adoption but realized that many of their existing systems would now be affected. At this stage, the company turned to its preferred IT supplier, a vendor with a very broad product line, with whom it had worked for many years. Resisting the vendor's instinct to develop a detailed fixed-price agreement, the company set up an enabling, resource-based contract. The project was completed successfully, providing competitive advantage for both the business and its supplier, which had established a reference site for its own imaging products.

We have mapped the two technical considerations—technology maturity and integration—in Figure 1.4. Of particular note is the absence of the term 'strategic partnership' from the contracting options. The strategic partnership contracting model has been widely recommended as the preferred governor of outsourcing contracts (Henderson 1990; McFarlan and Nolan 1995—see also Chapter 2). But we have also seen the rhetoric of strategic partnership used as an excuse to sign poorly constructed contracts, leading to failure in several total outsourcing cases (Kern 1999; Lacity and Willcocks 2000b). We argue that strategic partnerships require shared—or at least complementary—risks and rewards. In the five total outsourcing failures we studied, this requirement was missing. Instead, every dollar out of the customer's pocket in terms of excess fees or hidden contractual costs went directly into the vendor's pocket.

Instead of the term 'strategic partnership', we have labelled relationships based on shared or complementary goals as 'preferred contractors'. With a preferred contractor strategy, companies engage in a relationship with the vendor to help mediate risk. This strategy worked best for technically mature and highly integrated IT activities. Because of technical maturity, companies can negotiate a detailed contract in which the vendor is responsible for the management and delivery of an IT activity. Because of the high integration with other business processes, companies must develop a close relationship to maintain the integrity of interfaces. To ensure vendor performance, the company tries to construct an incentive-based contract that ensures shared goals. For example, when Philips NV, the multinational electronics company, decided to reduce costs by outsourcing data centre operations and support of existing systems, it mediated risk by entering into a joint venture with a software house. By establishing a jointly owned company, it created shared goals that prevented vendor opportunism.

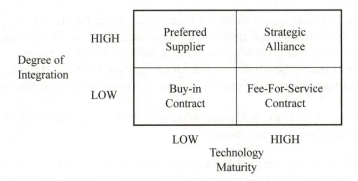

Fig. 1.4. *Strategic IT sourcing: technical factors*

Making effective IT sourcing decisions involves carrying out the analysis prompted by each of these matrices, then comparing the results, and making appropriate trade-offs. In practice there are inevitably trade-offs, as we shall see when we investigate the case studies in Chapters 3 through to 7.

MANAGING IT SOURCING: (2) EVALUATING TO CONTRACT AND BEYOND

In all our studies, assessment issues emerge strongly as critically affecting levels of success and failure in IT outsourcing. In particular, many respondents themselves noted four areas of weakness in their practice:

1. failure to establish adequate measurement of the pre-existing in-house performance;
2. limitations in the economic assessment of vendor bids;
3. failures in contracting in sufficient detail; and
4. inadequate attention to setting up measurement systems to monitor vendor performance.

This section, therefore, investigates the assessment issues in these areas, with a view to pointing the way toward how assessment practice could be developed. The section is organized to discuss findings on the economics of the vendor bid, setting up a measurement system for outsourced activities, and the major problems experienced on the assessment front after outsourcing (see also Graeser, Willcocks, and Pisanias 1999; Willcocks, Fitzgerald, and Lacity 1995, 1999).

Economics of the Vendor Bid

A proposed outsourcing evaluation process is shown in Figure 1.5.

This section will use the framework for discussing the more directly economic factors emerging from our research, namely the importance of the pre-existing evaluation process, the sources of hidden costs, some myths in the economics of IT outsourcing, and the central role of the contract in any outsourcing arrangement.

As detailed in Graeser, Willcocks, and Pisanias (1999), typical weaknesses in prior IT evaluation practice include:

- not fully investigating risk and its potential cost;
- understating knock-on operating, maintenance and human and organizational costs; budgeting practices that conceal full costs;
- lack of metrics to assess the business contribution of IT;

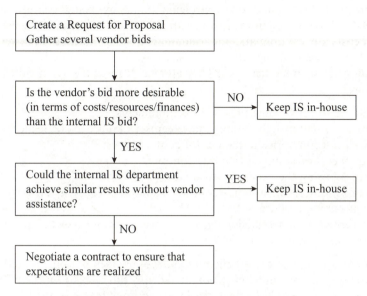

Fig. 1.5. *Proposed outsourcing evaluation process*
Source: Lacity and Hirchheim 1993.

● use of inappropriate metrics, given the objectives set for specific IT projects; inadequate approaches to dealing with 'intangible' benefits and for tracking benefits over long time scales.

For an organization contemplating outsourcing such weaknesses mean that a great deal of effort needs to be invested in understanding the costs and benefits of the existing IT operation so that these can be compared against vendor bids. Respondents found this can be best done in the lead up to the Request for Proposal (see Figure 1.5). Yet many organizations leave it until later; their experiences suggest, though, that it is rarely a good idea to postpone this analysis to the period after contracts have been signed. This can promote both subsequent hidden costs, and also opportunistic behaviour on the part of the vendor.

This detailed analysis needs to be carried out even where organizations have already moved to full in-house charging systems, have detailed in-house service level agreements and/or operate in-house IT as a cost or profit centre. Willcocks, Fitzgerald, and Lacity's (1999) findings indicate that failure to devote managerial effort to this evaluation task means not only poor assessment of vendor bids; there is also a knock-on effect of setting up inadequate measurement systems for subsequent vendor performance. These issues are pursued further below.

A consistent finding has been that outsourcing frequently carries hidden costs (Kern 1999; Lacity and Willcocks 1996). One extreme example by Lacity and

Hirschheim (1993) found one petroleum company being charged almost $500,000 in 'excess fees' in the first month into a new contract. More often the hidden costs are less dramatic but accumulate to a significant figure over time. As well as inadequate measurement systems, there seem to be five additional root causes of such hidden costs. They all relate to weaknesses in contracting. These are:

- failure to fully define present IT requirements;
- failure to define fully future requirements, or failure to create mechanisms for protecting price in the face of contingencies;
- loopholes or ambiguities in the contract;
- not allowing the vendor a reasonable profit; and
- unforeseen, rising, in-house contract management costs as a result of weak contracting practice.
- A lack of prior specified management processes and essential information exchanges in post-contract management.

The first three weaknesses left client organizations open not only to additional costs for services not previously contracted for, but also to higher prices for those services. Loopholes/ambiguities in the contract may also trigger conflicts with, and also opportunistic behaviour by vendors. That said, however, vendor opportunism can also be triggered by not allowing the vendor a reasonable profit. Vendor account managers then come under internal pressure to make their margins from the outsourcing deal.

Finally, in-house management costs in terms of new roles, time and effort are frequently higher than anticipated, and often fall between 4 and 8 per cent of the total value of an outsourcing contract (Lacity and Willcocks 2000*a*). Such costs may not be built into the preliminary assessment of a vendor bid, but they are typical rather than unusual outcomes in most outsourcing arrangements we have researched.

Detailed analysis of in-house IT performance together with assessing *all* the likely costs of outsourcing IT help to establish whether the vendor's bid is more favourable than any likely bid by the internal IT department. At the same time it is important to be aware of two central economic myths propagated by many vendors and trade press sources. One myth is that IT outsourcing vendors are inherently more efficient than internal IT departments. The second myth is that savings of 10–50 per cent can be achieved only through outsourcing (Lacity and Hirschheim 1995; Willcocks, Fitzgerald, and Lacity 1995). Let us look at these propositions in more detail.

Are IT outsourcing vendors inherently more efficient?
In practice, internal IT departments can be cost competitive with external vendors. The argument that vendors are inherently more efficient is usually based on notions of economies of scale. It is often considered that vendors achieve two types of scale economies over in-house departments: through higher

mass production efficiency and through labour specialization efficiencies. In practice, it is difficult to measure such efficiencies in IT settings. However, as pointed out above, our evidence is that the advantages vendors bring to bear are generally overstated, whether it be on mass processing efficiencies, hardware and software cost advantages, or labour specialization efficiencies (Willcocks, Fitzgerald, and Lacity 1995).

Taking the latter as an example, labour specialization efficiencies come from the wider access vendors can have to technical and business talent. In practice many companies outsource to access the vendor's pool of technical talent only to find that (*a*) they are supported essentially by the same staff, though sometimes at a lower cost, and (*b*) additional vendor expertise is expensive. We also found examples where after the first year of a contract a vendor moved their experienced, skilled staff off on to newer contracts, or where the better transferred staff with critical business knowledge of a company were nevertheless moved to other contracts run by the vendor. On business talent, many participants who outsourced felt a real loss of business expertise, as talented ex-employees were siphoned off by the vendor to assist in attracting other customers from the same industry. However, even where a vendor may be inherently more efficient on labour costs, the natural cost advantage still needs to be significant to cover the vendor's profit margin.

Can savings of 10–50 per cent only be achieved through outsourcing?
We found organizations achieving savings internally through a variety of measures. The organizations that were more hard-headed about IT outsourcing tended to drive down costs as much as possible internally before then considering outsourcing proposals. The alternative approach tended to allow the vendor to 'pick the low lying fruit', that is take, as an additional part of profit on the deal, those cost reductions that could have been achieved internally. As one high-profile example, it is probable that this happened in the 1988/9 Eastman Kodak/IBM deal.

Organizations can also drive down internal costs by consolidating data centres. As one example, Citibank in Europe did this before seeking an outsourcing agreement with a vendor to run those data centres. In several examples where organizations decided against outsourcing, costs were driven down by optimizing resource use, implementing strict cost controls, and by up-skilling existing staff rather than seeking access to more expensive technical staff available on the market. Again, even where a vendor may have inherent economies of scale in these areas, these usually still need to be significant in order to offset required profit margins (Currie and Willcocks 1998*a*; Lacity and Hirschheim 1995). That said, we found examples where there were political reasons why the IT department could not bring cost savings to bear, or where there were demands to reduce the IT headcount, or where the business required cash from the sale of information assets or needed to move IT from a fixed to a more variable expense. In such cases, the economic logic against outsourcing became intermingled and diverted through a variety of often conflicting stakeholder interests and perspectives (Currie and Willcocks 1998*b*; Lacity and Willcocks 2000*b*).

A major finding in research has been that, if an organization outsources IT, the outsourcing contract is the only certain way to ensure that expectations are realized (Kern 1999; Lacity and Hirschheim 1993; Lacity and Willcocks 1998, 2000*b*). In practice weak contracting, based on inadequate assessment of a vendor bid and backed up by poor monitoring systems, not only results in unanticipated, higher costs; it can create major problems for client organizations. In practice it is all too easy for all parties to a contract to agree broadly on what is required from a vendor. We also found parties all too frequently relying on 'partnering' notions to offset any difficulties arising from loose contracting. These rarely proved a sufficient base in themselves from which to run effective outsourcing arrangements (Currie and Willcocks 1998*a*; Lacity and Hirschheim 1993; Willcocks and Fitzgerald 1994). The issue is succinctly summarized by one of our respondents: 'Outsourcing contracts are agreed in concept and delivered in detail, and that's why they break down' (Vendor manager). When it came to drawing up effective outsourcing contracts we found that indeed the devil is in the detail. These issues receive further detailed treatment in Kern and Willcocks (2000*b*) and Lacity and Willcocks (1996, 1997, 2000*a*). Some more issues on the economic aspects of contracting are pursued in the next section.

Outsourced—Setting up a Measurement System

Once an organization has decided to outsource any aspect of its IT function, it will need to monitor vendor performance. In this section we extend the discussion on the importance of the contract as the fundamental building block for a measurement system, and look at respondents' experiences with different types of outsourcing contracts. We then focus on issues relating to measurement systems and service level agreements, and provide guidelines on these topics.

Where organizations are setting up and running measurement systems for vendor performance, the most common potential 'bad practice' areas observed were:

- over-reliance on the pre-existing standards and measurement systems; and
- failure to define comprehensively in the initial contract the detailed expectations of both sides on standards and how measurement will proceed.

These usually occurred either through time pressures or a belief in the 'good offices' espoused by the vendor. Much depends on the quality of the relationship between vendor and client. Several respondent organizations were still actually refining measures during the first six months of the contract. This worked reasonably well where, in the early stages of a contract, the vendor was anxious to demonstrate flexibility and good partnering.

However, in other contracts vendors were more concerned to keep very close to the original contract. This created contract management issues that became exacerbated where the contract was vague or did not cover issues arising. The problem arose from different perceptions by the vendor and client of the meaning and role of the contract (see also Xerox and ESSO in Chapters 3 and 6). In many cases, the client believed in the rhetoric of partnership much more than the vendor. The emerging lesson was that participants need to be clear as to what the relationship amounts to and how both sides understand it.

Another issue arises here. While clients had a tendency to believe that the quality of the vendor–client relationship would see them over limitations of performance measurement arrangements in the contract, in fact the latter could also come to affect the former adversely. In one contract it took some eighteen months of vigorous contract management finally to get the performance measures right and end disputes on service levels. In another case the client was disappointed that the vendor kept rigorously to the contract. The client felt that something more had been promised. The learning points, according to our respondents, were that the safe option in the period just before signing the contract is to get what is said actually written into the contract; and be prepared to spend time chronicling the agreement in monotonous detail. One reason is illustrated in a third case: the vendor kept rigidly to the contract deal because of very slim profit margins. In all three cases here described the vendor–client relationships became adversely affected because of problems with operationalizing the contract.

We have seen that it is possible to operate on a more flexible partnership basis, and also that some areas to be outsourced may be difficult to specify precisely in terms of service and performance required. However, in outsourcing, discretion may be the better part of valour. In reviewing thirteen organizations contemplating or undertaking outsourcing, Lacity and Hirschheim (1993) usefully suggest the following safety-first guidelines on creating a measurement system:

1. Measure EVERYTHING during the baseline period
2. Develop service level measures
3. Develop service level reports
4. Specify escalation procedures
5. Include cash penalties for non-performance
6. Determine growth rates
7. Adjust charges to changes in business.

The experiences recorded in other studies fit fairly closely with these guidelines (Currie and Willcocks 1998a; Kern 1999; Willcocks and Fitzgerald 1994). It is highly useful not to start a contract until current information systems services had been measured in a *baseline period*. There are a number of points here.

Some of our respondents left the contract incomplete with a view to carrying out measurement in a baseline period *after* the contract had started, or trusting to a good relationship with the vendor to deal with problems as they arise. Both approaches are hardly low risk and can leave an organization a hostage to fortune. Secondly, there may be time pressure to get a contract started. This may cut down on the time in which the baseline period for measurement is allowed to run. Lacity and Hirschheim (1993) recommend a six-month period to allow for fluctuations in service levels due to factors like tax season, seasonal business oscillations, and end-of-year data processing, for example.

A further stipulation about the baseline period is to *measure everything, not just what is easiest to measure.* The problem is less prevalent where what is being outsourced is an area that was being heavily measured before and is on the more traditional 'factory' or production side of IT operations. A more difficult area to measure, whether outsourced or not, is systems development. Our own view, argued above, is that these areas are probably best managed on an 'insourcing' rather than on a strict 'outsourcing' basis. The problem is that the end goal for systems development, and how to get there, can rarely be well defined. There also need to be in place measures of the productivity of vendor staff. However these should not be based merely on the speed with which development proceeds through a defined methodology and timetable. The outputs of development also need to be measured in terms of business impact—for example improvements in cost, quality, and service; systems reliability, ease of use, and ease of user learning.

These are difficult types of measures to formulate unless there are in-house systems people on the team, who already have key targets and measures in place before outsourcing (see below).

In addition to the above areas, there may be a series of services commonly provided by the IT department, but not documented. Before outsourcing it is important that these are analysed and included in the service agreement with the vendor along with measures of their delivery. What is not included in baseline period measurement will not be covered by the fixed price offered by the vendor and subsequently may be open to 'excess charges'. Examples of such services may be consultancy, PC support, installation, training services.

Clearly, *specifying service level measures* is critical. Lacity and Hirschheim (1993) point out that, while this is regularly done, a common mistake is to not then stipulate 100 per cent service accountability from the vendor. In one helpdesk support contract we researched in a major UK-based oil company, 80 per cent of service requests had to be responded to within 20 seconds and 90 per cent within 30 seconds. Financial penalties were attached to the failure to meet these criteria over a specified time period. However the vendor was also made responsible for reporting in detail on this performance and provide explanations where 100 per cent was not achieved. In a more critical area a measure would also be needed to ensure that the service requests not handled within the stipulated criteria were subsequently dealt with in an agreed and reasonable time. Note also in this example the importance of *detailed service level reports*. Also the importance of agreeing in advance what happens where problems escalate, for example providing explanations. This must lead on to *financial penalties for non-performance*. It is also important to look to the future when negotiating service levels and their price. A particular issue is underestimation of the rate at which service needs will grow. There is also a need to include realistic growth rates in the contract agreement's fixed price. Specific clauses may also be needed to cover large service volume fluctuations due to merger, acquisitions, or sale of parts of the business.

Overall, it is important for client organizations to make measurement work for rather than against their interests. Thus in one US manufacturing company the contract specified a two-second response time for key applications such as order entry and customer service. It also specified vendor support for up to twenty users at a given time using a Fourth Generation Language (4GL). However during the first week the eleven 4GL users were taking up more than 30 per cent of the machine cycles and making response times for critical applications unachievable. The vendor could have been forced to upgrade the technology provided, but the client, in this case, felt the demand would have been unreasonable. A tight contract reasonably handled by both sides was felt to improve the vendor–client relationship and levels of satisfaction all round.

Anticipating Problem Areas

In this section we signpost some further problem areas encountered. Some of the following issues are quite widely known about, but nevertheless are still experienced by client organizations (Lacity and Willcocks 2000a; Seddon et al. 2000). Other problem areas identified below would seem to be more difficult to predict. All are very real possibilities of which any organization contemplating outsourcing should be aware.

1. *Much effort may be needed to develop an adequate measuring system*
This was stressed earlier in the context of assessing vendor bids. We will see detailed examples of these difficulties in the later case chapters. Our other research shows that user involvement in the establishment of service level agreements (SLAs) is particularly important, if user needs are going to be properly identified, and if there is to be user buy-in to the measurement activity. However, more detailed service measures and costing procedures can have unanticipated effects on user behaviour, as will be discussed below. The sheer detail of the SLAs may also create a monitoring problem. It is important to focus on the key measures in any service level agreement.

2. *Outsourcing can require a culture change on measurement*
It is all too easy to underestimate how far outsourcing might require a fundamentally different approach to measurement and control. Many organizations,

at least in their early contracts, do not move that far away from their existing measures and standards for IT performance. This can leave latent problems and conflicts that will emerge across the life of the outsourcing contract:

The performance measures were not strong enough. This was because of the culture we operated in. I think they took us and I don't blame them, we weren't very professional. I think there have been some very good attempts at tightening up performance measurement. But once you've got a contract you've got a contract and if you are dealing with sharp guys like them, then it's very difficult. (IT director, UK public sector organization)

The fact that the manager here is getting a better deal on service towards the end of the contract suggests one reason why many organizations might choose to go for contracts of five years or less in length. The prospect of contract renewal reinvigorates vendor motivation to deliver service.

3. *The possibility of vendor opportunism*

This issue is hinted at in the previous point. In several studies we found a number of organizations operating a multi-vendor strategy explicitly to limit vendor opportunism (see also Chapters 5 and 6). Other organizations often learned over time about vendor opportunism and how to deal with it.

One case researched by Lacity and Hirschheim (1993) is very revealing about vendor opportunism. One ten-year contract began in early 1989. It was the product of senior management looking at ways to contain or reduce rising IT costs. A six-month baseline period was measured with the vendor contractually bound to deliver the average service level of this period. However, the contract was signed before the baseline measurement was completed. Therefore the services covered in the contract were not completely defined. In data centre operations the contract specified a fixed number of resources e.g. tape mounts, CPU minutes, print lines for a fixed price. On applications development and maintenance the company received a fixed number of man-hours of service. Other utility services were ill-defined in the contract. While the promised 20 per cent reduction off projected in-house IT budgets may be delivered by the vendor on the fixed price, in fact the 'excess' charges as a result of an incomplete contract may well cancel out any benefits. In fact, responses from the operating companies suggest that the vendor reduced its own costs by degradation of service, lack of responsiveness, 'excess' charges, and moving skilled staff transferred from the client on to other contracts. Additionally, despite promises, the vendor failed to develop service levels and performance measures after the contract went into effect. The vendor also took a strict view of the contract's 'change of character' clause, continually interpreting it in its own favour.

4. *Internal charging systems may create problems*

Even in a well-managed outsourcing contract, such as that between a major brewing company and a UK-based vendor, there can be latent problems between users in business units, the IT people managing the contract, and the vendor. In many examples the problems built around the charging system as it affected users. In this respect the company's experience in the first year of the contract is quite a common one:

The problems are around communications with our business which is the bit we are here to manage really. It's all around: are we buying a service level, is this time and materials, can I use X still on this, can I not use X on this, do things change or not? So it's all around communication with the business divisions and their understanding of the agreement. At the end of the day they will be paying, not directly, but I recharge to them. I am taking it into a central pot and reallocating it. Complexity of recharging is what's causing those communications challenges. . . . They (the business users) are very wary of it because they now realize that it's an outsider who's charging them and maybe there is a risk they will get charged more and people are going to get more commercial. (Senior manager, UK brewing company)

5. *Users may become more wary of the IT service*
In the cases of charging systems described above, users clearly became much more anxious about the service they were getting for the money they were being charged. In some respects this is often a healthy development, and may lead to users focusing on necessary rather than 'nice-to-have' services. It may also induce a much greater commercial awareness about computer use in their department. On the other hand there can be some less attractive outcomes in outsourcing situations:

I think when you talk about service level agreements and the sorts of terminology you start surrounding a lot of the services with then they tend to get in the way of true fast response, and a question of how much does it cost tends to be an issue. We are already finding that by charging internally for services then the idea that you have to locate a customer who has a budget that can pay, gets in the way of getting a fast response. It shouldn't do but it still does. It's magnified beyond reasonable proportions with an external agency. (Systems Development Manager, manufacturing company)

6. *IT costs may become too transparent*
This would seem to be a contradiction, in the sense that the transparency of costs as a result of outsourcing is usually proclaimed as a desirable outcome. However where there is still a large in-house IT capability, there may arise inflexibilities in the ways in which funds can be utilized, and additional IT work achieved:

One of the things that some of us were concerned about as part of the deal, but which was overlooked by senior management who signed up to the deal, was the fact that we know the way we operated here in IT. We could always fudge costs. . . . There's always a little bit of fat in any budget that allows us to take on something unexpected. I am talking about the ability to bring on a new software package which might enhance processing in an area, a systems software package, a new tool, which might cost you a licence fee plus £5,000 a year in maintenance costs. We could always do these simple things in-house. (IT manager, financial services company)

The irony here is that the in-house IT staff felt that the vendor had done too good a job of analysing costs and establishing what the price for different services would be. The problems are very much for operational IT staff rather than more senior management who in fact continue to see the non-degradation of contracted service plus large cost savings as very much a good deal.

Summary Points

The economics of IT outsourcing uncovered by our research suggests that organizations need to pursue in-house improvements first, identify full IT costs and establish performance benchmarks, pursue further in-house improvements, and only then make in-house vs. outsourcing comparisons. If the outsourcing option is initially rejected, it needs to be revisited at regular intervals, not least because the reassessment can act as an external benchmark on in-house IT performance. However, in practice we found a number of other objectives and interests often cutting across this economic logic.

Organizations found it difficult to assess vendor against in-house bids on a comparable basis, especially where prior evaluation practice exhibited the kinds of weaknesses discussed in, for example, Graeser, Willcocks, and Pisanias (1999). However respondent experiences suggested that the time and effort spent on fully assessing in-house performance, and revamping measurement systems proved vital in feeding into more effective contracting. All too often outsourcing deals can be based on varying degrees of 'voodoo economics'. Evaluation work, to enable comparison with and assessment of vendor bids, is best done before any contracts are signed, even where a specific vendor has been chosen. Organizations cannot safely assume that vendor opportunism will not occur. From this perspective, the contract has the central role in determining whether outsourcing expectations would be realized. Hidden costs in outsourcing arrangements are endemic, and these are most frequently the outcome of weak contracting.

However, even good contracting, based on detailed IT evaluation, and supported by comprehensive service measures and reporting systems, still did not avoid many problems arising during the course of any contract. This stresses again what emerge strongly from prior case and survey work: the importance of active monitoring and management of the vendor. As one respondent remarked ruefully about a particularly difficult outsourcing experience: 'The one definite thing I have learned is that it's not like ringing for room service.' So how can active monitoring and management of the supplier be assured?

MANAGING IT SOURCING: (3) CORE IT CAPABILITIES FOR POST-CONTRACT MANAGEMENT

The previous section has already detailed issues on evaluation, measurement, and control of vendors in IT outsourcing arrangements. In this section we deal with what our research has shown consistently to be the outstanding and major, neglected issue in IT outsourcing—that of retention of in-house capabilities. Our research base for identifying such core IT capabilities is described in detail in Feeny and Willcocks (1998). Here we will concentrate mainly on the findings and the emerging model of what we will call the emergent high-performance IT function required to manage IT successfully in the modern corporation.

The first step is to present the four faces of the emerging IT function (Figure 1.6):

- The business 'face' is concerned with the elicitation and delivery of business requirements. The domain of *Information Systems Strategy*, capabilities here are business-focused, demand led, and concerned with defining the systems to be provided, their relationship to business needs, and where relevant the interrelationships and interdependencies with other systems. A further focus here is on a strategy for delivery, together with actual IS implementation.
- The technical 'face' is concerned with ensuring that the business has access to the technical capability it needs—taking into account such issues as current price/performance, future directions, and integration potential. This is the domain of *Information Technology Strategy*, that is, defining the blueprint or architecture of the technical platform that will be used over time to support the target systems. IT presents the set of allowable options from which the technical implementation of each system must be selected. A further concern is to provide technical support for delivery of the IT strategy.
- The 'governance' face is concerned with *Information Management Strategy*, which defines the governance and coordination of the organization's IT/IS activity.
- The supply 'face' encompasses understanding and use of the external IS/IT services market. As such it is the domain of *IT/IS Market Sourcing Strategy*. Particularly critical here are decisions on what to outsource and insource, on which external suppliers to use and how. A further concern is ensuring appropriate delivery of external services contracted for.

In this section we develop the model of the future IT function by detailing nine capabilities required to render it dynamic and fully operational. These capabilities, expressed as roles, are shown in Figure 1.7. It should be noted that the nine capabilities populate seven spaces. These spaces are not accidentally arrived at. Three are essentially business, technology, or service facing. One is a linchpin governance position covered by two capabilities (see Figure 1.7—Leadership, i.e. CIO and Informed Buyer). Finally, there are three spaces that represent various interfaces between the three faces. The capabilities that populate these spaces are crucial for facilitating the integration of effort across the 'faces'. We now move to detailing each of the nine capabilities.

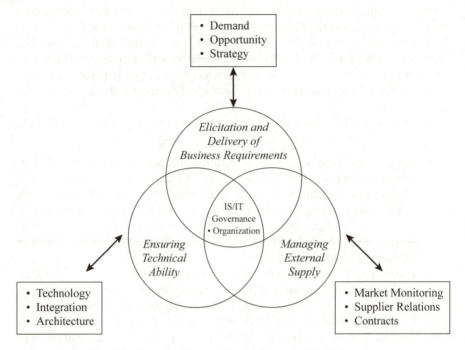

Fig. 1.6. *Four 'faces', or tasks, of the emerging IT function*

Capability 1—IS/IT Governance. IT leadership is required to 'integrate IS/IT effort with business purpose and activity'. The central task is to devise organizational arrangements—structures, processes, and staffing—to successfully manage the interdependencies, and ensure that the IT function delivers value for money. Provision of IS/IT governance capability is the traditional role of the IS/IT Manager or Director, the Chief Information Officer or 'CIO' of the local business.

Capability 2—Business Systems Thinking. This capability is about 'ensuring that IT capabilities are envisioned in every business process'. In best practice organizations, business systems thinkers from the IT function are important contributors to teams charged with business problem solving, process re-engineering, and strategic development. The information systems strategy emerges from these teams' recommendations, which have already identified the technology components of solutions to business issues.

Capability 3—Relationship Building. The need for relationship building is symbolized by the overlap between business and technical faces in Figure 1.7. While the business systems thinker is the individual embodiment of integrated business/IS/IT thinking, the relationship builder facilitates the wider dialogue, establishing understanding, trust, and cooperation amongst business users and

BUSINESS and IT VISION

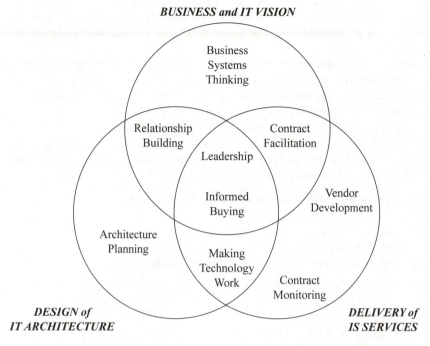

DESIGN of
IT ARCHITECTURE

DELIVERY of
IS SERVICES

Fig. 1.7. *Nine capabilities in the emerging IT function*

IT specialists. The task here is 'getting the business constructively engaged in IS/IT issues'.

Capability 4—Designing Technical Architecture. This is about 'creating the coherent blueprint for a technical platform which responds to present and future business needs'. The principal challenge to the architect is to anticipate technology trends so that the organization is consistently able to operate from an effective and efficient platform—without major investment in energy-sapping migration efforts.

Capability 5—Making Technology Work. Operating the overlap between the technical and supply faces of Figure 1.7 is the technical fixer. The fixer requires much of the insight found in the technical architect role, allied to a pragmatic nature and short-term orientation. In today's environment of high complex/net-worked/multi-supplier systems, the technical fixer makes two critical contributions: to rapidly troubleshoot problems which are being disowned by others across the technical supply chain; and to identify how to address business needs which cannot be properly satisfied by standard technical approaches. The need to retain technical 'doing' capability is recognized even amongst organizations that have 'total' outsourced IT.

Capability 6—Informed Buying. This involves analysis of the external market for IT services; selection of a sourcing strategy to meet business needs and technology issues; leadership of the tendering, contracting, and service management processes. In an organization which has decided to outsource most IT service, the informed buyer is the most prominent role behind that of the CIO. One respondent described their role in this way: 'If you are a senior manager in the company and you want something done, you come to me and I will . . . go outside, select the vendor and draw up the contract with the outsourcer, and if anything goes wrong it's my butt that gets kicked by you.'

Capability 7—Contract Facilitation—'Ensuring the success of existing contracts for IT services'. The contract facilitator tries to ensure that problems and conflicts are seen to be resolved fairly within what are usually long-term relationships. The role arises for a variety of reasons:

- to provide one-stop shopping for the business user
- the vendor or user demands it
- multiple vendors need coordinating
- enables easier monitoring of usage and service
- users may demand too much and incur excessive charges.

One contract facilitator noted: 'They (users) have been bitten a few times when they have dealt directly with suppliers, and it's a service we can provide, so now we do.'

Capability 8—Contract Monitoring. Another consequence of IT outsourcing complexity is the need for contract monitoring. While the contract facilitator is working to 'make things happen' on a day-to-day basis, the contract monitor is ensuring that the business position is at all times protected. Located in the exclusive space of the supply face, the role involves holding suppliers to account against both existing service contracts and the developing performance standards of the services market.

Capability 9—Vendor Development—'Identifying the potential added value of IT service suppliers'. The single most threatening aspect of IT outsourcing is the presence of substantial switching costs. To outsource successfully in the first place requires considerable organizational effort over an extended period of time. To subsequently change suppliers may well require an equivalent effort. Hence it is in the business interest to maximize the contribution of existing suppliers, which is the role of vendor development. Anchored in the supply face of our Figure 1.7 model, the vendor developer is concerned with the long-term potential for suppliers to add value, creating the 'win-win' situations in which the supplier increases its revenues by providing services which increase business benefits. A major retail multinational has a number of ways of achieving this, including an annual formal meeting: 'It's in both our interests to keep these things going and we formally, with our biggest suppliers, have a meeting once a year and these are done at very senior levels in both organizations, and that works very well.'

Comment on the Core IT Capabilities Model

The model has been used effectively as an analytical device in over sixteen corporations to date, to help organizations identify key IT management skills and appropriate human resource strategies. The model represents a number of serious human resource challenges. It requires high performers in each role. Furthermore, in contrast to the more traditional skills found in IT functions there needs to be a much greater emphasis on business skills and orientation in all but the two very technical roles. There is a significantly increased requirement for 'soft' interpersonal skills across all roles, all roles demand high performers, and each role requires a specific set of people behaviours, characteristics, and skills. In the research, we regularly found that where a particular capability was missing or understaffed, then problems arose. A typical issue was to conflate several of the capabilities and appoint one person to fulfil them. For example at one large bank we found a 'contract manager' responsible in practice for contract facilitation, contract monitoring, and IT governance. Not surprisingly, he underperformed in all these tasks. Chapters 3 to 7 will present additional examples of missing core IT capabilities in managing outsourcing, and the resulting complexities encountered by the client and vendor organizations.

The high-performance model also sets serious challenges for human resource policies. How do you pay these high performers at a level which is at least 'within striking distance' of that provided by alternative employers in a tight labour market? How do you provide them with the consistent level of challenge they look for in the job? And a career path despite their very small numbers in the organization? Few organizations develop the necessary human resource policies in an anticipatory way, partly because many still enter outsourcing believing that it is an opportunity to shed labour and run IT in-house as something of a residual rather than a core function. Against this view, we would argue, from the evidence, that in fact building and retaining these core IT capabilities form an insurance policy on retaining control over the organization's IT destiny, and will be the most likely source of any future competitive advantage the organization gains from its IT deployment.

CONCLUSIONS

In many countries in the world private and public sectors are wading into a series of further potentially large IT outsourcing waves, stimulated by moves to e-business, application service provision, business process outsourcing and the like, as well as more familiar forms of, and reasons for outsourcing. It is useful to stand back and look at what has been learned so far about IT outsourcing practices. It should be said that good and bad IT outsourcing experiences, like everything else in IT and its management, is *not* sector specific.

For example, financial institutions in all countries do not manage IT outsourcing any worse or better than any other organizations or sectors. Organizations fail when they hand over IT without understanding its role in the organization, and what the vendor's capabilities are. One rule of thumb is: never outsource a problem, only an IT activity or set of tasks for which a detailed contract and performance measures can be written. Too many client companies see IT outsourcing as spending—and as little as possible—and ditching their problems, not managing. In fact IT outsourcing requires a great deal of in-house management, but of a different kind, covering elicitation and delivery of business requirements, ensuring technical capability, managing external supply and IT governance. A cardinal insight from the research we have been reviewing up to early 2001 is that organizations still expect too much from vendors and not enough from themselves, or, put another way, vendors are still much better at selling IT services than their clients are at buying them.

The key is to understand and operationalize four capabilities necessary to pursue IT outsourcing effectively:

1. The ability to make sourcing decisions and arrive at a long-term IT sourcing strategy, building in learning, and taking into account business, technical, and economic factors. On this front, our research identifies two proven practices in IT outsourcing (Lacity and Willcocks 1998, 2000*b*). First, selective outsourcing decisions and total in-house/insourcing decisions achieve success more often than total outsourcing decisions. Secondly, senior executives and IT managers who make decisions together achieved success significantly more often than when either stakeholder group acted alone.

2. The ability to understand the IT services market place, the capabilities and weaknesses of relevant vendors, and what their business strategies are and imply in any likely IT outsourcing deal with an organization. Our research shows two proven practices here. First, *informed buying* is a core IT capability for all contemporary organizations. Secondly, organizations that invite both internal and external bids achieve success more often than organizations that merely compare a few external bids with current IT performance.

3. The ability to contract over time in ways that give suppliers an incentive and ensure that you get what you think you agreed to. Two proven practices here are that short-term (four years or less) contracts achieve success much more often than long-term contracts (seven years or more); and that detailed fee-for-service contracts achieve success more often than other types of contracts.

4. The ability to post-contract manage across the lifetime of the deal in ways that secure and build the organization's IT destiny, and effectively achieve the required service performance and added value from the supplier (Kern 1999; Willcocks and Kern 1998). The evidence is that this is one of the weakest areas in IT outsourcing practice and is rarely adequately thought through at the front of outsourcing deals. Typically, a minimum of nine core IT capabilities emerge as necessary in response to problems confronted during contract performance.

These cover leadership, informed buying, vendor development, contract facilitation, contract monitoring, technical fixing, architecture planning, relationship building, and business systems thinking.

Institutions need to assess their capabilities against these four vital components before outsourcing IT to any significant degree, and then build these capabilities where they are lacking. This chapter represents a summary of what research has told us so far about the effective management of IT outsourcing arrangements. However, in reviewing all the research on IT outsourcing, what has been particularly noticeable is the neglect of attention given to risks and their mitigation, and the role of relationships in IT outsourcing management. It is to these that we now turn.

REFERENCES

Currie, W., and Willcocks, L. (1998*a*). *New Strategies in IT Outsourcing*. Business Intelligence, London.

—— —— (1998*b*). 'Analysing IT Outsourcing decisions in the Context of Size, Interdependency and Risk'. Information Systems Journal, 8/2: 86–102.

Feeny, D., Earl, M., and Edwards, B. (1997). 'Organizational Arrangements for IS: Roles of Users and Specialists', in Willcocks, Feeny, and Islei (1997).

—— and Willcocks, L. (1998). 'Core IS Capabilities for Exploiting IT'. *Sloan Management Review*, 39/3: 9–21.

Graeser, V., Willcocks, L., and Pisanias, N. (1999). *Developing the IT Scorecard: Evaluation and Management Practices*. Business Intelligence, London.

Henderson, J. (1990). 'Plugging into Strategic Partnerships: The Critical IS Connection'. *Sloan Management Review* (Spring), 7–18.

Kern, T. (1999). 'Relationships in Information Technology Outsourcing: An Exploratory Research Study of a Conceptual Framework'. Unpublished D.Phil. thesis, University of Oxford.

—— and Blois, K. (2000). 'Norm Development: An Essential Ingredient to Outsourcing Relationships', 16th annual Industrial Marketing and Purchasing Conference, 7–9 September, Bath, UK.

—— Lacity, M., and Willcocks, L. (2001). *Strategic Application Service Provision: From Panacea to Business Solution*. Prentice Hall, New York.

—— Willcocks, L., and van Heck, E. (2000). 'Relational Trauma: Evidence of A Winner's Curse in IT Outsourcing'. *Erasmus University Working Paper*, Rotterdam.

—— and Kreijger, J. (2001). 'Application Service Providers: Exploring the Outsourcing Option'. *Journal of Strategic Information Systems* (forthcoming).

—— and Willcocks, L. (2000*a*). 'Cooperative Relationships Strategy in Global Information Technology Outsourcing: The Case of Xerox Corporation'. In D. Faulkner and M. De Rond (eds.), *Perspectives on Cooperation*. Oxford University Press, Oxford.

—— —— (2000*b*). 'Contracts, Control and "Presentation" in IT Outsourcing: Research in Thirteen UK Organizations'. *Journal of Global Information Management*, 8/4 (December).

Kumar, K., and Willcocks, L. (1999). 'Holiday Inn's Passage to India', in E. Carmel (ed.), *Global Software Teams*. Prentice Hall, New Jersey.

Lacity, M., and Hirschheim, R. (1993). *Information Systems Outsourcing: Myths, Metaphors and Realities*. Wiley, Chichester.

—— —— (1995). *Beyond the Information Systems Outsourcing Bandwagon: The Insourcing Response*. Wiley, Chichester.

—— and Willcocks, L. (1996). 'Best Practices in IT Sourcing'. Oxford Executive Research Briefing, Templeton College, Oxford.

—— —— (1997). 'IT Outsourcing: Examining the Privatization Option in US Public Administration'. *Information Systems Journal*, 7/2 (June).

—— —— (1998). 'An Empirical Investigation of Information Technology Sourcing Practices: Lessons from Experience'. *MIS Quarterly*, 22/3: 363–408.

—— —— (2000a). *Inside IT Outsourcing: A State-of-the-Art Report*, Templeton Research Report 1, Templeton College, Oxford.

—— —— (2000b). *Global IT Outsourcing: Search for Business Advantage*. Wiley, Chichester.

—— —— and Feeny, D. (1995). 'IT Outsourcing: Maximise Flexibility and Control'. *Harvard Business Review*, 37/3 (May–June), 84–93.

—— —— —— (1996). 'The Value of Selective IT Sourcing'. *Sloan Management Review*, 37/3: 13–25.

McFarlan, F. W., and Nolan, R. (1995). 'How to Manage an IT Outsourcing Alliance'. *Sloan Management Review* (Winter), 9–23.

Plant, R., and Willcocks, L. (2000). 'Sourcing Internet Development', in Willcocks and Sauer (2000).

Seddon, P., Rouse, A., Reilly, C., Cullen, S., and Willcocks, L. (2000). *Survey of IT Sourcing Practices in Australia*. University of Melbourne, Melbourne.

Strassmann, P. (1997). *The Squandered Computer*. Information Economics Press, New Canaan.

Willcocks, L., and Currie, W. (1997). 'IT Outsourcing in Public Service Contexts: Towards the Contractual Organization?' *British Journal of Management*, 8 (June) S107–20.

—— Feeny, D., and Islei, G. (eds.) (1997). *Managing IT as a Strategic Resource*. McGraw Hill, Maidenhead.

—— and Fitzgerald, G. (1994). *A Business Guide to Outsourcing Information Technology: A New Study of European Best Practice in the Selection, Management and Use of External IT Services*. Business Intelligence, London.

—— —— and Lacity, M. (1995). 'IT Outsourcing in Europe and the USA: Assessment Issues'. *International Journal of Information Management*, 15/5: 333–51.

—— —— —— (1999). 'To Outsource or Not?' In Willcocks and Lester (1999).

—— and Kern, T. (1998). 'IT Outsourcing as Strategic Partnering: The Case of the UK Inland Revenue'. *European Journal of Information Systems*, 7: 29–45.

—— and Lacity, M. (eds.) (1998). *Strategic Sourcing of Information Systems*. Wiley, Chichester.

—— Lacity, M., and Kern, T. (2000). 'Risk Mitigation in IT Outsourcing Strategy Revisited: Longitudinal Case Research at LISA'. *Journal of Strategic Information Systems* (September).

—— and Lester, S. (eds.) (1999). *Beyond the IT Productivity Paradox: Assessment Issues*. Wiley, Chichester.

—— and Sauer, C. (eds.) (2000). *Moving to E-Business*. Random House, London.

2

Risk Mitigation and the Relationship Advantage in IT Outsourcing

INTRODUCTION

Over the last decade the growth in significance and in the size of outsourcing deals has resulted in rising concern with the actual management of outsourcing arrangements, in particular with the twin issues of risk mitigation and relationship management. These have emerged as particularly fundamental issues to outsourcing management because of the mixed press and results regularly reported in both the trade and academic literatures on outsourcing ventures, and because they seem surprisingly difficult to get right.

Why focus on the specific risks attendant in IT outsourcing? We have already pointed to the large and rising expenditure on IT outsourcing, possibly reaching $150 billion by 2004. As reported in Chapter 1, by 2003, on average 30–5 per cent of a corporation's IT budget will probably be outsourced. Having a third of your IT under external control needs a clear understanding of the attendant risks, and how to mitigate these. Moreover, the research consistently demonstrates that, despite growing maturity of vendors and their clients, the practice of IT outsourcing continues to be a high-risk, hidden-cost process. Consider UK retailer Sears' experience. It outsourced most of its IT on a £344 million ten-year 'no tender' single supplier deal in early 1996. It was brokered largely as a financial rescue package for the troubled group. Within seventeen months, and with the resignation of the CEO, the Board could no longer see sufficient business advantage in the arrangement. The cost to Sears of implementing, then terminating, the deal was in excess of £55 million.

Most experiences are not so stark. One reason is that a majority of organizations take a selective outsourcing route. Nevertheless, surveys regularly find up to a third of organizations encounter serious and difficult problems in their IT outsourcing deals. Hidden costs, followed by credibility of vendor's claims continue to be the top single risks that actually materialize as significant negative outcomes in outsourcing (Lacity and Willcocks 2000b). Such risks are widely commented upon by, and a considerable matter for concern amongst practitioners considering or involved in IT outsourcing. Moreover, Chapter 1 revealed a range of practices adopted over the years in attempts to mitigate such risks. Nevertheless it is a surprising fact that risks in IT outsourcing have received little detailed and sustained attention. This chapter will fill this gap by developing and illustrating a risk analysis framework that will facilitate analysis and learning from the case studies in later chapters.

A related theme of this chapter is the relationship dimension in IT outsourcing. Study after study has respondents citing the importance of relationships, and their role in keeping an outsourcing arrangement on track, and for mitigating risks. Relationships in outsourcing evolve and take their shape—for good or ill—during the post-contract management phase, yet the post-contract management agenda is also all about operationalizing the contract (Halvey and Melby-Murphy 1995). Irrespective though of their form, these relationships—which we will call here the relationship dimension—are generally vital to the overall success of the outsourcing initiative. In fact, they are a primary source for mitigating risks and keeping the contract fresh and mutually useful (Alpar and Saharia 1995; Klepper and Jones 1998; Willcocks and Kern 1998).

It is thus surprising that this relationship dimension has received by far the least research attention to date in IT outsourcing. Past research has almost exclusively concentrated on outsourcing's determinants, benefits, vendor selection, and contracting. It is undisputed that these do affect the success of the outsourcing initiative. But case research highlights that the pre-contract phase in length is marginal in relation to the post-contract management period, which on average spans five years in terms of contract length (Currie and Willcocks 1998; Lacity and Hirschheim 1993*a*, 1993*b*). Ongoing relationship management forms, thus, an integral part of the post-contract management agenda, and its effective handling can make the difference between achieving the outsourcing objectives or not (Halvey and Melby-Murphy 1995). In this chapter, therefore we critique the little existing research available and then develop a framework for helping to understand and analyse the critical components of client–supplier relationships.

As will emerge, the juxtaposition of these two subjects—risks and relationships—is far from coincidental. Risk and relationships in IT outsourcing are undermanaged and understudied, and previous studies have never systematically linked the two issues. However, the case studies provide convincing evidence that managing the relationship dimension, as we define it, has also proven to be a major contributor to risk mitigation.

ANALYSING RISK

It is clear from the first chapter that IT outsourcing remains a risky business. Following Charette (1991) and Willcocks and Margetts (1994), risk is here taken to be a negative outcome that has a known or estimated probability of occurrence based on experience or some theory. In practice, the authors' detailed review of the last decade finds that there are all too few systematic academic studies of types of IT outsourcing risks, their salience and their mitigation. The main studies have been Earl (1996) and Klepper and Jones (1998), both of which are somewhat anecdotal in character; Ang and Toh (1998) with a detailed case history of a failed software development project, and derived guidelines; Jurison (1995) who provided a theoretical risk-return analytical model for making IT outsourcing decisions; Willcocks and Lacity (1999), who investigated risk mitigation tactics in a single case history; and Lacity and Willcocks (1998) and Willcocks (1998), who derived risk reduction guidelines from studying forty organizations and their IT sourcing practices. Outside these, there are many other studies that deal with IT outsourcing but do not choose to focus on providing a comprehensive analysis of salient risks and/or risk mitigation approaches (for example Ang and Straub 1998; De Looff 1997; McFarlan and Nolan 1995; McLellan et al. 1995).

Although there is a limited literature on which to draw for the identification of salient risks, an exploratory analytical framework can be distilled from case-study and survey work by Lacity and Willcocks (1998, 2000*a*, 2000*b*), and others (see below). Drawing on this work, the main reasons for failure/negative outcomes in IT outsourcing deals have been various combinations of the factors shown in Figure 2.1 (see also Ang and Straub 1998; Ang and Toh 1998; Auwers and Deschoolmeester 1993; Currie and Willcocks 1998; DiRomualdo and Gurbaxani 1998; Kern 1999; Klepper and Jones 1998; Kumar and Willcocks 1999; Lacity, Willcocks, and Feeny, 1995, 1996).

Apart from being built on prior research findings, an earlier version of the framework was also productively utilized and further developed for present use

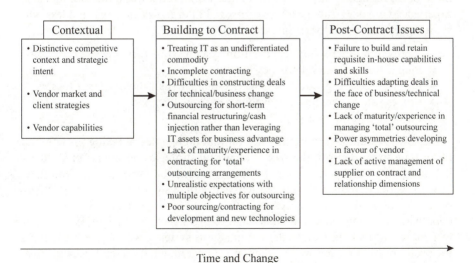

Fig. 2.1. *IT outsourcing: risk analysis framework*

in earlier case work (Willcocks and Lacity 1999; Willcocks, Lacity, and Kern 1999). A finding there in applying the framework was that it provided sufficient generic coverage of salient risks to allow complementary detail to be explored in an insightful, qualitative manner. Below we will illustrate the risks shown in Figure 2.1, beginning with contextual risks.

CONTEXTUAL RISKS: COMPETITIVENESS, STRATEGIC INTENT, AND VENDORS

In 1994 John Browne, CEO of oil major BP stated: 'Failure to outsource our commodity IT will permanently impair the future competitiveness of our business.' In a highly competitive sector, the risk here was loss of focus on core competencies if the company did not outsource. In the group, BP Exploration's total outsourcing contracts with three suppliers proved largely successful in this regard. As we shall see (Chapter 5) a 'best-of-breed' approach was adopted to supplier selection; contracts were kept to five years—considered a reasonable period to master the speed of business and technological change; and in-house measurement systems and retained capability proved largely up to the management tasks set by leveraging IT for business advantage and for monitoring and relating to multiple suppliers.

However, surmounting the contextual risks shown in Figure 2.1 can be elusive. Some studies suggest that strategic *disadvantage* can be one outcome from outsourcing. In a 1998 study of fifty-four businesses over five years, carried out by Weill and Broadbent in *Leveraging the New IT Infrastructure*, they found those outsourcing at a faster rate had indeed achieved lower costs, but had also experienced greater strategic losses compared to organizations that did less outsourcing. Some of the losses included:

- significantly increasing information systems staff turnover;
- longer time to market for new products;
- lower perceived product and service quality than their competitors;
- slower rate of increase in revenue per employee; and
- lower return on assets.

Our own research supports the notion that companies pursuing growth and faster time to market run the risk of incurring strategic and operational inflexibilities if they outsource principally for cost reduction purposes. For example, in 1994 Xerox (Chapter 3) signed a ten-year global single-supplier deal. Where cost reductions did take place, they may have restricted Xerox's ability to cope with a major change in their marketing structure. In late 1999 Xerox lost control of its billing and sales commissions systems, with big consequences for profitability. In other words, there must be a match between business strategy and what outsourcing is set up to achieve. Consider also Capital One, the US credit card group with 12,000 employees, 1,000 of them in IT. According to the president Nigel Morris: 'If you have a business that churns out products, then outsourcing makes sense. But IT is our central nervous system [. . .] if I outsourced tomorrow I might save a dollar or two on each account, but I would lose flexibility, and value and service levels.'

Further risks reside in not understanding a supplier's competitive and client strategies and its key capabilities. For example, while outsourcing remains a growth market vendors will be tempted to devote their attention and energies to winning new contracts rather than servicing existing ones. On the first issue, a supplier may well be keen to enter a new market place, as for example Perot Systems was in the early 1990s in the UK, or EDS in Australia in the mid-1990s. Alternatively, a supplier may seek increased rate of growth by offering favourable deals with the view that as other, more profitable contracts come along they can shift their key human resources to these, and can also find ways of increasing revenues and profits from the original contracts. When suppliers make losses or have slim margins—unless of course the client is a reference site—one must also look out for opportunistic behaviour, attempts to reinterpret contracts, and introduction of new modes of revenue generation. Checking that a deal is based on reasonable profit for the supplier can be a risk mitigating exercise here. Government agencies particularly need to heed this point. In the past, because of requirements to select the cheapest supplier, they may have secured fewer tenders in the first place. Subsequently they experienced difficult relationships with their vendors because the contract did not allow for reasonable profit.

Some large suppliers also have long-term strategies to dominate vertical markets, for example military logistics. In these cases a supplier may well offer very favourable terms and service over the early years of a deal, but the overall objective would be to make switching costs prohibitive and to build up a monopoly of experience and track record in that market in order to dissuade competition. The risk then is that power asymmetry develops in favour of the vendor who secures the client on a long-term basis, on price and service regimes over which the client has little real power to leverage behaviour (see Willcocks, Lacity, and Kern 1999 for an example). Clearly it is in their long-term interest for client companies to retain sourcing flexibility through encouraging competition, thereby retaining the power to influence the vendor.

Companies must also be wary of suppliers' claims on capabilities and resources. Even the largest suppliers, in fact, experience skills shortages, or 'stickiness' in making the skills they do have available to specific clients. When in the mid-1990s EDS claimed in its bid to South Australia government it had 100,000 people available worldwide, the challenge for the client was to determine how many were realistically not already committed, and able to travel to and work in Australia (see Lacity and Willcocks 2000*b* for a discussion of the case). Unless they stipulate otherwise, clients may well get their old staff hired back to them, gaining no real influx of new skills. Often suppliers have to subcontract. As Chapter 1 made clear, in the big deals we studied, frequently more than 30 per cent was a multi-supplier contract in disguise, especially in the areas of technical consulting, desktop hardware and installation, network specialists, and software specialists. There are a number of risks here. Suppliers do not always manage other suppliers better than the client could. They may charge more and add less value than if the client undertook the work. Moreover, responsibilities and intellectual property rights can be less than transparent. It becomes all too easy for responsibilities to fall through the cracks of these increasingly complex relationships as one supplier plays the client off against others.

Some companies have addressed these risks by taking an equity share in the supplier to whom they have outsourced IT. The best-known example is GM-EDS. Others include the Commonwealth Bank of Australia taking equity in EDS Australia and Lend Lease taking equity in IBM Global Services (Australia). This may prove an excellent business investment but the jury is out as to how far it helps mitigate outsourcing risk. Where the equity holding is managed by an asset management unit rather than the CIO as has sometimes been the case, that unit will support whatever strategy the supplier has for maximizing its returns ahead of pressing for better service for its own organization (see also Chapter 1).

BUILDING TO CONTRACT: PITFALLS AND PICK-ME-UPS

In our research, IT outsourcing deals in failure mode invariably exhibited all the practices shown in Figure 2.1 in their build-up to contracting. Problems and disappointments occurred if any one of these risky paths was selected. In 1992 East Midlands Electricity (EME) totally outsourced to a single supplier on a £150 million twelve-year deal. Within three years the Board accepted that significant parts of the IT viewed as an 'undifferentiated commodity' were in fact critical to the evolution of the company's business strategy. The company began to rebuild its in-house resources but was restricted by its outsourcing contract, the terms of which Perot showed no signs of breaking. Eventually the contract was terminated five years early in 1999, as EME's acquisition by Powergen triggered a let-out clause.

Bringing together many of the ideas in Chapter 1, some of the most disappointing deals were total outsourcing long-term, single-supplier deals signed in the early 1990s either as financial rescue packages, or to achieve cost savings. The failures exhibited a potent mix of characteristics. Contracting for ten years or more is done to establish the strategic nature of the relationship with the supplier. However, contracting for IT services for such a length of time is very difficult. As John Cross, IT director at BP (see Chapter 5) pointed out in 1999: 'In the course of five years we experienced two generations of technology.' Incomplete contracting is frequently the result.

Another feature of long contracts is that power asymmetries develop in favour of the vendor. In many of these deals the suppliers sought to recoup their investments in the second five years and found many opportunities to find excess charges for services not covered in the original contract. The explicitness of the contract and service measures emerged as critical, not least because in practice people move on, and contracts can be continually reinterpreted to favour one side or the other. None of this is helped when the client does not build requisite in-house capabilities to keep control of its IT destiny.

Success in total IT outsourcing has taken a variety of routes. On the evidence, it requires a lot of management maturity and experience of IT outsourcing, as we will see in, for example, the BP Exploration and British Aerospace (BAe) cases. It needs complete and creative contracting. As Chapter 1 indicated, we have seen successful creative risk mitigation uses of flexible pricing: for example shares in vendor savings, 'open book' accounting, third party benchmarking, reduced fees based on other customers. We have also seen long-term contracts begun with short-term, small ones and the use of competitive bidding for further work beyond the first contract in order to provide continuing incentives for the supplier. Effective contracts also allow for regular revisiting of price/performance criteria and benchmarking these against a fast changing IT labour and services market place.

Successful large 'total' outsourcing contracts are often mainly for stable, well-understood areas of IT activity such as infrastructure/mainframe operations. Less typically, Philips Electronics and Origin entered a strategic alliance, where the company spun off its entire IT function in a shared risk reward and joint venture with an existing supplier (see Chapter 1). Another success involved a short-term contract to wind down a public sector agency about to be privatized. Others have gone down the multiple supplier 5–7-year contract route, looking to spread their risks. Others, like British Aerospace-CSC and Inland Revenue-EDS, were single-supplier deals that took on board the above prescriptions, had detailed contracts, and were also high profile, with the suppliers wary of adverse publicity in specific countries or markets (see Chapters 4 and 7).

POST CONTRACT MANAGEMENT AS RISK MITIGATION

Failures in dealing with these issues of context and building to contract flow through into what actually happens at the post-contract stage—'when the rubber hits the road' as it were. But even if a deal is well set up, IT outsourcing can still seriously founder at the post-contract management stage. Risks arise from not staying flexible in the face of unexpected but inevitable business and technical change, not managing the relationship dimension well, not leveraging the relationship for business and mutual advantage, and not putting into place tactics for maintaining a power balance between the parties. Short-term contracts, multiple suppliers, the possibility of competition, the possibility of future work have all been used to incentivize the supplier. For example, one IT director, asked why he went for short-term contracts, commented: 'It's amazing the service you get when the contract is coming up for renewal.' The issue here is ensuring that the supplier's focus and priority is on your case. John Yard, IT Director in the 1993–2003 UK Inland Revenue-EDS deal, has made the point explicitly: 'I see myself as in direct competition for the supplier's attention with all its other customers' (see Chapter 7).

In all this, the most neglected area of risk mitigation and leveraging outsourcing for business advantage has been that of retaining requisite capabilities and skills. As Chapter 1 elaborated, Feeny and Willcocks in their June 1998 *Sloan Management Review* article 'Core IS Capabilities for Exploiting IT' spelt out the nine key capabilities needed to run any IT sourcing arrangement. Building these in-house resource capabilities remains the real way in which IT outsourcing arrangements can be kept on track. A major reason is that the existence of these essentially human high-performance capabilities leads to sound analysis and sourcing decisions, good contracting and management, and the development of productive relationships with suppliers—the foundations of what we call in this book the relationship advantage.

In practice, though, too many companies see IT outsourcing as an opportunity to offload headcount—a real risk if done indiscriminately. The core IS capabilities model implies far fewer staff but all with distinctive, high-performance capabilities. Frequently these are skills not available from existing, retained staff. IT outsourcing requires as much managing, in fact, but of a different kind from that in more traditional IT functions. As one IT director told us: 'Eventually we had to hire some new people; it really did require new skill sets.' It has also become clear, as Chapter 1 pointed out, that appointing one person, usually called the 'contract manager', to fulfil several of these roles detracts from the high-performance requirement, though this may be a necessary, pragmatic trade-off in smaller client organizations.

RISK PROFILING: SUMMARY

Generally, selective sourcing to multiple suppliers on relatively short-term detailed and regularly revisited contracts has been the more effective approach to mitigating the risks from using the external IT service market. On IT development projects, in situations where the technology is new and unstable, where there is little relevant IT experience of the technology, and business requirements are unclear or changing, we have found 'insourcing' the lower-risk approach. This is not to say that total outsourcing is not feasible; as we shall see in the cases, it means rather that risk analysis, and mitigation techniques, become even more compelling, required practices.

We have also seen a small number of organizations achieve strategic business goals by outsourcing IT on a large scale, for example facilitating and supporting major organizational change at British Gas in the 1990s (Currie and Willcocks 1998); achieving direct profit revenue generation through joint venturing with a supplier partner at Philips Electronics (Willcocks and Fitzgerald 1994); redirecting the business and IT into core competencies as at BP Exploration; and strengthening resources and flexibility in technology and service to underpin the business's strategic direction, as at Dupont (see Lacity and Willcocks 2000*b*). All underwent and managed the potential risks detailed in Figure 2.1.

As, in the new millennium, the IT outsourcing focus shifts to supplier-supported e-business projects, the use of application service providers, business service providers, managed network services, new forms of outsourced e-fulfilment, and customer relationship management, some really critical risk issues arise. As radical, new forms of large-scale IT outsourcing are mooted, and it is asserted that there are new management rules for the new economy, it should be remembered that the 'new' principles underlying large-scale outsourcing, for example at Cisco Systems, are not that far from those underlying the original 'virtual organization'—Benetton—in the late 1980s. Ignoring all we have learned about the risks in IT outsourcing and how to manage them would be a very risky business indeed.

THE RELATIONSHIP DIMENSION IN IT OUTSOURCING

Relationships in IT outsourcing have received even less conceptual and empirical research attention to date than risks—even though virtually all commentators allude to the critical importance of the relationship dimension—for mitigating risks, achieving productive and efficient operations, and leveraging the elusive 'value-added' anticipated from outsourcing. Most discussions on IT outsourcing relationships have frequently utilized terms such as partnerships or alliances as a means to characterize them. The appropriateness of these has often raised concern, as the terms not only seem to confuse, but also draw attention away from the contract:

Partnership is one of the most abused words in business English and no more so than in the IT industry. It is used as a political weapon. Partnerships are 'good'. So any relationship has to be presented as a 'partnership', especially by the party that stands to gain most from it. Heaven save me from some of the 'partnerships' I have seen. They are no more than the cut-and-thrust of ordinary commercial warfare dressed to be something they are not. (Handby 1996)

Fitzgerald and Willcocks (1994) found that the word partnership is so frequently used because it is a desired feature that client companies often look for. Their study revealed that partnership in outsourcing was usually seen as embodying:

- non-reliance on the contract as the basis of the relationship;
- a mutual desire to work things out and a give and take philosophy;
- a fair profit for the vendor, so that they do not seek to resort to what may be an inadequate contract;
- the ability to work together in personal relationship terms;
- the existence of a cultural fit between the client and vendor organization;
- good treatment of the client's transferred staff; and
- a perception that the vendor understands the client's business and problems.

Total outsourcing deals in particular have often been referred to as partnerships or alliances (Davis 1996; McFarlan and Nolan 1995; Michell and Fitzgerald 1997; Willcocks and Kern 1998). The logic behind such associations seems in part related to the complexity involved, the length of the deal, the costs, and the high degree of dependency on the vendor. The concern remains, though, whether such mega-deals merit the use of the term partnership or strategic alliance. In their study of three total outsourcing deals, Willcocks and Choi (1995) found that total outsourcing rarely has the characteristics of a strategic alliance, where there is usually 'a high degree of IT interdependence in primary internal areas of the organisations involved; and that there is a significant shared development and use of IT, focusing on external marketplace activities'. Moreover, Lacity and Hirschheim's (1993b) study similarly revealed that outsourcing relationships in their sample could rarely, if at all, be termed partnerships. In fact, 'the term "strategic partner" is unsuitable to characterise the relationship between an outsourcing vendor and its customer because the profit motive is not shared.' Consequently, the outsourcing relationship in most cases can neither be truly characterized as a partnership nor a strategic alliance. It rather seems that these terms are frequently used as analogies or as a shorthand, due to the lack of comprehensive research and conceptualization through which the intricacies of the relationship could be explained.

Previous Research on IT Outsourcing Relationships

This use of shorthand is not surprising. There is a dearth of studies in the parent discipline of Information Systems (IS), and all have limitations. Studies range from detailing prescriptive management tasks (Henderson 1990; Konsynski and McFarlan 1990), outlining evolutionary development (Lasher et al. 1988), prescription of relationship types (Elam 1988) through to leveraging IT for interorganizational coordination and cooperation (Bensaou and Venkatraman 1996; Kumar and Dissel 1996; Reekers and Smithson 1996). The prescriptive studies reveal few insights into the general dimensions of relations and potential underlying theory (see for example Henderson, 1990; Konsynski and McFarlan 1990; Lasher et al. 1988), whereas the others tend to be too limited in scope. Generally perplexing, though, was the fact that none explicitly addressed contracting and its management, perhaps because most were theoretically based, rather than true investigations into practice.

McFarlan and Nolan (1995), Klepper (1994, 1995), and Davis (1996) form the three main conceptual studies on the IT outsourcing relationship. McFarlan and Nolan's (1995) approach is more of an aggregation of helpful conceptual pointers, that has strong similarities to a checklist of the evolution, and hence handling, of an outsourcing alliance. The issues they raise seem good management practice, but are very general, with no empirical support to show how companies have handled the proposed parameters. Moreover, their generalization that outsourcing arrangements are in essence strategic alliances has been shown by Willcocks and Choi (1995) to be a dangerous assumption, as even total IT outsourcing ventures rarely possess the range of underlying characteristics integral to the alliance concept, for example risk-reward sharing (Child and Faulkner 1998; Doz and Hamel 1998; Faulkner 1995).

Klepper's (1994) first conceptual approach is based on a rigorous framework developed by Anderson and Narus (1990) in the marketing field, which he subsequently amends by integrating the concept of organizational adaptation to explain the dynamic and changing dimensions of the outsourcing relationship. The behaviourally focused model has at its core the dimensions 'outcomes' and 'relative dependence', from which unidirectional trust, influence, functionality of conflict, cooperation, and conflict are suggested to lead to satisfaction—all of which are particularly relevant to the outsourcing relationship (Kern 1997, 1999). The model is clearly restricted, though, in its focus on behavioural dimensions, thus providing little insights into exogenous and endogenous influences, such as the contract. Klepper's model also disregards the bidirectional influence that behaviours such as cooperation conflict (Axelrod 1984) and influence dependence (Emerson 1962) will have, which empirical findings have revealed (Kern and Silva 1998; Willcocks and Kern 1998).

Klepper's (1995) second relationship approach is again based on a conceptual model from the marketing field (by Dwyer, Schurr, and Oh 1987) which this time addresses the developmental stages of partnering relationships. He presents a life-cycle model of awareness, exploration, expansion, and commitment, which are pervaded by processes of attraction, communication, bargaining, development and exercise of power, norm development, and expectation development that supposedly lead to deeper relations. This constitutes an interesting approach, with a heavy behavioural focus. One dimension Klepper neglects completely this time is contracting and its effect on the resulting relationship; nor does he explain how structures and management processes evolve, even though they must surely underpin relationship development. It also seems that relations evolve in a vacuum unaffected by external factors or the other party.

Davis (1996) seems to follow Klepper's advice, elaborating an intricate web of economic and sociological theories to arrive at a 'straw man' model that supposedly aids decision makers in their analysis of the best control mechanism (price, trust, authority) to enforce in an outsourcing relationship. The precursor for the framework is the client's concern for the loss of control and future uncertainties. The resulting framework describes the outsourcing context (both endogenous and exogenous factors), the elements of organizational design (operating processes, structures, management systems, and human resource policies) in a matrix prescribed by control mechanisms (price, authority, trust), which, combined, are suggested to lead to sources of IT value creation. The three parts provide some of the essential ingredients of outsourcing relationships, alluding to the context, intention, structure, management processes, and likely outcome, but Davis too ignores completely the contract dimension. Moreover, the reasoning behind how the different dimensions are derived, and hence why only these three control mechanisms seem appropriate, is not apparent. Davis's theoretical eclecticism is confusing, as he not only relied on theory but also consultancy frameworks, and provides few justifications for his choices.

Auwers and Deschoolmeester (1993) and Willcocks and Choi (1995) provide empirically driven studies that attempt to explain their findings by using relationship frameworks from other disciplines. The underlying intention of each was to validate the adopted framework's explanatory potential. Auwers and Deschoolmeester (1993) present a single longitudinal case study of a Belgian chocolate manufacturer that entered into an outsourcing venture in the early 1990s for reasons of organizational restructuring, which they then analyse by use of Dwyer, Schurr, and Oh's (1987) evolutionary development model of a buyer–seller relationship (see above explanation). They conclude that the model can be adopted, but only if a number of critical changes are made to its developmental progression and its dimensions. Foremost, relational exchange was far more contractually formalized in outsourcing than in the model. In fact, the contract was of greater importance than indicated throughout the stages of the model. The stages also needed shifting to cater for multiple vendors and the lengthy selection process. Thirdly, the degree of trust also had a greater impact on relational development than considered in the model. Finally, a more general concern to raise about the case is whether it really presents a genuine outsourcing case or an insourcing deal. As it stands, the chocolate company essentially hired a vendor to provide mainframe computing services, which in light of today's understanding would most likely be considered buying-in services or an insourcing deal (Lacity and Willcocks 2000*b*).

On the other hand, Willcocks and Choi (1995) present an empirical study of three total outsourcing cases, characterized by some respondents as strategic partnerships. To analyse their empirical findings and assumptions, they use Henderson's (1990) strategic partnership framework. Henderson's prescriptive model identifies predisposition, commitment, and mutual benefits as factors in the 'context'; shared knowledge, mutual dependence on distinctive competency and resources, and organizational linkage are 'action' factors, that combined with the former determine partnerships. However, Willcocks and Choi (1995) identify a number of shortcomings of Henderson's framework, including:

- its neglect of the importance and centrality of the contract;
- its underestimation of difficulties and methods for building mutual dependence in outsourcing;
- its disregard of costs;
- the downplay of risk-reward arrangements;
- its disregard for external pressures and factors; and
- lack of detailed discussion on maintenance of a strategic partnership.

However, it should be pointed out that Henderson originally developed his partnering framework for in-house relationships between business units and the IT function, and it has only subsequently been applied, inappropriately, by others to outsourcing relationships. Willcocks and Choi conclude that Henderson's approach provides no more than a good starting point for understanding the basis on which total outsourcing relationships can be formed and developed as strategic relationships.

The above evaluation demonstrates, first, that our understanding of the outsourcing relationship is truly at an early stage, to the extent that no common framework has been identified or developed upon which to build our knowledge. Secondly, little overlaps exist between the different approaches and thus no common elements could be identified. Thirdly, the majority were found conceptually or empirically inconclusive. Fourthly, appropriating other relationship frameworks proved problematic, as they require considerable amendments before they can be used to investigate and explain the outsourcing relationship. Fifthly, the studies reveal a great deal of definitional ambiguity around the term relationship. To address this, the authors draw upon the *Collins Dictionary of English Language* (1986, p. 1289), which defines 'relationship' generally as 'the state of being connected or related; the mutual dealings, connections, or feelings that exist between two parties, countries, people, etc.' Furthermore, most discussions about the outsourcing relationship were found to be ambiguous because it is not always explicit whether they are referring to the relationship from an organizational or individual point of view. To cater for both levels, any definition has to integrate both. The following provides a basic definition of what the authors believe the outsourcing relationship involves:

The state where a client and vendor(s) organisation are connected or related via individual managers for the duration of the contract period of an outsourcing venture.

It is also the case that many studies fail to investigate the complexity of stakeholders and their relationships, assuming instead a straightforward client versus vendor dyad. Lacity and Willcocks (2000*b*) show a much more complex picture of eight types of stakeholder and their potentially differing expectations and goals. Finally, the frameworks did not present a sufficiently comprehensive approach that could be used to investigate and define outsourcing relationships. The most evident failing of all of them is the neglect of the contract dimension. But also the one-sided concern of some of the approaches for just behavioural aspects made them too narrowly focused to describe the outsourcing relationship holistically (see Kern 1999 for a more detailed critique).

ANALYSING OUTSOURCING RELATIONSHIPS: TOWARDS A FRAMEWORK

Since no existing framework has sufficiently integrated different perspectives and comprehensively delineated the outsourcing relationship, our research aims to address: *what constitutes a conceptual framework that adequately describes, and supports a detailed and comprehensive analysis of, an IT outsourcing relationship?*

The majority of research on relationships in IT outsourcing focuses on partnerships and their complexity. As discussed, researchers have often suggested that only total outsourcing warrants to be termed a strategic partnership or alliance (cf. Davis 1996; Saunders, Gebelt, and Hu 1997), yet this perspective has distracted from the fact that all outsourcing ventures entail a relationship that includes a common set of dimensions. As a departure from this and in an attempt to explore the relationship issue from a perspective that is perhaps more in line with concerns and priorities of managers involved in outsourcing, we need to raise a further question: *what does relationship management commonly entail in an outsourcing venture?*

The starting point for building an analytical framework are the extant studies of IT outsourcing relationships (Table 2.1). These contain three underlying

Table 2.1. *Prevailing views on IT outsourcing relationships*

Perspective	Theoretical orientation	Focus of concern	IS research examples
Economic	• Transaction cost theory	• Cost efficiency	Lacity and Hirschheim 1993*a*
	• Agency cost theory	• Benefits	Alpar and Saharia 1993
Competitive	• Contract	• Control	Halvey and Melby 1995
		• Legal security	Burnett 1998
Partnering	• Behavioural	• Relationship	Davis 1996
	• Sociological		Kleppers 1994 and 1995
			McFarlan and Nolan 1995

Source: Burnett 1998.

perspectives. The 'economic view' and its focus on economic efficiency alludes to the client's, but also the vendor's concern for the economic impetus in the relationship. The 'competitive view' arises from the client's concern for control, which stands threatened by outsourcing. Legal security through a formalized contract ensures clients can 'maximize control' in their relationship. Finally, the 'partnering view' argues that outsourcing does not follow completely the norms predicted by competitive rivalry or cost efficiency, but instead there is a sense of partnering given the long-term nature of these relationships: 'Organisations must strike a balance between maintaining competitive pressure and building strong relationships with selected vendors' (Hurst and Hanessian 1995: 106). Additionally there needs to be a focus on the sociological and behavioural factors that arise when developing a relationship. All three perspectives are fundamental to the outsourcing relationship, and all three need to be integrated into a comprehensive multi-dimensional framework, as each of the perspectives has a unique emphasis that contributes to the understanding of the outsourcing relationship in its entirety. Furthermore, this approach also endorses Klepper's (1995) and Willcocks and Choi's (1995) finding that research into outsourcing relationships needs to combine several theories and elements for a better understanding.

At this critical point, however, we need to go beyond the inadequacies of the extant IT outsourcing literature. Although the relationship could be studied from a range of theoretical perspectives, the present study brings to bear three influential streams of research from the broader organizational and management studies literature. These are transaction cost, relational contract, and interorganizational relationship theories. These correspond directly to the 'economic', 'competitive', and 'partnering' perspectives on outsourcing detailed in Table 2.2. Combined, they have the potential to capture much more richly a relationship's key dimensions, as well as provide a framework for assessing organizational impact. All three perspectives have extensive theoretical and empirical support. Let us look at them in more detail.

Transaction cost theory (TCT) emphasizes organizational concerns with efficiency (Williamson 1979). It examines the coordination and governance of economic actors in their transaction with one another. It focuses on how organizations choose to transact, based on the costs of production and transactions, and then determines the optimal governance structures that minimize total costs (Williamson 1975, 1985). Transaction cost theory essentially analyses conditions under which alternative governance structures between markets and hierarchies, i.e. classical, neo-classical, or relational contracts, are the most efficient forms of organizing economic activities (Ghoshal and Moran 1995). It provides a well-used approach for analysing the outsourcing option from an economic perspective and for investigating whether exchanges are conducted through market transactions or within hierarchical arrangements such as strategic partnerships or joint ventures.

Relational contract theory (RCT) highlights that all contracts include contractual relations (Macneil 1974*b*). The approach provides a means to analyse the behaviours and norms that are expected in particular types of contractual relations (Macneil 1980). At the centre of the theory are two key elements: first, the description of contract behaviours, i.e. norms that arise in exchange relations. Second, is the dimension of contractual discreteness, from discrete to relational. Contractual relations can be distinguished according to their discreteness along the former spectrum by considering the complexity of some of the behavioural elements of exchange relations (Macneil 1987). In IT outsourcing the spectrum is defined as arms-length market-based relationship and strategic relationship (Ang and Beath 1993; Klepper 1995). RCT provides the crucial legal perspective and a highly usable approach through which to analyse the contractual relations in outsourcing (see Kern and Blois 2000).

Interorganizational relationship theory (IOR) is concerned with the reasons and conditions for forming relationships (including socio-political and economic aspects), and their structural, behavioural, and process dimensions (Oliver 1990; Van de Ven and Ring 1994). Although the focus of most IOR studies has been on the isolated dyad, a number of scholars have argued for an extended view that includes relational networks (Aldrich and Whetten 1981; Anderson, Hakansson, and Johanson 1994). Of interest are the reasons and conditions for formation that describe the intent of a company for entering into such relationships (Oliver 1990), the structural characteristics that prescribe the overall pattern of relationships between the parties (Van de Ven and Ferry 1980), the exchange behaviours that influence the relationship (Anderson and Narus 1990), and the types and characteristics of interactions (Aldrich and Whetten 1981; Tichy 1981). IOR theory provides a useful approach for understanding and analysing the causes and conditions for the formation of a relationship, and the structural, behavioural, and interaction dimensions.

Other theories considered, but disregarded, were social exchange theory (Blau 1964; Emerson 1972; Homans 1961) and resource dependency theory (Pfeffer and Salancik 1978). Social exchange theory was abandoned as it underlies and hence pervades IOR theory and relational contract theory. Even though exchange theory defines the dominant paradigm of IORs, it was found too narrowly focused on the structural dimension of exchange relations (Blau 1987; Turner 1987). On the other hand, the concepts of politics, power, and dependence inherent to resource dependence theory are ingrained in all three of the above paradigms. Although resource dependency theory provides a powerful approach to analysing the political dimension in organizations and the interactions between organizations, it was disregarded as its core argument that organizational survival depends on acquiring resources is negligible as a reason for outsourcing alone.

Each of the theoretical perspectives has a unique emphasis that contributes to a broad understanding of the outsourcing relationship, but each is primarily concerned with a specific part of a larger phenomenon. In particular, IOR theory describes and analyses exchange and its influence on organizational behaviour and structural dimensions. TCT explains the efficiency of institutional

Table 2.2. *Three perspectives informing the relationships framework*

	Interorganizational relationship theory	Transaction cost theory	Relational contract theory
Paradigm	(Social) exchange theory Industrial marketing	Classical and neo-classical economics	Classical and neo-classical contract theory Social exchange theory
Unit of analysis	Dyadic interorganizational relationships	Relational transaction costs	Contractual relations
Basic assumption	Inter-firm relations arise for a number of reasons and entail a particular set of behavioural and structural dimensions	The cost of transactions is critical for the choice of an optimal governance structure	Business contracts inherently are relational and entail a number of norms
Strengths	Examines the reason(s), exchanges, and behavioural and structural dimensions of dyadic inter-firm relationships	Analyses the efficiency and costs of governance structures	Holistic approach that considers the behaviours and dimensions of different contractual relations
Weaknesses	Determinants covered are fragmented, broad ranging, and heterogeneous Studies focused primarily on public and welfare sector	Narrowly focused on economic aspects Discrete and static analysis that assumes the existence of an optimal structure	Discusses only the polar archetypes of discrete and intertwined relations Lack of empirical studies to support relational concept
Contribution to study and framework	Analysis of the reason for formation, exchanges, and structural and behavioural aspects of interorganizational relationships	Conceptualizes efficiency of the interorganizational relationship	Investigates the essence of contractual relations and the pattern of behaviours

governance structures. RCT focuses on contractual behaviours and those dimensions that distinguish between different types of contractual relations. Together, the theories cover an organizational, behavioural, economic, and legal perspective of the outsourcing relationship. All in turn imply different perspectives on the nature of outsourcing relationships.

As we would expect, each individual theory has a range of weaknesses/preoccupations that leave certain aspects uncovered or unexplained (see Table 2.2).

Consequently, the outsourcing relationship may be inadequately explained by any single theoretical perspective. As others before have argued, a single approach tends to be too narrow to address the complexity of the observable phenomena at hand (Bensaou and Venkatraman 1996; De Looff 1997; Grover, Teng, and Cheon 1998).

Linkages of multiple perspectives for research provides useful opportunities for synergy, and improves the efficiency of social science research. Indeed, multiple-perspective research is particularly appropriate in situations where the area of research is relatively unexplored. However, there are a number of problems inherent in using multiple perspectives. Multiple paradigms offer both 'potential richness, but also the dangers of theoretical confusion and complexity in the possible routes forward' (Willcocks and Lacity 1998). In their review of outsourcing research, Willcocks and Lacity identified three potential dangers in adopting an eclectic approach. One issue is the concern for the degree of compatibility between theories; the second is the appropriateness of the theories for the phenomena studied; and the third is the adoption of theories without being aware of the critique and controversies surrounding the approach in its own discipline.

In our approach we attempt to minimize all three dangers. One way would have been to analyse the outsourcing relationship from each perspective separately, but this would result in considerable ambiguity, overlap, and redundancy. Although each of the theoretical perspectives has a distinct view and sheds a different light on the outsourcing relationship, the approaches are intertwined. For example, transaction cost theory shares with relational contract theory an interest in opportunism and asset specificity. Interorganizational relationship theory considers power and conflict in a way which seems synonymous with power and conflict in relational contract theory.

In fact, across all three theories a behavioural dimension exercises a greater or lesser influence. Often similar elements play different roles in the three theories. For example, efficiency in interorganizational relationship theory determines the reason for outsourcing, whereas efficiency in transaction cost theory analyses the governance mode and costs of operations. Uncertainty is considered by all three theories. However, it influences the outcome in different ways. In relational contract theory uncertainty influences the degree of presentiation, the type of contractual relation, and the pattern of behaviours, whereas in interorganizational theory it describes a reason for forming relations. All three theoretical perspectives concentrate on dyadic relationships (Davis and Powell 1992; Ring 1996), the difference being that interorganizational relationship theory is concerned with the reasons for relations, structural, exchange, and behavioural issues, while transaction cost theory looks at the economic, i.e. efficiency aspect, and relational contract theory concentrates on the contract behaviours and legal issues.

We proceeded by applying each theoretical perspective and concept to the outsourcing relationship then selecting what seemed on balance, taking into

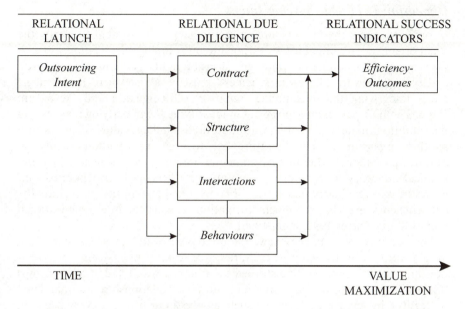

Fig. 2.2. *The relationship advantage: overview of the conceptual framework*

account strengths and weaknesses, the most suitable for specific purposes, using a contingency approach (Grover, Teng, and Cheon 1998). Each of the theories and concepts is integrated to the extent that it is found best to address a number of specific issues, thus ensuring good use is made of the strengths of each theory, while duplication and overlaps are minimized. The remainder of this chapter discusses the main dimensions and elements of the analytical framework that can be built in this way from previous IT outsourcing relationship studies and from the application of concepts and issues dealt with in interorganizational relationship, transaction cost, and relational contract theories. A full discussion of the theory-building process used here can be found in Kern (1999). Figure 2.2 presents an overview of the resulting framework's structure and its six interrelated dimensions, which we will now proceed to detail.

THE RELATIONSHIP ADVANTAGE: RELATIONAL LAUNCH

Every relationship is launched with particular guiding objectives, reasons, and intentions. These define often not only the short-term, but more importantly the long-term objectives for entering, forming, and maintaining a relationship. For the suppliers it is about facilitating these goals to achieve ultimately relational success and customer satisfaction.

Dimension 1: IT Outsourcing Intent

In order to assess the IT outsourcing relationship it is essential to clarify the client organization's intent for venturing into outsourcing: 'the relationship with the vendor—for example, contract type, decision rights, performance measures, and risk-and-reward allocation schemes—must be aligned with the strategic intent underlying the outsourcing initiative' (DiRomualdo and Gurbaxani 1998). The IOR paradigm is powerful in identifying the underlying reasons and the conditions under which organizations establish linkages and exchanges with another organization. The literature has focused its attention mainly on resource procurement due to environmental, internal, or task uncertainty and political advocacy as reasons for formation. Others have also pointed out, however, that regulatory necessities, organizational legitimization, reciprocity, and efficiency are also prominent formation reasons for interorganizational relationships (Oliver 1990; Ring 1996).

The resource procurement view (voluntary necessity) provides significant insights into problems that arise from resource scarcity and asymmetry in relationships, as well as suggesting strategies for coping with these in relationships (Galaskiewicz 1985). In some situations, however, relationships are mandated (necessity) by higher authorities, such as the industry or government. In contrast, reciprocity alludes to an organization's motivation to cooperate or collaborate with another organization. Cooperative interorganizational relationships are formed for a multitude of reasons and have become an important business option in the form of alliances, partnerships, or joint ventures (Doz and Hamel 1998; Faulkner 1995). Realization of political interests through organizational legitimization of particular practices, procedures, processes, or functions can also define an important reason for fostering interfirm relations (Benson 1975; Lacity and Hirschheim 1993a, 1993b).

For evaluation purposes, the intent for outsourcing in this study refers to the objectives and scope pursued through contracting with a vendor. The motivation of organizations to outsource in the past primarily concentrated on cost reduction (Lacity and Hirschheim 1993a, 1993b; Willcocks and Fitzgerald 1994), although more recently this has shifted to an emphasis on improving organizational performance (Willcocks and Currie 1997). In their study of outsourcing deals worldwide, DiRomualdo and Gurbaxani (1998) found that the traditional justification of vendor economics of scale and specialization had become less convincing as the key reason for outsourcing. Instead, others such as improving IT's contribution to the organization's performance within its existing lines of business and the commercial exploitation of IT, by leveraging technology-related assets such as applications, operations, infrastructure, and know-how in the market place through the development and marketing of products and services have become prominent. However, cost efficiency continues to be a decisive factor, in addition to a number of reasons, such as technical issues, lagging IT performance, business objectives, vendor pressure, and political reasons (Willcocks and Currie 1997; Lacity and Willcocks 1998; McFarlan and Nolan 1995). Multiple reasons more often determine the motivation for outsourcing. Table 2.3 summarizes the four components of intent and the basis for launching into an outsourcing relationship.

Necessity. The necessity to form exchange relations arises commonly from the need for particular resources. Ongoing specialization of organizations has become a primal cause for relationships, as organizations no longer produce internally all the materials and products necessary to continue business. In the 1990s, specialization gathered further pace through the push to focus on the organization's core competencies.

In the context of the necessity element we here distinguish between 'mandatory' and 'voluntary' reasons for entering into exchange relationships. In some situations organizations may find themselves mandated by 'higher authorities', such as government agencies, legislation, industry, or regulatory bodies to form linkages with other organizations (Oliver 1990). By contrast, 'voluntary necessity' involves restricted forms of choice. Once stakeholders make decisions on an organization's objectives and purposes, then, in the light of resource requirements, and business, technical, economic, and political imperatives another decision may well need to follow, to 'buy rather than to make' products or services and hence form a relationship with another organization.

The next paragraphs give some understanding of these latter voluntary reasons. In general, the necessity to outsource will become clear in the antecedent conditions and organizational objectives.

Reciprocity. In many situations organizations form collaborative or cooperative relationships with others, because there are significant mutual benefits to be gained by doing so. For example, R&D activities in high-technology industries such as aerospace and biotechnology are often so capital, time, labour and resource intensive that by collaborating with others these costs can be shared. Other benefits are available by generating a resource synergy, in which two organizations combine the strengths and overcome the weaknesses of their resources (Ring 1996). The implicit and explicit motive for any form of cooperative IOR is reciprocity. Indeed, 'motives of reciprocity emphasise cooperation, collaboration, and coordination among organisations, rather than domination, power, and control' (Oliver 1990).

The degree of reciprocity depends on the expected benefits that are available by cooperating or collaborating. Benefits such as business or technical improvements will increase reciprocity. According to DiRomualdo and Gurbaxani (1998) improving business performance by exploiting technology through the vendor's 'state-of-the-art' technical expertise and capabilities influences the degree of cooperation. Similarly, the conjoint commercial exploitation of technologies, IS products, practices, or processes by launching a new business will also significantly effect reciprocity. Irrespective of these scenarios, a common level of reciprocity is implicit, and the breakdown of this is likely to strain the relationship and lead to conflict.

Legitimacy. The pressures to legitimize organizational operations, activities, or outputs present at times strong reasons to form interorganizational relationships. According to Oliver (1990) the formation of an interorganizational relationship to increase legitimacy can originate from an organization's motives to demonstrate or improve its reputation, image, prestige, or congruence with prevailing norms in its institutional environment. Few empirical studies have been undertaken to relate the legitimacy aspect specifically to interorganizational relationships. In IT outsourcing, an interesting aspect has been the strong degree to which share price increases have been related to announcements of large-scale outsourcing, indicating such decisions may sometimes be a legitimation tactic to persuade investors and analysts about the strategic direction and value of the company (Loh and Venkatraman 1992*a*, 1992*b*; Lacity and Willcocks 2000b).

For the purpose of our framework, the focus on legitimacy is at the organizational level of the client company. Legitimacy refers to the underlying political motivations that influenced the organization to legitimize its internal IT operations by outsourcing. In the case studies, we will evaluate legitimacy through respondents' views of the outsourcing arrangement and how it develops.

Efficiency. The outsourcing relationship is most often formed to enhance the efficiency of the IT resource and reduce costs, though this is increasingly

Table 2.3. *The IT outsourcing intent dimension*

Element	Operational definition	Evaluation pointers
Outsourcing intent	Objectives and scope pursued through contracting with a vendor	
Necessity	Distinction between 'mandated' and 'voluntary'	• Mandated pressure to outsource • Voluntary—chosen goals make outsourcing an imperative
Reciprocity	Anticipated benefits by cooperating or collaborating with the vendor	• Degree of expected cooperation and collaboration • Technical improvements • Business improvements • Financial improvements (e.g. percentage of revenue)
Legitimacy	Underlying political motivations	• Perception of politics involved
Efficiency	Expected cost reductions	• Cost reductions achieved • Improved cost control • One-off cash injection

one of multiple objectives an organization will pursue (see also Chapter 1). Clearly, the efficiency contingencies are internally oriented and prompted by an organization's attempt to improve its internal input/output ratio (Oliver 1990). Some reasons for forming interorganizational relationships to arrive at efficiency are inspired by an organization's expectations of increases in return on assets, reduction in unit costs, benefits from economies of scale, and general improvement of operations at lower costs. Related to IT outsourcing, the efficiency intent is seen as a means to capitalize on the firm's intangible IT assets, reduce costs, strengthen the firm's balance sheet, receive a cash injection, change a fixed-cost to a variable-cost structure, and improve overall cost control (Lacity, Willcocks, and Feeny 1995; McFarlan and Nolan 1995). An indication of the efficiency motive is revealed by the degree to which an organization expects to reduce costs by outsourcing. Other efficiency evaluation pointers are improved cost control and one-off cash injections.

THE RELATIONSHIP ADVANTAGE: 'RELATIONAL DUE DILIGENCE'

Relationship management depends on carefully planning and formulating the contract, devising operational structures, outlining the interactions and leveraging and forming relational behaviours. These define the 'relational due diligence' criteria that need consideration prior to the post-contract management phase, but also describe the relationship dimensions that need ongoing management throughout the venture.

It is about setting the ground rules for the relationship and making sure in subsequent operations that the relationship works.

Dimension 2: Contract

The Relational Contract paradigm offers an understanding of the essential differences between contractual relations along a number of contractual and behavioural dimensions. Discrete contracts describe the basis upon which the majority of contractual relations are formed in interorganizational relationships (Dwyer, Schurr, and Oh 1987). Discreteness is associated with the level of contractual completeness. Conversely, a contract is relational according to Goetz and Scott (1981) to the extent that it embodies clauses in which important terms of the arrangement are not reduced to well-defined obligations. Long-term ventures will have a tendency towards a relational contract form, since contracts in business are often impossible to plan completely for the duration of the deal. Consequently, parties to a continuing contractual relationship depend not only on the legal, i.e. stipulated terms, but also require the use of extralegal mechanisms (for example behavioural aspects—see below) to cater for incompleteness and to reduce the information and enforcement deficits. Remembering that contract is a promise or a set of promises that are legally enforceable and binding for the duration of the contractual relationship. A promise is: 'the manifestation of intention to act or refrain from acting in a specified way, so made as to justify a promisee in understanding that a commitment has been made' (Macneil 1974*b*: 713).

In their study of software outsourcing contracts, Ang and Beath (1993) empirically showed that unlike the suggestions of discrete contracts, parties to a contract in reality dynamically interact, commit to, and reinterpret their agreements with one another to assure necessary flexibility. Therefore, promise used as a projector for future exchanges is not always the most effective means, as it suffers from the bounded rationality of individuals (Barnett 1992). Furthermore, depending on the complexity of the contract, anticipating all future events and covering them by making them present in the promise—called 'presentiation'—is impossible (Macneil 1974*a*). Non-promissory accompaniments become mandatory to ensure contractual relations continue and promises are kept. Relational contracts depend on a balance between promises and non-promissory accompaniments to project exchanges into the future. Promise is the more visible and anticipated factor, whereas non-promissory accompaniments represent the gel and unnoticed gap-fillers that are difficult to define because of the great diversity in contract relations. The three elements of the contract dimension are summarized in Table 2.4.

Promises. A promise in this study refers to the assurance or obligation to perform the expected and required exchanges in the relationship. Contract as promise suffers from a number of problems including enforcement rationale, reliance on promise, and gaps left. Promises are made irrespective of potentially expecting to be compelled to keep them. In turn inherent to promissory commitments is a degree of ambiguity, which needs consideration when contractually pressuring a party to enforce them (Barnett 1992). Related is the reliance on the promises made. Promises are made in situations where they should not be perceived as an absolute (Macaulay 1963). Perceiving them as absolute can have a detrimental effect, as promises may, should, and will be broken.

In outsourcing, promises determine the contractual obligations and the sources of the exchange content, i.e. service levels, pricing arrangements, the formal information requirements, and other exchanges for the present and future. Promises depend on the degree to which they have been exactly specified and agreed. Their measurement indicates the extent to which promises are being kept. Relating this to outsourcing, monitoring the vendor's service performance and payments describes part of the client's key management tasks (Feeny and Willcocks 1998). Although keeping a promise is critical as it defines the reason for the contractual relations, in some cases developments require parties to break promises. This depends on the degree to which change is necessary to assure promises continue to be mutually beneficial. In addition, some promises made in a contractual relationship may have stopped serving their usefulness and are substituted by others, so that promises no longer should be kept.

Non-promissory accompaniments. Contracts are shadowed by non-promissory accompaniments since contracting parties often fail to cover all foreseeable contingencies. Customs, standards, industry practices, bureaucratic patterns, and other internalized practices of an organization can fill gaps in the expressed agreements of parties. A decisive means to fill gaps is the use of a third party for arbitration or even a court hearing. Macneil (1974*b*) emphasized, however, that often the most important non-promissory accompaniments are the expectations that future exchanges and other future motivations arising out of the dependence on the ongoing exchange relation will cause exchange to occur in a predictable pattern. Expectations in effect take a role of projecting exchange into the future without having detailed all of the elements' specificity or measurements. In IT outsourcing contractual completeness is likely to be influenced by the clarity of content (e.g. detail of service levels) and the clarity of organizational expectations.

'Presentiation'. As defined by Macneil (1974*a*): 'to presentiate is to make or render the present in place or time; to cause to be perceived or realised as present.' Presentiation identifies the degree to which the future requirements have been brought into the present contract. No individual, however, can know

Table 2.4. *The contract dimension*

Element	Operational definition	Evaluation pointer
Contract	A promise or a set of promises that are legally enforceable and binding for the duration of the contractual relationship	
Promise	The expected and required exchanges in the relationship	• Contractual obligations • Source of exchange content • Degree of exchange specificity • Measurements to monitor promises are kept • Necessity to change promises
Non-promissory accompaniments	The degree of contractual completeness	• Clarity of content • Clarity of expectations
'Presentiation'	The degree to which future requirements are imbedded in the present contract	• Bindingness of promise • Contractual completeness

all the causes affecting results in any complex sequence of events, so that the ability to presentiate is always a limited one. In effect, this limitation leads to projecting the present into the future, rather than bringing the future backwards into the present. Contracting intentions thus have a tendency to concentrate on how the present will affect the future, and whether the present arrangements will continue to be sufficient in the future. Any outsourcing relationship necessarily has to strive to assure the highest degree of presentiation to preserve the venture's efficiency and hinder any opportunistic behaviour from the parties involved (Ang and Beath 1993; Kern and Willcocks 2000).

Dimension 3: Structure

Interorganizational Relationship Theory offers a lens for examining the structural dimension of an IT outsourcing relationship. Although little about structures of outsourcing relationships has been discussed so far, some suggestions come from their close association with buyer–supplier relationships (Klepper 1994; Davis 1996). Buyer–supplier relationships entail a set of structural properties such as size, centralization, specialization, and configuration (Hakansson and Snehota 1995) that can be assumed to broadly correspond to the outsourcing relationship. The elements we identify from the literature as describing the structural dimension of the outsourcing relationship are summarized in Table 2.5.

Size. Two factors are of main concern. First, the sheer size of the outsourcing arrangement, in terms of the number of organizations directly contracted to deliver services to the client organization. Secondly, the actual size of the organizations, especially that of the client organization. In both cases increased size will increase the complexity of the deal. Of course, measuring an organization's size is problematic and ambiguous. These ambiguities have resulted in a large number of indices for measuring size, including for example number of employees, resources for disposal (e.g. funds and property), production turnover, and annual turnover.

In general, organizational size influences the level of power (or control) in the interfirm relationship. Klepper (1994) noted that in outsourcing power and 'dependence increases with the size and importance of the client's business to the vendor, with the proportion of the vendor's business represented by the client firm, with the difficulty the vendor would have in replacing this business, and with the image of the client firm (high visibility firms give status to the vendor and make it easier for the vendor to win other business).' Thus, the number of exchange partners, and the size and status of the organization in its industry are important structural elements.

Complexity. This refers to the variety of services and the multiplicity of exchanges between the client and vendor. The influence of complexity on the organization is in terms of management structures, divisions of labour, and coordination efforts. Child (1973) established that as an organization's task volume increases, the internal structure will become more complex. Relating this to the outsourcing relationship, as the variety of the IT functions and projects outsourced and hence the exchanges increase, so will the complexity of the relationship. An increase in complexity is likely to have a number of effects. Child (1973) found that the number of hierarchical levels is likely to increase, as well as the number of specialist functions, the standardization of procedures, while the centralization of decision making will most likely decrease. In IT outsourcing the greater the complexity, the more intensive the demand for interorganizational interactions and hence the higher the transaction costs (Williamson 1975).

Vertical and occupational management structure. Complexity clearly influences the vertical and occupational management structure of the relationship. In IT outsourcing several individuals from different functional areas, at

Table 2.5. *The structural dimension*

Element	Operational definition	Evaluation pointers
Structural Dimension	Structure of the client–vendor relationship	
Size	A. Number of organizations directly contracted to provide IT services and size of deal B. The actual size of the client organization	A. Number of service providers Number of contracts B. Annual turnover Status in the industry The proportion of the vendor's business represented by the client firm Importance of the deal to the vendor
Complexity	The variety of services and multiplicity of exchanges	• Complexity of service exchanges • Task volume of outsourcing
Vertical and occupational management structure	The impact of outsourcing on the organization and the density of the relationship management structure	• Individuals involved in managing relationship • Management focus of individuals • Number of individuals transferred
Stability	The continuity of the relationship	• Length of contract • Frequency of change in individual relationships

different levels in the hierarchy, and fulfilling different roles generally become involved (see Chapter 1). In respect to outsourcing, McFarlan and Nolan (1995) explained that:

the interfaces between customer and outsourcer are very complex and should occur at multiple levels [. . .] At the most senior levels, there must be links to deal with major issues of policy and relationship structuring, while at lower levels, there must be mechanisms for identifying and handling more operational and tactical issues.

Outsourcing relationships will vary in the density of vertical and occupational involvement according to the size of the undertaking and its complexity. The density determines the management structure for the outsourcing relationship. In addition, the number of individuals transferred and the number of individuals actively involved gives an indication of the organizational impact.

Stability. The stability of an interorganizational relationship has been seen as a coping strategy 'to forestall, forecast, or absorb uncertainty in order to achieve an orderly, reliable pattern of resource flows and exchanges' (Oliver 1990). Here, stability refers to the continuity of the outsourcing relationship. Stability focuses on two aspects. First is the contractual time frame and/or expected continuity of the outsourcing venture. Second is the continuity of individual relations, as an indicator of the stability of the relationship. The overall time frame can be evaluated by the length and history of the outsourcing relationship. The use of the length of contact has been successfully applied in outsourcing studies as a structural indicator (Lacity and Hirschheim 1995).

Dimension 4: Interactions

Exchange is the dominant process underpinning interorganizational relations (IOR). It determines the essential reason for entering into relations and becomes the focal event of the relationship. Interactions among cooperating parties may cast a positive, neutral, or negative overtone on the relationship, influencing the parties' behaviours toward each other. Exchange also forms a focal point for identifying the social structure of individuals and organizations that participate in the exchange's formation and execution; is a critical event in the market place allowing the careful study of antecedent conditions and process of interfirm exchange; and also provides an opportunity to examine the domain of the objects or psychic entities that are transferred. Exchange as such does not necessarily only involve elements of economic value, but it may also include services, symbols, and economic units.

Relevant elements for study include the actual exchange content, the normative content which pervades both implicit and explicit exchanges, and the communication content, which supports and underlies most exchanges and will vary between formal and informal. Together, these interactions define the basic elements of processes in and between organizations (Van de Ven and Ferry 1980). In respect to outsourcing, the exchange content describes the service, technical, product, and financial exchanges, whereas the communication content is defined by formal information exchanges such as service reports and accounts (Willcocks and Kern 1998). The resulting interactions can be characterized by their degree of standardization, reciprocity, and formality. The entire relationship has to be viewed against the interaction backdrop. The four elements that operationalize the concept of interaction are summarized in Table 2.6.

Exchange content. In the outsourcing relationship, as in other IORs, the focus is on the utilitarian exchange. Goods or resources are exchanged in return for money or other goods. As Bagozzi (1975) noted, the motivation behind the actions taken by individuals participating in the exchange relationship lies in the anticipated use or tangible characteristics associated with the objects in the exchange. Therefore, the exchange content in most instances can be referred to as economic and essentially identifies goods and payments.

Normative content. This element refers to the expectations organizational stakeholders have of one another because of some social characteristics or attributes (Aldrich and Whetten 1981). The normative content underpins the economic exchange. In interfirm relations they involve the mutual transfer of psychological, social, or other intangible entities that smooth interactions (Bagozzi 1975). Relating this element to the outsourcing relationship, the normative dimension exists primarily at the individual or group level and concentrates on their perceptual degree of satisfaction with the services provided.

Communication content. The information that is passed from one organization to another has several interesting aspects in interfirm relationships. First is the degree to which technical, economic, or organizational information content dominates the exchange. In their study of 140 dealer–manufacturer relationships, Mohr and Spekman (1996) found that the quality of communication content—defined as timeliness, adequacy, completeness, and credibility —had a positive impact on the relationship's overall success. Second is the degree of formality of the communication, which applies to all interactions and exchanges (see below). Finally, the means of actual communication—either personal or impersonal—matters. Personal communication is suggested to be used to discuss and transfer 'soft information'; for example, information concerning an institutional operating custom. Impersonal communication is often used to transfer basic technical and/or commercial data (Hakansson 1982).

Type of interaction. The type of interaction refers to the characteristic of the exchange link. Three types characterize the link in outsourcing—formality, reciprocity, and standardization. Formality refers to the degree to which activities and exchanges are clearly prescribed and codified. This will depend on a range of factors, including the type of information communicated and the degree of contractual completeness.

Reciprocity refers to the degree to which relations and hence exchanges are symmetric (Tichy 1981). Relating this to the outsourcing relationship, it is evident that for the services the vendor delivers it receives a set amount of money, thus it may be termed symmetric. On occasions, however, exchanges

Table 2.6. *The interaction dimension*

Element	Operational definition	Evaluation pointer
Interactions	The process dimension and focus of the outsourcing relationship	
Exchange content	The economic exchanges in the relationship	• Goods and resources exchanged • Money or goods in return as payment
Normative content	The expectations one organization has of another because of some social characteristics	• Perceptual degree of satisfaction with exchanges
Communication content	The information that is passed from one organization to another	• Degree of technical, economic, and organizational information • Extent of impersonal and personal communication
Type of interaction	The characteristic of the exchange link	• Degree of formality • Degree to which relations are symmetric • Extent of standardization

may be asymmetric, especially in those instances of failed service delivery. The third indicator is the degree of standardization, which indicates the extent to which exchanges are non-specific and routine or highly specific and clearly case-dependent. In respect to outsourcing, standardization depends on the complexity of the technology and services outsourced. A high market maturity with standardized practices exists for some IT functions such as data processing or software development which simplifies contracting and hence management of the interactions (Willcocks and Fitzgerald 1994*a*).

Dimension 5: Behaviour

Both the Relational Contract and Interorganizational Relationship paradigms are powerful in identifying the major elements representing behaviours in interorganizational relationships. The behaviours adopted can have both a positive and negative influence on the relationship. Generally, they can establish the standards of conduct and set the ground rules for future interactions (Dwyer,

Schurr, and Oh 1987; Macneil 1980). Relevant elements here identified from the literature are dependence, power, conflict, cooperation, and trust. Dependence indicates the extent to which exchange partners depend on each other in terms of delivering the volume and quality of services contractually agreed. Power defines the degree of influence a party has over another, and to what extent political tactics can be employed by a party to gain an advantage over the other. Conflict and cooperation are opposing elements referring to both a behavioural dimension and relationship status. Resolving conflict amicably is crucial for the preservation of the relationship. Trust evolves as a result of a number of the former elements and relational continuation. Trusting another party is about confidence that they will undertake actions favourable to you. These elements defining the behavioural dimension in the framework are summarized in Table 2.7.

Dependence. Of concern is not only the degree of dependence in relationships, but also the extent to which the dependence is on one particular source. In fact, the more an organization is dependent on a single source, the greater the likelihood is that that source will control the necessary resources. In IT outsourcing it is the desire of the client organization to control the vendor which is likely to effect the relationship's structure (De Looff 1997).

Dependence can be evaluated through the degree of mutual dependency on the particular relationship, the client's dependence on services, expertise, and capabilities of the vendor, and the importance of the relationship to the parties involved (Kern and Willcocks 1996). Additional indicators are prestige of the client and the proportion of turnover it comprises. Others have used the ease with which an exchange partner can be replaced as an empirical measure.

Power. This can be a key influence on dependence. Determinants of organizational power include organization size, access to and control over resources, control over the rules governing the exchange and the ability to choose a 'do without' strategy because of the existence of alternative sources (Dwyer, Schurr, and Oh 1987; Oliver 1990). Power can range from little power, through balanced power to imbalance and centralized power. Measuring exercised power directly is very difficult. Traditionally, power has been distinguished as: coercive, non-coercive, influence, authority, and force (Anderson and Narus 1990; Kumar 1996). Power is enforced both unilaterally and bilaterally in relations (Macneil 1980). In IORs power has been recognized to exist in two general types: perceived power and actual control (Reve and Stern 1979). The latter is actually regarded as something that can be objectively measured, whereas the former can only be evaluated in a subjective manner.

Power in this study refers to the degree of control and influence a stakeholder has over a client organization's IT strategy, and outsourcing destiny (Kern and Silva 1998). Contractual completeness influences the client's level of control and its power to assure the vendor does not resort to opportunistic behaviour (Hart 1995). Suggested means of evaluation focus on the perceived extent to which the client exercises unilateral power over the vendor. This is affected by

Table 2.7. *The behaviour dimension*

Element	Operational definition	Evaluation pointer
Behaviour dimension	Standards of conduct and ground rules for future interactions	
Dependence	The degree to which participants depend on each other to achieve their own objectives	• Importance of relationship to either party • The criticality of the exchanges, e.g. services, expertise, and capabilities • The proportion of turnover • Easiness of switching relations
Power	The perceived degree of control and influence	• Perceived power use • Level of dependency on vendor and/or relationship
Conflict	Negative perceptions about the exchange relationship with the vendor	• Constraints of effectiveness • Frequency of conflict • Intensity of conflict • Measures taken to preserve relations
Cooperation	The undertaking of complementary activities	• Effective communication • Exchanges leading to satisfactory outcomes
Trust	The client organization's belief that the vendor will perform the required contractual exchanges and actions that will result in beneficial outcomes	• Performance of obligations and commitments • Perceived benefits, satisfaction, and equitableness • Motivation to continue the relationship

the level of dependency, actual or perceived, either party has on the other and the relationship (Hakansson 1982).

Conflict. Both the desire for maximizing control and the reluctance to lose control reflects the most common motive for conflict. Interfirm conflict is a common area of study in both IOR theory and the channels of distribution field. It is said that conflict can be alleviated by increased control and cooperation (Frazier 1983; Anderson and Narus 1990). In effect, both conflict and cooperation exist simultaneously in IORs and are found interdependent (Axelrod 1984). Mitigation of conflict is essential to preserve the relationship and ensure ongoing collaboration (Macneil 1980).

Conflict arises in a number of ways. Lusch (1978) described conflict as manifest, affective, or latent. 'Manifest' conflict arises out of a process in which a party seeks the advancement of its interest in the relationship over others. 'Affective' conflict defines feelings of stress, tension, or hostility of an organization towards another, and 'latent' conflict determines the antecedent conditions of conflictful behaviour. Robecheaux and El-Ansary (1976) describe conflict as either functional (healthy and requisite for efficiency) and dysfunctional (requires cooperation for resolution). The opportunities for conflict in IORs are plenty, as lack of information, disagreements, or misunderstandings suffice for conflict. Conflict can evolve from interdependence as either organization strives to keep control over its interests in the relationship. Other sources identified are those of economic rewards, access to scarce resources, 'differing perceptions of reality', 'goal incongruence' and the expectation of a reciprocity that does not happen (Robecheaux and El-Ansary 1976). Structural arrangements to handle the relationship can also present a possible source of conflict, for example if there is no clear point of contact or appointed individual to manage the relationship.

Conflict can be seen as a means of 'clearing the air' of potentially harmful tensions. In turn, conflict has been found to be productive and functional in promoting cooperation and fostering open and cordial relations (Frazier 1983). Harmonization of conflict can strengthen and assist stability of the interorganizational relationship (Robecheaux and El-Ansary 1976). Conversely, an organization that is in conflict with its partner because they were provided with poor goods, services, and other contractual arrangements including finance, tends to invoke strong and controlling means of influence, i.e. power (Reve and Stern 1979).

For the purpose of this study conflict as 'behaviour' refers to the overall level of disagreement with the partner over the working of the exchange and execution of the contract (Klepper and Jones 1998). Conflict in outsourcing involves negative perceptions about the exchange relationship with the vendor, constraining and making the achievement of effectiveness difficult. Similar to other elements, conflict is difficult to evaluate, but surfaces in terms of its frequency and intensity, and the extent of action needed to preserve the relationship.

Cooperation. Although in many instances it actually outlines the underlying motivation for relations, there is a tendency not to address the cooperation element explicitly (Hakansson and Snehota 1995; Ring 1996). In the organization literature many treat cooperation simply as the opposite to conflict. Consequently, little attention has focused on developing empirical measures of cooperation. Cooperation plays an important role in managing uncertainty and achieving organizational goals. High cooperation exists when interfirm communications are perceived to be effective in reducing uncertainty. Frazier (1983) suggests that perceptual measures such as high levels of ideological agreement, goal compatibility, and role satisfaction, and the use of power in a non-pressurized fashion contribute to high levels of cooperation. Underlying cooperation are the concepts of mutuality and reciprocity (Axelrod 1984; Macneil 1980). In exchange relationships any actions or exchanges by one party will necessarily result in a form of reciprocation; if not, relations are likely to break down. Cooperation in turn influences the future course of exchange and the relationship.

For our purpose, cooperation refers to the undertaking of complementary activities to achieve mutual outcomes for both parties. Underlying cooperation is the concept that joint efforts will lead to benefits that neither party could have achieved alone. Effective communication and exchanges that lead to satisfactory outcomes for both parties suggest high cooperation.

Trust. Trust in IORs is frequently defined as 'confidence or predictability in one's expectations' and 'confidence in the other's goodwill' (Ring and Van de Ven 1992). It is a necessary ingredient for any exchange transaction. Williamson (1985) acknowledged the importance of trust, noting 'idiosyncratic exchange relations that feature personal trust will survive greater stress and will display greater adaptability.' Indeed, trust can help mitigate the extent of uncertainty that exists in the IOR, by discouraging opportunistic behaviour. In terms of contractual behaviour, trust reflects 'the extent to which negotiations are fair and commitments are upheld' (Klepper 1994).

The concept of trust in organizations has received multidisciplinary research attention. However, by nature trust is exceedingly elusive and exists in many facets and at different levels, making it a complex phenomenon to research (Gambetta 1988). Williamson (1993) distinguished trust as calculative, personal, and institutional. Calculative trust refers to a rational form of trust, which has strong similarities to taking an informed risk. Personal trust identifies altruistic behaviours of individuals and exists primarily in close relations. Finally, institutional trust emerges from 'social and organisational embeddedness' (Powell 1996), but can be calculative. According to Van de Ven and Ring (1994), trust generally emerges in two ways in IORs. First, trust may be based on norms of equity that define the degree to which one party judges that another party has the required expertise to perform tasks effectively, reliably, and equitably. Secondly, trust will emerge as a consequence of repeated interactions between the parties observing equitableness in the process. Related to a vendor's reliability is the incompleteness of contracts, which may require adaptation to cater for unanticipated contingences (Bakos and Brynjolfsson 1993).

Based on the above insights, the trust element is included in the framework to describe a stakeholder's belief that the other party will perform the required contractual exchanges and actions that will result in beneficial outcomes, and will not undertake any unexpected actions that could potentially result in negative outcomes. As Handy (1995) stressed, unlimited trust in practice, especially in interfirm relationships, is unrealistic. Therefore, the trust element will be used to look at whether stakeholders in the relationship, and in particular the vendor, have fulfilled their obligations and commitments. In addition, the element is used here to suggest whether a relationship is worthwhile, equitable, and satisfying (Frazier 1983). Trust will have a positive influence on the level of satisfaction and motivation to continue the relationship.

THE RELATIONSHIP ADVANTAGE: RELATIONAL SUCCESS INDICATORS

Relationships have a number of perceptive and measurable outcomes that indicate their relative success to both customers and suppliers. Using these success indicators gives customers a means to see whether their relationship is delivering the expected benefits and value-added. On the other hand, vendors can gauge whether they are succeeding in their relationship efforts.

The objective for client and supplier will be one of mutual 'value maximization' over time. Achievement of value depends very much on the efficiency and outcomes of the relationship.

Dimension 6: Efficiency Outcomes

Evaluating relationships is the most complex task in achieving the relationship advantage. Here we are interested in capturing how efficient and productive relationships have been, and, relatedly, how far this has fed into overall satisfaction with the outsourcing arrangement. There are many ways these issues could be tracked and evaluated. One good key is looking at the transaction costs of setting up and managing the relationship. In allied case research we found these to be anything between 4 and 8 per cent of the total outsourcing costs, but we are also interested here in qualitative judgements of transaction costs from participating parties. Transaction costs can also be assessed by comparing strategic intent against the above discussed Dimensions 2 to 5 of our framework (see Figure 2.2). Two other relationship outcomes we can usefully isolate from the literature and our previous research experiences are uncertainty reduction and customization of service. Finally, we are concerned with assessing the overall levels of satisfaction with the relationship, and, critically, the relationship advantage achieved, that is, how far relationships are positively leveraging outsourcing performance. We do this by relating outsourcing performance back to strategic intent, then seeking qualitative assessments from stakeholders and ourselves, on the impact of relationships and on the levels of performance achieved. Table 2.8 summarizes the efficiency-outcomes dimension of the outsourcing relationship.

Transaction costs. As noted earlier, the primary theoretical construct of TCT is efficiency. The theory argues that if one institutional governance mechanism is more efficient than another in decreasing the cost of exchange then there is a tendency towards that form of governance (Williamson 1975). Van de Ven and Ferry (1980) evaluate efficiency on the perception of the parties' judgement about whether the relationship is worthwhile, productive, and satisfying. Alternatively, some suggest that efficiency is associated with quality, flexibility, and innovation (Lundvall 1988). The outsourcing relationship probably has its greatest efficiency benefit in the latter type of arrangement. By reducing the costs of IT services and technology and improving quality and innovation, outsourcing enables the client company to save money and access new skills, expertise, and competencies, without having to invest in acquiring the necessary resources.

For the analysis in this study, the concept of efficiency focuses on the economic motivation behind outsourcing and the impact the outsourcing relationship has on costs. But costs divide into both production and transaction costs. For transaction costs we limit ourselves initially to those factors related to setting up (i.e. selection process, negotiations, and contract formulation), operating, monitoring, and maintaining the client–vendor relationship. But of course the entire relationship in turn needs to be viewed against the economic backdrop, including production and operational costs.

The economic dimension is complex, since the total transaction costs are often difficult to determine (Williamson 1975). As a result—following previous studies' operationalization—a number of factors influencing transaction costs also have to be employed, those being uncertainty, specificity, and transaction frequency (Hakansson 1982; Klepper 1994; Davis 1996). Williamson's (1975) bounded rationality issue is treated as a contingent factor of uncertainty, without which there would not be any contracting problems. Any behavioural factors, such as power, control, cooperation, trust, are generally not regarded as being at the centre of transaction cost analysis (Ghoshal and Moran 1995), even though they may influence efficiency. Instead the behavioural issues are addressed separately (see previous section).

Uncertainty reduction. The organization and institutional economics literature highlight that uncertainty is a key environmental dimension affecting IORs and the mode and cost of transacting (Aldrich, 1976; Pfeffer and Salancik 1978). Uncertainty is strongly related to the concept of bounded rationality, because it is caused by incomplete information about the environment (Williamson 1975).

In the literature distinctions are made between environmental and task uncertainty. Environmental uncertainty refers to the variability and the degree of stability dynamism of resources and the influence of the environment. Task uncertainty refers to the uncertainty surrounding the execution of a particular task, which suffers from unpredictability because the outcomes are unknown for a long period. According to Van de Ven and Ferry (1980) task variability and task difficulty are sources of uncertainty. Task variability refers to the number of exceptions and problems encountered in performing tasks, which affects the degree to which work processes can be structured in a standardized way. Task difficulty refers to the degree to which tasks can be analysed and their outcome predicted, and influences the amount of expertise and mutual adjustment needed to perform them.

Within the outsourcing relationship the broader environmental as well as the narrower task uncertainty is highly relevant (Kern and Willcocks 1996). Additionally, there is a concern with the client–vendor relationship's uncertainty (Bensaou and Venkatraman 1996). Uncertainty in the outsourcing relationship context is defined as a perceptual element that reveals an organization's perception about change and ambiguity in the environment, the execution of tasks and the relationship with its vendor partners.

Transaction uncertainty refers to the clarity, predictability, and frequency of the actual transactions. Possible sources of uncertainty are the client organization's unanticipated service requests, peaks in service demands, and the uncertainty that the vendor has the ability to meet additional service requests. IT services uncertainty arises with quality of services, changes in volume, frequency of new requirements, new technology, and technology compatibility as the organization grows in size, business, and complexity. Looking at task variability and difficulty in IT services, three factors can be distinguished: volume uncertainty (volume fluctuations in services and their estimates introduce uncertainty), new service requirements uncertainty (additions and changes in service requirements), and technology uncertainty (new systems, computers, and applications). What we are interested in here is the extent to which relationship dimensions assists in managing levels of uncertainty.

Customization. Also called specificity in the literature; here we evaluate the degree to which investments in an exchange relationship can be used for alternative purposes or whether they are idiosyncratic investments, such as know-how, particular technology, process, or the choice of location (Williamson 1975). Additional sources of specificity are the time and effort needed to become familiar with operating the outsourcing relationship with a particular vendor. Asset specificity may represent highly specific investments to the relationship that make it expensive and difficult for the client, but also the vendor, to switch to another vendor.

Here, service and/or product specificity refers to the expertise, skill-set, and tools required for the specific client and is reflected in the changes and investments the vendor has to make to tailor its services to the client's demands. On the other hand, transaction specificity refers to the customization of services, applications, organizational structures and process that need to be put in place to specifically support transactions with the client. Our concern here is to assess the extent to which the outsourcing relationship produces advantages in sought-after levels of customization.

Satisfaction. Van de Ven (1976) introduces the concept of outcome as the belief by an organization that 'relationships are worthwhile, equitable, productive, and satisfying'. The focus of outcome in this context is on the perceived effectiveness of the relationship. Anderson and Narus (1990) contend that satisfaction is not only a close proxy for concepts such as perceived effectiveness, but may also be more predictive of future actions by managers of the partnering organization. Satisfaction is said to reflect a party's cognitive state of feeling about whether it has been adequately or inadequately rewarded in the relationship: 'If achieved rewards (losses) compare poorly to deserved and expected rewards, the target will be relatively dissatisfied with exchange because it has not provided the firm with what he/she expected and feels it deserves' (Frazier 1983: 74).

Generally, we posit from the prior research evidence that high levels of satisfaction with the relationship will translate to some degree into better leveraging of outsourcing performance, but also that outsourcing effectiveness will influence levels of satisfaction with the relationship dimensions. The case studies will explore these possibilities and links in detail.

Table 2.8. *The efficiency outcomes dimension*

Element	Operational definition	Evaluation pointers
Efficiency and outcomes	Performance of outsourcing relationship	
Transaction costs	Costs of setting up and managing the outsourcing relationship	• Setting-up costs (includes selection process, negotiations, contract formulation) • Operating costs • Monitoring costs • Maintaining costs
Uncertainty reduction	An organization's perception about change and ambiguity in the environment, the execution of tasks, and the relationship with its vendor partners	• Reliability of daily service delivery • The frequency of changes • Exceptional demand cases • Clarity and predictability of service requirements • Extent of service changes • Demand for technology
Customization	The degree to which services, applications, organizational structures, and process are made specific to the customer	• Dedicated organizational arrangements • Specifically tailored services, processes, and procedures • Expertise and specific technology required
Satisfaction	Degree of satisfaction with relationships and outsourcing performance	• Relationships expectations achieved—contract, structure, interactions, behaviour • Perceived adequacy of outsourcing performance—strategic, financial, business, technical

Satisfaction in an interfirm relationship refers to a 'positive affective state resulting from the appraisal of all aspects of a firm's working relationship with another firm' (Anderson and Narus 1990). Related to outsourcing, greater or lesser satisfaction affects the client organization's perception of the worth, benefit, and willingness to sustain relations (Klepper 1994). Individual and organizational behaviour is influenced by the level of satisfaction. Indeed, dissatisfaction negatively influences the level of cooperation and trust; so will the use of power in a coercive fashion. We explore such linkages, but also address satisfaction and its causes not just with relationships, but also with outsourcing performance overall, linking satisfaction back to strategic intent, and using both quantitative and qualitative measures. For the purpose of this study, then, outcomes refer to the degree of satisfaction with both the relationship dimensions and overall outsourcing performance.

THE RELATIONSHIP ADVANTAGE FRAMEWORK FOR IT OUTSOURCING ANALYSIS

We have outlined the proposed dimensions and elements of a conceptual framework of the client–vendor relationship, with its theoretical foundation in interorganizational relationship theory, transaction cost theory, and relational contract theory. A combination of perceptual and objective pointers are used to capture the numerous and complex aspects that prescribe the various elements and dimensions.

Our aim in this chapter was to develop frameworks for studying and understanding IT outsourcing risks and relationships. Risk analysis is enabled by Figure 2.1. On relationships, our intention was to integrate three research paradigms on interorganizational relationships with the IT outsourcing research literature, in order to arrive at an analytical tool to investigate the outsourcing relationship. The resulting multidimensional framework is shown in Figure 2.3 One additional aspect is built into the framework, and needs comment. This relates to the effect of time on the relationship, which we perceive essential to imply mutual 'value maximization' of the relationship. Time in the outsourcing relationship is imbedded in the processes of ongoing interactions. Time, process, and changing contexts, intents, relationship dimensions, and stakeholders are vital elements in outsourcing, which requires that outsourcing arrangements and the relationships they embody are investigated, as here, longitudinally.

At the relationship level, one interesting aspect here for us to study is the process and the effect of institutionalization. Repetitive interactions and patterns of behaviour become institutionalized as relations progress (Cunningham 1980; Cunningham and Tynan 1993). Institutionalization is an indicator of the closeness of the parties:

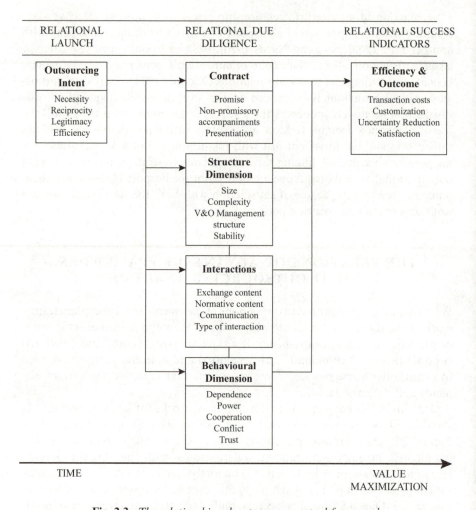

Fig. 2.3. *The relationship advantage: conceptual framework*

However, 'businesses must always seek to balance the advantages of a close relationship, perhaps in terms of cost reduction and ease and speed of interaction, against the opportunity costs of that single relationship and the dependence it involves.' (Hakansson 1982)

Signs of institutionalization are apparent in the outcome of long-term interactions. Examples are those of cultural closeness or normalization (Klepper and Jones 1998). McFarlan and Nolan (1995) suggest that a shared approach to problem solving, similar values, and good personal chemistry among key staff are indicators. Others suggest that adaptations of the ways in which one or both parties modify behaviours to accommodate the other party are clear signs of institutionalization (Anderson, Hakansson, and Johanson 1994; Hallen, Johanson, and Seyed-Mohamed 1991). Modifications can occur in a seemingly unconscious manner, but Hakansson (1982) suggests these may also sometimes be regarded as strategic moves.

Since the literature has not yet put forward a model which could be used to analyse outsourcing relationships comprehensively, our multidimensional framework draws a link between the different bodies of theory and research to achieve a more comprehensive overview of outsourcing relationships. The next step is to illustrate the use of the framework in an empirical context as an explanatory and prescriptive tool.

CONCLUSION

This chapter has covered much preparatory ground. From a detailed analysis of prior theoretical and empirical research studies, including our own, we have developed two robust, analytical frameworks. These, of course, simplify the phenomena observed and commented on, but if used judiciously, also help to make sense of a highly complex set of findings. The first, for analysing risk, will be applied to each of the case studies in the next five chapters. The purpose here will be to provide a consistent lens for viewing where the likely weak points are in each outsourcing arrangement, and where practices have been adopted to mitigate risks. Eventually, in Chapter 8, we will then pull together the findings and identify common patterns, mistakes, and prescriptions that can be derived from looking across the case studies.

Each case study will also be subjected to a detailed analysis from the relationship dimension perspective, utilizing the Five Dimension framework developed in this chapter. The objective here will be to identify how each outsourcing arrangement has developed along these relationship dimensions. This will enable us to identify where relationship aspects are considered crucial, where they are missing or present and the effect this would seem to have, and the extent to which relationship issues influenced the levels of risk experienced, and the outcomes being achieved.

The two analytical tools will be inevitably interrelated when applied to specific case studies, not least because there are some obvious overlaps between the frameworks. Moreover, each is constructed on a time-line, allowing analysis from the origin of the outsourcing idea, through to its operationalization in subsequent years. More importantly, our own sense, based on prior research, is that risks and relationships are inherently related in IT outsourcing. The next five chapters will substantiate this strongly, but also provide the detail as to exactly how risks and relationships interrelate, enabling detailed suggestions on how IT outsourcing arrangements can be constructed and managed.

A risk-relationship perspective on IT outsourcing has been long overdue.

We have argued here that both are highly neglected, even though each is invariably presented, separately, as forming a critical set of issues. We operate here from the conviction that applying and developing further tools for understanding risks and relationships in IT outsourcing, and applying them to longitudinal case studies, takes the study of the phenomenon a significant step forward.

REFERENCES

Aldrich, H. (1976). 'Resource Dependence and Interorganizational Relations: Local Employment Service Offices and Social Services Sector Organizations'. *Administration & Society*, 7/4: 419–54.

—— and Whetten, D. A. (1981). 'Organization-Sets, Action-Sets, and Networks: Making the most of Simplicity', in P. C. Nystrom and W. H. Starbuck (eds.), *Handbook of Organizational Design*. New York, Oxford University Press, i. 385–408.

Alpar, P., and Saharia, A. N. (1995). 'Outsourcing Information System Functions: An Organization Economics Perspective'. *Journal of Organizational Computing*, 5/3: 197–219.

Anderson, J. C., and Narus, J. A. (1990). 'A Model of Distributor Firm and Manufacturer Firm Working Partnerships'. *Journal of Marketing*, 54/1: 42–58.

—— Hakansson, H., and Johanson, J. (1994). 'Dyadic Business Relationships within a Business Network Context'. *Journal of Marketing*, 58 (October): 1–15.

Ang, S., and Beath, C. M. (1993). 'Hierarchical Elements in Software Contracts'. *Journal of Organizational Computing*, 3/3: 329–61.

—— and Straub, D. (1998). 'Production and Transaction Economies and IS Outsourcing: A Study of the US Banking Industry'. *MIS Quarterly* (December), 535–42.

—— and Toh, S.-K. (1998). 'Failure in Software Outsourcing: A Case Analysis', in Willcocks and Lacity (1998).

Auwers, T., and Deschoolmeester, D. (1993). *The Dynamics of an Outsourcing Relationship: A Case in the Belgian Food Industry*. De Vlerick School voor Management, Case Study series, University of Gent: 1–25.

Axelrod, R. M. (1984). *The Evolution of Cooperation*. New York, Basic Books, Inc.

Bagozzi, R. P. (1975). 'Marketing as Exchange'. *Journal of Marketing*, 39 (October): 32–9.

Bakos, Y. J., and Brynjolfsson, E. (1993). 'From Vendors to Partners: Information Technology and Incomplete Contracts in Buyer–Supplier Relationships'. *Journal of Organizational Computing*, 3/3: 301–28.

Barnett, R. E. (1992). 'Some Problems with Contract as Promise'. *Cornell Law Review*, 77/5: 1022–33.

Bensaou, M., and Venkatraman, N. (1996). 'Inter-Organizational Relationships and Information Technology: A Conceptual Synthesis and a Research Framework'. *European Journal of Information Systems*, 5/2: 84–91.

Benson, K. J. (1975). 'The Interorganizational Network as Political Economy'. *Administrative Science Quarterly*, 20 (June): 229–49.

Blau, P. M. (1964). *Exchange and Power in Social Life.* John Wiley & Sons, New York.

—— (1987). 'Microprocess and Macrostructure', in K. S. Cook (ed.), *Social Exchange, Theory.* Newbury Park, Calif., Sage Publications Inc.: 83–100.

Burnett, R. (1998). *Outsourcing IT: The Legal Aspects.* Gower Publishing. Aldershot.

Charette, R. (1991). *Application Strategies for Risk Analysis.* McGraw Hill, New York.

Child, J. (1973). 'Predicting and Understanding Organization Structure'. *Administrative Science Quarterly*, 18: 1–17.

—— and Faulkner, D. (1998). *Strategies of Co-operation: Managing Alliances, Networks, and Joint Ventures.* Oxford University Press, Oxford.

Cunningham, C., and Tynan, C. (1993). 'Electronic Trading, Interorganizational Systems and the Nature of Buyer–Seller Relationships: The Need for a Network Perspective'. *International Journal of Information Management*, 13/1: 3–28.

Cunningham, M. T. (1980). 'International Marketing and Purchasing of Industrial Goods—Features of a European Research Project'. *European Journal of Marketing*, 14/5–6: 322–38.

Currie, W., and Willcocks, L. (1998). *New Strategies in IT Outsourcing: Major Trends and Global Best Practice.* Business Intelligence, London.

Davis, G. F., and Powell, W. W. (1992). 'Organization-Environment Relations', in M. D. Dunnette and L. M. Hough (eds.), *Handbook of Industrial and Organisational Psychology.* Consulting Psychologists Press, Inc., San Diego, Calif., iii. 315–75.

Davis, K. J. (1996). 'IT Outsourcing Relationships: An Exploratory Study of Inter-organizational Control Mechanisms'. DBA thesis, Graduate School of Business Administration, Boston, Harvard University: 310.

De Looff, L. A. (1997). *Information Systems Outsourcing Decision Making: A Managerial Approach.* IDEA Group Publishing, Hershey, Pa.

DiRomualdo, A., and Gurbaxani, V. (1998). 'Strategic Intent for IT Outsourcing'. *Sloan Management Review*, 39/4: 67–80.

Doz, Y. L., and Hamel, G. (1998). *Alliance Advantage: The Art of Creating Value through Partnering.* Harvard Business School Press, Boston.

Dwyer, F. R., Schurr, P. H., and Oh, S. (1987). 'Developing Buyer–Seller Relationships'. *Journal of Marketing*, 51: 11–27.

Earl, M. J. (1996). 'The Risks of Outsourcing IT'. *Sloan Management Review*, 37/3: 26–32.

Elam, J. J. (1988). 'Establishing Cooperative External Relationships', in J. Elam, M. Ginzberg, P. Keen, and R. Zmud (eds.), *Transforming the IS Organization.* International Center for Information Technologies, Washington DC, 83–98.

El-Ansary, A. I., and Stern, L. W. (1972). 'Power Measurement in the Distribution Channel'. *Journal of Marketing Research*, 11 (February): 47–52.

Emerson, R. M. (1962). 'Power-Dependence Relations'. *American Sociological Review* 27/1: 31–41.

—— (1972). 'Exchange Theory, part I & II', in J. Berger, M. Zelditch, and B. Anderson (eds.), *Sociological Theories in Progress.* Houghton-Mifflin, Boston, ii. 38–87.

Faulkner, D. (1995). *International Strategic Alliances: Co-operating to Compete.* McGraw-Hill Book Company, London.

Feeny, D., and Willcocks, L. (1998). 'Core IS Capabilities for Exploiting IT'. *Sloan Management Review*, 39/3: 1–26.

Fitzgerald, G., and Willcocks, L. (1994). 'Contracts and Partnerships in the Outsourcing of IT', in *Proceedings of the 15th International Conference on Information Systems*, ICIS, Vancouver, 91–8.

Frazier, G. L. (1983). 'Interorganizational Exchange Behavior in Marketing Channels: A Broadened Perspective'. *Journal of Marketing*, 47 (Fall): 68–78.

Galaskiewicz, J. (1985). 'Interorganizational Relations'. *Annual Review of Sociology*, 11: 281–304.

Gambetta, D. (ed.) (1988). *Trust: Making and Breaking Cooperative Relations*. Oxford: Basil Blackwell.

Ghoshal, S., and Moran, P. (1995). *Bad for Practice: A Critique of the Transaction Cost Theory*. 55th Academy of Management Conference, Vancouver.

Goetz, C. J., and Scott, R. E. (1981). 'Principles of Relational Contracts'. *Virginia Law Review*, 67/6: 1089–2054.

Grover, V., Teng, J. T. C., and Cheon, M. J. (1998). 'Towards a Theoretically-Based Contingency Model of Information Systems Outsourcing', in Willcocks and Lacity (1998), 79–101.

Hakansson, H. (1982). *International Marketing and Purchasing of Industrial Goods: An Interaction Approach*. John Wiley & Sons, Chichester.

—— and Snehota, I. (1995). *Developing Relationships in Business Networks*. Routledge, London.

Hallen, L., Johanson, J., and Seyed-Mohamed, N. (1991). 'Interfirm Adaptation in Business Relationships'. *Journal of Marketing*, 55 (April): 29–37.

Halvey, J. K., and Melby-Murphy, B. (1995). *Information Technology Outsourcing Transactions: Process, Strategies, and Contracts*. John Wiley & Sons, Inc., New York.

Handby, J. (1996). 'Outsourcing: Perfecting Partnerships'. *Management Consultancy* (11 December), 11–20.

Handy, C. (1995). 'Trust and the Virtual Organization'. *Harvard Business Review*, 73/3: 40–9.

Hart, O. D. (1995). *Firms Contracts and Financial Structures*. Oxford University Press, Oxford.

Henderson, J. C. (1990). 'Plugging into Strategic Partnerships: The Critical IS Connection'. *Sloan Management Review* (Spring): 7–18.

Homans, G. C. (1961). *Social Behaviour: Its Elementary Forms*. Harcourt Brace Jovanovich, New York.

Hurst, I., and Hanessian, B. G. (1995). 'Information Technology/Systems—Navigate IT Channels: Integrate or Outsource'. *McKinsey Quarterly*, 3: 103–11.

Jurison, J. (1995). 'The Role of Risk and Return in Information Technology Outsourcing Decisions'. *Journal of Information Technology*, 10/4: 239–47.

Kern, T. (1997). *The Gestalt of an Information Technology Outsourcing Relationship: An Exploratory Analysis*. 18th International Conference on Information Systems, Atlanta, Ga.

—— (1999). 'Relationships in Information Technology Outsourcing: An Exploratory Research Study of a Conceptual Framework'. Unpublished D.Phil. thesis, University of Oxford.

—— and Blois, K. (2000). 'Norm Development: An Essential Ingredient to Outsourcing Relationships', 16th Annual Industrial Marketing and Purchasing Conference, 7–9 September 2000, Bath, UK.

—— and Silva, L. (1998). 'Mapping the Areas of Potential Conflict in the Management of Information Technology Outsourcing'. European Conference on Information Systems, Aix-en-Provence.

—— and Willcocks, L. (1996). 'The Enabling and Determining Environment: Neglected Issues in an IT/IS Outsourcing Strategy'. European Conference of Information Systems, Lisbon.

—— —— (2000). 'Cooperative Relationships Strategy in Global Information Technology Outsourcing: The Case of Xerox Corporation', in D. Faulkner and M. De Rond (eds.), *Perspectives on Cooperation*. Oxford University Press, Oxford.

Klepper, R. (1994). 'Outsourcing Relationships', in M. Khosrowpour (ed.), *Managing Information Technology with Outsourcing*. Idea Group Publishing, Harrisbury, Pa., 218–43.

—— (1995). 'The Management of Partnering Development in IS Outsourcing.' *Journal of Information Technology*, 10/4: 249–58.

—— and Jones, W. O. (1998). *Outsourcing Information Technology, Systems & Services*. Prentice Hall PTR, Englewood Cliffs, NJ.

Konsynski, B. R., and McFarlan, W. F. (1990). 'Information Partnerships—Shared Data, Shared Scale'. *Harvard Business Review* (September–October): 114–20.

Kumar, N. (1996). 'The Power of Trust in Manufacturer–Retailer Relationships'. *Harvard Business Review*, 74/6: 92–106.

—— and van Dissel, H. G. (1996). 'Sustainable Collaboration: Managing Conflict and Cooperation in Interorganizational Systems'. *MIS Quarterly*, 20/3: 279–300.

—— and Willcocks, L. (1999). 'Holiday Inn's Passage to India', in E. Carmel (ed.), *Global Software Teams*. Prentice Hall, Englewood Cliffs, NJ.

Lacity, M. C., and Hirschheim, R. (1993*a*). *Information Systems Outsourcing: Myths, Metaphors and Realities*. John Wiley & Sons Ltd., Chichester.

—— —— (1993*b*). 'The Information Systems Outsourcing Bandwagon'. *Sloan Management Review*, 35/1: 73–86.

—— —— (1995). *Beyond the Information Systems Outsourcing Bandwagon: The Insourcing Response*. John Wiley & Sons Ltd., Chichester.

—— —— and Willcocks, L. P. (1995). 'Are Information Systems Outsourcing Expectations Realistic? A Review of US and UK Evidence'. Oxford Institute of Information Management, Templeton College, Oxford. RDP95/1: 1–23.

—— and Willcocks, L. P. (1998). 'An Empirical Investigation of Information Technology Sourcing Practices: Lessons from Experience.' *MIS Quarterly*, 22/3: 363–408.

—— —— (2000*a*). *Inside IT Outsourcing: A State-of-Art Report*. Executive Research Report, Templeton College, Oxford.

—— —— (2000*b*) *Global IT Outsourcing: Search for Business Advantage*. Wiley, Chichester.

—— —— and Feeny, D. F. (1995). 'IT Outsourcing: Maximize Flexibility and Control'. *Harvard Business Review*, 37/3: 84–93.

—— —— —— (1996) 'The Value of Selective IT Sourcing'. *Sloan Management Review*, 37/3: 13–25.

Lasher, D., Ives, B., and Jarvenpaa, S. L. (1988). 'USAA-IBM Partnerships in Information Technology: Managing the Image Project'. *MIS Quarterly*, 15/4: 551–65.

Loh, L., and Venkatraman, N. (1992*a*). 'Diffusion of Information Technology Outsourcing: Influence Sources and the Kodak Effect'. *Information Systems Research*, 4/3: 334–58.

—— —— (1992*b*). 'Determinants of Information Technology Outsourcing: A Cross-Sectional Analysis'. *Journal of Management Information Systems*, 9/1: 7–24.

Lundvall, B. A. (1988). 'Explaining Interfirm Cooperation and Innovation: Limits of the Transaction-Cost Approach', in G. Dosi, C. Freeman, R. Nelson, and L. Soete (eds.), *Technical Change and Economic Theory*. Pinter, London, 52–64.

Lusch, R. F. (1978). 'Intrachannel Conflict and Use of Power: A Reply'. *Journal of Marketing Research*, 15 (May): 275–6.

Macaulay, S. (1963). 'Non-Contractual Relations in Business: A Preliminary Study'. *American Social Review*, 28/1: 55–67.

McFarlan, F. W., and Nolan, R. L. (1995). 'How to Manage an IT Outsourcing Alliance'. *Sloan Management Review* (Winter): 9–23.

McLellan, K., Macolin, B. L., and Beamish, P. W. (1995). 'Financial and strategic Motivation behind IS Outsourcing'. *Journal of Information Technology*, 10/4: 299–321.

Macneil, I. R. (1974a). 'Commentary: Restatement (Second) of Contracts and Presentiation'. *Virginia Law Review*, 60/4: 589–610.

—— (1974b). 'The Many Futures of Contracts'. *Southern California Law Review*, 47/3: 691–816.

—— (1980). *The New Social Contract: An Inquiry into Modern Contractual Relations*. Yale University Press, New Haven.

—— (1987). 'Relational Contract Theory as Sociology: A Reply to Professors Lindenberg and de Vos'. *Journal of Institutional and Theoretical Economics/Zeitschrift für die gesamte Staatswissenschaft*, 143/2: 272–90.

Michell, V., and Fitzgerald, G. (1997). 'The IT Outsourcing Market-Place: Vendors and their Selection'. *Journal of Information Technology*, 12/3: 223–37.

Mohr, J. J., and Spekman, R. E. (1996). 'Several Characteristics Contribute to Successful Alliances between Channel Members'. *Marketing Management*, 4/4: 34–43.

Oliver, C. (1990). 'Determinants of Interorganisational Relationships: Integration and Future Directions'. *Academy of Management Review*, 15/2: 241–65.

Pfeffer, J., and Salancik, G. R. (1978). *The External Control of Organisations: A Resource Dependence Perspective*. Harper & Row, New York.

Powell, W. W. (1996). 'Trust-Based Forms of Governance', in R. M. Kramer and T. R. Tyler (eds.), *Trust in Organizations: Frontiers of Theory and Research*. Sage Publications, Thousand Oaks, 51–67.

Reekers, N., and Smithson, S. (1996). 'The Role of EDI in Inter-organizational Coordination in the European Automotive Industry'. *European Journal of Information Systems*, 5/2: 120–30.

Reve, T., and Stern, L. W. (1979). 'Interorganisational Relations in Marketing Channels'. *Academy of Management*, 4/3: 405–16.

Ring, P. S. (1996). *Networked Organization*. Uppsala University, Uppsala.

—— and Van de Ven, A. H. (1992). 'Structuring Cooperative Relationships between Organizations', *Strategic Management Journal*, 13: 483–98.

—— —— (1994). 'Developmental Processes of Cooperative Interorganizational Relationships'. *Academy of Management Review*, 19/1: 90–118.

Robiecheaux, R. A., and El-Ansary, A. I. (1976). 'A General Model for Understanding Channel Member Behaviour'. *Journal of Retailing*, 52/4: 13–30.

Saunders, C., Gebelt, M., and Hu, Q. (1997). 'Achieving Success in Information Systems Outsourcing'. *California Management Review*, 39/2: 63–79.

Tichy, M. N. (1981) 'Networks in Organizations', in Paul C. Nystrom and William H. Starbuck (eds.), *Handbook of Organizational Design: Remodeling Organizations and their Environments*, Volume ii, Oxford University Press, New York, 225–49.

Turner, J. H. (1987). 'Social Exchange Theory: Future Directions', in K. S. Cook (ed.), *Social Exchange Theory*. Sage Publications, Newbury Park, Calif., 223–38.

Van de Ven, A. H. (1976). 'On the Nature, Formation, and Maintenance of Relations among Organizations'. *Academy of Management Review*, 1/4: 24–36.

—— and Ferry, D. L. (1980). *Measuring and Assessing Organisations*. John Wiley & Sons, New York.

—— and Ring, P. S. (1994). 'Developmental Processes of Cooperative Interorganizational Relationships'. *Academy of Management Review*, 19/1: 90–118.

Willcocks, L. (1998). 'Reducing the risks of Outsourced IT', in Financial Times (ed.), *Mastering Global Business*, Financial Times/Pitman, London.

—— and Choi, C. J. (1995). 'Co-operative Partnership and Total IT Outsourcing: From Contractual Obligation to Strategic Alliance'. *European Management Journal*, 13/1: 67–78.

—— and Currie, W. (1997). 'IT Outsourcing in Public Service Contexts: Towards the Contractual Organization?' *British Journal of Management*, 8: (June) S107–20.

—— and Fitzgerald, G. (1994). *A Business Guide to Outsourcing IT: A New Study of European Best Practice in the Selection, Management and Use of External IT Services*. Business Intelligence, London.

—— and Kern, T. (1999). 'IT Outsourcing as Strategic Partnering: The Case of the UK Inland Revenue'. *European Journal of Information Systems*, 7: 29–45.

—— and Lacity, M. (eds.) (1998). *Strategic Sourcing Of Information Systems*. Wiley, Chichester.

—— —— (1999). 'IT Outsourcing in Insurance Services: Risk, Creative Contracting and Business Advantage'. *Information Systems Journal*, 9: 163–80.

—— —— and Kern, T. (1999). 'Risk Mitigation in IT Outsourcing Strategy Revisited: Longitudinal Case Research at LISA'. *Journal of Strategic Information Systems*, 12/8: 285–314.

—— and Margetts, H. (1994). 'Risk Assessment in Information Systems'. *European Journal of Information Systems*, 4/1: 1–12.

Williamson, O. E. (1975). *Markets and Hierarchies: Analysis and Antitrust Implications. A Study in the Economics of Internal Organization*. The Free Press, New York.

—— (1979). 'Transaction-Cost Economics: The Governance of Contractual Relations'. *Journal of Law and Economics*, 22: 233–61.

—— (1985). *The Economic Insitutions of Capitalism: Firms, Markets, Relational Contracting*. The Free Press, New York.

—— (1993). 'Calculativeness, Trust, and Economic Organization'. *Journal of Law & Economics*, 36 (April): 453–4.

3

Global Relationship Management at Xerox Corporation

INTRODUCTION

Xerox Corporation contracted EDS for $3.2 billion in 1994 to handle its information technology (IT) requirements worldwide. The deal was part of Xerox's strategic restructuring initiative to halt its dwindling turnover and to redevelop its global competitiveness. To succeed, large investments were required to replace existing legacy and proprietary information systems. These were urgently necessary to insure that Xerox's information infrastructure could support the new business processes needed to compete against strong Asian business pressures (Kearns and Nadler 1995).

This case is of particular interest because, first, it was reputed at the time to be the largest outsourcing deal ever, and the first to be implemented on a global scale. Only a few suppliers could support such a contract. Secondly, the complexity of the undertaking made it necessary to pursue outsourcing as a cooperative strategy, where the contract would not limit or demarcate the venture excessively. As noted by Jagdish Dalal,[1] head of Xerox's global outsourcing team, in 1994:

> The term outsourcing is inappropriate. This is really more of an integration of two separate businesses. We wanted to take the best parts of each culture and put them together. The same goes for structure, strategy, and people. We will realise substantial economic value if we can achieve commitment to a high degree of integration. It is the spirit of the agreement that creates this commitment; there are no 'mechanisms' that can be put into place as a substitute for the spirit.

However, the intention to cooperate strategically and implement the contract on this basis took a particular twist during post-contract management. Operationalization of the contract at the local level proved exceedingly difficult, due to the lack of service detail following the centralized negotiations. In turn, the relationship became very much caught up in alleviating service issues and defining the contract, while relationship management for Xerox became focused on managing EDS. Still, early relationship successes were evident in areas such as the rapid roll-out of the new information infrastructure. Reflecting

---

[1] Quoted in Davis and Applegate (1995).

on two and half years of operating the outsourcing venture the Global Head of IT for Rank Xerox noted in 1997:

Generally the reasons that drove us to outsource are still valid. Some of the things we've done over the last couple of years we would not have achieved without an IT partner. But, I think we were naive the way we went into the relationship and we are now having to almost do it again, redefine big areas of the relationship based on the knowledge we now have. Some areas we are probably not getting great value-added. I'm not sure we've achieved anything through outsourcing. If we did it again we would probably be more selective, about what we did and what we didn't do. All of that with 20 : 20 hindsight.

This case presents the story of Rank Xerox UK in light of the Xerox's global outsourcing initiative. In many parts, it is representative of the local level complexities encountered more widely, in other Xerox geographical regions, as a result of the formalization of the global outsourcing venture centrally.

Relationship Lessons

The case illustrates the complexities of global outsourcing. Contracting for such a large-scale deal was found only possible by centrally negotiating the terms, yet the resulting lack of local and operational service detail became a major problem for operationalizing and managing the venture. The pressure on local relations became one of defining requirements, identifying future service requirements, and handling daily service demands, while in parallel developing relations with EDS and operationalizing the contract. The eventual breakdown of relations was, to a degree, predictable. Lacity and Willcocks (2000), for example, note that very few large-scale deals escape significant restructuring eighteen months to two years into the contract. Only with fundamental re-negotiations to define the detail were both parties able to alleviate some of the problems. One consequence, though, of these early complexities and renegotiations were unanticipated cost increases. This does serve to raise serious questions about the economics of such undertakings and their comparability to in-house service costs, though, as we shall see, the Xerox–EDS deal was not just about cost issues.

The case further highlights that customers, in this case Xerox, need to enforce a management structure and possibly impose the management processes on its supplier. Only with the specification of the management team that EDS had to put in place to handle the local operations did Xerox's managers feel more confident in working together. Only with the resulting control balance shifted towards Xerox again, did relations begin to settle and improve over time.

BUSINESS CONTEXT AND OVERVIEW

Xerox Corporation is a leading global document processing organization, with revenues in excess of $19.4 billion in 1999/2000. It develops, manufactures,

THE DOCUMENT COMPANY XEROX

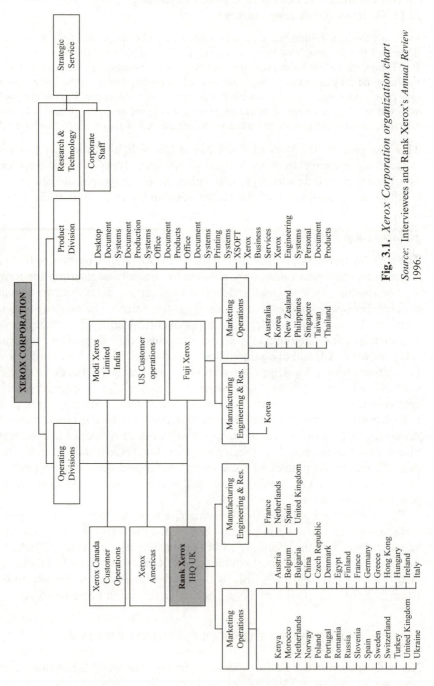

Fig. 3.1. *Xerox Corporation organization chart*

Source: Interviewees and Rank Xerox's *Annual Review* 1996.

markets, services, and finances a range of products for handling documents around an organization. Products include photocopiers, digital publishing systems, printers, facsimile machines, scanners, document handling networks, document software management, and associated products and services (Xerox Corporation, *Annual Review* 1999). Xerox's business objective is to build easy-to-operate, integrated systems for scanning, storing, retrieving, viewing, and distributing documents to simplify the document process and improve the effectiveness of all tasks that office workers perform (Rank Xerox, *Annual Review* 1996). Its operations network spans 130 countries using both direct marketing and a network of dealers, agents, and distributors. It employs approximately 103,000 employees worldwide. Figure 3.1 presents an overview of Xerox's global structure.

Xerox's History

With the revolutionary introduction of the first plain paper photocopier in 1959, Xerox experienced a phenomenal growth in profitability. In 1976 with the forfeit of its patent protection and the push to license the technology, all was suddenly to change for Xerox. Early market dominance dwindled through competition. Its golden years from 1960 to the mid-1970s saw it acquire an estimated 80 per cent of the US copier market, only to see it diminish to 13 per cent by 1982. Profits had plummeted from $1.15 billion in 1980 to $600 million in 1982, as Japanese companies such as Cannon, Minolta, Ricoh, and Sharp entered the lower end of the market (Walker 1992).

Xerox's struggle to survive required another internal revolution. A strategy of competitive benchmarking, employee involvement, and quality management was designed to make Xerox competitive once again (Kearns and Nadler 1995). In the early 1980s extensive competitive benchmarks were undertaken on product development, product costs, distribution, marketing, sales, billing, after sales support, and general organizational properties. Results proved poor on all accounts and costs were generally far too high: 'Xerox's unit manufacturing cost was equal to the Japanese U.S. selling price—and they were making a profit' (Walker 1992). Production cycles were also twice as long, with 30 per cent more defective parts than competitors.

The introduction of the 'Leadership through Quality' philosophy and programme was to form part of the turnaround. The restructuring programme meant a total change of Xerox from a classical command and control structure, consisting of discrete hierarchical functions, to a cross-functional participative organization, with a strong team-oriented work ethic (Walker 1992). Implemented via benchmarking, employee involvement, and greater commitment to customers requirements, Xerox was able to regain some of its lost market share and improve its profitability. The programme initiated in the early 1980s was the single most significant initiative that reversed Xerox's demise (Kearns and Nadler 1995). However, profitability was never to reach similar staggering growth rates as in the 1960s and 1970s. In fact, profitability remained a challenge to such an extent that in 1992 and 1993 Xerox recorded losses.

Following the quality restructuring of the 1980s, the early 1990s entailed further reorganizations as a consequence of spiralling losses. Xerox was also preparing for the year 2000. Paul Allaire, Xerox CEO explained: 'each Xerox division [was to have] end-to-end responsibility for a set of products and services, a set of primary market segments, an identifiable set of competitors and an income statement and balance sheet' (Xerox *Annual Review* 1992, p. 9). Re-engineering efforts were mounted to change the organization into customer-focused business lines, on both operations and management processes. As part of these efforts Xerox also re-evaluated its core competencies. As a result, in early 1993 Paul Allaire announced the sale of its finance and insurance business: 'We've decided to disengage from our remaining insurance and other financial services business. . . . With the decision to exit from financial services, we can now focus clearly and unencumbered on our Document Processing business' (Xerox *Annual Review*, 1992, p. 6). In June 1994, Xerox globally out-sourced its IT functions to EDS. Combined, these radical changes led to an upswing in Xerox's profitability in 1995, which continued for several of the subsequent years. Xerox is one of the few companies who survived the Japanese onslaught and continued to be a strong global player.

Rank Xerox (RX) Joint Venture: 1956–2000

Some understanding of the early history of the formation of Xerox Corporation is useful. In 1956 Rank Organization and Haloid Xerox (which became Xerox Corporation in 1961) established a joint venture to bring photocopiers to the European market and to develop some simple manufacturing capabilities. Since the early days, Rank Xerox has remained primarily a marketing, sales, and after sales operation. It has been a huge success in terms of Rank Xerox growing to 22,000 employees with numerous representations in Europe, Africa, Eastern Europe, and Asia and an annual turnover of £3.673 billion (Rank Xerox *Annual Review* 1996). The initial equity split was 50–50, but over the years Xerox slowly bought Rank's share. Up to mid-1997 Rank Organization held a minority share of 20 per cent, but generally had no influence on the day-to-day running of the business. According to the Global IM Manager, Rank had two advisory directors on the main board, whose main interest focused on their investment and maximizing its return. In June 1997 Xerox bought Rank's final share for $1.5 billion, and intended to change Rank Xerox to Xerox Limited in the near future. By 2001 Rank as a name had altogether disappeared in the corporation.

Information Management (IM) Context

The restructuring initiatives of the early 1990s significantly impacted the global IM function of Xerox to the extent that existing systems were found unable to supply the required technological support. Walker (1992) observed during Rank Xerox's restructuring efforts 'our data processing did not support the process view [. . .] A major overhaul of our system strategy was therefore required.' In this section IM management at Xerox[2] and its IM2000 strategy, that eventually led to outsourcing, is briefly described.

In the early 1970s Xerox[3] established its corporate information management (CIM) unit, which was placed in charge of handling the company's data centres and networks. In 1987, CIM's technology was hived off into the general services division. CIM was to take charge of Xerox's strategic technology direction, for which Patricia Barron was appointed in 1987. She explained the mission of CIM as 'to develop the information technology strategy for Xerox and ensure that it was implemented in all the business units'. However, it soon become evident that existing technology and its structure would not support Xerox for the future. Drastic changes were needed. In 1988, together with an IT strategy consultancy, CIM undertook an audit, which revealed a number of grave concerns. In particular, as Davis (1996) noted, the diffusion of authority in IT decision making had created many IT problems at Xerox. Indeed, the consultants had found:

there was no overall coordination or management of the hundreds of millions of dollars spent each year and no corporate-wide management of IM investment priorities. The CIM organization at Xerox was not positioned, chartered, or staffed to perform many of the CIO functions. Overall, CIM was a peripheral player in the IT management picture because they were not chartered to direct or manage infrastructure nor resourced to furnish leadership. The IT function at Xerox possessed a narrowly focused IT talent pool, reported to senior managers, who viewed IT infrastructure investment as an expense to be avoided, required redundant and overlapping efforts to find or reconcile the most basic information, and lacked effective development mechanisms.

In other words, CIM and the existing IM infrastructure was unfit to support Xerox's IM needs for its strategic intentions in the 1990s. Barron's management team spent the next few years addressing some of these issues, but changes were slow. In 1992, Patricia Wallington was newly appointed as head of CIM and IM worldwide. As part of Xerox's subsequent realignment and restructuring efforts in 1993, IM authority was centralized in an effort to support the data needs of the divisional organization structure the CEO had been pushing to implement. Spend was increased on technology: 'we invested at least 90 per cent of all IT related spend in data and voice and less than 10 per cent in document management' (Walker 1992: 17). However, it was apparent that IM was still unable to provide the data needed for the divisional structure. Figure 3.2 illustrates Xerox's divisional information management organization structure.

---

[2] Xerox's IM management and subsequent IM2000 strategy is applicable to all of its operating units including Rank Xerox (UK). The only difference in IM management lies in the interpretation of centrally decided policies at the operating units.

[3] See Davis and Applegate 1995.

*Corporate Officer

Fig. 3.2. *Xerox's information management organization, December 1993*
Source: Davis and Applegate 1995.

Xerox's IM2000 Strategy

In an effort to address IM's deficiencies, CIM initiated the IM2000 project in mid-1993. The IM2000 strategy defined IT's future role and its contribution to Xerox's global re-engineering effort. To implement the strategy, various teams were established in charge of identifying problem areas and suggesting strategies for alleviation. These were then to be implemented by transitional teams, and ultimately led to the new infrastructure.

An internal study sponsored by senior management in mid-1993 found most of the current systems needed renewal since the existing proprietary technologies and hence legacy systems were no longer flexible enough to guarantee Xerox's competitiveness. More importantly, it was unable to support the requirements of the new functionally structured organization and systems were taking up too much time to keep operational: 'IM managers were probably spending 80% of their time managing legacy systems and 20% of their time worrying about new developments' (Senior IT Manager). Renewal of the current infrastructure was estimated as very costly and would undoubtedly require additional investments; especially since the current rate of new system

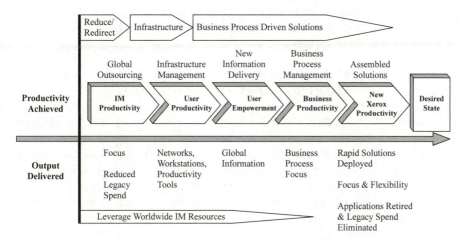

Fig. 3.3. *Xerox's IM2000 key strategies*

Source: Adapted from Jagdish Dalal (Vice President, Information Management Director, Global Outsourcing Management Xerox Corporation), 1994 presentation.

implementation was not meeting the businesses requirements. IM appeared to be trapped in a spending spiral based on outdated legacy systems.

Financial pressures on IM became even stronger in 1993, due to Xerox's profitability slow-down. In effect, new investments into IM changes stagnated, and overall funding to implement a new infrastructure was reduced: 'We were asked to do that [implement new technology] by the business without spending a ton more money, we'd already spent a lot of money. So that meant pulling investment away from those old applications into the new' (Head of IT, Xerox). The expected costs for implementing a new infrastructure, that being just the hardware, was estimated at $55 million. On top came applications, training, and reskilling.

Internally, IM was seen as providing a very ineffective service and costing a lot of money without significant measurable returns. IM customers were in most cases dissatisfied with services and cared little for changes or improvements in IM, which further complicated requests for investments. Internal politics, especially on cost matters and increase of headcount, constrained the speedy turnaround of the IM2000 strategy. In fact, many IM managers believed as long as the IM function remained in-house, they would always be asked to provide services that exceeded their facilities capabilities, while at the same time being hindered by too tight a budget.

Global outsourcing, in turn, was seen as the solution to implementing the IM2000 strategy. Outsourcing was the bridge strategy, as it would help support current business while IM2000 focused on the future. It would enable retirement of the outdated infrastructure and applications, and provide the foundation to support the new IM2000 strategy. Figure 3.3 presents an overview of the revised IM 2000 strategy.

MOVING TO IT OUTSOURCING

In-house talks about IT outsourcing began in earnest in early 1992, leading to a provisional draft of functions to be outsourced. It took the company a long time to identify the final functions and to decide to go through with it. In August 1993, Xerox kicked off its outsourcing project. Following a seven-month selection process, EDS was chosen as the vendor, and in June 1994 the global contract was signed. In return, EDS agreed to pay Xerox approximately $170 million for transferred IT assets, and accepted 1,900 IM employees. From Rank Xerox 550 people were transferred, and in the UK alone 103 people transferred to EDS.

Vendor Selection

To find the right partner, an outsourcing team was formed that consisted of both technical and senior managers. The team's initial task was to evaluate a list of ten pre-selected vendors according to past experiences and available information. From these, five were eventually sent a 'Request for Information' (RFI) in September 1993. The information received was then internally evaluated through benchmarking exercises of existing outsourcing ventures the suppliers were currently operating. For this, a number of supplier sites were visited. In addition, Xerox managers analysed the suppliers for their strategy, processes for contracting, transitioning, ongoing management, vendor references, and human resources impact. Once the team was satisfied with the vendors' capabilities, vendors were issued a 'Request for Proposals' (RFP) between December 1993 and February 1994. Three bids were received in total—one from EDS and two from alliance groups, i.e. CSC, Andersen Consulting, and partners and IBM-ISSC and AT&T. The bids were then put through an in-depth review, and scored according to predetermined criteria that focused on the particular vendor's qualifications, human resources, technical solutions, financial, and 'soft' issues. Table 3.1 describes some of the selection criteria.

The selection criteria aided the process of judging which of the three bids presented the best option. The selection criteria enabled Xerox to eliminate one of the three vendor bids. Following intense negotiations with the remaining two vendors, Xerox eventually chose EDS for a number of reasons. First, EDS was found to have the superior global presence. Secondly, EDS offered a better human resource programme for transferred staff, and, finally, EDS had entered a very competitive bid. Although, one of the other bidders had the better cultural match, EDS was the preferred choice. In general, the selection process

Table 3.1. *Xerox's selection criteria*

Vendor qualifications
- Global Presence
- Capability to manage 'globally'
- Experienced in large-scale outsourcing
- 'Core' strengths in various frameworks
- Desire to 'create' a different outsourcing environment (for Xerox)
- Management processes and strengths

Human resources
- Treatment of Xerox employees
- Human resource values

Technical solutions
- Overall productivity commitment—% and credibility
- Support for existing Xerox diverse environments
- Capability to help 'migrate'

Financial
- Translation of productivity to savings to Xerox
- Flexibility in meeting Xerox financial requirements (globally)
- Experience in 'engineering' financial environment (worldwide)

'Soft' criteria
- 'Congruence' with positive Xerox cultural traits
- Provide benchmark for desired Xerox cultural traits

Source: Adapted from Jagdish Dalal (Vice President, Information Management Director, Global Outsourcing Management Xerox Corporation), 1994 presentation.

undertaken seemed a rational and objective process, except it was to become questionable whether single vendor total outsourcing really was the best choice. Figure 3.4 summarizes Xerox's outsourcing process.

Outsourcing Scope and Expectations

Xerox outsourced all of its desktop computing, mid-range, and mainframe systems, the worldwide data centre operations (mainframe and midrange), helpdesks, network operations (both voice and data), legacy applications (maintenance and enhancements[4]), desktop systems support (current and future) and telecommunications services (private networks and use of public networks). Xerox retained the overall planning role, but EDS is very much involved in the detailed configuration, operation, and management of the

---

[4] The legacy applications defined 95% of the existing applications.

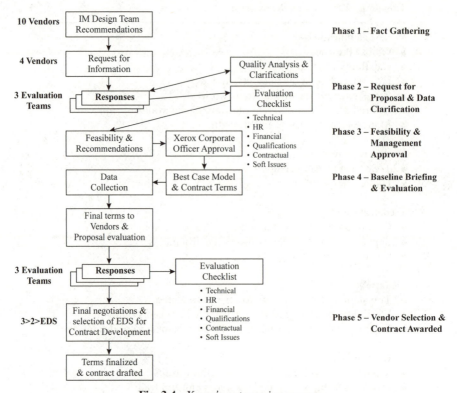

Fig. 3.4. *Xerox's outsourcing process*

Source: Adapted from Jagdish Dalal (Vice President, Information Management Director, Global Outsourcing Management Xerox Corporation), 1994 presentation.

services. The strategic direction, selection of hardware and software and definition of standards, and the overall planning remains with Xerox:

What we've retained within Xerox and RX is the whole strategic direction and control, and we still obviously control investments and the level of investment and where we want to spend it. We generally control our technology definition of standards, so we decide where we want to go in terms of technology. In some cases right down to the vendor. (Head of Global IT, Xerox)

Xerox entered outsourcing with a particular set of expectations in mind. The IM2000 strategy generally informed these expectations and objectives (see above, Figure 3.2). Table 3.2 summarizes Xerox's outsourcing objectives.

Outsourcing was to address initially the infrastructure area where Xerox was at the beginning of an exercise which involved replacing something like 60,000–70,000 users on their worldwide network and office environment. Xerox planned to move the whole office infrastructure from the Xerox proprietary software and hardware to industry standard PCs and networking. They were looking to find an IT partner who could help with this changeover: 'We certainly

Table 3.2. *Xerox's outsourcing objectives*

- Concentrate IM resources on future, business critical information management solutions

- Provide a framework where the information technology investment becomes a 'variable' cost rather than the current 'fixed' cost

- Reduce/redirect Xerox IM spending on information management activities and optimize yield on our assets

- Improve IM service levels

- Access to technology to facilitate transition to the new IM environment

---

Source: Adapted from Jagdish Dalal (Vice President, Information Management Director, Global Outsourcing Management Xerox Corporation,) 1994 presentation.

didn't understand what it would take to do that [change the infrastructure]. One of the key reasons for outsourcing was just that, that we felt we needed some help in doing that' (Senior IT Manager, Xerox). Xerox in turn looked to EDS for help on managing this new technology environment; the continuous effort put into managing legacy systems had resulted in very few managers finding time to acquire the necessary skills to handle the envisaged client/server infrastructure: 'We felt that we needed access to new skills that we didn't have. If you think about the picture when you've got hundreds of IT people, but they are buried in taking care of today, how on earth do you release them to give them the skills and move them on to new projects?' (Global Head of IT, Xerox.) So on the one hand Xerox looked to EDS for client/server and other advanced technologies, whereas, on the other, they needed training and skilled people to manage these new technologies.

Outsourcing was also seen as a means to improve the cost issue for CIM. The intention was to reduce costs by cutting the headcount, by diminishing IT spend on legacy systems including applications, and by changing the cost structure from fixed to variable: 'We really wanted to redirect what we were spending away from the old legacy applications which frankly no longer supported the business' (IT Executive, Xerox). In general, the aim was to free up money for investments in new applications and technology. With the introduction of new technology a new skill set was required, subsequently demanding additional personnel, especially at the operational level. However, as the General Manager of Information Management at Rank Xerox (UK) noted, 'this being an American company there is always a phobia about headcount, and its costs. [. . .] in American companies they tend to measure headcount very thoroughly and always want a reduction on headcount.' So outsourcing was expected to provide access to the new skill set without incurring an increase in staff numbers and personnel costs. As a positive side-effect it diminished the political battle of justifying new staff. Finally, the outsourcing objectives corresponded to corporate management's overarching, stated strategic intent:

Xerox, The Document Company, will lead by providing innovative, intelligent document services—products, systems, solutions and support—that enable individuals and organizations to be more effective and productive.

The IM2000 strategy is clearly aligned to these business goals; likewise is the outsourcing initiative.

On the other hand, for Rank Xerox UK the overarching objectives were defined by three expectations. According to the Financial Director of Rank Xerox (UK) these were 'to save money but without losing our service levels. [. . .] to get certainly as good and hopefully better service, better expertise, better provision of availability of resource and a flexible availability of resource. [and] to tap into specific skills, whatever you need to tap into more easily because you've got a specialist provider.' These local objectives, of course, differed to a degree from the global objectives. Though those at the operational level had little influence on the outsourcing decision, they still had their own expectations of a specialist IT service supplier like EDS.

THE CONTRACT

In June 1994 Xerox signed a ten-year global contract for an estimated value of $3.2 billion with EDS. The contract was split into two global parts: (1) Xerox North and South America and Canada, and (2) Rank Xerox North and Western Europe. Parts not outsourced were Eastern Europe, Africa, and Asia (except Hong Kong), as they were still very much a developing part of the business.

The importance of the contract was recognized early on by Xerox, and every effort was made to formulate a comprehensive contract. Two lawyers were integrated into the outsourcing team and it was decided to involve an external legal adviser in the contract development. John Halvey,[5] a specialist lawyer for outsourcing from Millbank, Tweed, Hadley & McCloy was hired to advise on legal matters and to countercheck the contract. The contract eventually became a very lengthy document exceeding 1,000 pages in length. The length reflected the complexity and the concern for control. It was intended to cater for most unforeseen events, and give Xerox sufficient control to terminate, if necessary.

However, at the time it was very difficult to write a detailed contract for an arrangement of this magnitude: 'A number of outsourcing criteria were completely unpredictable and unspecifiable because we had no experience with the technology we needed' (Head of Global IT, Xerox). In fact, Xerox was sure of its technology objectives, but unsure about how to achieve them both in terms of hardware, software, and time needed. Consequently, Xerox's management decided to write a very open framework contract with financial arrangements

---

[5] Co-author with Barbara Melby-Murphy of a seminal legal text on Outsourcing in 1996, *Information Technology Outsourcing Transactions: Process, Strategies, and Contracts*, John Wiley & Sons, Inc., New York.

Table 3.3. *Xerox-EDS contract specifics*

- 'Evergreen' contract terms—new concept
- Contract terms—some 'unique' in the industry:
  - * Global contractual terms
  - * Human resource terms
  - * Pricing mechanism—benchmarking and indices
  - * Service Level Management—'Service Level Variance' Concept (adaptation of Xerox Quality Processes/tools)
  - * Ongoing relationship terms built on 'partnership' rather than establishing a 'supplier/buyer' model
  - * Future business relationship terms
- Contract is kept confidential (internally and externally)

Source: Adapted from Jagdish Dalal (Vice President, Information Management Director, Global Outsourcing Management Xerox Corporation), 1994 presentation.

that would encourage both organizations to move in the same direction. The decision was made in half an hour, and as Global Head of IT noted: 'ever since we have been struggling.' Table 3.3 highlights some of Xerox's distinct contract arrangements.

The contract framework integrated a distinct and new 'Evergreen concept', which described a flexible mechanism through which the relationship could cater for the uncertainty of the changes to be implemented with the infrastructure changeover. The idea behind it was to ensure the contract always stayed representative of Xerox's requirements. The IM Strategy Manager at Xerox UK explained how it works at the operational level:

We have an IM strategy which is called 'Evergreen Strategy' in that it sits in an electronic document that we both have access to and it defines our infrastructure and IM goals in about an 18 month to 2 year planning horizon. So it's targeted at people like programme managers, departmental managers, who want to make investments in their area, this acts as a guideline for them over their planning period to determine how and where they should make their investments. That also acts at the next level down as our projects and programme plan with EDS.

Similar arrangements were introduced globally and at different strategy planning levels.

In line with the Evergreen concept, an adaptive pricing scheme was integrated, with a general emphasis on decreasing the overall costs. Figure 3.5 below illustrates the general price reduction EDS proposed, in order to give Xerox certainty in forecast savings. Moreover, EDS had committed to pay cash for assets, expense reductions, and the provision of year-on-year productivity improvements. To assure pricing remained in line with EDS's proposal, the contract incorporated an annual price benchmark against a set of organizations

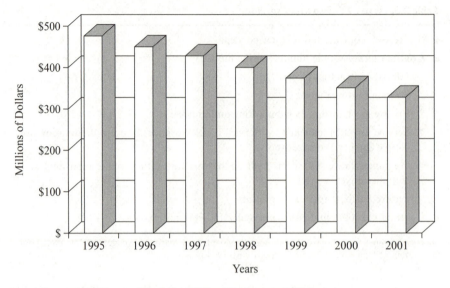

Fig. 3.5. *EDS's price proposal 1995*

Xerox had pre-specified. This guaranteed that EDS's prices remained globally competitive. The price benchmarks consisted of forty different price elements rather than an aggregate price. These were then measured against a price index previously compiled. This mechanism diminishes the possibility of dramatic price swings and avoids renegotiating the contract to adjust pricing, since every year prices were adjusted, or not, according to the benchmarks.

Xerox entered the contract with the intention of cooperating and collaborating closely with EDS. In fact, the contract had been formulated to encourage partnering, and both EDS and Xerox's senior managers had committed to this notion. The justification for partnering came from the perceived similarity in the organizations' strategic intents. Both wanted to become the leading organization in their particular industry and they would support each other to achieve this. But that meant that in other areas the contract had to be written very loosely to give ample flexibility:

It has to be very loose because you are into a contract that says EDS will manage our whole IT operation for us, here are some objectives. And you are down to saying things like we want our IT costs to be 2% of revenue or something, get on with it. And some arrangements have been set up this way where the vendor will make investments, or if you like take some of the financial risk associated with IT. But they will also then take a piece of any gain that comes out of it. The vendors are making some fairly substantial investments on behalf of Xerox, but then assuming that those investments pay off then they have a big piece of the action in terms of benefit. (Contract Manager, Xerox)

This extreme relational contracting approach would demand considerable trust in the partnering supplier to undertake those investments favourable to the client organization. Xerox management had this confidence in EDS, and felt secure in EDS undertaking those IT investments that ensured its productivity would improve.

POST-CONTRACT MANAGEMENT

The Transition Period: 1994–1995

As EDS had proposed in its bid, the transition activity only took six months. Through the creation of a transition alliance team, staff and asset transfers had been completed for the twenty countries in a record time by December 1994. EDS's integration was well on its way. Having taken ownership and accountability of the outsourced IT functions, the next steps were migration and closer integration. At this stage, and in accordance to both parties' intentions, a new organization was to be established referred to as X*EDS, that essentially outlined the overarching structure of the strategic relationship. Figure 3.6 presents an overview of X*EDS. The planned time frame to integrate and develop X*EDS was eighteen months. To achieve integration, actions were take that supported changes in processes, people, structure, strategy, and culture.

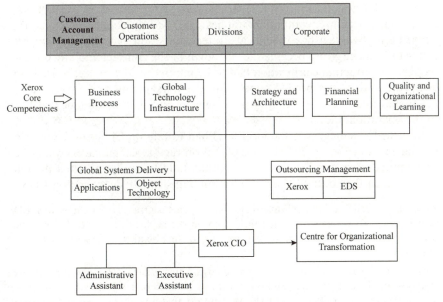

Fig. 3.6. *Envisaged X*EDS structure*
Source: Xerox presentation 1994.

Indicators of integration were to be read into how far the services delivered value to Xerox's customers.

The importance of achieving integration led EDS to establish a separate global strategic business unit (SBU) dedicated entirely to Xerox. Closer integration for EDS was to entail:

- appointing Xerox as a preferred supplier and thus increasing internal EDS spend;
- outsourcing its North American and European printing services to Xerox Business Services;
- using joint on-demand publishing facilities offered by Xerox's Document Production Systems; and
- possibly integrating into their service portfolio printing technology and document handling facilities offered by Xerox's Office Document Systems, Printing Systems, Personal Document Products, Xerox Engineering Services, and XSOFT.

In parallel, at the local level post-contract management focused on operationalizing the service level agreements, clarifying the contract, establishing rapport, and implementing management infrastructure and processes. EDS also initiated programmes locally and globally to consolidate, standardize, and change the proprietary and legacy systems.

Within the X*EDS structure central IT was placed in charge of coordinating standardization, and generally controlling the strategic direction. For each part that was outsourced a separate strategy framework was established, e.g. for infrastructure, computing, applications, and telecommunications, that defined on a two-year basis the local strategic direction. Additionally, the central management group became the custodian of the contract and any disputes requiring contractual clarification had to be referred to the centre. Indeed, any clarification that was needed concerning the outsourcing venture was to be negotiated and agreed by central management and then communicated back to the operational level.

In turn, IT managers at the local level had to rely on EDS to take the lead in implementing the stipulated terms of the contract. Local managers were given only limited access and sight of the contract, and basically inherited the relevant parts of the contract. Their understanding strongly depended on EDS:

Xerox negotiated and initiated this worldwide contract centrally, corporately with EDS in the States. So we have then just picked up on the back of that, and that has then been implemented in each country on the back of this blanket contract (RX Finance Director)

I can't go to EDS and renegotiate the charges, the pricing structures or charging methods, or basic terms and conditions of the relationship. They are set. So when we meet with our local EDS counterpart, we can't do anything about changing the structure in the terms and conditions in which we are operating, all we can do is try and

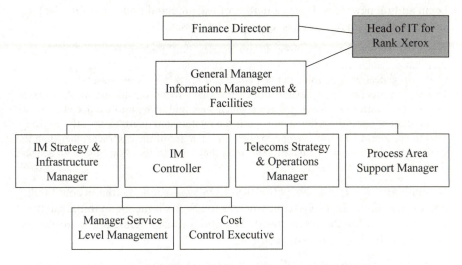

Fig. 3.7. *Rank Xerox IM group organization chart 1997*

work together to make sure that we get the best out of the structure that we are presented with in terms of contract and cooperation (RX IT Manager)

Continuity of services in the transition phase was guaranteed through the residual group of IT managers and the former employees who had transferred from
the IM department to EDS. Total reliance on this management infrastructure
was, however, not possible as some of the former colleagues were geographically relocated early on. Relations rather sooner than later faded away and
new relations had to be built with EDS people. The local infrastructure generally consisted of retained IM managers. For example, at Rank Xerox (RX) UK
seven managers were retained, and each was placed in charge of a particular
area, e.g. infrastructure, cost control, service level management, telecoms strategy and operations, IM strategy, and process area support. Figure 3.7 presents
an overview of RX UK's local management structure.

EDS's global strategic business unit, in theory, was to handle all service
delivery, whereas the individual customer-facing groups would interact with
managers and users at the local level. For example, at the local level for
RX UK, EDS's management infrastructure consisted of an account manager,
an operations manager, and a number of managers who previously were part
of the IM department at RX UK. This structure was to ensure managers were
culturally in touch with Xerox and would be aware of the organizational
pressures.

Similar arrangements were made by EDS for the management processes.
Initially, of course, EDS worked with the existing processes, before they would

begin adding new ones. It was a matter of learning and understanding the local situation and demands, before changing processes:

When you take over an operation in outsourcing you don't understate the processes that you are going to take over. A lot of the customers say oh we thought you'd bring your own processes. But you can't just come and break what's there and throw it away and impose processes, you have to work with what's there to some extent. And maybe we could do with some other processes which we could bring into the account. So we are dependent upon the relationship and if the relationship doesn't start off well things tend to deteriorate. People become focused on the letter of the contract rather than the spirit of the contract or the intent. And then they start to focus on 'it's us and them'. (EDS Account Manager)

In summary, the transition period for EDS was about taking accountability and ownership of the IT systems, whereas for Xerox it meant an initial payment of a lump sum for the assets transferred and a drastic reduction in headcount and assets. It also meant cost control:

Looking at it with an accountant's eye I would probably say for two reasons: I suspect that it's provided us with cost advantages in that we are paying less for our IT. Plus it's enabled all the costs to go above the line. So we have absolutely much better control. (IM Strategy Manager, RX)

In addition, integration procedures were set in gear to formalize X*EDS, which included implementing an infrastructure and taking over the management processes. In general, both Xerox and EDS were very pleased with the transition.

Post-Transition Period: Migration and Operationalization at RX UK (1995–1996)

Following the successful transition, Xerox was now expecting EDS to truly overhaul its existing centralized mainframe systems and roll-out the new decentralized IT infrastructure. Desktop computing and client-server systems were to replace existing proprietary systems. Local area networks, wide area networks, and telecom systems were to be changed in accordance with the installation of new PCs and the new client-server architecture. In addition, relations were to be fostered and strengthened, and management processes formalized. This would entail making sense of and revising the contract at the local level and shaping it to the idiosyncratic operations.

EDS's revamping of the infrastructure was progressing rapidly; 60,000–70,000 new desktop computers were expected to be installed and integrated into a corporate wide network architecture. The undertaking was of an enormous size:

The new infrastructure roll out is going very well. We will complete the whole thing in 2.5 years which everybody in the industry told us we are crazy to even attempt. People talked about it taking 3–4–5 years to do that, and we will have done it in 2.5 years and it's working. It's well accepted now by the general population. So in that sense it's been very successful. We could not have done that before the contract, we could not have done that at the time even if we'd wanted to. Equally well we could not have got as far as we have as quickly as we have in building that new infrastructure without an IT partner. (RX Global IT Manager)

In early 1995 at RX UK, EDS began implementing a new Novel-based local area network architecture, which eventually had to cater for approximately 2,000 industry standard desktop computers running Microsoft Office. This was a considerable step towards phasing out the Xerox XMS-based workstations. To manage this changeover key dates were agreed and integrated into an electronic 'evergreen strategy' that outlined when implementations were to be completed, and when new projects were to begin. The online documentation guided management on both sides for a two-year planning horizon. It also allowed managers oversight and the ability to finally forecast in detail the annual IT costs and budget requirements.

On the other hand, daily problem resolutions and request issues were taking up considerable time. Overall management was complicated due to insufficient flow of information between the parties at the local level. In fact, IM managers had become reliant on EDS to provide them with the information to monitor service performance, which at times was sporadic and sometimes only given when Xerox managers asked for it:

One of the areas that does cause me problems is where there is no follow-up, so I put in the request and he passes it on and there would be nothing coming back, it would be up to me to chase it. He just passes the request on he doesn't actually chase it because presumably he's got so many other requests coming in he doesn't have time to chase the ones that haven't come back yet. So it's up to me to keep following it up and say what's happening with this. (Contract Manager, RX)

If I ask them to give me information on certain charges they've made to us like tell me where all these PCs are that you've charged me for, they can't do it. Things like that. Also lack of timely and accurate information. So they charge for the amount of the mainframe that we use, I want a report that explains what I spent it on. So we are getting information but it's not timely and it's also wrong. So for me to try and manage the business [. . .] I haven't got the right information to be able to put that under control. (IM Controller, RX)

It is important that if they haven't fixed the problem that they phone and say I'm sorry it hasn't been fixed. [. . .] communicating even though there's nothing to communicate in a positive sense, is far better than not communicating at all. (IM Strategy Manager, RX)

Communication difficulties emanated from the management process, which was taking a long time to be formalized. It was RX's view that EDS's account team was in charge of implementing appropriate management processes, not least because they were expecting to benefit from EDS's expertise. In addition, they were expecting EDS to formalize an appropriate account management structure. The complexity of the global deal presented, however, a number of structural difficulties: 'I'm not sure how their [EDS] organizational structure works, because that's one of the problems we've got is that it is a bit of fragmented structure where separate specialist sections operate in separate locations. It's one of the things that we are wrestling with at the moment' (Finance Director, RX). The complexity is exemplified when a problem in the telecoms area arises:

If we have a problem with telecoms in terms of the responsiveness, our local manager has got to go to [EDS]. So if there was a telecoms issue he's got to go to his telecoms organization within EDS, which is like another arms length organisation from him, and he's got to go and bring them in, kind of subcontract them in. So they are far removed from us. And that starts to get quite a bit removed from what we feel is an immediate on-site responsive type of approach that we've been used to.

To smooth operations, efforts were made to foster relations. For this, IM managers gave EDS managers appropriate space to adapt and adjust to their idiosyncratic operations. Where necessary, IM managers helped by coaching and advising them on their former practices:

After a while though it was clear that things weren't happening the way we would have liked, so we had a look to see what was going on. Then I carried out a coaching and guidance role with former members of my team, if they had a problem they would speak to me about it. [. . .] I would talk to one of my old staff about a problem and I used to word it very carefully and say, 'well if I was EDS I would do this and this'. I didn't say this is what you have to do because otherwise it would be me giving them instructions to do something and I didn't see it my place to give them direct instructions. (IM Strategy Manager, RX)

If there is a problem I'll say have you tried this or that, have you contacted this person. And you coach them along giving them additional pointers to try and work with them to resolve the problem. To an extent it is a bit of a team effort—united in adversity. (IM Manager, RX)

In addition, a number of social activities were instigated by the parties. These team-building exercises were supposed to give both sides the opportunity to actually meet their counterpart outside work. It was an important part of fostering interpersonal relations, and was in the spirit of developing X*EDS:

In the early years for example we had a bowling evening, both with EDS and the IM side. That was quite good. It helped you to relax and to get to know the human side of the people you're dealing with. I suppose in a lot of areas it's helped some of the ways of working. When you've got a particular problem I might phone and ask for a status report on what's happening about this. (RX Telecoms Strategy Manager)

A big part of early post-contract management at the operational level focused on localizing the contract. In many cases parties had to agree an additional informal understanding of the contract:

There are still a few glitches but only through differences of interpretation of some of the small print in the contract. But again in the UK, I can't speak for other operating units, we had a number of hot house sessions with EDS when they take the contract apart and said what do you understand by this. And where there's been differences we've worked it out and documented our interpretation of it. (Telecoms Manager, RX)

This was essential for determining how best to implement the agreement. For example, the contract specified a single charge for the software installation. So, if a user wanted five programs loaded on a PC that would be one charge. RX UK's interpretation of this software installation for five PCs with a single software requirements in one room was also interpreted as a single charge. EDS however interpreted this situation as five separate charges. A mutual understanding had to be reached by using PCs as the charging measure. More complicated matters were referred to central headquarters. By late 1996 the amount of interpretations the agreement demanded slowly began to subside.

Throughout this time, the relations between EDS's management team and RX UK's IM group remained tense. EDS was encountering serious management difficulties, as a result of which service levels had been suffering:

After the transition relations were low. In many areas service levels went to 'hell in a hand basket', [and] there were lots of issues in the business about IT costs. (RX Head of Global IT)

Although the revamping was progressing rapidly, problems were not being adequately addressed. For example, the high demand for desktop computing resulted in networks being so overloaded that they eventually crashed. EDS was 'fire fighting' to fix problems and not truly addressing the root causes of problems:

Over the year we must have installed well over 2,000 terminals on to the LAN and during that time nobody has been looking at what's happening with the traffic. Consequently most of the services have ground to a halt. Users are complaining that it takes 5 minutes to get a response back on your terminal. Not long ago the network in Oxford just collapsed. When they came to fix it they found that it was running the traffic levels at 87%. Just to give you an example, I would expect an average network to run at 15%. When it gets to 20% you are talking about it being overloaded and you ought to start looking at ways of reducing the traffic, segmenting it to keep some of the traffic off. (RX Telecoms Strategy Manager)

In effect, EDS's managers were unable to manage the migration and integration, while handling in parallel the day-to-day problems and requests. IM managers realized their difficulties and tried to help as much as they could, but circumstances were generally not improving:

I didn't bother complaining anymore because it's a waste of time. There was a stage even in the early days, 6 months into the contract, where the IM team sat down and prioritized what we wanted to talk to EDS about—which problems. And although we'd got major problems in one area we said alright we will just ride that and not say any-thing we will just give them these because we don't want to swamp them with too much to do. (RX Strategy Manager)

The reality has been they [retained IM staff] are spending more time managing EDS than we anticipated. And I guess that's going to be the reality. (Global Head of IT, RX)

As a result, frustrated RX managers began to micro-manage their former staff, taking control of service delivery management. This was, however, clearly contrary to the idea of freeing RX managers from routine service management to enable them to focus more on strategy formulation and oversight of EDS. In addition, they were doing EDS's account team's job:

It was clear that things weren't being addressed, so we started creeping back in. [. . .] And I gradually crept back in carrying out that management role. But it's very difficult because you maybe are not supposed to be doing that role, but nobody else was doing that so there was a need. Why outsource and then carry on doing it yourself, it beats the object. And by the way while I was carrying on that role I wasn't doing the job I was paid to be doing. (RX Telecoms Strategy Manager)

The consequences of IM managers' actions in micro-managing staff was to increase the pressure on the already strained relationship:

I think the overall relationship between the EDS management and the RX management was strained, because the EDS management got the impression that we were meddling in things that we didn't ought to be meddling in. [. . .] So we got situations where there would be resentment between me and the EDS management, because they would resent what I am doing. At one stage they actually banned me from the computer room. To some extent that's where this chaperoning thing came in. The account team would accompany any of the technicians if we had to have a meeting. (IM Contract Manager, RX)

EDS was being held culpable for the problems. Indeed, some were even being put down to the inadequate management infrastructure EDS had implemented at RX UK. One respondent commented:

they [EDS] promoted their best programmers to managers so producing a community of poor managers and deficient programmers. So this led to a very weak supervisory capability, which still exists to a certain extent. (RX Strategy Manager)

In fact, EDS had appointed only one operational manager to be responsible for facing off against six IM managers—each with a different and specific set of queries and requests:

We have this simple hierarchy so that the customer always has a single point of contact. (Account Manager, EDS)

Figure 3.8 presents an overview of this simple hierarchy that defines the account management structure.

The operation manager as the key interface became inundated over time with demands and requests, and was seldom able to follow any of them up.

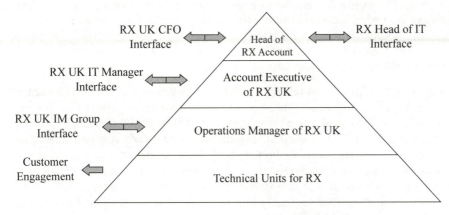

Fig. 3.8. *EDS account management structure 1997*

Source: Interviewees.

There is one interface within EDS and he handles everything. All requests for change, all the service level problems, literally every request that I have, I have to put through this one person. (Telecoms Strategy Manager, RX)

In the background EDS as an organization did, however, have sufficient specialist managers and technicians to handle the demands but they were not supposed to interface with the customer directly. Only the account management team was to be the interface. Indeed, when RX managers wished to discuss an issue with a technical manager they had to go through the account team, before actually speaking to the specialists.

Due to these ongoing frustrations, EDS's account manager and RX UK's IT manager eventually ran into relationship difficulties by mid-1996. Both had to be subsequently replaced, as positions on certain issues had become rigid. This was symptomatic of the general relationship, which at the local level had become adversarial and loggerheaded. In fact, end-user IT services satisfaction levels in the UK had reached an all time low of 52 per cent in 1996 (Johnson 1998). The initial high level of confidence following the transition was totally eroded by now. Trust was at an all time low, and similar problems in the X*EDS venture were mounting across the globe.

It turned out that neither party at the highest levels had really planned the actual operationalization of the contract at the local level. The vagueness of the contract complicated matters for the IM managers, as they were dependent on EDS to implement the specifics. Indeed, the visionary perspective of what EDS was to do for Xerox was there, but the detail of the management processes was missing:

I think in some areas Xerox and Rank Xerox haven't necessarily understood outsourcing at the local levels. So there has been conflict and sometimes EDS haven't been getting their margin, sometimes Rank Xerox haven't been getting their service levels or afford-able costs or both, because of the terms of the global contract. Because then at a global level it's fine and at an operating level you get problems. I think every major operating company we are talking about within Rank Xerox has gone through a level of problem. (RX IT Manager)

The severity of these and related problems had simmered through to the senior levels at EDS, and senior management was subsequently forced to become actively involved in developing relations at the operational levels. No direct blame was to be apportioned, as expectations had clearly not been managed. More attention should have been initially paid to clearly defining roles and responsibilities, services, levels of services, and pricing. The lack of doing so made it very difficult to establish effective management processes. As a result, Xerox decided in 1996 to clarify and renegotiate the individual frameworks, and the first one to be addressed was the infrastructure framework. The others were to be renegotiated at a later stage and regularly revisited over the con-tract's lifespan.

Global Contract Renegotiation (1996)

After only one and a half years, contract renegotiations were initiated by Xerox for three reasons: first, it became possible, following the revamping of the legacy infrastructure, to specify in detail the service levels. Secondly, both parties found that the contract in totality should have been more robust on a number of issues, which were to be clarified in the renegotiation. And thirdly, Xerox's IM management had concluded that integration, i.e. partnering, was not going to work as initially envisaged, and relations would have to become more formalized:

The middle of last year (1995), maybe a bit earlier, the IM management team across Xerox really came to the conclusion that we were going to have to change the way we were trying to manage the relationship and move it to a strict supplier relationship. And that's really when we got into redefinition of the whole infrastructure agreement. (Head of IT for Rank Xerox)

In effect, in the coming years each framework was to be formalized. The first area to be addressed was service requirements and pricing for the 'global desktop management services (GDMS)'. This new GDMS agreement focused purely on the new infrastructure and included network architecture, comput-ing (PC, mid-frame, and mainframe), software, and new developments:

The contract is laying out the standards of services that they will provide to us. It goes into a lot of detail specifying the types of PCs we should have, the software that can go on it, when we get things done free on PCs, where we charge for things, when things are in scope and out of scope, where additional fees are charged. (RX Contract Controller)

Prior to the GDMS, services were sparsely documented. In some cases simple rules guided infrastructure services and pricing. In large parts, these were based upon Xerox's IM2000 infrastructure intentions, but exact service levels could not be formalized. Prices were calculated on a time rate and a minimum charge was raised for call-outs, including software and PC installation. These unprecedented costs pushed the cost up and since the infrastructure after two years had been more or less complete, pricing and services became formalizable. By having an agreement that outlined the charges and services it was hoped that the amount of local negotiations and disputes could be diminished:

With the GDMS we can understand now what each side is talking about. In there you find everything about services. It's down in writing now so we can refer to a page and say it does mean X or Y, because it was agreed with EDS locally. Whereas before there wasn't anything. (RX IM Controller)

The importance of the GDMS for Xerox has been that services come to work out cheaper to run because the agreement defines certain activities as being for free; for example, standard software upgrades on PCs are no longer charged for. Moreover, the service levels stated in the GDMS became better defined and more precise, giving the residual IM groups at the local level some means for monitoring service performance:

We can measure against service levels and both sides can judge and see whether we are getting the service, and EDS can see what they need to do to get up the service level that they've got to provide. The down side of it is that service levels are only measured at a very high level so we don't have a separate measure for RX UK, it's a measurement for the whole of RX Europe. So we are trying to push for those same measures done locally. So we should be measuring how EDS are doing here locally rather than doing it overall at the European level. It should be done at a local level. That's the only thing I've got against it. It's very detailed, it's all in there. But then it's measured at too high a level to be meaningful and to give us a reassurance that we are having a bad service but it's being acted upon. (RX Control Executive)

The initial lack of local consideration comes back to the nature of the contract being global, and negotiated centrally. Outsourcing, as well as all other service changes, such as the GDMS, are imposed on each subsidiary. The logic was economies of scale and avoidance of duplication, but the subsidiaries that are forced to implement the outsourcing terms tended to grapple with the obscurity of the details of the contract:

We didn't have an option either way and we've got to try and live with it and work it and if it is causing problems try and push it back. (RX Finance Director)

In many circumstances, centralized IM management was too detached from the operational level of the subsidiaries. In turn, input from the operational level was marginalized. But operational managers realized that a globally negotiated agreement might be the only option for large-scale outsourcing ventures.

Throughout 1996 Xerox's central IM group proceeded with its in-depth evaluations of the other functions outsourced. In particular, they looked into telecoms and its service agreement:

There are some other services under the telecoms umbrella where it's difficult to see what value EDS have added. All that has happened in that area is that EDS collects the bills from whoever the carrier is and passes them on to us. So we've said what value added is there in this. Are they really incentivized in any way to make sure that we are getting the best deal, which is a serious concern in Europe right now with deregulation and the growing competition. Tariffs are changing so rapidly and vendor offerings are changing so rapidly. And that's an area where we are in discussions with EDS. (Global Head of IT, RX)

Also, the support agreement of the client-server applications environment came under discussion. Through the renegotiations, Xerox aimed to be able to manage EDS more in line with other service procurement arrangements they had operated prior to the total outsourcing venture. Indeed, they hoped that EDS's commitment to the service agreement would help to rebuild the confidence in IT services all round.

Maturing Relations (1997–1998)

As a result of the management difficulties in the UK, relations at the local level became more structured in 1997. To a similar degree globally, relations became more formalized. The GDMS now specified in detail service requirements, allowing both parties to operate more along the lines of the contract. Processes were implemented to ensure these were being achieved. The venture to date had been successful in a number of areas and has provided some real benefits to Xerox's end-users. According to Johnson (1998), Xerox's end-users now had access to IT capabilities that allowed them to:

- develop and share spreadsheets, databases, and correspondence with Xerox, customers, and suppliers;
- use powerful graphics for better communication;
- work virtually anywhere with a laptop computer;
- communicate with other employees, customers, and suppliers from anywhere with a laptop and modem;
- access CD-ROM based information; and
- browse both the Internet and Xerox Intranet, and take advantage of this new communications medium to keep up with competitors and colleagues.

In parallel, by 1998 EDS had retired 38,000 proprietary global view workstations and had installed 40,000 PC workstations at over 700 Xerox locations worldwide. In addition, several thousand new file, print, e-mail, and remote access servers had been set-up (Johnson 1998). Combined, the resulting benefits of these changes were said to add significant value for Xerox. The changes had created a new high-end service offering for the Xerox engineering community, and moved the cost structure of the IT infrastructure to one that can be price benchmarked against 'best in class' industry systems. According to several respondents, the changes had brought Xerox closer to its customers; enhanced their ability to position their products better in the market place; generally improved computer literacy in the organization; and enabled the development of new applications for the evolving common infrastructure (Johnson 1998). Most crucially EDS had rolled out a new infrastructure in line with its IM2000 strategy requirements. However, operations at the local level, especially in the UK, remained strained. To resolve some of the problems, in early 1997 Xerox initiated dramatic changes that saw the IM group in the UK take control of the account. For this, IM managers called for an 'exception review', as the amount of continuing problems had peaked and a number of issues truly needed urgent attention. Over a number of months a root cause analysis identified eighty-two areas requiring urgent action/attention. This included, for example, technology requirement specifications, a review of the wide area network, changes for network links between different sites, local area network upgrades, new telecoms technology, and so on. EDS acknowledged the urgency of this exception review and fully cooperated and collaborated with the analysis. As one respondent noted:

It was very much a two-way thing. We identified the issues and EDS recognized and reacted very positively to them. It could have gone differently. If our relationship with EDS hadn't been particularly good it could have been just a head-to-head stand-off [. . .]. But they didn't at all, they worked with us in a quality manner, went through the quality process, brought people in with experience to identify the root cause and came up with recommendations. They went through a process of clearance with us, we agreed them and now they are implementing them. (RX IT Manager)

Of the 82 areas identified as requiring actions, 41 had been completed by EDS, 29 were in progress, and 11 were on hold by late 1997. An area that demanded particular attention and change was EDS's account structure.

Following EDS's difficulties with the formal account structure, RX now requested EDS to mirror its management structure by appointing an operational manager in charge of each technology framework, i.e. application service delivery, infrastructure, telecoms, computing, and contract coordinator:

They are looking to recruit a telecoms person to work opposite me, be my counterpart in EDS. And there is a manager in each discipline right through. I think that will be a lot better when you've got somebody who is a specialist with technical background and who effectively knows what he is talking about in the area and will take ownership of that service. (RX Telecoms Manager)

Previously they had one point of contact which was becoming a bottleneck [. . .] They are now, to a certain extent, mirroring what we call the frameworks. So the framework is applications, infrastructure, telecom and computing. And that's just the coordination of key parts. (RX IT Manager)

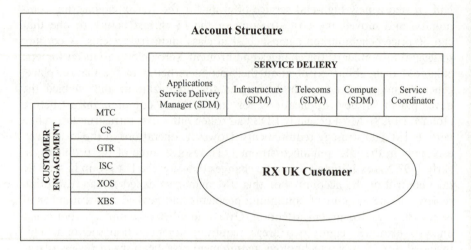

Fig. 3.9. *EDS revised account structure*

Source: Adapted from EDS and Xerox UK's *Account Review* 1996.

Establishing a formal structure was an important step. By late 1997 a new structure had been formalized by EDS to respond to Xerox's demands (see Figure 3.9).

At least now dedicated managers would focus on issues in specific areas, and by 1998 these managers were in place. In addition, the IM group formalized the management processes, which they also imposed on EDS. This specified the regularity of meetings, i.e. weekly, monthly, quarterly, and yearly, the type of review meeting, i.e. infrastructure, finance, SLA, or account review, the managers that needed to attend, and the required documentation and information that needed to be exchanged (cf. Figure 3.10). The management processes enabled managers to table problems, requests and specific issues, and new procedures were agreed on how to handle these. For example, all change requests and quotes by EDS had to be authorized by both parties, so disputes could no longer arise about pricing and changes. As noted by an interviewee:

We've brought in a process where any work has got to be mutually approved. That's helped really and takes away the issues of who authorized that, we are not paying for this you've changed the quote, because they've signed a bit of paper so we've no argument. If there is an argument it's them who it was signed by, so we know who to bring in to resolve issues. The overall state of the changes are then reviewed at the monthly meetings. (RX Contract Manager)

In addition,

The review process also says what EDS have done very well this month. So it's a balance between not just recognising is everything okay or are there problems, but also saying this has gone well. Which again is an important part, especially for building an effective relationship. (RX IT Manager)

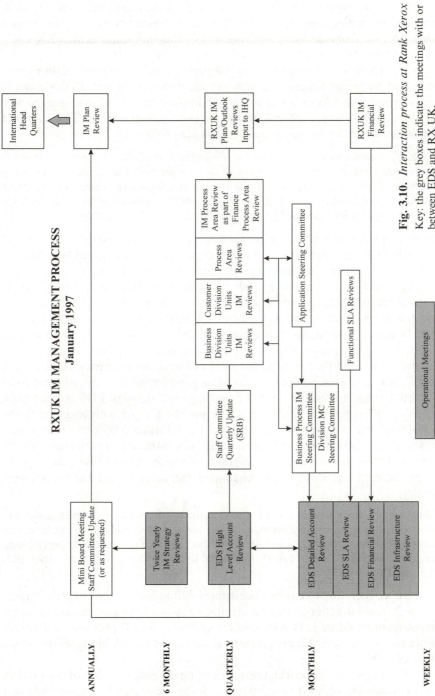

Fig. 3.10. *Interaction process at Rank Xerox*
Key: the grey boxes indicate the meetings with or between EDS and RX UK.

EDS was committed to improving relations at the local level, as was evident through the willingness to take the changes on board and enforce the actions that emerged from the exception review. For this they implemented RX UK's specified management processes as depicted in Figure 3.10.

In addition, EDS's eagerness to cooperate and to improve relations was enforced by senior management's active involvement. In fact, EDS's endeavours to improve relations had a positive impact on the IM managers at RX UK. Confidence improved and trust in the new account manager's honesty and openness about certain issues was reciprocated with a similar openness:

we had a new account director who came into the part of the UK, and he was much more dynamic and far more customer and client orientated. That made over probably the year of 1998 and into 1999 the relationship at a local level much more palatable much less contentious and much more 'we'll satisfy the users' needs' rather than we are one big organization. (Senior IT Executive, Xerox)

In fact, the new account manager turned around the adversarial relations and in early 1998 end-user satisfaction had improved by 23 per cent to a level of general satisfaction with service performance (Johnson 1998).

The maturing of relations by 1998 had a twofold effect. On the one hand, it formalized relations and pushed the emphasis on contract management. Yet, on the other, it improved each party's understanding of the other's internal pressures and frustrations. For example, EDS's account team appreciated that certain systems at certain times in the year needed to be 100 per cent operational. As a result they planned for extra vigilance and resources at these peak times. IM managers, on the other hand, began to appreciate the inherent complexities of the strategic business unit arrangement the local EDS account team faced. For example, in situations where problems arose with telecoms at the local level, the account team was totally dependent on EDS's telecoms organization to resolve them. Of course, this subcontracted organization is very removed from the actual site, as a result of which the response rate to problems had been very slow. Urgent changes to this arrangement had become necessary:

What we are doing now is that EDS have come in to conduct a complete audit and operational analysis of our telecoms networks and structures and back-up facilities and contingency plans. Because again we've had back-up facilities and contingency plans, and low and behold when they've been called upon they haven't worked either. (RX Finance Director)

In turn, cooperating to ensure problem resolution had become of great importance in these situations, because in some cases not even the account management team could be held completely responsible for all problems. Of course both parties and senior management were aware of the inhibiting matrix structure of EDS.

Nevertheless, the overall changes, including the renegotiation of the GDMS in 1996 and the planned renegotiations of the other frameworks in 1997 and

1998, were clear signs given by Xerox's senior management that relations were to be formalized. It was a matter of implementing structure and processes to assure EDS could respond and deliver the necessary service requirements. The Global Head of IT for Rank Xerox noted that this was to become part of future strategy:

> The route we are going down now is moving more towards a supplier relationship I think we've pretty much given up any ideas we had that this was going to be a partnership or closer to the partnership end of the scale. What that means to us is we will have to go back and more closely define some of the services, we will have to review the pricing, we will have to be much more formal in the way we deal with EDS in terms of giving them a demand case for what we want, in terms of setting expectations very clearly and in terms of measuring their performance against those service level agreements and project agreements. But that will cost us in resources for sure, because when we outsourced we didn't plan to manage the relationship as closely as we are actually doing, and will do in the future. So we didn't keep a resource to do that. We will almost certainly have to put some back in place.

Significant Relational Challenges and Contract Breakdown (1999–2000)

By early 1999 the contract had reached its five-year mid-term point. Taking stock of EDS's past developments and performance, interviewees commented that although relations had significantly improved with the contract formalization, performance remained below expectations. Clearly service improvement expectations across all the legacy services outsourced to EDS had not been achieved to what had initially been anticipated by entering into a strategic partnership with a leading IT services company. Nevertheless, looking back, Xerox at the time of signing the deal was in no position to rapidly implement and roll out the necessary new IT infrastructure that was urgently needed to replace Xerox's proprietary systems. To this extent the deal was often quoted as being strategically a success, yet at the operational level service performance remained in many areas—for example, telecoms and laptop support services—far below expectations.

The halfway mark of the contract, therefore, gave both parties an option to reflect on the status of the deal. For both parties, the relationship development over the last five years at the operational level had been particularly difficult, raising not only considerable extra costs by having to formalize and renegotiate service level agreements, but also requiring considerable additional management resources. All of these problems and the additional costs, stood in the light of the fact that EDS was not achieving the kind of returns it had expected to be making:

> Xerox were already pretty lean and mean in systems and systems development and the architecture so there wasn't that much opportunity there. So as opposed to suddenly be able to make big margins because they were getting good money and they didn't need

as many people, the margins weren't coming through so therefore it was a bit tense. (Senior IT Executive, Xerox)

Xerox, on the other hand, was equally not totally happy with all parts of the outsourced IT services. In fact, by late 1998, Xerox had decided to withdraw from EDS the services and support for laptops due to rapidly increasing internal demands, but also consistently low service performance. EDS responded to this by initiating in February 1999 legal proceedings against Xerox for breach of contract and non-payment for services. According to Caldwell (1999):

the complaint says Xerox was paying discounted fees for EDS services and support of laptops used by Xerox customer-service engineers in the field. Xerox has 24,000 of these personnel worldwide. The discount was conditional upon an agreement that Xerox would begin paying the full fee as of Jan. 1, 1999. But in November 1998, Xerox stopped paying for those services, now provided by Xerox employees. EDS argues Xerox should pay the difference between the discount and the full fee for 1998, 1997, and 1996, since cancelling the services nullifies Xerox's entitlement to lower the rates.

The case went to litigation in early 2000. In the meantime extensive discussions at senior levels about EDS's approach to resolving the disagreement had led Xerox to further minimize EDS's involvement in developing Xerox's future strategic IT direction. In many ways it had soured the relations, and EDS had become more and more a service provider for necessary legacy systems, until they are eventually phased out in 2004. However, at the operational level the disagreement between EDS and Xerox had little direct impact or effect:

I'm sure there are lots of heated discussions on this [litigation case] in lots of parts of the corporation on both sides. But on an operational basis that is left to one side because of the day-to-day business. EDS is still fulfilling all the parts of the rest of the contract and we need them to, because otherwise we can't operate. (IM Manager, RX UK)

Operational relations to this extent remained cooperative and ongoing. In fact, some noted they measurably improved once EDS in 1999 was able to improve its profitability on the account through additional services. The reason for this being that from as early as 1998 Xerox was becoming increasingly aware and concerned that they would have to make all their existing legacy systems Y2K safe. This posed a significant challenge as their current applications were still largely operating on legacy-based systems, yet all had been outsourced to EDS. In turn they had become dependent on EDS, which inherently implied that all negotiations for programming and conversion rates had to be done with them at non-market rates. This gave EDS the long awaited opportunity to realize some of the expected margins:

Now year 2000 appears but certainly in the UK we had massive legacy systems, nothing to do with EDS they inherited them from us. So all of those legacy systems needed either re-mediation or replacement or just to be closed down. [. . .] So that gave them a massive opportunity to get money out of Xerox at decent year 2000 rates. Clearly we at Xerox didn't like it but it wasn't EDS' fault so we accepted it and found the money to actually change because no one had an option but to change for the year 2000. (Senior IT Executive, Xerox)

According to interviewees, the resulting dependency and the increasing margins for EDS saw EDS's managers become more cooperative and willing to undertake, for example, voluntary work to resolve minor problems without charging for it. The relationship became more focused on mutual gain:

the relationship from my point of view became in 1998 less confrontational more business footed because we had this joint goal with EDS that they had signed up to do all the work on year 2000. We were managing that project with them and we put a programme office in to manage it with them, and we stopped building other things and doling new development and focused all our attention on getting through that key date of year 2000. (IM Manager, Xerox)

Of course, Xerox had little choice in whom they could truly select to handle the essential Y2K conversions. Yet looking back, they were very pleased to have had EDS on board to handle the transition period across the millennium. In fact interviewees noted that without EDS in this case their systems would most likely not be operational by late 2000. They had truly added value by applying vital IT capabilities, as noted by a senior IT executive at Xerox:

Had we faced year 2000 without a supplier of quality and capabilities to attract programmers we would never have got through year 2000. Or if we did we would have struggled a hell of a lot more than we did. I think that was one big value add. If you stand back from it and say would we have done it on our own, I doubt we would have got there but by the skin of our teeth. We wouldn't have been able to attract people and would have had to go out and find people, and it's not our core discipline.

This was explained as being another good example of the value EDS was adding. Others were the fact that EDS was able to introduce the kind of change initiative necessary to roll out the desktop infrastructure. The value here was again EDS's core IT capability. Also, the ongoing refresh rate of desktops and new applications (such as upgrading from Windows 3.1. to Windows 95) was something Xerox internally would have found very difficult to undertake at the speeds EDS was able to. So in terms of operational value, EDS was doing well. However, in terms of the strategic, value-added ambitions, e.g. selling cross company services to customers, these were found to be unachievable:

We certainly again in the UK had several meetings with our sales manager, managing director and the equivalents on EDS looking to see where the two companies on the selling side could partner and move forward. There were a couple of joint bids they put together to see if that would work and there was an amount of success but not an enormous amount of success. (Sales Executive, Xerox)

By early 2000, relations in the UK were to face two major challenges for the coming years. First, Xerox was undertaking a major roll-out of an SAP system in excess of 20,000 users with PriceWaterhouseCoopers that had to be integrated with the outsourced legacy systems EDS was covering. The system was to be taken further than the UK and rolled out across Europe. The challenge became the need for seamless integration, to be completed in two years:

So if you consider that if you've got 50 countries across Europe all with different systems, and within 2 years the landscape will have changed completely that everyone is effectively on common SAP systems. That is a massive change and requires many partners not just EDS to achieve that. And clearly the investment case for SAP systems across Europe is absolutely massive and it has to be a success. (IM Manager RX UK)

In parallel, EDS would have to continue its support and evolution of new technologies on the data and telecommunication networks. The increasing importance of fast and large data transfers across the globe had become fundamental to Xerox's business. This posed a considerable challenge as EDS would become increasingly dependent on subcontracting third party telecommunication companies to handle Xerox's needs. EDS needed to cope with these challenges, and maintain existing service levels in order to ensure operational relations would continue to progress cooperatively.

CASE ANALYSIS AND DISCUSSION

The Xerox case demonstrates some early successes, and ongoing difficulties with total outsourcing on a global scale, and also illustrates the challenges of fostering relationships at operational levels, constrained by contractual incompleteness and technological uncertainty. It is useful to analyse the case in terms of the main dimensions of the two analytical frameworks presented in Chapter 2.

Risk Profile

In retrospect, Xerox took a high-risk approach to using the IT service market. Total outsourcing ran the risk of outsourcing too much too soon before building up understanding and capability to manage a changed style of 'doing' IT. At the same time Xerox sought ambitious, multiple objectives ranging from traditional service delivery to a business alliance with EDS to sell mutually developed products and services on to the external market place. How realistic were these multiple ambitions? A large risk also rested with scoping the outsourcing deal as global, and contracting for it centrally, because this severely limited the number of suppliers that could come close to claiming they could deliver on the requirements, thus restricting choice and the influence of competition on subsequent supplier behaviour. A global, total deal also brought with it much complexity, in terms of management and operationalization, stakeholders, multiple and changing objectives over time.

Furthermore, it is probable that no one supplier could have delivered on the requirement anyway. EDS was responsible in 1994 for running mainframes, legacy systems, worldwide data and voice communications, and infrastructure support and renewal. Certainly EDS itself had to subcontract, including most of the, unhappy, telecoms part of the arrangement. Looking at it even just three years in, some interviewees suggested that a selective, multi-vendor approach would have been a more realistic route, mitigating risk and allowing management experience to accumulate at a more suitable rate on both sides. Total outsourcing on a long-term contract also made switching costs prohibitive for this massive, complex deal, even quite early on. This, in turn, ran the risk of shifting power to the vendor over time, unless countervailing management capabilities, arrangements, and controls could be developed and applied to the right degree.

Not surprisingly, the length and size of the contract inevitably resulted in a lot of incomplete contracting even of immediate work, but especially for future requirements and for technical and business change. This incomplete contacting combined with a lack of experience in handling total outsourcing in general, and EDS in particular, to create some real performance and relationship and process issues within major parts of the contract. In time Xerox's active management of the contract and relationship dimensions came to redress the problem areas to a considerable degree, but parts of the deal remained problematic into the new millenium. With the benefit of hindsight, and using the risk profile framework from Chapter 2, developments during the contextual and building to contract phases would, indeed, seem to be heading for this finding of very mixed results over halfway into the contract term. But how did relationships develop? What role did Xerox have in this, and how far did the relationship dimension mitigate risk, and leverage business advantage?

Relationship Overview

Generally, in terms of forming a relationship it is fairly clear that Xerox and EDS started with high hopes of a 'strategic partnership' based on integration, trust, and close relations. However, the complexity of the global deal led Xerox's senior managers over time to secure a more traditional client–supplier relationship based on a much more formalized and detailed contractual basis. On one view, this could be interpreted as a straightforward progression of filling out the contractual details that were not available at the beginning, due to high degrees of uncertainty about what was technically and organizationally required and could be expected. On another view, indeed the retrospective view of many senior Xerox managers, the 'strategic partnering' concept was always a flawed one. It was an over-generalized approach, inducing too little attention to contract detail, performance measurement, and the formalization of management processes and arrangements necessary to operationalize and deliver such a large-scale mutual undertaking. The need to renegotiate in 1996 underlines the plausibility of this second interpretation. Indeed, it became clear that a poor contract did not help in securing good relationships, but that the improved (and still developing) post-1996 contractual arrangements were a better basis on which to develop cooperative relationships.

Outsourcing Intent

The conditions underlying Xerox's outsourcing initiative were essentially those of financial difficulties, brought on by strong Japanese competitors and resulting in a drive for operational efficiency and a refocus on core competence. To cope with the competitive market pressures a more nimble and responsive company was needed, built around a divisional organization structure that would be spanned by modern information and communication systems and which would enhance communications throughout the organization and with its customers. The investments needed to implement a new systems infrastructure that would be technologically capable of supporting the operational efficiency drive and Xerox's envisaged IM2000 organization exceeded the financial liquidity of Xerox. The pressure on the IM department in an environment of financial constraint to perform and implement such a new infrastructure led to a search for alternatives. Xerox's chosen goals made some form of outsourcing a 'voluntary necessity', but senior managers may well have closed off the full range of IT sourcing options too soon.

Outsourcing presented a viable option to bridge the financial and technological uncertainty, to legitimize IM's practices, and to provide a much needed cash injection and necessary technological expertise. In addition, senior management's attraction to outsourcing was informed by the espoused efficiency benefits of reducing the headcount and eliminating assets. Outsourcing at Xerox was meant to be transformational, in the sense that Xerox had some twelve separately identifiable major objectives it wished to achieve. The question was whether they were indeed achievable through this type of arrangement. The answer by 2001 would seem to be that a minority of them were, but the supplier's capabilities were overestimated, and the contractual complexity, and relationship management required, considerably underestimated.

In essence, Xerox planned to outsource a problem and some highly uncertain areas, but expected through close collaboration to attain technical, business, and financial improvements. Their chosen option reflected the high degree of reciprocity required in their collaboration with the supplier to deliver very ambitious goals. Previous research warns of such undertakings, since they give suppliers too much control and the chance to act opportunistically (Lacity and Hirschheim 1993; Currie and Willcocks 1998). In research into similar cases, almost all encountered serious problems, but especially those signed early in the 1990s (Lacity and Willcocks 2000; Willcocks and Lacity 1998). Chapter 1 also pointed out that all too often the 'value-added' element in such deals as Xerox–EDS is too small a part of the contract to actually become a priority, and for these reasons fails to influence positively the levels of reciprocity and collaboration experienced in other parts of the contract—precisely what happened in this case.

Contract

Two key factors influenced the shape of the outsourcing contract. First, Xerox and EDS's decision to form a 'strategic partnership' based on closer integration. Secondly, the technological uncertainty and hence unspecifiability of Xerox's exact requirements. Consequently, both parties had to agree at the highest levels to form a 'strategic partnership'. In fact, Xerox felt with EDS as its partner contractually very secure in not being able to define the exact details initially, and to base the relationships on the strategic frameworks of what it expected from EDS. These frameworks defined the overarching obligations, whereas the more specific requirements were then to be developed at each subsidiary. In general, there was a high degree, in places a complete reliance, on the partnership to compensate for contractual incompleteness. For these reasons, certainly at the front end of the deal, there was much talk about the 'spirit' of the contract. As the head of the global outsourcing team put it in 1995: 'Article 1 of the contract covers the spirit of the agreement. . . . It is the spirit of the agreement that creates this commitment; there are no "mechanisms" that can be put into place as a substitute for the spirit.' On the other hand, in other studies, we have found that it is precisely having good contracts and mechanisms in place that leads to good relations and 'spirit' developing. An alternative, if such contracts and mechanisms could not be put in place for some activities, was to postpone outsourcing until they could. More likely, talk about the importance of the 'spirit' of the contract actually persuaded Xerox managers to go into outsourcing in some places without the appropriate contractual details and processes in place. Although the contract frameworks gave EDS the necessary flexibility to achieve the high-level framework objectives, at the local level the contractual incompleteness hindered operationalization. The lack of detail made it difficult to determine whether EDS was keeping its promises; at least at the local level (from the IM manager's perspective) it seemed, according to former service levels, EDS was not keeping its promises. In fact, the contractual framework representing the global account had several adverse effects on relationships. In many IT areas, especially those being developed, the open contract and the 'Evergreen' strategy failed to make clear the responsibilities, service levels, and penalties for non-performance. On the other hand, the contract was arrived at and controlled from the centre, building in too much inflexibility for local levels to fill in the detail or adapt the contractual arrangements to particular circumstances and needs. This too had to be dealt with in the renegotiations of 1996.

The renegotiation led to a detailed redefinition of the whole infrastructure agreement, and much more detailed definitions of service levels, equipment, and pricing. All the other areas were also looked at with a view to tightening up on service levels, charging, and competitiveness of EDS's performance. Subsequent experience demonstrated that these issues were dynamic and continually and regularly had to be revisited.

Structure

Few suppliers were sufficiently resourced to handle the size and complexity of Xerox's proposed undertaking. Indeed, the bidding process highlighted that such mega-deals are restricted to only the largest outsourcing service suppliers, and even for those players it still presents an enormous business venture. The selection of EDS as the sole vendor presented EDS with the largest global outsourcing deal ever in 1994, and in turn a considerable proportion of their business. Their response was to create a separate strategic business unit dedicated entirely to Xerox, signalling clearly the importance of the deal to them. In addition, they agreed to closer integration, which can be interpreted as EDS's objective of benefiting from Xerox's long-standing industry excellence for quality and leading edge technology in handling documents around an organization. This became even more evident through the integration of Xerox's business services into the EDS service portfolio and in appointing them as the preferred supplier for document-handling technology. All this had implications for both Xerox and EDS in terms of developing matching structures that could deal with these size and complexity issues. Not surprising then, that the newness of these large structural demands created challenges for both companies. The impact of uprooting 1,900 employees through outsourcing at Xerox was far reaching, touching every management level in the organization.

The implemented organizational management structures reflected these changes. Xerox's overall IM management structure had flattened and seriously decreased in numbers. The management structure at the local level corresponded to the negotiated contract frameworks and included, additionally, a manager in charge of the contract. The key relationship managers were the head of the IM group and, for EDS, the account executive. EDS's lack of a structure that matched RX UK's local structure led to bottlenecks in information flows and eventual breakdown of relations. This reflected, in part, a consequence of the over-reliance on goodwill and the 'strategic partnering' approach to outsourcing. This reliance proved misplaced and led to renegotiations. An exception review at RX UK saw IM managers impose a management structure on EDS. In turn, a more traditional, structured relationship was introduced at both central and local levels in Xerox, but also within EDS to match the management structures in Xerox. Subsequently, the management structures had to be continually flexed and adapted to fit with developing business requirements and supply challenges.

Interactions

It is evident from the case that the contract negatively influenced the interactions in the relationship at the local level. The lack of contractual clarity concerning exchanges made it very difficult for the local management groups to refer to the agreement for guidance on what EDS was expected to deliver and what the exact performance requirements were. In fact, Xerox's lack of experience with certain new technologies prevented them from specifying the exchange content, making them overly dependent on EDS. All this created large tensions in the formal and informal interactions, especially as EDS ran into performance problems once the transition period was over. Evidence of continuing performance problems was apparent in the record low end-user service satisfaction results in the UK in 1996, for example.

Up to 1996 a large number of interactions were governed by contractual arrangements of various degrees of incompleteness. This was true between EDS and central IM, and as a result at the local level in-house IT managers became highly dependent on EDS for their understanding of contracts negotiated centrally. Indeed, guidance and direction for interactions were primarily outlined in the overarching and broad ranging contract frameworks and 'evergreen strategy' documents. Only with the renegotiation of the first contract framework, the 'global desktop management services', did Xerox add the necessary exchange detail that outlined expected service performance from EDS for the infrastructure and applications. This marked the beginning of a phase of contractual and relational formalization, that would eventually span all the technology frameworks.

At Rank Xerox UK, a particular problem causing frustration was the lack of information exchange. In fact, communication between IM and EDS's managers had been particularly strained, and was only beginning to be resolved in early 1997 with the formalization of the 'management process' and the description of the necessary information exchanges underlying each process. By imposing a new management structure upon EDS, Xerox evolved a degree of standardization and structure that assured regular information exchanges.

With the institutionalization of the management processes, the necessary operational exchanges presented less of a concern to managers on either side. Instead, of greater concern now were the services levels that remained often below most user expectations. Through the improvements in the interactions, though, by 2000 the level of control over service performance had improved as essential information was now more readily available to Xerox's managers giving them the opportunity to define more precisely service requirements. Was it though a matter for the customer to define the management process for the relationship or should the supplier have introduced 'best practice' arrangements?

Behavioural Dimensions

Underlying the outsourcing venture at the highest levels at Xerox was a strong sense of cooperation and collaboration to foster a 'strategic partnership'. It was planned that the centrally negotiated contract and the 'spirit of the strategic partnership initiative' would inform how relationships globally were to evolve, but it soon became apparent that operations at the local level essentially fostered their own behaviours according to how the relationship was working out. As noted by a local account executive:

The approach taken of 'let's work together' probably was the correct approach but maybe it was done a little naively; because two people can work together who have built a relationship in the centre, but then you are assuming that that relationship, which has been built up over a few months, not just like this, can just be delegated to people locally. (Account Executive, EDS)

In RX UK's case, behaviours clearly did not conform to the central management's 'strategic partnership spirit'. Despite initial attempts to foster relations through social events and team-building exercises, the management arrangements on both EDS's and Xerox's side were not appropriate for developing and sustaining cooperativeness, and developing behavioural dimensions to the relationship such as trust, mutual confidence, a sense of identity, and commitment to mutual objectives. The arrangements made were that EDS had appointed only one manager to face off against six IM managers in the RX UK area and EDS had promoted good programmers to managerial levels, resulting in deficiencies both in managerial performance but also in programming skills—both compounding the informal relationship problems.

As a result the failing service levels and management problems at RX UK diminished the levels of confidence, trust, and willingness to cooperate with EDS's managers, resulting in IM managers circumventing EDS managers and taking charge of their former staff. Conflict levels eventually peaked with the falling out and replacement of both the account executive and the head IM manager. The consequence was that from 1996 local level relations and interactions were formalized and structured. At the same time, EDS's account structure was developed to reflect the Xerox management structure, and the Xerox IM central group imposed more formal management processes specifying the regularity of meetings, type of meeting, required documentation and people expected to attend. While all this proved necessary, at the same time it was clear that EDS responded positively to the 1996 renegotiation and the call for subsequent tightening of management and control mechanisms. This, together with the detail of how Xerox managers supported EDS people through their difficulties during the post-transition period, indicated a renewed maturing of the spirit of cooperativeness on both sides.

By 2000, following the difficult Y2K phase, operational managers were fairly comfortable with the relationship and the outsourcing venture. Trust had increased to the stage where confidence had regrown in EDS service provisions, knowing that EDS would always endeavour to provide contractually specified services to the best of their capabilities. Cooperation was now very much the basis of relations. Xerox managers knew by now that they could not operate nor function effectively without EDS at this stage. Again, this became particularly evident with the Y2K compatibility and transition phase. Adversity in turn had now moved from the operational level to the senior levels. Disputes about overall performance, the pending court case, and in general the failure of 'strategic alliance' approach gave plenty of material for relational adversity and mistrust at senior levels. Cooperation at senior levels in Xerox were at an all time low, giving rise to rumours of early contract termination.

Efficiency and Outcomes

In terms of outcomes at the macro-level EDS's achievements were significant. The transition period was handled successfully within six months. EDS resource competence and experience led to the successful deployment of a new infrastructure within two and half years, contrary to a rough industry standard of four years. The enormity of the changeover of the centralized structure to a decentralized structure with the roll-out of approximately 70,000 PCs is unusual in outsourcing cases (but see also BP Exploration in Chapter 5) and EDS was revealed as relatively competent at large-scale changes in the sense that very few suppliers could have handled the magnitude and complexity of Xerox's undertaking. EDS did also give access to technology that would otherwise not have been available so quickly, if at all, to Xerox.

However, at the micro-level it became clear that outsourcing only partially allowed the refocusing of IM attention. In a not untypical finding (Feeny and Willcocks 1998) in-house staff still found themselves doing a lot of the IT work, this being partly an indicator of the underestimation by Xerox of management time and effort needed to manage long-term mega-deals. Research suggests that such management can cost between 4 and 8 per cent of total outsourcing costs, and, as in the Xerox case, is rarely fully catered for in the early in-house arrangements and costings (Lacity and Willcocks 2000).

On efficiency, the running of legacy systems and the base services did reflect controlling of costs and yearly productivity improvements. However, the new areas were much less cost controlled, and the need to renegotiate the contract in 1996 was one indicator of the need for detailed contracts and monitoring, if IT costs were to become really variable as intended, rather than fixed and/or rising. After the transition, service levels started deteriorating in many areas as EDS was reduced to 'firefighting' rather than addressing the root cause of problems. This put additional pressure on Xerox managers to take more control of service delivery management. It also led to the recognition of the need to renegotiate the contract in detail and put in more measurement and control mechanisms.

By 1997 Xerox users had much greater access to IT capabilities than ever before, and the issues and procedures for handling them were becoming much more clarified, with positive effects on EDS–Xerox relationships, but increasing the overall costs on the other hand. At the same time, Xerox seemed to be taking an active line in a degree of 'backsourcing'—adjusting their exposure to the main supplier by bringing more control and tasks back in-house or buying in other resources from the market. This is most clearly seen in the withdrawal of the laptop service from the EDS remit in late 1998—and represents a commentary on the original outsourcing scope and choice of supplier, but also on the adequacy of outsourcing performance in certain areas. Outsourcing was designed to allow Xerox to refocus IT on business critical applications, while the supplier facilitated routine operations, applications, telecoms, and the move to a client/server infrastructure. It proved less successful in the applications and telecoms areas. Moreover, where cost reductions did take place they probably incapacitated the ability of Xerox to cope with a major change in marketing structure. In late 1999, Xerox lost control of its billing and sales commission systems with big consequences for profitability. By early 2000 Xerox market share value had dropped from above $90 to under $20. In some circumstances, one effect of IT outsourcing can be to contribute not to business advantage but to strategic disadvantage (Lacity and Willcocks 2000).

CONCLUSIONS

Outsourcing of any IT function—but even more so in mega-deals like Xerox—requires a cooperative strategy to convert the objectives into reality. The case revealed the complexity of total outsourcing at a global level, and the complex impacts of business and technical uncertainties and contractual incompleteness. At the same time the impacts of size and complexity of the undertaking of global IT outsourcing is revealed as considerably underestimated both by the vendor and client—a frequent feature of other such deals we have studied. The declaration of a cooperative strategy supported by a contract negotiated at the centre, and with many incomplete aspects—partly arrived at in the spirit of 'partnering' and mutual commitment—led to a contract renegotiation within the first two years. It also led to a rethink about the level of detail needed on services, expectations, and pricing across Xerox activities, and senior managers actively pursuing a more formal, traditional type of client–supplier relationship.

Amongst some senior managers, with the benefit of hindsight, it was felt that a more selective IT sourcing approach would have been more appropriate right from the beginning. It was also clear that both the client and vendor underestimated how much work was needed on securing appropriate management processes and procedures, though these were eventually being revamped and invested in, and were manifestly then helping the cooperative strategy three years into the contract. In all this global IT outsourcing deal is revealed as high risk and heavily dependent not just on the will to cooperate, but on the many detailed contractual and monitoring arrangements, management procedures, and processes that act as the foundation for the behavioural and informal interactions needed to generate and support an effective cooperative strategy. This is not to detract from what was achieved in this case; however, the whole construction of the deal: the outsourcing arrangement's success across the board, over such a long time horizon, makes an unlikely occurrence.

REFERENCES

Annual Review 1992—The Document Company Xerox Corporation.
Annual Review 1996—The Document Company Rank Xerox.
Annual Review 1996—The Document Company Xerox Corporation (Internet Version).
Annual Review 1999—The Document Company Xerox Corporation.
Caldwell, B. (1999). 'Revamped Outsourcing: American Express Bank, CNA Financial, and Xerox Cut Back Deals', News in Review, *InformationWeek*, 26 April, pp. 26–8.
Currie, W., and Willcocks, L. (1998). *New Strategies in IT Outsourcing*. Business Intelligence, London.
Davis, K. J. (1996). 'IT Outsourcing Relationships: An Exploratory Study of Interorganizational Control Mechanisms'. Unpublished DBA thesis, Graduate School of Business Administration. Harvard University, Boston, 310.
—— and Applegate, L. (1995). 'Xerox: Outsourcing Global Information Technology Resources'. *Harvard Business School* 9-195-158: 1–31.
Feeny, D., and Willcocks, L. (1998). 'Core IS Capabilities for Exploiting IT'. *Sloan Management Review*, 39/3: 1–26.
Johnson, M. (1998). 'Local versus Global: Managing the Local End of the Xerox Global Outsourcing Contract', Proceedings of the 1st Annual Outsourcing Management Group Conference, 28–9 April, London, England.
Kearns, D. T., and Nadler, D. (1995). 'Prophets in the Dark: How Xerox Reinvented Itself and Beat back the Japanese'. HarperCollins Publishers, New York.
Lacity, M. C., and Hirschheim, R. (1993). *Information Systems Outsourcing: Myths, Metaphors and Realities*. John Wiley & Sons Ltd., Chichester.
—— and Willcocks, L. (2000). *Global IT Outsourcing: Search for Business Advantage*. Wiley, Chichester.
Walker, R. (1992). 'Rank Xerox—Management Revolution'. *Long Range Planning*, 25/1: 9–21.
Willcocks, L., and Lacity, M. (eds.) (1998). *Strategic Sourcing of Information Systems*. Wiley, Chichester.

4

Relational Dynamics at British Aerospace

INTRODUCTION

Like other major defence organizations in the 1990s, British Aerospace (BAe) experienced considerable financial difficulties following the end of the Cold War and the global economic recession. As a response, BAe initiated a dual strategy to revamp its financial situation to: (1) focus on its core competencies in aerospace and defence, and (2) push for operational efficiency to refinance the entire balance sheet. Information technology (IT) spending in turn came under close scrutiny, resulting in a benchmarking exercise for the IT function. After a two-year decision process, BAe selected Computer Science Corporation (CSC) to manage its yearly £120 million operating budget and £250 million worth of IT assets. In April 1994, BAe then contracted with CSC for a fixed-price, £900 million, ten-year total outsourcing IT contract.

BAe's hard-nosed experience in third-party procurement led BAe to negotiate a very favourable and extensive contract. CSC was obligated to provide all baseline services for a fixed fee, regardless of volumes. During contract negotiations CSC assumed that BAe's volumes would eventually decrease over time as the company downsized and processes became standardized. In fact, CSC expected its margins to increase over the period of the contract. In reality, BAe recovered speedily, to become one of the most profitable aerospace groups in Europe. As at end of 2000, its order books were full for the coming years and numerous aerospace and defence alliances had been formed, helping to diversify BAe's product offerings:

BAe got an exceptional deal when it signed its agreement with CSC. It was also an agreement signed at a time when the business prospects of BAe looked very different. Since the signing of the agreement BAe has spent considerably more on IT . . . and it is doing much more particularly, in, say, desktop computing. Most of the contract bid was fixed price rather than variable price. That would have offered CSC protection if BAe's business had perhaps been in decline but in reality BAe's business has been in growth and as a result BAe has had phenomenal value out of the fixed price contract. Because what they'd got is far more work content—and therefore CSC cost—at a fixed price. That's a contracting issue that CSC lives with and manages. We are prepared to operate it at a low margin, even though the rate of growth in BAe at the moment means that it is a tough contract to execute. But despite the fact that we've not been making significant returns, CSC continues to invest heavily in the account. So it's an investment account for us. Still, this contract is very, very important for CSC's growth in Europe. (Vice President, CSC, 2000)

Overall, CSC has delivered the envisaged cost savings and is meeting the contractual service requirements. Still, both parties had to realign the contracts to meet changes in business and technical demands. As in other large-scale outsourcing ventures, the BAe–CSC relationship is an evolving and dynamic relationship that required settling down. At first, managers on both sides fought hard over contractual issues, services, and prices, but as time progressed the IT teams developed a rapport. They have worked together to determine realistic expectations of CSC's contractual obligations, and to focus on more strategic issues such as exploiting IT for business advantage.

RELATIONSHIP LESSONS

This total outsourcing scenario highlights a number of interesting relationship pointers. First, although BAe has long-standing experience in procuring services, has excellent in-house legal representation in writing tight procurement contracts, and had spent considerable efforts on writing a detailed contract for the outsourcing venture by use of external lawyers, advisers, and auditors, nevertheless it was eventually pressured to realign the contract after two and a half years. The realignment highlights the importance of the formal contract in relationships, and also the inherent incompleteness of agreements in long-term ventures. Alleviation has been sought through two- to three-year recurrent realignment phases to ensure adequate representation of business and technological changes.

Secondly, building trust is based on a solid track record of contractual performance. Contracts initially define the performance requirements, and as such serve as the foundation of the relationship. However, after the supplier builds a track record of delivering stipulated terms, the relationship can evolve more strategic and intimate roles. In British Aerospace, after a number of years, CSC was invited to participate in strategic planning and in undertaking strategic projects and change programmes. Both parties now collaborate to deliver added value from the relationship.

Finally, both parties had to work closely together to foster realistic user expectations about the supplier's contractual obligations versus additional costs for service capabilities. Users, in turn, must understand that additional IT products and services above the baseline cost CSC money that must be recovered in some way. BAe and CSC had to create a mutually agreed number of innovative processes to assess and mediate user expectations and keep them realistic.

CONTEXT AND OVERVIEW

British Aerospace, the United Kingdom's biggest exporter, stood on the brink of collapse in 1991, but has since been able to turn around its business and operations to one of the strongest aerospace companies in Europe. This remarkable transformation has involved, amongst other things, extensive restructuring programmes, and a revolution in its manufacturing techniques and management style (Gray 1995).

British Aerospace's History

BAe was formed as a nationalized company under the Labour government in 1977, following the merger of several disparate defence businesses, i.e. British Aircraft Corporation, Hawker Siddeley Aviation, Dynamics, and Scottish Aviation. Early problems of uniting such disparate businesses into a single company demanded radical reorganization, as the businesses were, and largely still are, culturally diverse. BAe continued to foster this decentralized culture, making each unit responsible for its own profitability and support services, including IT. In part, the decentralized culture continues to be required because each business unit operates under drastically different production, marketing, and legal environments. For example, the Military Aircraft Division may produce two to three products (aircraft) per year, whereas another division, like Matra Dynamics, may produce hundreds of products (missiles) per year.

In 1985 BAe was floated on the stock market under the Conservative government's privatization initiative. Following privatization, BAe faced the dilemma of a too small balance sheet, providing insufficient financial strength to support its businesses and future uncertainty. To make up for the lack of financial strength, BAe entered into a takeover and diversification strategy in the late 1980s with massive cash outflows. By early 1990 BAe had acquired organizations and stakes in businesses in excess of £1.3 billion, and was then confronted with dramatic changes in its markets and world politics. The civil aircraft market stagnated; the Cold War abruptly ended; the Berlin Wall fell; the COMECON Pact was dissolved; and the UK was in a deep economic recession. Cash hampered as a result of its diversification strategy, BAe entered the 1990s with serious cash-flow problems and declining markets, pushing it to the brink of bankruptcy: 'The company's near collapse came as such a shock to the outside world. BAe, after all, appeared to be blessed with strong cash flow, a solid balance sheet and healthy order book' (Gray 1995). The slump in orders resulted in immediate large-scale redundancies of approximately 5,000 jobs, affecting almost every business unit of BAe, except for Airbus (Betts, Leadbeater, et al. 1991). In parallel, extensive internal reorganization programmes were initiated to change the management structure to enable BAe to focus on its main business activities, i.e. aerospace and defence.

First signs of recovery came in late 1993, after BAe had shed over 45,000 jobs and sold a number of non-core businesses, including Rover Group and Ballast Nedham. En route to consolidation, BAe was able to present a £20 million pre-tax profit for the first half year, compared to a £129 million loss the previous year (Betts 1991; Betts et al. 1991). The emphasis for the next years remained on cash generation and cost reduction to boost longer-term profitability. In 1994, as part of the restructuring plan, BAe changed its operating companies into separate subsidiaries and entered into a total outsourcing venture with CSC. In line with cash generation, the intention was to keep costs under control, improve flexibility, and continue to focus on BAe's core competencies:

British Aerospace has, as a result of these changes, been refocused back on its roots of aerospace and defence. Within these roots lie the core engineering and technological strengths upon which the management of our business can build British Aerospace as Europe's leading aerospace company (Dick Evans, CEO, *Annual Report* 1994)

These changes were part of BAe's consolidation drive, and its attempt to improve the group's culture. The goal was to introduce team thinking and new working methods—building on open management, accountability, transparency, and tight cost control. By 1996 BAe had downsized and restructured. Bob Bauman, Chairman of BAe, stated:

the drive to rebuild the balance sheet, following the substantial expenditure on restructuring our businesses and the extensive programme of disposals to focus on our core strengths, has been successful. In particular the emphasis on cash management has contributed to the strengthened financial base. (*Annual Report*, 1996, p. 2)

In the course of reorganizing, and driving for operational efficiency, BAe was able to show by mid-1997 a reduction in staff numbers from 125,000 to about 45,000. Its refocus saved the company from near bankruptcy, and BAe's healthy £8 billion turnover in 1997, and outstanding orders worth an all time high of £19.4 billion, made it one of the most profitable aerospace companies in Europe. BAe's strength was further boosted in December 1999 with the completion of the merger with Marconi Electronic Systems, adding not only significant numbers of employees, business, global presence, but also substantial revenues. By 2000 BAe was known as BAe Systems, as the corporate IT director explained:

that's adding about another £3–4 billion of turnover to the business and another 50,000 people. So we've gone from the order of 50–55,000 to the order of 105,000. With a presence now of about 18,000 people in North America and 3–4,000 in Sweden, and 5–6,000 in Australia, 5–6,000 in Saudi Arabia, and thousands of people in Germany, France and so on. We have become both much larger and much more international.

Information Management (IM) at BAe

Historically IM had been handled by each individual business unit, causing each unit to formulate its own particular IT demands, systems, and strategy. Little technological compatibility existed across BAe, as each unit always added new 'bits and pieces' as needed. Moreover, IT as a whole was marginalized with a very low input factor. Duplication of systems across the divisions was extensive.

BAe realized that as a result of this organization they were paying several times over for their IT because each of these small units was developing its own IT capabilities to support its business. The centre couldn't get hold of any of the information to collate it, because it operated in different formats and on different platforms and so on. (CSC Quality Manager)

The resulting spiralling IT operating costs led BAe in the mid-1980s to attempt centralization of IT services. The central information technology unit (CITU) was established and pressured to achieve greater efficiency. In charge of developing a common operating platform that would improve internal communications, CITU's initial efforts focused on telecommunications and data networks. In the late 1980s CITU developed a mainframe-based architecture that was referred to as the Overall Business Architecture (OBA). OBA was to be introduced as a standard for all business units to achieve a common language and compatibility. However, the OBA initiative never took off. Two reasons were put forward for its failure. First, the business units did not see the benefit of standardization and largely rejected it:

The business units turned around and said: why should I change this? It's going to cause me nothing but grief. I'm quite happy doing things the way I want to do them. I do not need a new operating platform. (CSC Quality Manager)

Secondly, the business units that had implemented the OBA insisted on modifying it to their specific requirements, rendering it incompatible with others.

In the 1990s CITU had to consider alternatives after realizing that OBA was failing. In short, a committee was established in charge of formalizing an IT strategy for BAe's future. It consulted widely, reflecting upon whether to keep it in-house or outsource the technology. In 1992, BAe's total IT budget across the division was approximately £120 million, with about 1,800 IT employees. Because of the decentralization, it was difficult to identify the exact number of IT assets, but the 1993 IT infrastructure amounted to an estimated £250 million and included:

- 20,000 Desktop computers
- 1,400 Workstations
- 400 Mid-range computers
- 8 Mainframe IBM data centres (850 Mips)
- 350 DEC machines in Military Aircraft Division, and more in other design focused units
- 1 Cray supercomputer
- Wide Area Network operating voice, data, and e-mail

There were many bespoke and packaged software applications dispersed throughout the divisions. Regarding packaged software, there were approximately 350 to 400 different software licence agreements. But even packaged software had been modified within each division. The user community was very computer literate. The majority of BAe's employees are actually qualified engineers with extensive IT experience. In some divisions, users actually designed their own systems. One respondent noted:

Some end-users specify requirements better than service providers ... the Automated Airborne System, [the users] specified their own workbenches and code generators. They design at the chip level and don't even rely on a packaged operating system. Their main concern is the system better keep the aircraft up. (Client Manager)

IT OUTSOURCING

Following an eighteen-month evaluation period, British Aerospace signed a ten-year total outsourcing contract with Computer Science Corporation in 1994 for £900 million. Some justified it as an urgently needed cash inflow and others suggested it was the best option to handle the decentralized and inefficient IT situation. The importance of outsourcing, together with the other internal transformations BAe undertook, was its contribution to saving the company from near bankruptcy.

During BAe's financial crisis in 1992, EDS approached the Corporate Finance Director with an unsolicited bid to take IT assets of the balance sheet. Although the EDS offer was attractive initially, BAe felt they needed more data: 'We were very ignorant of outsourcers' capabilities and track records' (Purchasing Director). A full-scale investigation of the outsourcing option was initiated in 1992.

Vendor Selection

It took BAe an estimated eighteen months to decide, and select Computer Science Corporation (CSC) as their sole supplier. The process involved the use of a number of external experts including lawyers, financial modellers, auditors of the RFP and in-house proposal, and technical experts. BAe's long-standing experience with procuring services, materials, and products strongly influenced this process. Indeed, culturally BAe has always been a hard-bargaining and cost-conscious company in procurement. BAe's supplier contracts reflect this tradition:

BAe, say for Military Aircraft, 70% of the cost of the Eurofighter is brought in from somewhere else. So they are used to, and their whole culture is around, one of deal-making and negotiating and hard-bargaining. And they are brought up in that and they play hard ball extremely well. (Military and Defence CSC Account Executive)

Interestingly, BAe's contracts also showed that there is always a Prime Contractor. The supplier may subcontract, so long as they deliver on the contract: 'The advantage of this approach is to organize the coordination, control, and accountability around a single supplier rather than have multiple suppliers' (BAe outsourcing report). Before BAe engaged in the selection process two independent teams were created: a six-person outsourcing evaluation team reporting directly to the board, and a team to develop an in-house proposal. According to a BAe report, the in-house proposal was not intended to be a bid to compete with other suppliers. Rather it was to inform the company what might be possible internally, and also to provide useful benchmarking information for the discussion with the other outsourcing parties.

The actual outsourcing process began in earnest in December 1992 with the issue of a 'request for information' (RFI) to twenty companies. After a brief evaluation, ten companies were selected to attend a bidder's conference at which BAe presented the details of their outsourcing intentions. By March 1992, five companies had responded with a short proposal. They were asked to present their proposal which was to be videotaped for future reference:

They then invited firms to qualify themselves. We had to write a 20-page maximum description of who we were and what we were going to do for them. And we then gave a presentation, again they were limited to an hour and they were videotaped to the committee which included not only the people in the central team, but also representatives of all the business units. (BAe Client Manager, CSC)

Of the five companies that had presented their proposal, CSC, EDS-Scion, and IBM-DEC were eventually chosen and sent a 'request for proposal' (RFP) in June 1993. The RFP entailed not only a detailed bid, but also reference visits and further presentations. The scope of the RFP included most of the infrastructure, application developments, and support. It also gave cost estimates for in-scope resources, including approximately 1,500 IT employees. The estimates were based on the in-house proposal. Suppliers were told: 'Here's what we can get costs down to ourselves, so don't bother bidding if you can't beat this' (BAe Purchasing Executive). Although BAe planned to outsource the majority of applications, BAe felt that a supplier could not provide software cheaper. Instead, they were looking for 'value-added', such as getting free software developed which a supplier could then use with other clients.

Following the distribution of the RFP in June 1993, BAe invited the three bidders for on-site tours. Kevin Howley from CSC hired a bus, nicknamed the 'Battle Bus', to enable his team of forty people to visit the sites (Collins, 1993). In return, the bidders invited BAe to visit a number of reference sites. These reference sites highlighted the need for BAe to define a comprehensive and detailed contract. In particular, the outsourcing team needed consistent cost data, service data, including standard service level agreements for 500 services. BAe also rejected the idea of forming a 'partnership', as IT suppliers and Bae would not share revenue, nor would they be responsible for each other's debts.

For the evaluation of the final bids, BAe reshaped its outsourcing team by involving the IT managers from its two biggest business units:

We then set up a central team. Then we involved our two major business units, who got about 70% of the total services, as a partner to assessing the remaining bidders. So that was very much a cultural check do we fit. (BAe Purchasing Executive)

On receipt of the final bids in July 1993, an initial evaluation eliminated IBM-DEC, because its bid was 20 per cent higher in price than the other two suppliers. Interestingly, IBM knew BAe the best because of its past business with them. The reason for the higher price was simply because they did not believe it could be done at a lower cost: IBM found the claims of the others questionable. Hence only CSC, EDS-Scion, and the internal proposal remained. A BAe manager had estimated that each supplier had on average thirty employees working on each bid, and that they spent approximately £2.5 million during the process so far. Hence, losing the contract at this stage would come at a considerable cost.

The remaining two bids and the in-house proposal were very similar in price (only 1 per cent difference). The in-house proposal showed that BAe could compete with external suppliers on price, but that CSC and EDS were able to do a number of things that BAe could not do internally. The in-house proposal served its purpose of increasing BAe's negotiating power. At this stage, the main outsourcing objective shifted from cost reduction to value-added:

The focus had shifted to one which is described as 'value-added'. In looking at a comparison of the cost model between internal and external performance, it became clear that either option could be equally cost effective. However, the key question for the company was: Is there something which a third party (whose capability lay with exploiting IT) could bring to the business that we could not otherwise acquire? This question was considered for a period of two to three months. (BAe outsourcing report)

The RFPs issued by BAe were found to be very demanding, especially for CSC, which at the time was not well established in Europe:

CSC, which at that time was a consultancy organization in the UK, did have one or two outsourcing deals but they were small scale and we obtained the BAe contract primarily using our American parent company's resources. (Airbus Account Manager CSC)

BAe requested the suppliers to present a number of innovative proposals concerning the transferral of hardware, software, and assets of which no exact lists existed, and for the development of a company-wide information technology infrastructure, which highlighted the value-added they could deliver. As one respondent noted:

Having sent us the request for proposal they then sent us covers for the supplementary documentation saying what they'd got. And they said to us, all right given our projections and given what we've told you about what we've got, what is your strategy for taking these clumps of IT and turning it into a system which is going to support the whole of our business and our strategy. So we had to produce proposals which said

Table 4.1. *Assessment process*

Central team
- Quantitative review
- Many questions of clarification
- Overall views formed
- Commercial negotiations

Business units
- Two largest units represent the other 11
- Direct contact with outsourcer
- Users become aware of benefits
- Develop ownership scheme
- Develop strategic approach to IT

HOPING FOR CONSENSUS DECISION

Source: Presentation by Henderson-Begg.

what we were going to do with the network, what we were going to do with the data processing, what we were going to do with the applications, the mid-range machines, all that stuff. (CSC Quality Manager)

From August to November of 1993, the divisions became actively involved in the evaluation of EDS's and CSC's bids (see Table 4.1). Some of the divisions would not financially benefit from outsourcing, and argued against the bids. The Corporate IT Director forcefully argued that the entire IT functions across all business units had to be on offer to attract external suppliers. The bids were very carefully scrutinized, evaluating every part with the aid of the external auditors:

No sooner had we delivered the four volumes than almost immediately the questions started coming back, in paragraph so and so you say this, and in paragraph something else you say this, these subjects appear to be incompatible please explain. They'd got an army of people going over the words to find out their reaction and they were comparing our bid to two other bids as well. So they were able to use the statements made in one bid to test the other bids. It helped them do a better job of finding out what they were really being offered. (CSC Quality Manager)

BAe asked for numerous rounds of clarifications from both bidders. In addition, both external bidders were asked to undertake further presentations to the managers of a number of business units:

BAe said now we need to involve the business units, so they asked us to go around the business units and make presentations on the basis of what it's going to be like for you, and allow the managers, not the IT managers, the managers running manufacturing and design and things like that, to ask us questions. Some of these managers were very hostile to begin with. They couldn't imagine how anybody could do a better job than they'd been doing for years. Some of them were very open, many of them were quite happy for this process to happen, provided that they got whatever was their pressing concern. (BAe Client Manager, CSC)

Following extensive comparisons, the outsourcing team selected CSC as the best offer and preferred partner choice. In November 1993, the final report was made and approved at the Board level. The reason why CSC was selected was put down to a number of reasons. First, they offered the best costs savings, cash input and value-added benefits. Secondly, their culture seemed fairly agreeable: 'One of the things of confidence we have in CSC is they were a reasonable cultural fit with the way we operated, a feeling of confidence that we could do business with them' (BAe Senior IT Manager). Thirdly, CSC had extensive experience in the aerospace industry, in particular with operating one of the largest aerospace accounts—General Dynamics. One respondent noted:

Senior managers within BAe, and even more the managers within the business units, by and large didn't want to hear people talking pure IT. What they wanted was to hear people talking their language, the language of making aeroplanes. And we were able to do that, we were able to produce these people who talked their language. (BAe Client Manager, CSC)

Computer Science Corporation (CSC)

CSC is an American-based organization that originated from the computer programming arena. It has been involved in outsourcing since 1961, at which time NASA contracted it to support their computer systems that guided and tracked telemetry data from unmanned lunar and planetary probes (CSC 1996a, 1996b). CSC offers services in strategic management consulting (through CSC Index), systems integration, outsourcing, SAP implementation, client-server systems, legacy system management, data warehousing, custom software, and concurrent engineering solutions. By 1996 CSC was managing three of the largest outsourcing contracts ever awarded in the aerospace industry—British Aerospace, General Dynamics ($3 billion), and Hughes Aircraft ($1.5 billion):

If you go through our project abstracts and you total up the amount of work we've done at cost, it's upwards of $15B worth of business in the aerospace world. (BAe Client Manager, CSC)

Combined with its numerous other contracts in diverse industries, CSC was by 1996 the second largest outsourcing vendor globally with an annual turnover of $4.2 billion. By 2001 it continued to be in the top four of largest IT suppliers globally.

Outsourcing Scope

British Aerospace outsourced its complete infrastructure and the majority of its applications. CSC eventually took over the information technology sections

Table 4.2. *Outsourcing scope*

- Total IT business £120m per annum
- Each business unit autonomous
- Some businesses buy services from others
- 8 mainframe 'IBM' data centres (850 Mips)
- Large number of DEC machines particularly in design area
- A large Cray Supercomputer facility
- WAN connects sites, except Royal Ordnance unit, includes voice, data, and email
- Network connections to Europe, USA, and Partners, e.g. Saudi Arabia
- 20,000 PCs, 1,400 Workstations
- Applications varied but large number based on 1980s big common systems
- Design organization use CATIA and ANVIL 4000
- 1,500 people

Source: Presentation by Purchasing Executive.

of thirteen business units including the central information technology unit, twenty-four manned sites such as airfields, and 1,500 people (see Table 4.2).

BAe retained 300 people to manage what were identified as core IT capabilities, including IT strategy, contract administration, relationship management, and specific IT systems perceived as strategic. According to several BAe reports, the company has within its mainstream engineering organization genuine leading-edge capabilities in some IT-related areas, e.g. product embedded software within airplanes and missile systems. Such capability and skills would not be outsourced under any circumstances. Indeed, they were considered to be a core competence. The company boasted (and to some extent continues to retain) a software development capability that went far beyond anything that external suppliers were able to provide. In this capacity, IT was seen as part of the business:

Some of the engineering IT is not outsourced. British Aerospace has some IPR in air-force software. So the avionics area is something special for British Aerospace which our aircraft pride themselves on and it has a real market value. (Military Defence Head of IT services BAe)

Outsourcing Expectations and Objectives

British Aerospace's outsourcing objectives, and hence expectations, in 1993–4 were strongly informed by their financial situation and core competency initiative. There was an urgent need for a cash injection. In addition, outsourcing offered the kind of cost reductions in IT spend that corresponded to BAe's general operational efficiency drive: 'One of the very clear directions in outsourcing was to drive down IT cost, and, as well as drive it down, make sure we'd got it under control . . . and therefore through the life of the contract there was a control issue over IT cost' (BAe IT Strategy Manager). The added benefit of outsourcing was that IT assets could be taken off the balance sheet and converted into controlled, variable costs according to business demand rather than having a fixed cost. These accounting possibilities were a key objective for senior management.

BAe also looked to IT outsourcing as a means for focusing on their core competencies. They realized as part of their operational efficiency drive that they had to focus on what they do best—defence and aerospace. In line with this endeavour they hoped outsourcing would help them to improve their businesses' overall flexibility, by using it as a means to restructure: 'CSC had to deliver on reduction of cost. And they therefore expected to see CSC doing reorganizations, rationalization of data centres and stuff like that, which we did' (CSC Quality Manager). Of course, by changing the IT infrastructure they also expected to benefit from the suppliers' IT expertise. Their objective was to reorganize with the intention at the same time to establish a 'world-class' IT service. CSC's view was: 'BAe sought not only single-point accountability for the provision of its IT services, but also a partner whose management of the service would add real value to BAe's business' (Tom Williams,[1] President of CSC-BAe Account). The world-class service demanded considerable improvements on the service quality. This meant improvements on the efficiency and effectiveness of services, but also access to the newest technology. In line with this objective was the need to improve confidence in the IT sections. Most end-users perceived IT services very negatively and as a cost factor.

They saw the big advantage of outsourcing as being able to access wider expertise and get better IT, better support of their business objectives, into the business. They expected to consolidate geographical dispersed IT functions, standardize systems, and divest commodity activities. (CSC Quality Manager)

THE CONTRACT

In April of 1994, BAe and CSC signed a ten-year, £900 million contract. CSC paid BAe £75 million for IT assets and transferred 1,500 employees (Harris 1994). The contract was structured as an umbrella agreement covering two main parts: the general contractual terms including the sales agreement for a number of assets and the specific service level agreements. 'The contract was in two parts, there was a sales agreement which was for the transfer of the assets and the people; and there was a services agreement which was about—what services are you going to provide, and how are you going to provide them' (BAe Purchase Manager). The sales agreement was split into four infrastructure packages and priced as follows:

[1] Quoted in White and James (1996).

Table 4.3. *Service agreements*

Master service agreement	Business unit annex
• Asset protection plan	• Asset protection plan
• Account management	• Account management
• Business recovery	• Business recovery
• Exit management	• Exit management
• Open book accounting	• Quality policy
• Quality policy	• Transition plan
• Risk management	• Key personnel
• Property licences	• Site locations
• Price matrices	• Statement of work
• Transition plan	• Change management
• Escrow	• Problem management
• Performance assessment	• Corporate process
• Performance bond	• SDSs/SLAs
• Statement of work	• Financial report
• Change management	• Operating plan
• Problem management	• Retained assets
• Corporate process	
• SDSs/SLAs	
• Financial report	
• Extended enterprise	
• Schedules	

Annex—separate service agreement from each business unit including Airbus, AMO, BASE, Matra-Dynamics, Flying College, Headquarters, Jetstream, MAD, Regional, Royal Ordnance, Sowerby, Space Systems, SSD.

Source: Presentation by Purchasing Executive.

- Data centres (35% of annual cost)
- Networks (14% of annual cost)
- Distributed computing (26% of annual cost)
- Applications (25% of annual cost)

The service agreements were constructed in layers. The main agreement was with BAe Plc and then additional specific agreements—not as elaborate—were formulated with each business unit. Table 4.3 lists the dimensions of the service level agreement (SLA). Over 500 SLAs are provided in the master service level agreement: 'There was a central agreement about what the services were and how they would then be paid for, and if you like policies about how they were going to be measured. It was then up to the individual business units to put in the numbers and any special needs they had' (BAe Client Manager, CSC). In all, twelve business units specified additions and changes to the master agreement. If CSC failed to meet the SLAs for critical services, then they would have to pay a cash penalty. CSC, on the other hand, was unable to negotiate a clause that rewarded CSC for over-performance beyond stated service levels. In other words, no further incentives.

To mediate BAe's risks in a long-term, single-supplier agreement, the Corporate IT Director hired Arthur Andersen to help identify and negotiate contract amendments. In total, 140 technical, human resource, and commercial risks were addressed between the parties. On the human resource side, BAe committed CSC to retain all transferred staff for the first year to ensure a smooth transition. Similarly, BAe was concerned about the appointment of new managers into key functions, so they implemented a veto clause in the contract.

On the commercial side, BAe specified at length the different security requirements that had to be integrated into an asset protection plan. Specific precautions had to be taken to protect business unit data against not only external threats, but also other business units:

The assets protection schedule outlined that CSC is going to protect BAe's information because it's commercially sensitive. This was latched onto by the business units who said yes and you are going to protect our information not only from the world at large but from all the other parts of BAe because we are an independent business. (BAe Procurement Manager)

Similarly, to ensure a consistent level of services across the divisions, BAe contractually enforced an ISO9001 quality standard for all operations:

BAe supplies equipment to British government, and it requires its suppliers to be qualified to ISO9001. So BAe put into the services agreement you will take all of these bits of IT scattered about the company, you will put them together under one quality management system and you will get it qualified to ISO. (CSC Quality Manager)

Pricing Structure and Arrangements

The contract budget per annum was approximately £120 million, to which the various business units were to contribute in a range of percentages according to their baseline measures in the contract. The following three units defined the largest percentage share of the costs:

- Defence Military Aircraft 47%
- BAe Airbus 20%
- Matra BAe Dynamics 12%

The pricing mechanisms integrated into the contract are very complex. BAe chose to group certain costs together in a particular way, with the intention to recover costs early on. In addition, the contract obligated CSC to provide all baseline services at a fixed price. Due to BAe's financial predicament, both parties assumed during the contract negotiations that volumes would most likely decrease as non-profitable businesses were sold. For CSC, a decline in volumes would mean an increase in their margins.

However, BAe wanted the fixed fee to reflect market prices over the ten-year period of the contract. BAe was fully aware of the rapid price-performance curve in IT, and provided a number of mechanisms for altering the fixed price. The contract stipulates that the four infrastructure areas previously outlined will be benchmarked every year by a named third party. CSC is obligated to match the top 10 per cent best-of-breed performance and cost standards:

We knew that because we'd gone through this competitive process, that we need to establish the best price performance from CSC and compare it to the industry. Two Excel databases ascertain whether the price-performance we are now receiving is industry top and if it isn't then CSC have to reduce their prices which will match industry best in class. (BAe Purchasing Executive)

However, both parties realized that benchmarking was very immature in the areas of distributed computing and applications, so open book accounting of CSC's costs was introduced, as well as a profit cap on CSC's margin:

It's open book accounting. So [BAe] get to look at our costs and they get to measure us independently on productivity benchmarking. (Airbus Account Executive CSC)

On the whole, there is a limit on the margin CSC is allowed to charge for its service provisions. Although the margin is not applicable to individual services, BAe felt that open book accounting would serve to increase their negotiation power. In addition, BAe included the possibility of other vendors bidding for services, to promote fair market pricing for services beyond the agreement: 'This enables the company to periodically ask other suppliers to compete with the major supplier for a specific project' (BAe outsourcing report).

POST-CONTRACT MANAGEMENT

Post-contract management was fraught with problems in the first year. The complexity of the contract, the diversity of the business units, and the due diligence process were held responsible for the early difficulties. In the second year the amount of contractual disputes and interpretations settled down, but the levels of satisfaction and expectation remained low. An early contract alignment was necessary in 1996 to address a number of issues that had been neglected, and to alter a number of aspects that hindered CSC from achieving stipulated terms and benefits. Throughout this time the central information technology unit (CITU) remained the custodian of the contract, overseeing the commercial relations.

The Transition Year (1994–5)

The transition year focused on operationalizing the contract and integrating CSC. It was expected to be complex. The initial tasks focused on interpreting the contract for the user population, establishing a post-contract management infrastructure and processes, implementing consolidation, rationalization, and standardization, validating services, costs, service levels, and responsibilities for baseline services, managing additional service requests and supporting transferred employees to adapt to CSC.

The contract, and especially the complexity of the legal language, did not exactly lend itself to easy implementation. In the early days, BAe's central contract management team had to spend considerable time on deciphering and interpreting the agreement for the user population. User guides were developed to describe what CSC is obligated to provide under the fixed fee structure in user terms. Still, the guides remained in part ambiguous and open to interpretation as, in practice, not all contingencies could be foreseen. Questions thus arose about what is in and out of the contract, demanding in many cases further clarification, for example:

Networking, the actual ports you put the computers in, something that's called a network extension is down to BAe's cost. So if we take this network into another portakabin it quite clearly is their cost. Something called the network enhancement is CSC's cost. Now the difference between an extension and an enhancement, say that next door didn't have the network. Is that an extension or an enhancement because it's giving it to my secretary and it's the same network in theory. (Military and Defence Account Executive CSC)

In some situations lengthy discussions were necessary to alleviate the discrepancies. Both parties initially took a tough stand on contract interpretations because these set precedents for the entire ten-year relationship. As precedents were established, the central contract management published them in a jointly formulated document. As other resolutions led to precedents, they too would be filtered into this document:

Unfortunately in my view, it wasn't possible for the central document to take account of all the nuances of the business level agreements required. So that no sooner was the services agreement in operation, than there were meetings of people about interpretations of the contract. What did it actually mean? And that was built up so there is one supporting body of agreed interpretations. (CSC Quality Manager)

To oversee the contract, both parties established a post-contract management infrastructure. In the area of administration, BAe's Corporate IT Director manages the master service agreement, whereas the central contract management group interprets the contract, mediates disputes, resolves problems, and identifies opportunities for new business. According to a BAe presentation, the duties of the Corporate IT Director and his contract team include:

- Assisting user organizations in reviewing business processes and identification of IT needs
- Definition of overall IT architecture across business
- Providing training to business users and awareness of potential benefits
- Ensure IT strategy is consistent with partners', customers', and suppliers' needs
- Ensure quality, security, and health and safety requirements are met
- Management of outsourcer.

Each business unit has its own BAe contract manager and support staff. The size of the support staff depends on the size of the unit. Military Aircraft Defence unit's contract management group, for example, had fourteen people: six IT commercial managers, seven IT managers, and one strategic manager. IT commercial managers focus on financial management. IT service managers focus on demand management and service levels, including annual benchmarks. As with all outsourcing arrangements, residual IT staff must learn new skills and capabilities to carry out contract administration roles. BAe recognized that the staff needed to develop two key skills:

These skills fall into two broad categories . . . [Retained IT] people were largely responsible for managing the relationship with the supplier. The competencies and skills were managerial and technical in nature. Firstly, people were needed with the skills of negotiating, influencing, and coordinating. It was necessary to articulate business requirements to a supplier on a continuing basis. Secondly, people were needed with good technical skills who could also undertake an internal consulting role. These people were needed to articulate the IT-related solutions within a business context to the supplier. (BAe outsourcing report)

Several units actually provided training in the areas of negotiating and managing supplier relationships. In areas where training would not suffice, BAe moved IT employees around the organization to develop IT expertise. They also considered recruiting these skills from the market place.

On the CSC side, there is a general account team that oversees the entire relationship. In each BAe unit, CSC has an Account Executive, business and technical account managers, and business and IT strategy analysts. Distributed across BAe, CSC's Professional Service and Technical Management Unit handle application development, software maintenance and support, consulting, utility services, data centre, networks, desktop, and helpdesks.

The structure of BAe-CSC's account management teams, however, can vary by business unit. In Airbus and Aerostructures, for example, the roles of the IT Director and Account Executive are embodied in one CSC person who is 'seconded' back to BAe. The reason for keeping this person as an official CSC employee is to allow access to CSC worldwide resources:

If you ask me to go join BAe, I'm cut off from CSC. I can't call Index [consulting branch of CSC]. I can't call the States. I can't call other people consulting in the UK and say, 'listen, I'm working on this, can you do this and that?' . . . anyway we had a chat openly between the CSC Vice President and BAe Executive. And I said, 'it's going to be very difficult, we can't write terms of reference.' It's very difficult to do that here. It's basically the shake of a hand and we've got to trust that this will work. (BAe-CSC Head of IT and Account Executive)

This dual role may work well for two business units, but other units rejected this structure as politically unfeasible: 'I don't think anyone can serve two masters with competing environments' (Military Aircraft BAe Head of IT Services). The interorganizational structure was essential for establishing the post-contract management processes. Service levels are tracked within each unit. Using the service delivery specification (SDS) system, services are measured by a colour scheme—red (10% or more below target), yellow (less than 10% below), green (on target or less than 10% above), and blue (10% or more above). Most business units, however, focus only on a few of the 500 defined service levels:

I think our conclusion is that we seek no more than a dozen key performance indicators. Yes, the relationship is more complex than that. But unless you pick the 12 maximum most important keys, you again will have something which is unmanageable because you are trying to manage too many points. (BAe Purchasing Executive)

In general, CSC has consistently delivered on the SLAs, but both parties' managers found at this time that user expectations and service needs were not always met:

So what you can do firstly, you can see if CSC are making the contract or not and sort that as an issue. But, secondly, you could see if that contractual level met customer need. So CSC might be exceeding the contract requirement, but not the customer need. (BAe Head of IT services)

BAe and CSC recognized the need to supplement the quantitative contractual SLA with qualitative performance assessment. The process is called customer performance assessment reporting system (CPARS). Users are asked to rate CSC's service using similar colour codes as the SDS scheme. Blue indicates 'excellent', green indicates 'fully satisfied', yellow indicates 'some problems', and red indicates 'poor and/or unacceptable'. As one respondent elaborated:

You may have heard talk about the CPARS process that we use. We use that quite extensively here actually, and it's one of our main sources of contact with the customer. It looks at how we are performing, where we can improve, and then, if there are major issues, they will bring that to the table if we haven't already heard about it through some other means. One of the things about the sessions is that they are quite subjective. (Military Aircraft Account Manager, CSC)

Key users of IT in the business areas then meet monthly with CSC to discuss their perceptions of recent performance:

There are two key objectives underpinning these meetings. The first is for both parties to agree how the service will be provided in the coming month or quarter. This discussion will exclude the application of hard measures such as SLAs because it is intended to generate new ideas rather than simply discuss what is already in place. The second objective is to formulate an agreement acceptable to both parties. It will then be implemented and will be the subject of the next meeting. So far, the company has set up some 250 meetings between key users of the services and the relevant representative from the supplier organization. (BAe Outsourcing Report)

The CPARS process has become a crucial tool for both parties to manage service performance. It has to be carefully managed, as users may be motivated to give a red rating in order to get immediate attention. One of the BAe IT Managers noted they have to act as a mediator sometimes between the users and CSC to ensure the problem resolution process is fair:

If a customer gave a red score, completely unacceptable service performance this month, and CSC committed to solve that problem in the month following. . . . It could easily have been just a non-policed process: 'I'll get my job fixed by giving you a red', because we are talking about people, human beings. 'I'll give them a red so I'll get my job done.' Whether it was really on a yellow, green. 'I'm not terribly happy, I'll give them a red, they'll go fix it.' So what we did, we actually had the CSC account manager sit down with the customer representative and the IT team put somebody in between and said, 'You didn't deliver your commitment CSC', or alternatively, 'You were being unreasonable, service customer.' And so they had an arbitrator. (BAe Defence Head of IT services)

Both parties consider the CPARS process an overall success. By 1998, some four years into the contract, few disastrous problems existed and CPARS very seldom hit red: 'We find now it's exceptional to get a red. We might find yellow in 10% of the cases' (BAe IT Director). In parallel to establishing the post-contract management structure and process, CSC consolidated, rationalized, and standardized to reduce costs, and thus increase its own margins. CSC was able to progress rapidly with consolidation and rationalization, but was contractually prevented from standardizing, because they would fail to deliver service levels (see Table 4.4).

Table 4.4. *Early changes (1994–1995)*

- Consolidation of BAe's eight expensive large mainframe data centres into two at different locations
- Redesigned and restructured BAe's internal data network
- Phasing out of old legacy systems and introduction of new more reliable and economical equipment
- Overhaul of BAe's telephone service
- Rationalization of development methodologies, project management, legacy systems re-engineering and applications development
- Investments in training of the transferred staff
- Productivity and cost saving schemes had been introduced

Source: According to interviewees.

CSC was successful in consolidating the data centres in the first year of the contract:

There were about eight data centres prior to outsourcing. And within 15 months of outsourcing, we had two. And that was done very professionally and certainly better than we could have done. (BAe Purchasing Executive)

By October 1994, CSC consolidation had reduced the headcount by 250 people. Such cost reduction tactics were vital in order for CSC to make a margin. Thus, transferred employees felt their instincts about outsourcing leading to redundancies were correct. But CSC's Director of human resources, Gordon Bottoms[2] noted: 'We are looking ahead to six months and there are 100 jobs vacant in CSC UK, in firms such as Ford and BHS, plus offers of training and redeployment.' CSC was also able to rationalize, by implementing new procedures and methodologies. For example, they implemented their own system development methodology. From BAe's perspective, this too had been successful:

They've introduced a development methodology. And I understand it to be a particularly good methodology for system development. And that's now well spread around the organization. It's really now that we are starting to see the real business benefit. (BAe IT Director)

In the case of BAe, CSC cannot reap the full benefits of standardization because each business unit has idiosyncratic service requirements. For example, when CSC tried to centralize the PC procurement process, they were not meeting some of the business units' requirement. Each required a customized approach.

---

[2] Quoted in 'Ex-BAe staff to go as CSC Revamps Centres', *Computer Weekly* (13 October 1994).

During the transition a number of services, costs, service levels, and responsibilities for baseline services had to be validated. In large-scale deals, such as at BAe, validation can be expected to discover undisclosed baseline items that trigger excess costs. But BAe catered for such eventualities by obligating CSC to cover undiscovered baseline items. CSC failed to discover a number of items in the due diligence, and rushed their evaluation:

CSC was completely innocent. They didn't know the complexity of the business. They'd got General Dynamics, and they thought that was the same with CSC. . . . They had no idea what they were taking on, they just wanted to have it, they didn't really care what it was exactly. (Airbus Business Analyst CSC)

CSC thus found £600,000 extra software that they would have to support within the fixed-fee structure:

There is a huge discrepancy in the amount that we pay for software maintenance and the revenue we get from BAe. It makes it very difficult for me to be charitable or generous when it comes to dealing with software maintenance issues. So I want to take bit harder line on that. Most other areas, it's not really a big deal. (Dynamics Account Executive, CSC)

CSC also claimed to have found £30 million worth of liability for hardware leases, software licences, pension costs, and British Telecom lines. Of course, these costs cut significantly into CSC's profits, and created significant challenges to the relationship:

I believe because of the way the contract was structured that automatically put us in a bad position in order for us to be profitable. We had to stick to the contract as closely as possible and try to take advantage of that to get revenue where we could because I don't believe that contract was set up in a way that enabled us to do that immediately. (Dynamics Account Executive, CSC)

The dilemma CSC has faced is that contractually they are obligated to provide baseline services for a fixed price. In some areas, such as desktop computing, the increase in demands has caused CSC to lose money. As such, they cannot financially provide the level of service they would like to:

We have a particular rough ride on desktop. And this is a very difficult area to deliver in BAe. There are a number of factors for that. One is that we are not resourced to meet BAe's requirement and in a sense we've got no ability to financially meet the requirement. Every PC in BAe last year we moved on average more than once, nearly twice. And because they are all networked, we had to re-cable because they don't have quality infrastructures. That's a huge demand on us because we are doing most of that at our own cost. (CSC Vice President and Account Director, 1997)

In part, this complicated the management of additional service requests. New projects are obviously beyond baseline services and subject to additional fees, so a line could be drawn. However, both BAe and CSC managers found it difficult to explain to end-users that CSC fairly prices new requests. Users compared service quotes with market prices, found the service quotes much higher, but failed to consider total cost of ownership and maintenance:

[The purchase cost] is the only cost the individual user sees. Maintaining it costs five times as much as it does to purchase. The purchase price is 20% of the whole thing. And the current head of the central IT unit who manages this whole process for BAe, went into print, he had to go into print to explain [that] to BAe's users. (CSC Quality Manager)

In general, though, users began to understand the cost-service trade-offs for additional service requests:

Where previously it was viewed that they didn't pay for a service before, now they are paying for a service. It made it more invisible [before] and perhaps they expected more [after outsourcing]. I think that might initially have strained the relationship. (Airbus Account Executive, CSC)

For example, one business unit manager requested a shop control system that would save him £250,000. But the BAe IT Director pointed out that it would cost £500,000 to build. Users also came to realize the cost of changing legacy systems, and do not now spend as much on trivial enhancements. BAe personnel improved their behaviour in relation to becoming more cost conscious in their service and change requests.

Both parties perceived the first year as difficult, but successful. CSC was able to accomplish an immediate cost saving of 10 per cent in most areas of technology expenditure. In addition they were able to relieve BAe from one of its non-core activities:

The first year was just about doing the drains and bogs, the networks, mainframe availability, and reducing the price and also paying a big lump sum of money because they were strapped for cash at the time. So that was what the contract and the outsourcing deal was framed around. Do what we are doing now, but do it cheaper and provide the same level of service. (Military Aircraft Account Executive, CSC)

In summary, the transition period focused on the parallel tasks of stabilization and reduction of the baseline service costs, and progressive infusion of CSC's management and technological expertise (Williams[3] 1996). CSC was expected to deliver costs savings and meet the service level requirements. As such, they were initially treated as a traditional procurement based relation, where exchanges according to the agreement are paramount. A number of disputes resulted in strict contractual governance and performance measurement.

Post-transition (1995–1997)

Due to the complexity and scale of the deal, the transition period continued far into the second year. In the post-transition period CSC had to spend addi-

---

[3] Dr Tom Williams was the President of the British Aerospace account for CSC (1994–7).

tional time on clarifying the contract, formalizing the process and the infrastructure, and fostering realistic expectations of its performance. This was a critical time for both parties because, following the high expectations, user service satisfaction and confidence dropped dramatically.

Even though by now many of the early contractual disputes and misunderstandings had been clarified, a number of fundamental service management issues persisted: 'There was a rash of work building contract resolutions over the first 12 months, which then slowly dissipated away in the next year' (Head of IT Services, BAe Military Aircraft). It was expected that the development and institutionalization of the necessary management processes would require additional time. Transferred employees had to adapt to changes in working methods, and CSC managers had to learn to cope with the cultural diversity of the numerous business units. Early signs of management processes settling down were evident in the decreasing number of disputes escalated to the central IT unit. The consequence was a decreasing amount of contract reinterpretations. By mid-1996 it was possible for BAe and CSC to publish a booklet comprising the collected interpretations and contract dispute resolutions:

So there was a joint booklet, and the interesting thing is that booklet doesn't get added to any more. I've not seen any for last year. Which means the contract is settling down and becoming less pressured. (Head of IT Services, BAe Military Aircraft)

A major task CSC faced was to foster realistic end-user and IT staff service expectations. As in other cases, users usually expect that the IT service supplier will deliver an exceptional service at marginal costs as 'they are the IT experts'. For some users, in turn, it was difficult to embrace the notion that suppliers are really only contractually obligated for baseline services:

I don't feel like the end-user really understands the contract and what we are contractually required to provide. So there is a perception that the service ought to be much greater than what is actually required in the contract financially. . . . In particular, some of our engineering customers who I believe are already very technically able and so I think they expect a much higher level of service than perhaps the SLA may actually warrant. (Account Executive Dynamics, CSC)

The gap between expectations and reality was particularly large at the outset, since both parties had the difficult task of selling to the users and IT staff the concept of outsourcing. Yet, as in most total outsourcing contracts, the size of the undertaking did not permit radical services and operational changes right away. The CSC Airbus account manager explained:

At one stage on this site, when we had something like 400 people here, there were actually only two of us on this site who had worked for CSC anywhere other than here. They were all transition staff. That was BAe's specific request. They wanted the changes in the transition to be—I think the words were 'evolutionary' rather than 'revolutionary'. But at the same time the [service expectations] were going to be fantastic. So the end customer had got this expectation of a step-change, but you were doing it with the same workforce, doing the same things. They've just got a CSC mug and their pay-checks have a CSC logo on it.

Interestingly, even though CSC was achieving almost all of its contractually required service levels for critical systems, it generally received a low service level satisfaction rating, and there was a general feeling of disappointment on the 'value-added' side.

Overall, I think statistically, if you look at things in terms of performance against SLAs and things like that, in general we are meeting the terms and conditions of the contract, but I think expectation within the customer is much higher than what the contract actually states. What we can't do is always go running back to the contract for protection. So we have to move the relationship on. And even if it's not required of us by the contract, we need to be able to work to support the customer. But he also needs to recognize that in providing and receiving a service, there needs to be some compensation. So I guess overall in outsourcing, I think a lot of it revolves around understanding each other's expectations. (CSC Account Executive, Military Aircraft)

In mid-1996, the parties realized that the growing gap in expectations was largely due to the different definitions of 'value-added'. Users defined 'value-added' as getting more IT products and services under the fixed price arrangement of the contract. BAe managers defined 'value-added' as accessing IT to exploit business advantages, whereas CSC's managers defined 'value-added' as delivering the cost savings, meeting contractual service levels, and providing BAe with technical skills. Alleviation came only through mutually agreeing to what the areas of value-added would be:

- *business value-added*, in which the supplier applies their expertise to help the customer exploit IT for business advantages;
- *capacity value-added*, in which the supplier infuses new skills and technologies in an effective manner; and
- *utility value-added*, in which the supplier provides cheaper IT services.

To further clarify and alleviate the expectation disparity, CSC instigated seminars and visits to clients in the USA and elsewhere to assess a number of business solutions using advanced information technologies that BAe could benefit from (Williams 1996). Additional benefits were made available through CSC's access to scarce technical resource. For example:

one thing that CSC have been able to do because of their overall international size of operation, they've actually been able to recruit on a scale that we would never have been able to as BAe. To actually draft a team of 40 people in within weeks, I've never seen happen in terms of IT (Head of IT Services, BAe Military Aircraft).

These benefits were slowly permeating into the business units, drawing attention to CSC's capabilities. However, some problems still clouded CSC performance. In particular BAe's IT managers were frustrated by the amount of promises not fulfilled through lack of expertise and attention: 'CSC was actually quite poor on a lot of things and aspects. They just said oh yes we'll do this and that and they didn't understand what they were saying, they didn't know what they were promising' (Systems Analyst at Airbus, CSC). Both parties were struggling with issues such as:

- CSC not seeing a big enough profit, resulting in strains in the relationship;
- Procurement procedures for desktop computing services insufficient across the business units;
- CSC lacked an internal structure, causing communication problems;
- Benchmarking did not provide effective measures for comparing services;
- Open book accounting was initially inconclusive; and
- Liability on Year 2000 conversion was unclear.

The lack of profit put substantial pressure on CSC, as they had made sizeable investments, but were not recuperating sufficient revenues to balance their investment. In the meantime, CSC was delivering utility and capacity value-added benefits, but their overall low profit margin was straining relations:

Value-added, it's one of the goals. It's value adding but has to be done on both sides. CSC has to turn a profit and has to allow BAe to turn a 'profit'. If you were signing up a partner, you wouldn't want your partner to lose money. You want your partner to be successful. So I think the value-added term is used with the implicit understanding that CSC is also prospering to some level. (CSC Account Executive, Airbus)

On the other hand, staff development of the transferred people was progressing well. Many had been able to change to CSC's operational style, and adopt CSC's values and practices. They were now coming up through the organization in a way probably not possible if they had stayed with BAe. However, following the initial year of near full employment for transferred employees, CSC had to embark on reducing its headcount to ensure its profitability. In turn, there were increasing redundancies, and dissatisfaction on both sides between employees:

We haven't been given a big picture by the company on redundancies and I've asked the Union representatives formally to ask for the big picture and whether they will be given it I don't know but they should ask. There's a lot of people disappearing right left and centre from different bits of the business and I also want to know what the age profile is. (Business Analyst and Acting Pension Trustee, CSC)

In summary, the post-transition period saw a continuing phase of settling a number of contractual problems, while, in parallel, processes were implemented and by now had begun to settle down. CSC was delivering the baseline services as expected. A track record of solid service performance boosted IT staff's and users' confidence. The relationship as such was moving steadily into strategic and value-added areas.

Rejuvenation: Contract Realignment (1996–1997)

Two and a half years into the deal both parties jointly agreed that the contract needed a realignment. Both perceived it as having become unrepresentative of the business and technology changes that had occurred since 1994. This was a radical step as new costs would emerge and initial contract management plans had not considered such an updating necessary as the relationship progressed:

We've come to the conclusion that actually the contract itself has to be a much more dynamic, moving, changing thing rather than something set in stone. And so what we've gone through in the last 12 months is a process of contract realignment where we've looked at the way the contract works, particularly in the way some of the contracting mechanisms work. And without wishing to change the past and our relationship, we've jointly been working to realign the mechanisms so that they produce results which are more in keeping with what we went after. (BAe Purchasing Executive)

Actually, three areas were of particular contention that demanded careful re-negotiation. First, the general composition of IT services had shifted from legacy mainframe systems to client-server technology, and business units were overly keen to implement such systems:

From the day the contract was signed we have had a major issue on both sides—this isn't BAe or CSC's fault—about how do we deliver our client server. And the contract realignment exercise takes account of client server now, but it's only through this process of going back to the contract because the contract itself doesn't recognize these things. (Head of IT Services, BAe Military Aircraft)

(Indeed) BAe predicted that there would be a fall off in the requirement for mainframe services. But the prediction was inadequate as individual business units suddenly became hell bent on getting into client server systems because they think it's cheaper. What they don't realize is that they are trading one form of cost for another form of cost. And one of the reasons why we are doing a realignment contract is because client server was not adequately dealt with in the original contract because there wasn't a lot of it about. The long and short of it is we need even more people rather than less. (CSC Quality Manager)

Secondly, deregulation in the telecommunications industry radically reduced telephony prices, to such an extent that costs calculations were off by up to 50 per cent:

If you look at the fixed prices in the contract they pay no account to technology change or market demand for telecoms and the competition, so the prices are outrageous . . . I think we've halved our telephone prices by choosing different providers, that's not recognized by the contract. The contract is not recognizing emerging technologies. It's all based around static volumes. There is room for growth but not in the dynamic sense that it actually happened. (Head of IT Services, BAe Military Aircraft)

Finally, desktop computing demands increased manifold, beyond the forecasts. In turn, CSC had to absorb all these additional costs for desktop demands:

Desktop services, this was an area incidentally where BAe miscalculated. They did not realize just how fast the take-off into a PC on every desktop was going to happen, and they underestimated the number of PCs that were going to be bought, that needed to be bought, and the size of that aspect of the business. This is something that is now being put right. (CSC Quality Manager)

They stopped the procurement of desktop and said well we are going to outsource in 6 months' time so just hang on until then. They were building up this demand behind a dam. And then on April 1st the dam burst and we were hit by a wall of demands—nobody foresaw it. (CSC Client Manager)

These changes had to be undertaken to ensure the contract remains fair. In fact, both parties accepted that the fixed price for baseline services no longer reflected IT usage. It was found, for example, that mainframe consumption was supposed to remain static over the life of the contract, whereas in reality the demand in certain units significantly increased. BAe initially wanted mainframe costs to decrease with volume. Another typical example in the business units was that CSC would normally charge a fixed fee for office moves. This would involve PC relocation and network connection, but the actual explosive growth in desktop demand required CSC to absorb all costs of moves and invest in substantial cabling for networks. There was thus a strong pressure to move towards variable-based pricing, for the benefit of both parties:

By mutual agreement, we are trying to make it a little more related, but overall it won't change the bottom line of profitability. It's really a readjustment of the pricing mechanisms within the contract, and provides protection for both sides. . . . I see realignment as an ongoing, healthy, fresh aspect of the relationship. (Vice President and Account Director, CSC)

Price alignment focused on cost drivers such as client-server, telecommunications, and emerging technologies. In addition, price adjustments were needed for work packages and man-hour rates for skill expertise. For example, the contract only covered one standard man-hour charging rate for all CSC people. This was causing problems in terms of getting people onto the account as the flat rate was often too narrow. In instances of specialist or scarce skills, CSC would lose money on the hourly rate. In instances of remedial skills, BAe was paying above hourly market rates. It was thus agreed that man-hour billing should be split into three skill categories that would reflect the market and technical expertise costs better, especially since the existing pricing mechanisms were encouraging bad practice:

We found, for instance, that some of our pricing mechanisms encouraged bad behaviours, and bad behaviours are things like the buyer being almost incentivized not to give the service provider due notice of his requirements. The service provider not being incentivized within the contract to provide the client with an efficient service. Things that you can only determine in practice given the way the two organizations work. (BAe Purchasing Executive)

Discussions were also held about an incentive structure for users to standardize processes. CSC's problem was a lack of standardization of technology across the account, diminishing the possibility of achieving any true economies of scale. This in turn often led to open discussions about CSC's level of profitability. However, no changes were made in favour of CSC during these re-negotiations (Moxham 1997).

Nevertheless, both parties did find that the 'realignment' was a helpful way of clearing the air and it was not perceived as a negative event. It also helped to clarify and rejuvenate the relationship. Indeed, it was regarded widely as a progression in relationship management:

> But the important factor is that we anticipate to do the same thing [alignment] again in 2–3 years time. And then 2–3 years after that we will do the same thing again. Not because we got it wrong, but because the change in technologies, changing typologies, and changing user requirements, and satisfaction drivers. We know that we have to do it, we might as well get ourselves into the mindset that says this is the sort of things that outsourcing relationships present. (BAe Purchasing Executive)

It is important to note that the contract still remained critical to the relationship at this stage, and was widely accepted as providing the foundation of operations in form of prices, services, processes, and expectations.

Towards Mature Relations (1997 and 1998)

Realignment highlighted that pricing and emerging technologies were to become of greater importance to British Aerospace in the coming years. Indeed, management processes in the form of, for example, the ongoing benchmarking exercises highlighted the service control pressures on CSC. At this stage, participants explained that post-contract management processes and the management infrastructure had become quite institutionalized. Management procedures like CPAR had proved their worth by smoothing operations and alleviating problems. Still, further emphasis was needed on monitoring to strengthen the management processes—for example, benchmarking was often found immature in measuring distributed computing arrangements and new applications:

> Our experience, being honest, is that I haven't been terribly happy with the benchmarking process. This is not happy for CSC or BAe. It's just the process seems to be a little bit naive. (BAe Military Aircraft, Head of IT services)

For example, application productivity, quality, and cost are benchmarked using function points. CSC is obligated to be 10 per cent of best-of-breed, but best-of-breed is based on a management process that allows for software standardization and economies of scale able to yield such results. However, since CSC could not standardize the software, technology, or procedures in the face of

Table 4.5. '*1997—'IT changes in the last 3 years*'

- Tremendous growth in desktop and client/server systems beyond that forecast
- BAe concentrating on IT strategy related to business strategies and major investments being made
- Growth in the use of the Internet
- Setting-up of the BAe Intranet
- Less retained IT staff, more CSC staff in BAe jobs
- Looking for value beyond efficiency (some positive—most disappointed)
- Introduction of 60 CSC Consultants to advise on IT strategy and specific projects

---

Source: Presentation by Moxham (1997).

idiosyncratic business demands, it was unreasonable to expect CSC to deliver best-of-breed results.

At this stage, the capabilities of CSC in some business units had been acknowledged, and strategic discussions had been sparked. The formal definitions of value-added served to align expectations and focused strategic discussions. As Table 4.5 illustrates, CSC had so far implemented a range of new technology, with significant effects all around.

However, it now became increasingly necessary to move away or beyond the contract and to further integrate CSC strategically. Two issues were of importance: first, to benefit from CSC's expertise to help formulate BAe's future IT strategy, and secondly, to become more flexible as requirements arise:

Now phase three is upon us which is all these major IT strategy activities such as the stuff that we are doing here and other places in BAe. So that's an evolution in terms of where the focus of energy has been. (CSC Military Aircraft Account Manager)

CSC called upon its consulting subsidiary—CSC Index—not only to present a number of innovative ideas, but also to advise strategically (Moxham 1997). The resulting strategic initiatives underway focused more on exploiting IT for BAe's benefit. CSC has become involved in strategic IT planning, re-engineering projects, and major change programmes. Though these were initiated by BAe, both parties realized the mutual financial benefits:

What we are trying to do in the strategic arena is really, we've got a programme called the Operation Efficiency Improvement. And it's really a step change. And CSC work is at the heart of that with BAe staff, and what we tried to do is make the thing strategic in not a financial sense, but in a benefit sharing sense. . . . We've actually developed, speaking about the contract, we've just developed another attachment to the contract which is trying to formalize the principles around benefit sharing. But it's still not tangible enough, but it's an attempt. (BAe Military Aircraft, Head of IT services)

In another example, CSC was instrumental in a planned replacement of 200 mainframe legacy systems in five divisions. They conducted a fifteen-month evaluation of packages and selected Baan, the Dutch counterpart to SAP. A team of CSC and BAe staff were identified to implement the system. CSC's ongoing participation on strategic projects, however, does not mean that BAe places less emphasis on costs:

Today (1998), as a result of the strategic work we did, we are implementing a whole client-server environment, and buying a lot of PCs. We can demonstrate why we are going to spend all this money, why BAe needs to spend all this money. They bought into it. But we are now negotiating how we can get the price per PC down as low as possible. But they have agreed that the client-server architecture that they transferred over to CSC really will not support their business. (CSC Airbus, Account Executive)

The second issue, namely the level of flexibility BAe was looking for from CSC, persuaded managers to place efforts on moving past a transactional focus:

The flexibility comes through being able to put long-term plans together, long term being a year or more. So if you give CSC a year's notice then on a contractual basis they can actually raise their rewards in our books. Some of the aircraft bits for instance, suddenly we need to resource with 70 people, that's a major issue having 70 people from an account team of 40–50. Increase the manning level by 30% at short notice, it's not gone through the planning process and the contract doesn't recognize that issue. It recognizes planned increase and decrease on a 1–2 year horizon, it recognizes a very slow rise and fall. But if you win a bid like Nimrod where there's 1,000 BAe staff wanting new IT, there's an enormous demand for IT staff. And we've got to put an IT system together for next month, maybe. The contract doesn't recognize that. (Head of IT Services, BAe Military Aircraft)

Although CSC and BAe operate more as collaborators on strategic projects, the relationship can still be (and into 2001) adversarial when debating operational issues:

We have a schizophrenic relationship. And two compartmentalized debates. So one is entirely a service contract, service level agreement, delivery, value, price and performance debate. And there, compared with other clients, they are very strong and aggressive in that area. On the other end, they have high expectations that we will be strategic, help them change their business. We are involved in some of their most intimate programs. (CSC, Vice President & Account Director)

This 'schizophrenic' relationship was commonly experienced by managers actively involved in the management of the relationship. The nature of the relationship seemingly varies from adversarial to cooperative to collaborative, depending on the task at hand. By this stage, however, even 'adversarial' tasks were based in part on a foundation of confidence and trust earned through ongoing interactions and solid performance.

Marconi Systems Integration and Upcoming Challenges (1999–2001)

Throughout most of 1999 the additional challenge was one of integrating Marconi Electronic Systems. There were significant opportunities to be harnessed from Marconi's extensive IT systems knowledge, but there were also a number of challenges around making Marconi's existing systems compatible with BAe's almost completely rolled-out industry standard IT infrastructure. How could integration be achieved with the existing outsourcing contract, especially as Marconi's IT unit was still entirely in-house, with quite a sizeable expenditure?

To minimize the integration complexity, BAe decided in favour of extending CSC's contract to include Marconi's IT services. The driving reasons for this were the working relationship and high satisfaction levels with CSC's service performance. Of course, an additional factor was that BAe did not have the necessary IT skill sets (having outsourced them to CSC) nor management resources to handle such a large-scale IT function and hence its integration with CSC. The deal with CSC involved the transfer of 1,000 Marconi IT staff and the integration and management of service provisions across the globe involving e-mail, office productivity, ERP systems, mainframe and mid-range computer servers, desktops, helpdesks, applications, and Internet services.

By early 2000, BAe Systems (renamed following the merger) needed to improve its overall strategic control over its now global business, and in some way try to set a group-wide IT strategy. For this BAe Systems decided to develop a stronger centralized IT group that would take organization-wide responsibility for setting the IT agenda. This implied a number of changes in terms of strategy and service definitions for the existing account management structures throughout BAe's business units. The corporate IT director further explained that:

we have significantly reduced the strategic concept there [in the business units] and the content there, whilst upping the central amount. So if one looked at say 15 people in the businesses when we add them up, one would now find 4 in the business and 6 in the centre as it were, so the total weight has radically changed. [. . .] In a positive way it's dismantling some business unit structures and focus, be they within the business unit or in CSC, and a positive building up of a previously relatively small central organization.

In parallel to the merger with Marconi Systems, the central IT group completed the one-year audit for its second contract realignment phase. As before, it was based on ensuring ongoing cost reductions and flexing the contract to match current service changes across the account. This process had by now become very much accepted as reoccurring in 2–3 year phases over the rest of the contract life. An IT director for BAe explained the second alignment phase:

Again, as previously, it wasn't born out of take some cost out, it was born out of getting the right balance of service and support and cost and so on. I think it's a recognition in the maturity of the relationship that we can go through those things again and probably will do again in a couple of years' time.

However, due to the ongoing commercial discussions and the pending changes that would result from the merger with Marconi Systems, the contract realignment changes had not been implemented by mid-2000. Instead they were to be further amended by the addition of Marconi's IT services:

So we have another package of realignment we've done, quite successfully we believe, which is sitting on the shelf temporarily while we go through the rest of the broader commercial debate. (IT Executive, BAe)

In the coming months and years BAe Systems faced the major challenge of integrating Marconi Systems and outsourcing it to CSC. It also embarked on radical change in terms of business development and procurement of supplies for its core business of military, aircraft, and defence. Together with Boeing, Lockhead, and Martin it had agreed to jointly develop an on-line aerospace exchange market place. The objective was shared procurement, over time expanding into areas of new business development and customer support. CSC was to provide BAe Systems and its partners in the project called 'Zephyr' with the necessary technology support and expertise. In fact, CSC was expected to become a major participant in developing the market place:

We would expect CSC to play a role in helping shape what that solution might be rather than just responding to a requirement to deliver [the Zephyr] solution. And therefore they may ultimately take, for example, some risk in that element or maybe paid on a reward type basis at the end of the day rather than payment on a here's the money for the software and hardware and solution. So we move towards—or potentially move subject to agreement—towards something which is much closer to the business.

CSC, in turn, was expected to take on more risks in developing and delivering services to BAe Systems in future, but in return would also receive significant cost rewards. More importantly though, it mirrored the existing state of the relationship. CSC had truly become, and was considered at every level of the organization as, a strategic partner in developing mission critical services that would shape and define the future of BAe Systems operations.

Case Analysis and Discussion

Total outsourcing at British Aerospace was driven by a core competency initiative, and hence a focus on operational efficiency and effectiveness. Both cost reduction and value-added services were expected from their supplier. BAe's relative success with outsourcing is in part related to their experience of procuring services externally. Early on, BAe ensured through a rigorous selection process the best bid and closest cultural match. CSC's eventual selection as the prime contractor assured single responsibility for all IT-related services. The

sophistication of the contract gave BAe control over much possible opportunistic behaviour. In fact, the contract was written so that CSC had agreed a
fixed price for baseline services, because at the time CSC expected in the long
term BAe's service volume to decrease with diminishing business. Instead, it
dramatically increased with BAe's financial regeneration and business improvement. Hence, as it stood for many years the contract has been strongly in favour
of BAe, giving CSC little opportunities to make a profit. In some units the relationship has increasingly moved towards a value-added relationship. In these,
CSC's integration at the strategic level presented a number of operational
improvements and innovations, and new opportunities for business, and hence
profit, for CSC. In others it remained at the buyer-supplier service procurement level, with for the first five years in particular a strong focus on cost containment. By end of 2000, the annual BAe cost of IT was exceeding £220 million,
compared to some £120 million in 1992.

Risks at BAe

BAe-CSC ran similar risks as other large-scale single-supplier contracts signed
in this period. These risks have been spelt out in earlier chapters, and will not
be repeated here. BAe also ran the risk of being over-influenced by its poor
financial position and the need to alleviate immediate profitability and cash-
flow problems. Also, there were all too few suppliers who could credibly deliver
such a large contract at this time, thus reducing the options, but also potentially the ease of switching supplier, if outsourcing went radically wrong.

However, compared with Xerox-EDS, these risks were alleviated by (*a*) very
detailed contracting and service level measures at the beginning, together with
subsequent 2/3 year revisions; (*b*) the deal was about half that of Xerox-EDS
and therefore less complex, especially in terms of less global roll-out; (*c*) the
supplier had a core capability in defence/aerospace IT outsourcing, learned on
an ongoing basis at General Dynamics; (*d*) the supplier saw this as a vital long-
term contract to succeed in, not least for building perception and attracting
other European clientele. Additionally, BAe's considerable procurement and
contracting experience fed into a more risk-averse set of arrangements than the
ones Xerox adopted (see Chapter 3). Nor did BAe pursue quite as many multiple objectives as Xerox, and in some ways had much more realistic goals for
its outsourcing, given its supplier's capabilities.

A major risk for several years lay with the supplier not making 'reasonable'
profits, exacerbated by a strong cost consciousness in some business units,
though this began to change some five years into the contract, and was offset
by BAe's strong contractual position. CSC, in fact, spent a lot of the first few
years just working to get the inherited IT organized and straight, and got frustrated by the lack of other more profitable work coming through. Contracting
for the future and for new developments and technologies is always difficult in
outsourcing, and BAe proved no different in this respect. However, its constant

revisiting of the contractual position, pricing, benchmarks, and service levels, supported by a plethora of retained core IT skills and capabilities ameliorated many of the risks here.

Post-contract, both parties proved willing to learn, and to develop the relationship, once a long transition phase was concluded. Having many highly IT-literate user groups also set up countervailing power in the face of the dangers of ceding too much technical prowess to CSC and not retaining enough technical skills in-house. In time, the relationship dimensions developed considerably, thanks to active management of the supplier. This enabled considerable business leverage to be gained from the outsourcing, though the business value-added beginning to come through from 1998 on could certainly not be perceived as cheap.

Outsourcing Intent

BAe's financial crisis in the late 1980s and early 1990s demanded dramatic changes involving cutting its workforce by half and the sale of a number of businesses not contributing to its defined core competency in aerospace and defence. BAe's decentralized information management sections were not excluded from these challenges. The drive for operational efficiency demanded investments to impose a centrally organized IT infrastructure, which business unit managers, however, were unprepared, and unwilling, to implement. In this context, outsourcing was to provide an urgently needed cash input and clearing of assets from the balance sheet, and to enable central IT management to impose operational efficiency on the IT sections across the divisions. For the BAe board, in the terms of our framework, total outsourcing was a 'voluntary' necessity.

However, 1993 marked an upturn in business, allowing BAe to make a profit. In part, this relegated BAe's cost-driven focus for outsourcing; 'value-added', and so more intense 'reciprocity' with the supplier became much more a priority. Cost did remain critical, but bidders were also asked to present innovations and operation improvements. A shift from 'cost saving' to 'value-added' and 'business leveraging' became apparent early on, even before the contract was signed (Currie and Willcocks 1998). CSC should have subsequently revised its cost calculation, as its envisaged profit expectation of decreasing volumes of service requirements was flawed in light of BAe's business upswing. It also called for expectation management early on, as end-users and management expected to see areas of 'value-added', while at the same time many remained very cost conscious.

Of course, BAe's business recovery resulted in higher requests for services, which CSC had to cover as it had agreed to cover baseline services for a fixed price. The subsequent financial tightness of the contract for CSC meant relations in the first instance had to focus on service delivery according to the contract, with CSC trying to charge back for any services not covered in the agreement. Clearly, the early development of the relationship was in part hampered by the restricted profit margin, hindering CSC from recuperating its financial investment, and making it think carefully through resource provision. This was potentially dangerous for both parties, as CSC's failure to deliver, and clashes over cost/service trade-offs would interdependently affect BAe.

Contract

Contract negotiations at BAe were extensive, involving both in-house and independent third-party lawyers, plus auditors of service level agreements. BAe realized early on that once they signed the deal there was no going back. BAe's procurement culture pushed them to invest considerable effort in ensuring that the contract catered for as many contingencies as possible. Subsequently, the contract had for example 500 service levels and was rumoured to be one metre thick. The lawyers advising them were naturally sympathetic to an approach of great contractual detail. In line with BAe's procurement tradition, they advised for strict penalty clauses for non-fulfilment of stipulated terms and no real incentives for exceeding performance:

So her [the lawyer's] guideline in formulating the services agreement was for every promise of delivery there shall be a penalty for non-conformance. And when CSC said, 'Okay we will accept that in the case of business critical service promises, but how about a bonus for exceeding the promise', she said 'No'. So the initial contract knee-capped us if we didn't perform, but it didn't give us any incentive to over-perform. (CSC Quality Manager)

As it stood, the contract was written as adversarial in nature. This, of course, had an effect on the level of 'value-added' BAe could expect from CSC, as the contract made it clear that only service delivery according to the agreement would be acceptable.

The incompleteness of the contract in the case influenced the potential of both parties to refer to it for guidance. In addition, the nature of contracting is time dependent, so much so that, once formulated, contracts actually become outdated. For BAe the contract governs their perspective of the relationship. Hence, it was critical to ensure alignment of the contract to existing business and technology changes. On the other hand, CSC saw alignment as a possibility to address a number of areas that (*a*) diminished their potential to make a profit margin and (*b*) were also seen as unfair. In turn, the contract continued to govern the relationship and it was reasoned that realignment should occur recurrently as an updating practice to assure it still went on adequately reflecting the venture and the parties' objectives.

Structure

The management infrastructure implemented in post-contract management varied in size across the business units; no common interorganizational structure can be generalized for BAe. The residual group formed BAe's management groups, whereas CSC's account teams were spearheaded by CSC personnel and supported by transitioned staff. There was a common management hierarchy handling IT services in each business unit:

- Senior managers: Account Executive (CSC)—Head of IT Services (BAe)
- Middle managers: Operation managers overseeing specific service areas, IT strategy, contract, and pricing (CSC and BAe)
- Line managers: Business and Technical Analysts (CSC)—Business line managers (BAe)

CSC has to relate to many different 'customers' ranging from senior managers, business unit managers, IT managers, and a population of end-users that can amount to nearly 16,000 users in a single unit e.g. MAD. These stakeholders possess different needs, expectations, desires, and measures of 'success'. Thus in the venture, client–vendor relationships vary according to the stakeholder groups. Perceived beneficiaries of IT outsourcing are sympathetic and supportive of the supplier's performance, whereas losers may be aggressive and attack the supplier's performance. Much of this happened in the BAe-CSC deal, as found in other deals, for example by Lacity and Willcocks (2000).

Of great interest were the arrangements made at the Airbus and Aerostructure units. In each, the role of the Account Executive and IT Director has been filled by the same person. This poses a number of management complexities not only for the manager, but also for BAe and CSC. It demands complete trust in the person to judge and undertake whatever is best for either of the organizations, meaning at times choosing between who benefits and who loses. It also requires confidence in the person in the business unit and across BAe, because this person will become involved in business meetings, have sight of documents, and access to information, that a CSC manager would normally never be exposed to. This arrangement is further complicated by the fact that no guidelines or contractual references can be formulated. Its complexity is revealed by a respondent:

He's a CSC employee who works for BAe, i.e. account manager and head of IT role, and he's not a happy man. He grapples with how to solve the internal conflict. This is what is best for BAe and this is what is best for CSC [. . .] To save his sanity he's taken the BAe route. My prime responsibility is to make sure that the IT management function with BAe Aerostructures is like this. No matter what grief it causes him within CSC, he can handle the grief and he can handle getting it right for BAe, but what he can't handle is the conflict of working for both sides. So you shut your mind to one of them, and get on with the other. (Head of IT services)

The infrastructure is dependent on retained capabilities and skills. Early on BAe recognized the importance of developing new skills for managing the outsourcing contract, particularly managerial and technical competencies. According to Currie and Willcocks (1998) additional people were needed at BAe with the skills for negotiating, influencing, and coordinating. In particular, it was necessary for managers to be able to articulate business requirements to CSC on a continuing basis. Both business and technical analysts were in demand, as these had the skills to articulate the IT-related solutions within a business context to the supplier. Most of BAe's technical line managers, however, had transferred to CSC.

Although the company had retained a sufficiently large group to manage the outsourced relationship in terms of service delivery, it was missing the people with the necessary interpersonal skills to manage the relationship as it progressed into strategic areas. People with relationship management skills were becoming essential, but tended to be scarce at BAe. As a result managers with a proven relationship management track record were moved around to other units to handle more senior positions needing a well-working relationship. Additionally, as new technologies and services came to be implemented, so new needs arose for experienced people with knowledge of mainstream areas, one obvious example in BAe being client-server technologies.

Interactions

The detail of the service level agreement, but also BAe's early consideration of the post-contract management processes, had a positive effect on the operationalization of the contract. Although only an extract of the 500 service levels could be monitored, the specifics of the service level agreements allowed management by SLAs. Control and monitoring in post-contract management honed in on the baseline services and continued to be the chief concern in the relationship. Institutionalization of the exchanges became evident with the change in focus on additional services and value-added services. Of concern for BAe was avoidance of opportunistic behaviour by stakeholders. This remained as a potential, because, in time, gaps opened up that could be exploited by interested parties. Regular realignment of the contract, pricing, and service levels attempted to close these gaps, and throughout the contract continued to serve as the key governance structure.

As far as 'normative content' is concerned, a number of interactions are of particular interest: pricing, benchmarking, hard and soft service measures. Pricing was of grave concern to BAe as their large service demand could potentially entail fluctuating prices. Alleviation was sought by imposing a fixed price for baseline services and by negotiating pricing algorithms that would cater for unforeseen changes in IT services. These processes paid out in post-contract management, catering, for example, for the unforeseen growth in desktop, computing requests. Contractually, this growth was covered by the baseline services. Independent benchmarking was there to ensure that service prices would always correspond to the industry's best-of-breed. In practice this benchmarking proved a naive process; realistic benchmarking of prices across BAe's autonomous business unit structure was found to be near impossible.

Both parties concluded early on that service monitoring and management could not be dealt with solely through the quantitative SLA measures. CSC was delivering the stipulated service levels, but user perceptions did not correspond to this performance. The introduction of the CPARS method allowed CSC to capture subjective end-users' perceptions of services provided. It is a time-consuming procedure, as separate meetings have to be arranged between users and managers. The abuse of CPARS is also an area of potential power wielding, demanding further management attention. By late 2000 an estimated 300 plus such meetings had taken place, and the procedure was being perceived as highly successful. CPARS's usefulness lies in its strength to gauge the users' overall satisfaction with IT services, which is critical to temper expectations, to identify opportunities, and to build trust among the end-user population:

The issue is not so much whether there is trust between CSC and the IT community; it's whether there is trust between the IT community for all CSC and BAe on the one hand and the business users, the real point of consumption as it were. And I think we are far from achieving that. We don't have trust between IT as a whole and the business community. (Account Executive, 1998)

Clearly CPAR has been a mechanism that has contributed subsequently to building more trust, through productive interactions.

Behavioural Dimensions

Over the first seven years of the contract the parties increasingly grew interdependent. While, by 2000, switching costs out of the contract were far too prohibitive, and BAe were overly dependent on the supplier, at the same time it retained many sources of countervailing power, not least by means of the contract, and its active in-house management of many aspects of the supplier performance, measurement, user requirements, and relationships.

Furthermore, in practice, CSC's commitment to the venture was largely unaffected by their inability to make a sufficient profit margin in the early years. The BAe account is perceived by CSC to be a flagship often presented as a reference site to potential clients. Internally, it attracts the best staff and continues to receive full commitment and attention by CSC's senior management:

When you are running at very low margins it becomes more difficult to make business cases for investments. It hasn't though here at BAe, and this is something I think may be surprising. To some extent it surprises me. It hasn't constrained CSC's investment in making sure it's got a very strong team running the account. I think we have some of the brightest and best people in CSC who have spent time with this account. Despite the low levels of profitability the account does get star billing if you like within our pulling power within the rest of the corporation. (Account Executive)

CSC's commitment has been recognized by some BAe managers and reciprocated through greater cooperation. In some business units, however, relations are still adversarial. It varies across BAe, and in some units there can be a mix of cooperative and adversarial relations (see Lacity and Willcocks 2000). One respondent elaborated:

I have two discussions when I go and visit a managing director. Ten minutes might be criticizing me or asking me to take action on the fact that PCs haven't been delivered, then having cleared that conversation, we will move on to probably quite an earnest debate about where his business is going and how IT is or can support him. So you tend to end up with quite compartmentalized debates. (Haines, Vice President)

The issue at stake is clearly closer cooperation to move the relationship towards a strategic relationship. To achieve this, debates should be mainly about how CSC can add value and innovative benefits rather than discussions about baseline services. Indeed, after the transition phase, BAE and CSC invested time and effort in building a track record that fostered confidence in CSC. Confidence has had a positive effect on relations, as managers began to trust CSC. As trust was built, CSC was invited to expand their responsibilities to more strategic functions. In Airbus for example, CSC had initially suggested to the manager to expand the scope of the contract to include engineering systems in the scope of the plan. At first, the BAe Unit Manager responded: 'And he said, "When you can deliver a PC when you say you are going to deliver a PC, then we'll talk about outsourcing more people to you"' (Account Executive). Four years into the venture, CSC had achieved a record of performance. When CSC presented a strategic plan to the same BAe Unit Manager, he asked the CSC Account Executive to include the engineering systems in the scope of the plan.

He said, 'What about all the engineering software? Who is looking at that? Your strategy isn't covering that.' I said, 'Hey, you were the one who told me not to look at it, that's engineering's.' He said, 'No, you should look at that. We are spending a lot of money on engineering software, that's got to be part of your work.' So without knowing it, the trust needle switched over to the other side. (Account Executive)

Because trust has been built on an operational performance record, CSC has increasingly been given more responsibilities in IT strategic planning, reengineering, and change programmes. The level of trust varied, however, across the account, and depended on whether the task was operational or strategic. Moreover, as Lacity and Willcocks (2000) point out, in outsourcing, relationships between stakeholders can vary all the time between adversarial, cooperative, collaborative, depending on the task at hand, and the specific interests being pursued. Certainly this has been the observable phenomenon in the BAe–CSC deal over the first eight-year period.

Efficiency and Outcomes

The success of the IT outsourcing venture for BAe can be assessed according to the initial objectives specified in the context of the venture. They acknowledge both in public presentations, but also internally, that the outsourcing venture has been successful in realizing several expected benefits. First, reduction of costs was critical for achieving their operational efficiency drive. Claims were made by various interviewees that baseline costs have been decreased by up to 30 per cent. As we have seen by 2000 the annual costs had greatly increased, though CSC was doing a lot more in BAe than in 1994. Secondly, BAe was able to remove a substantial amount of IT assets from the balance sheet. According to Harris (1994), CSC paid some £75 million to BAe for assets that they had taken over. Thirdly, BAe were able to focus their attention on its core competencies—aerospace and defence. Much less concerned about IT demands, and supply, they were able to focus their efforts on bidding for projects. So when awarded, for example, the Nimrod (plane) project they could rely on CSC to provide the necessary flexibility to suddenly resource seventy IT specialists to the project—something BAe would have found impossible to resource before outsourcing. Fourthly, BAe were able to improve their service quality through a more rationalized approach to service requests and a process of expectation management, but also by imposing an ISO9001 quality standard on CSC, and across the business units. End-user satisfaction began to reflect the improved service quality in higher CPARS ratings. Finally, BAe has benefited from a revamp of its diversified technology. The legacy systems were changed over to a desktop computing and client-server infrastructure, improving compatibility.

Further benefits have been in the 'value-added' that BAe initially presumed would evolve for free. BAe expected 'world-class' services in technologies and skills. Once the three-tiered definition of the main areas had been clarified, and it was accepted that 'value-added' meant that both parties had to benefit from these transactions, then extra benefits from the relationship started to flow. Thus, CSC has been able to draw on its consultancy subsidiary (CSC Index) and other resources to present a number of technological innovations and advisory services. By 2000 it was involved in business re-engineering, IT strategic planning, and change programmes within BAe, as well as providing more traditional IT operations and services.

CONCLUSIONS

The British Aerospace-CSC case study presents an example of a total outsourcing contract, where the client company has successfully manœuvred itself into a win situation, and by doing so is slowly improving the suppliers' economic situation in the venture through additional and new areas of business. This case highlights the importance of a detailed contract in a long-term exchange-based relationship, and especially the important role of the contract in providing a continuing governance structure for the relationship. Because of the centrality of the contract, it was recognized that realignment procedures needed to be mutually implemented to ensure the contract properly represented BAe's business and technological changes, but also the shifting basis on which CSC could provide services at a reasonable profit.

Both parties began to institutionalize the relationship by implementing structures and processes to resolve issues in a fair manner. Trust among the parties developed as the record of supplier performance mounted. Disputes were settled in a financially neutral way that benefits both parties overall, sidestepping in most cases the penalty clause arrangements in the contract altogether. The early difficulties have been settled and the relationship is moving towards new, strategic projects. Both sides are hoping to devote less time to the operational issues in the future and more time on exploiting IT for business advantage. By late 2000 the move continued to be towards a mutually beneficial relationship, while accepting that such a complex set of arrangements, and moving targets would inevitably experience a number of fluctuations in relationships and how they were handled and adjusted in different parts of BAe.

REFERENCES

Annual Report (1996), 'British Aerospace'.

Betts, P. (1991). 'Survey of Aerospace: On a Wing and a Prayer—for the First Time in its Highly Cyclical History, the Industry is Having to Adjust to a Slump'. *Financial Times* (12 June).

—— Leadbeater, C., White, D., and Fazey, L. (1991). 'British Aerospace to Cut 4,700 jobs'. *Financial Times* (22 March).

CSC (1996a). 'Brochure: Designing the Future of Aerospace'. *Computer Science Corporation*, USA.

CSC (1996b). 'Annual Report: Adding Value for Our Clients'. *Computer Science Corporation*, USA.

Currie, W. L., and Willcocks, L. (1998). 'Managing Large-Scale IT Outsourcing Contracts: The Case of British Aerospace Plc'. Conference—United Kingdom Academy of Information Systems, 15–17 April, Lincoln University.

Gray, B. (1995). 'Special Report on British Aerospace: How BAe Pulled Back from the Brink'. *Financial Times* (18 December).

Harris, D. (1994). 'How BAe is Spending £1 Billion to Save Money'. *The Times* (5 September), 21.

Lacity, M., and Willcocks, L. (2000). *Global IT Outsourcing: In Search of Business Advantage*. Wiley, Chichester.

Moxham, B. (1997). 'Presentation: British Aerospace and CSC after 3 Years', in A. Shepherd (ed.), *Seminar on the Management of Change in an Outsourcing Environment*, Oxford Institute of Information Management, Oxford.

Williams, T. (1996). 'CSC Computer Sciences Ltd', in R. White and B. James (eds.), *The Outsourcing Manual*. Gower Publishing Limited, Aldershot, 201–6.

5

Alliance Management at British Petroleum Exploration

INTRODUCTION

British Petroleum's (BP) rapid growth and extensive diversification in the 1970s and 1980s caused BP to suffer from serious cash flow problems in subsequent years as the oil market and the UK economy entered into a severe economic recession. Faced with financial difficulties in the early 1990s, and with an organization that was overly bureaucratic and personnel intensive, BP initiated the strategic '1990s Project'. The project would see a radical change in the organizational and management structure, a refocus on core competencies, a phase of high employee redundancies, and a revamping of the information technology (IT) infrastructure. In combination, these changes would see it becoming a 'lean and mean' competitor once again in its global markets.

BP Exploration (BPX), the second largest and most capital-intensive division, exemplified BP's radical IT changes, highlighting in particular the innovative use of IT outsourcing to overhaul its infrastructure. In the 1990s, through multiple suppliers, BPX hoped to maintain best-in-class service and technology levels, but also benefit from economies of scale, improved flexibility, and access to innovations that would raise overall operational efficiency. Compelling suppliers to work as a 'strategic alliance' to deliver a seamless service globally, BPX negotiated five-year contracts at an annual cost of $US 150 million. Although the contract was structured on principles of partnering that included risk-reward arrangements, and principles to which all parties had agreed, suppliers found it increasingly difficult to work as an 'alliance team'; in reality they remained latent competitors in an extremely competitive IT market. By 1998, even though relations had evolved to a stable and trusting level between BPX and the Alliance, it was decided that the original conceptualization had not worked:

When you look at outsourcing in hindsight we find that almost everywhere we rarely meet any cost saving targets for outsourcing, it almost always costs us at least as much money, if not more. On some kind of per-unit basis where you can measure it, it is always hard to achieve. So our conclusions recently have been that alliances don't work. You don't assemble a group of vendors and say be nice boys and go off and do good things for us. It just hasn't taken off at all. There's got to be a prime contract or some-body among the contractors has got to step forward and say I'm going to be the lead contractor. People just don't cooperate out of altruistic behaviours and so on. We rarely saved the kind of money we had hoped to save. (Head of Business Information and Process International Systems Programme, BP)

Consequently, as the contracts came to their natural end in March 1998, BP Exploration decided to drop the alliance approach. The subsequent strategy adopted was one of single sourcing for specific areas globally. For example EDS was given a five-year contract to deliver global infrastructure services. Yet this venture ran into difficulties resulting in some outsourcing confusion. Following the merger of BP and Amoco Corporation in the late 1990s, the strategy moved into something of a hybrid, with the addition of more local-ized selection of the best supplier to provide the particular IT services required.

Relationship Lessons

BPX's experience illustrates the complexity of managing multiple suppliers as an alliance, where each party was selected for their 'best-of-breed' IT expertise in a particular area and together cover all of BPX's IT service requirements. The expectation that, with little direct relationship management involvement, suppliers would cooperate as an alliance and provide a seamless service proved to be unrealistic. The approach resulted in the need to introduce focused partner/relationship managers at significant costs, and in the eventual post-contract realization that the alliance approach as conceptualized actually did not work and, in some respects, raised additional costs.

Although all parties had committed to a pre-contract alliance agreement on critical relationship issues, and thus entered the venture with strong partnering intentions, the relationships between the suppliers themselves and with BPX still turned adversarial and contract-focused in many instances. Only with the introduction of dedicated relationship managers, as in the other cases, was BPX able to control and alleviate many of the interface problems, service lapses, and relationship difficulties. Again, the positive influence of full-time relationship managers to resolve disputes, enforce management processes, and identify new business and value-added benefits actually helped to keep the deal on track.

Finally, the case provides insights into challenges clients and suppliers face with the integration of substantial IT services following a merger. The result-ing pressures on suppliers to cooperate on, and integrate, service delivery pre-sents not only challenges in terms of managing supplier–supplier and client–supplier relationships, but also in terms of ensuring the continuity of critical business IT services.

Table 5.1. *BP's operations by turnover 1997*

Sector	Turnover (£m)	Share of total (%)	Investments (£m)
Exploration and production	7,909	16.8	2,108
Refining and marketing	35,728	76.3	667
Chemicals	3,123	6.6	169
Others	58	0.3	34
Total	**46,818**	**100.0**	**2,978**

CONTEXT AND OVERVIEW

In 1997, before its merger with AMOCO, British Petroleum was the third largest petroleum and petrochemicals company globally, and in Europe was quoted as the fifth largest company by turnover (Petrocompanies 1997). In 1997 BP had a turnover of £46 billion, with 56,450 employees and operations in twenty-eight countries worldwide. In 2001 BP's main activities continued to be exploration and production of crude oil and natural gas; refining, marketing, supply, and transportation; and manufacturing and marketing of petrochemicals (BP Amoco 1999). Table 5.1 depicts the 1997 turnover of BP's business divisions, indicating the importance of each to the organization.

As the table illustrates, critical to BP's future, and to most other petroleum and oil organizations, is the ongoing production and exploration of oil. With the 1999 merger with AMOCO Corporation, the fourth largest oil firm in the USA, BP strengthened its market position and access to exploration sites globally. BPAmoco together now operated in over 100 countries and had an annual revenue of $108 billion (BPAmoco 1999). Finally, in April 2000 ARCO also joined BPAmoco, making it the second largest petrochemicals group in the world (Horizon 2000).

British Petroleum (BP): History

BP was incorporated in 1909 as Anglo Persian Oil Company (APOC) to exploit oil reserves it had discovered in Iran. Searching for funds, the British government invested in the company with two-thirds equity, making BP in essence nominally state-owned. In the 1960s and 1970s BP continued its expansion in the Middle East and Europe, especially in the North Sea. Growth in the 1970s involved acquiring 25 per cent of Standard Oil (BP 1990). However, the oil price shock in the 1970s caused many problems for oil firms. The most troublesome was the lack of direct access to crude oil supplies. As a result BP decided in the 1980s to diversify its business portfolio to diminish its dependence: 'Retrospectively it can be seen that this strategy [diversification] was not always a wise one, and by late 1980s BP was actively divesting its noncore businesses' (Jones 1991: 379).

Its diversification involved expansion of its nutrition business (animal feed and breeding, consumer foods, and related products), of its minerals interests, and acquisition of Scicon (a computer services organization). However, the world recession in the early 1980s halted BP's diversification, and led to extensive rationalization of its refining and chemical business to maintain its profitability. Speedy growth and diversification had resulted in a very large, inflexible, people-intensive, hierarchically structured organization, that consumed considerable capital to stay operational. Indeed in 1992, as a direct consequence of rash investments, BP spiralled into a loss (Mortished 1998). Fundamental changes to the organization had become necessary, especially in its management and organization structure, to ensure competitiveness and operational efficiency for the future:

In 1990 BP announced a fundamental change of its corporate structure, known as Project 1990. The main aims were to reduce organisational complexity, re-shape the central organisation and reduce its cost, reposition BP for 1990s. [. . .] At the heart of the scheme was a conviction that BP had become over-bureaucratic, and that strategic flexibility was handicapped as a result. (Jones 1991: 378)

Changes involved abolishing some 90 per cent of the corporate centre committees, and instead empowering individuals to take responsibility for their own decisions. These changes entailed replacement of the hierarchically organized departments with small flexible teams with more open and less formal lines of communication. Combined with these changes, 'Project 1990' aimed to position the company for new opportunities in the twenty-first century.

The '1990 Project' not only resulted in extensive cultural changes, improved flexibility, and decentralization of management, but also implied a renewed focus on its core competencies. The crucial driving force for these changes was the need for operational efficiency: 'Browne [Chief Executive] said BP aimed to lift its annual profitability by $2 billion (these days the company thinks in dollars) over the five years from 1997 to at least $6 billion by 2002, based on the assumption that Brent oil prices averaged about $16 a barrel over that period' (Lorenz 1998). Continuing projects in 1998 included making the different parts that comprise BP—exploration, production, retailing, and chemicals —self-governing while ensuring the transfer of best practices across the organization:

Browne says: 'the organization must be flat, so that the top is connected to the people who actually make the money; it should be divided—BP has 90 business units—so that the manager of a unit can actually feel possession of that unit, not get lost in a great big organization. But those units must also be connected, so that people are persuaded to do something for the good of the whole. (Lorenz, 1998)

In those areas where third party organizations are superior, BP has endeavoured to gain access to their wealth of knowledge by forming alliances, through, for example, outsourcing their IT functions (in 1993) or collaborating on the retailing of petrol and oil, as had been the case with Mobil (in 1996). More recently in 1998 BP entered into merger discussions with Amoco in an effort to improve its accessibility to the American market (Mortished and Durman 1998). The merger was finalized in late 1999, strengthening BPAmoco's position as the third-biggest petrochemicals group (Marsh 1999). Finally, in April 2000, ARCO, another large US oil firm, merged with BPAmoco making it, by 2001, the second largest petrochemical group in the world (Horizon 2000).

British Petroleum Exploration (BPX)

BP's exploration and production operations are focused on a number of key fields in sixteen countries around the world. The main fields are located in the North Sea and North America. Crude oil production from North America accounts for 47 per cent of the company's total while the UK production amounts to 33 per cent of the company's total. For natural gas, on the other hand, the UK presents the major source of production and amounts to 67 per cent of the total globally.

Exploration as such is a high-risk and very capital-intensive undertaking, with a lot of unknown variables. Frequent change in the form of new exploration areas around the world is inherent to this business. The exploration business is also mostly about a series of big projects:

you are always starting over and rebuilding something whether it's a new exploration, producing a new field, or whatever. It is very discontinuous in those project phases, exploration, drilling, production, and then operations. There is no real integrated value chain in there other than there is a highly intellectualized value chain between the first act of exploration and producing wells five years later and retiring a field 25 years later when you've exhausted it. (Head of Business Information, BP)

Exploration for and production of crude oil and natural gas does, however, demand a variety of skills and expertise, backed up by advanced equipment and techniques (BP 1996: 5). Key has always been communication, which IT facilitates. Over time IT became an essential ingredient for improving overall productivity: 'Swift application of technology and our people's expertise, increasingly with others, have been the keys to getting to the most effective results from both exploration and production' (BP 1996: 2).

BPX'S INFORMATION TECHNOLOGY OPERATIONS

BPX's IT users tend to be knowledgeable about IT and are always looking for new advances. IT expenditure in turn has tended to be high and very personnel intensive at BPX:

The exploration people—the systems are specifically specified and used by technical professionals, geologists, petro-physicists, mechanical engineers, designers. And the function of IT in those areas is to supply the infrastructure and some aspects of support and choice of systems by the geologists. The geologist is an articulate user of computer systems, trained in their use at school and so on, and they know what kind of practices they want. The IT function in BP has always been a check on their appetite for packages. They'd spend a lot of money on it if they could. (Head of Business Information, BP)

In 1989 BPX's IT infrastructure was primarily based on large VMS mainframe systems with approximately 1,400 personnel. IT had suffered in the 1980s from BP's weak economic performance and poor internal perceptions about IT's competence. In many ways, IT operations had outgrown their usefulness following the acquisition of Britoil, Standard Oil, and Lear Petroleum. To improve operations and perceptions, BPX decided in late 1989 to embark on an extensive IT change programme:

Browne believed that IT was key to creating a global organization and delivering higher productivity. He also sensed that the IT function was top heavy, pursuing its own agenda and not fully exploiting the IT marketplace. So he selected IT as the first function for transformation and a new General Manager, John Cross, was appointed to lead it. (Cross et al. 1997: 402)

The driving force behind the changes were cuts in IT costs while preserving the IT service to the business. The routes selected for achieving these changes involved (Currie and Willcocks 1998):

- eliminating human resources duplication;
- making large reductions in staff numbers;
- forming single 'centres of excellence' to provide support for all sites;
- rationalizing applications; and
- IT outsourcing.

In the years following 1989, BPX consolidated seven of its IT departments into one global department, standardized a range of systems across BP, and closed down all but two data-centres. Other changes occurred:

they used outsourcing and restructuring of IT as part of that agenda to radically restructure and simplify, rationalize, the amount of money they spent on computers. And when they started they had three Cray computers for example and they went from three to zero in a 3-year timeframe. So they did an important task here—rationalization, radical downsizing, cut the budget by a huge amount and so on. People sometimes attribute that to outsourcing. Outsourcing was simply an artefact of how we did it, the real answer was they fired a lot of people and there would have been a lot of overlapping redundancy. (Head of Business Information, BP)

The underlying objective behind these changes was operational efficiency, leading to a reduction in costs from $360 million to $170 million by 1992. Irrespective of the cost cutting during this period, computing power increased and new technologies were still implemented.

By 1992, BPX had reduced the headcount to 390 people, working essentially in a distributed client-server environment where the majority of services were delivered via desktop computing. In a matter of three years the whole IT infrastructure had been revamped. The prime responsibility of the remaining people was now the architecture, planning, and overseeing the infrastructure (Cross, Earl, and Sampler 1997). In parallel to simplifying the complexity of the architecture, BPX decided to enforce regional responsibility for systems and consolidate, rationalize and standardize a range of systems: 'For example, eight different simulation systems were reduced to two. Geophysical applications were allocated to London, drilling applications to Aberdeen. "Shrinkwrapped" software replaced in-house development of software for reasons of cost and standardisation' (Cross, Earl, and Sampler 1997: 404). Overall, BPX reduced its computing applications from 175 to 75 with few actual complaints by the business lines. In addition, the applications development budget was reduced by 69 per cent from 1989 to 1995 (Cross, Earl, and Sampler 1997). A driving objective behind this transformation was BP's organizational problems and economic difficulties. Consequently, in 1993, in pursuit of further cost savings and other objectives, BPX looked towards large-scale IT outsourcing. Outsourcing was to contribute financially towards the restructuring project, which was extensive and far reaching (see Table 5.2). The overall budget had been reduced by 63 per cent and the headcount of the former IT section by almost 90 per cent. In combination, the changes were said to have delivered BPX with $460 million savings without diminishing the value or benefits of the IT function.

The transformation programme involved extensive outsourcing and by 1995 the IT function was not only transformed to decrease costs, improve operational efficiency, and maintain the value and benefit of IT, but was expected to make an active contribution to the future business of BPX (Cross, Earl, and Sampler 1997). IT outsourcing formed an integral part at BPX as the company believed it no longer needed to own the technologies. As John Cross stated:

the market for technology services had matured during the previous decade, and it now offered companies like ours a broad array of high-quality choices. Additionally, the problems encountered in most internal IT departments, with their mix of old and new

Table 5.2. *BPX IT statistics 1989–1995*

	1989	1992	1995
IT budget	$360m	$170m	$132m
IT personnel	1,400	390	150
IT applications	170	110	75
% Desktop MIPS to mainframe MIPS	20%	85%	99%

Source: Cross et al. 1997: 402.

machines and skills and their traditional tendency to focus on business issues, distracted senior IT management and frustrated executives.

And anyway IT services did not define BP's core competencies:

By definition more and more stuff will be outsourced in the world, there's no doubt about that. The big companies, particularly companies like ourselves that are capital-intensive businesses, not a bank or financial services, information is not our stock in trade. The days of running big IT departments are over. (Head of Business Information, BP)

BPX'S IT STRATEGY

In line with corporate wide changes under the '1990s Project', BPX formulated its future vision and strategy as 'the right information, of the right quality, available to the right people at the right time' (Cross, Earl, and Sampler 1997: 421). BP's commitment to this strategy was emphasized by the Board's decision to standardize the software environment on Sybase, to implement open standards that facilitated information sharing and systems portability, and to agree to a unified desktop strategy and e-mail system worldwide. In particular BPX's strategic IT goals for the 1990s concentrated on (cf. Cross, Earl, and Sampler 1997):

- Data sharing between business activities;
- Data managed independently of applications;
- Common definitions of business processes and data;
- Information indexed for easy reliable access;
- Data responsibilities clearly documented and understood;
- Portability of data and systems; and
- Significant improvements of the quality of information products and services.

These changes to be implemented throughout the 1990s aimed at operational efficiency and cost reductions:

Information management (IM) contributes directly to IT's role as an agent of change, adding value to the business. The IM strategy and work program will also contribute to cost reduction through elimination of duplication and complexity. IM will support the introduction of open systems, the client-server architecture, and the 'buy, not build' policy for application software. (John Cross, Group Head of IT)

In the long term, underpinning BP's restructuring and outsourcing initiatives, was the development of a common operating environment (COE). Russel Seal, BP's group managing director responsible for IT noted:

The COE will create proper 'roads' through the company. Once the COE is in place, we shouldn't have to worry about our IT infrastructure. It should be taken for granted, like the telephone. The COE must be reliable, cheap to maintain and easy to upgrade. We will be looking for simplicity, productivity and low-cost operation. (Keith 1996)

Outsourcing was to be an important facilitator for this common operating environment. However, BPX argued that no single supplier could possibly offer best-in-class for all IT areas. BPX thus pursued a selective multiple supplier outsourcing strategy on a global scale.

IT OUTSOURCING

BPX had mixed experiences from their initial IT outsourcing activities in the late 1980s. The majority of selective ventures operated during this time were inherited from BP's acquisition of Standard Oil, Britoil, and Lear Petroleum. Additional short-term contracts had also been signed with a number of suppliers for items including desktop equipment maintenance, maintenance of selected applications, and helpdesk services (Currie and Willcocks 1998). These early deals presented BPX with important experiences, and although these contractors often performed their individual tasks to an adequate level, overall the effectiveness of the deals in terms of business benefits and performance was poor. According to Currie and Willcocks (1998), the contracts were drawn up in ways that did not encourage cooperation between the suppliers and in turn left BPX with a range of contractual and management problems.

In the early 1990s BPX decided to re-examine its outsourcing options. A lengthy study of the market opportunities was undertaken, which involved evaluating whether long-term outsourcing to a single supplier would be beneficial. Such arrangements were found to be too inflexible, as changing business requirements demanded a continuous cycle of innovation and rejuvenation of technology. Nor did BPX's managers believe that a single supplier could provide all their IT requirements to a best-in-class level. Eventually BPX decided to outsource selectively, but to a consortium of outsourcing suppliers.

Vendor Selection

In late 1991 BPX began in earnest its search for a consortium of suppliers. The selection process for Sema, SAIC, and BT Syncordia as the eventual preferred suppliers took an estimated fifteen months. It began in November 1991 with the mailing of approximately 100 Requests for Information (RFI) to large and small service providers both in the United States and Europe. Suppliers considered ranged from niche providers in areas such as data centre management, applications development, and telecommunications groups, to every major service provider in the market. Essential to preselecting possible candidates, BPX had asked thirty focused questions in its RFI (see Table 5.3) to discover how service companies operated, their culture and their flexibility.

Not every supplier met the key criteria, but by February 1992 sixty-five suppliers had responded. To evaluate the numerous responses, an outsourcing team of twenty people was established, which included IT managers, specialists from

Table 5.3. *BPX's RFI questions*

BPX's RFI Focus

- Experience and approach to outsourcing
- Geographical reach
- Technical capabilities
- Policies for improving efficiency
- Culture
- Business strategies
- Human resource policies
- Service philosophies
- Quality initiatives
- Experience as lead supplier
- Experience as subcontractor to other suppliers
- Service provision partnerships with other suppliers

Source: Cross (1995).

BPX's internal audit, contracts, materials, and commercial departments. Overseeing the whole IT selection process was John Bramley, BP Exploration's chief financial officer. The evaluation procedure involved assigning each team member three to four supplier responses; he/she would then have to champion the companies in discussions and presentation. Suppliers were individually evaluated for their strengths and weaknesses and then compared to the others. Discussions led to the selection of sixteen possible suppliers. Over the next months the team visited each of the suppliers to assess the company's management staff and culture, the level of understanding about the outsourcing industry, their strategic long-term vision, their ability to be innovative and flexible, their service orientation and aggressiveness to keep overhead costs down, and how receptive they might be to novel price arrangements. Encouraged by the capabilities of several of the service suppliers, senior management decided to expand the scope of the original tender to include the IT service provision for BP Company's offices in the UK.

BPX encouraged an incremental outsourcing approach, getting each decentralized businesses to buy into the advantages of IT outsourcing (Currie and Willcocks 1998). By mid-1992 evaluations led to the final shortlist of six US and European service suppliers. BPX early on had decided to selectively outsource and now it wanted an alliance of suppliers to formulate a proposal to meet their service specifications. The objective was to obtain a seamless service for the totality of the outsourcing scope. The alliance had to consist of more than one and fewer than five of the short-listed companies. The challenge was to present a proposal with the best cost-performance target: 'As we hoped, suppliers met round the clock to explore what each could do—testing capabilities, forming alliances, dissolving them, and forming new ones' (Cross 1995: 98). BPX had concluded from their previous outsourcing experiences that it needed different suppliers with differing skills for different activities, but all with the ability to effectively work together to eliminate the difficulties managers had with maintaining a coordinated interface. The key to BPX's relationship was in not only itself having good relations and hence interfaces with the suppliers, but also developing the interface between these suppliers.

Five different proposals were submitted consisting of a range of alliances. The six suppliers each had cooperated and collaborated to provide proposals for the service scope. In October 1992 the proposal submitted by Sema, SAIC, and BT Syncordia was accepted by BPX as meeting all of the team's expectations. It was found that these three suppliers best complemented each others' expertise and capabilities. In addition, all three had the capabilities to provide BPX with services globally, something identified as a critical competency. Moreover, the Sema Group excelled in managing traditional data centres and commercial engineering applications. SAIC excelled in implementing modern distributed computer systems and developing leading edge technologies and applications that could be used for BP's oil business. BT Syncordia had the experience, reach, and flexibility to handle BP's intricate telecommunications services. Finally, in April 1993, BPX signed contracts worth a total of approximately $35 million per year with Sema, SAIC, and BT Syncordia.

Supplier Alliance—SEMA, BT Syncordia, and SAIC

Sema Group was one of the top five service suppliers in Europe with approximately 9,400 employees in 1996. The Group's main business areas (as at 1997) were consulting (11%), systems integration (52%), outsourcing (30%), and IT products (7%):

Sema is in the delivery of technical consulting and services. I think where you can get mileage from a company like Sema is saying take this service whatever it is and use your skills to provide it in a smarter way, and there are smarter ways of running desktop support for example or helpdesks. [. . .] So Sema operates at the implementation level, that's the nature of the company. (Account Manager, Sema)

Its biggest markets have been the United Kingdom and France, and in 1995 Sema achieved a turnover in excess of £677 million.

Science Applications International Corporation (SAIC) is a diversified high-technology research and engineering company based in San Diego. It offers a broad range of expertise in technology development and analysis, computer system development and integration, technical support services, and computer hardware and software products. SAIC has been one of the world's largest employee-owned organizations with approximately 34,000 employees in 134 cities worldwide. In 1997 it achieved an annual turnover of $3.1 billion. The hallmark of SAIC through the years has been the principle that 'Those who contribute to the company should own it, and ownership should be commensurate with that contribution and performance as much as feasible' (Dr J. Roberts, CEO and Founder, SAIC).

British Telecommunications (BT) Syncordia was established in 1991 in Atlanta USA with the intention of forming a joint venture between BT, NTT, France Telecom, and Deutsche Telecom. However, the companies could not agree, so BT incorporated Syncordia wholly into its own organization. Syncordia offered global networking solutions for voice, data, video, and computing. Essentially, it has been BT's outsourcing brand:

BT Syncordia, we have £250 million revenues, we have £1.2 billion contract value which implies that most of the contracts are between 3–5 years which leads into the revenues of that. And we have a headcount of approximately 1,500. All of this is in the UK headquarters division. (Senior Contract Manager, BT Syncordia, 1997)

Outsourcing Scope

Sema Group was initially contracted to operate the UK data centres in Glasgow, the computer centre in Harlow, and to provide IT services for BPX's offices at Stockley Park and BP's head office in London. They were also to provide helpdesk and PC support.

SAIC was contracted to manage the IT facilities at BPX's European Headquarters and all the company's other applications. That included all the technical applications such as UNIX applications for seismic assessment. In addition, it was to manage desktop and local area network services in Aberdeen.

BT Syncordia was contracted to manage BP's telecommunications and telex networks worldwide providing data, voice, and video communications services: 'the scope of that was a wide area network and voice and what we call external connectivity. In other words telex and X400 networking went to Syncordia' (Senior Contract Manager, Syncordia). In total an annual budget of £105 million was allocated to the global service provisions of the alliance. That represented approximately 80 per cent of the total IT expenditure of BPX.

Outsourcing: Objectives and Expectations

According to BPX's senior management, outsourcing was not only targeted at simply reducing costs, but also at rebuilding all IT functions and services on a different and more effective basis:

when I joined BP Exploration at Sunbury to complete the outsourcing of the IT services there the aim was to reposition the internal IT team to create much more value rather than having them deliver IT services themselves. (Deputy Head of IT, BP)

I've always said you've got to look beyond the simple commoditization of today's service, it's not good enough. This is a model, in fact I find most IT organizations don't look beyond that. They simply see it as swapping out an internal service for an outside service. To me that's ludicrous. I think the issues for me are, what are the things we really need future access to that are part of the components of the way our business needs to operate. And so I look for distinctive capacities in the organizations we are going to deal with. (Head of IT, BPX)

In other words, by partnering with the vendors, BP hoped to gain higher value and significant benefits from the relationship. Outsourcing was also a key part of BP's strategy to restructure its IT function and to develop a common operating environment with standard packages:

BPX's IT strategy is to migrate to a client-server model which facilitates information management. A challenge is to contain operating costs throughout the transitional period in which our legacy of existing applications, based on central computers and character-cell terminal, must continue to be supported. Our suppliers must be ready and able to participate with us in developing the new computing environment while continually improving the efficiency and quality of service from the old. Within three years, our environment will be based on open systems platforms thus diminishing dependence on proprietary technology. (Quoted in Cross, Earl, and Sampler 1997: 406.)

We tend to use more standard packaged software which suits very well in the up-stream because it's broke down into different stages there are many companies that make exploration software, and seismic software. Many companies do most of our drilling analysis for us, put special services out in the field and bring all the computers with them. So it's a business that inherently is modularized and packaged and uses packaged software. (Head of Business Information, BP)

Together with BP's internal restructuring efforts, management expected the outsourcing arrangements would also help to diminish the costs of finding new oil fields, improve productivity, and provide an additional £10 billion cash influx.

BUILDING TO CONTRACT

The contracts and arrangements BP negotiated with the three vendors took a great deal of time to finalize and agree. Agreements were influenced by European 'anti-trust' law, which hindered the three suppliers from formally joining in an alliance to deliver services to BP: 'the European Commission of Fair Trading, as I understood it prevented the partners from forming contractual relationships between each other and forming a cartel effectively' (Senior Contract Manager, Syncordia). Therefore, BP was forced to contract each individual supplier, but with the implicit agreement that they would have to conjointly provide services for the variety and diversity of BP's needs:

The trio agreed to a plan to provide the seamless service that was so important to us. For each of our eight major business sites—London, Aberdeen, Houston, Anchorage, Bogota, Stavanger, Stockley Park, and Sunbury-on-Thames—one of the three suppliers serves as the primary contractor and coordinates the services the trio provides to most or all of the businesses supported on the site. (Cross 1995)

To ensure the suppliers would work as partners with BP, senior managers from SAIC, Sema, Syncordia, and BP formalized the Aston Clinton Principles in late 1992, which encapsulated what these parties believed were the characteristics of a successful partnering relationship:

in terms of the intent for the relationship, all companies signed for us what was called the Aston Clinton Principles of relationships. It was something which we all wanted to adhere to, it wasn't a contract but it was the spirit in which we wanted the relationship to move forward. [. . .] It's the characteristics of what a partnership arrangement is. So that's about long-term relationships, mutual commitment, sharing the rewards and risks, commitment to each others' success, creating win-win relationships and scenarios. Totally dependent on one another. [. . .] This is about working together in a way that was different. (IT Director, BPX)

These principles formed a vital addendum to the actual contracts. Yet it was only a guiding framework, and had no true legal force. The principles encapsulated:

- Simplicity of practice;
- Visibility of costs;
- Trust between the parties;
- Common understanding between the parties;
- Creation of a win-win relationship;
- Fair returns for Alliance members;
- Long-term relationship but no legal partnership between the parties;
- Site targets will be agreed locally. These targets will include the margin;
- Risk/reward arrangements will apply to the difference between the costs included within the target and the actual costs as demonstrated via an open book policy;
- Principles will generally apply on a site-by-site basis as well as on a global basis;
- From time to time, benchmarks will be established by BP to validate 'best in class' performance, not necessarily just financial performance; and
- Other alternative financial arrangements for ad hoc activities can apply where appropriate, for example: fixed fee or incremental cost.

As BPX incrementally outsourced across its sixteen sites worldwide, business managers negotiated with the IT suppliers their own specific contracts, specifying the scope of services, service levels, and performance targets. BPX agreed five-year framework agreements with Sema Group and SAIC and a two-year agreement with BT Syncordia which was later renewed in 1995 for another three years:

Syncordia has five main contracts which we call COG contracts. The original one would be Exploration was COG 1 which went from April 1993 to March 1995. We didn't have a COG 3. COG 2 is with BP Finance. COG 4 is with BP Chemicals. COG 5 is with BP Exploration and COG 6 is with BP Oil. BPX is a 3-year contract from March 1995 to

March 1998. And we call it a one year rolling contract. The reason I'm telling you that is that COG 1 was renegotiated and became COG 5 in March 1995 because they wanted a different approach to the contract and some different terms and conditions. So as you can see it was originally a 5-year contract and will come up to renewal in March 1998 at the end of the 5-year term for all the partners. (Senior Contract Manager, Syncordia)

These arrangements emphasized BP's intention to regularly revisit contracts, in light of the high price volatility for IT services, especially for telecommunication services.

   These framework agreements in general covered generic and specific services, legal provisions, general commercial principles, financial targets, margins and incentives, quality assurance, and performance reviews. Each of the sixteen sites then negotiated for customized services. In turn, each business unit had to pay for its IT services, for which suppliers directly invoiced the different sites, and the sites then had to recover their costs from the individual business units to which services were delivered. These costs were very closely scrutinized:

The three suppliers' books are open to us; they itemise all costs clearly in quarterly or annual invoices, distinguishing among direct, allocated and corporate overhead costs charged to BPX. [. . .] Our agreement stipulates that we can audit our suppliers' accounts of services to us, if it proves necessary. (John Cross, quoted in Currie and Willcocks 1998: 211)

In effect, all accounts are viewable as BP's explicitly agreed open book accounting:

We allow our customers to audit our books with respect to their spending. [. . .] we will sit down with a client and talk about remunerations and talk about mark-up on our costs, on his costs, and we will come to an agreed matrix of what there should be based on the market. (Account Manager, SAIC)

And we had open book accounting, literally sat down every month with the finance people and went through payrolls, expenses, maintenance, really open book. [we gave] them our spreadsheets each month and said you can pick anything you want and we will discuss it. So they had that absolute knowledge that the financial side of it was almost an open book. (Account Manager, Sema)

In addition, suppliers were required to itemize all costs clearly in quarterly and annual invoices. These also had to distinguish among direct, allocated, and corporate overhead costs charged to BPX. BT Syncordia was further required to present detailed records of all the telephone charges with third party operators that BP used worldwide.

   New performance contracts were negotiated annually for price rates, services, and performance levels. This was critical as multiple supplier relationships were found to be very dependent on regular updates. To simplify negotiations standard IT procurement terminology, such as response time, mean time between failures, and time to fix, were used for the service agreements. In addition, the initial performance metrics were amended and updated over the years to a balanced scorecard approach: 'suppliers are assessed on things of value to the business, for example financial management, innovation, customer focus, organisational learning. The results of which influence the profit margins suppliers earn' (Currie and Willcocks 1998: 211). Also included in the framework agreements were benchmarking provisions. The suppliers were required to deliver best-in-class services for specific areas. In circumstances where another provider could supply an important service more cost effectively, BP could then insist on the relevant supplier being subcontracted and managed by the existing vendors. These arrangements ensured in effect that BP could always take advantage of the newest technology.

BPX also operationalized a risk/reward sharing arrangement. On an annual basis suppliers could be paid an additional agreed rate, which could be increased at any time as improvements were presented:

on the surface it would appear like they are willing to be part of the journey and take some risks, and have a go. I'm not sure that there is that much risk taking in terms of the way our contract is structured—we can come on to that because it's a cost plus a margin which means there is no risk to an outsource company. Whatever their costs are they will always have a margin on top. (Deputy Head of IT, BP)

In fact, in those situations where the alliance did achieve cost savings the results were to be evenly split between BPX and the responsible vendor. This required an annual renegotiation for performance targets. Conversely, in those cases where either of the suppliers did not achieve the target they agreed, penalty payments arose, which in some cases could be quite substantial:

I would say the relationship on the whole is a relationship that is born of elements of trust, elements of real risk and reward sharing where we put in hard dollars, and we have paid up this year on projects where we have not delivered and overrun. We take those. And I know our fellow suppliers have equally paid up, or paid up from the perspective when they are under-run. (Account Manager, SAIC)

POST-CONTRACT MANAGEMENT

Transition Period (1993–1995)

The start-up period was particularly difficult for all parties involved. It was expected to be difficult, but not to the level encountered: 'Our outsourcing strategy has not always worked smoothly; we have encountered some bumps. Indeed the first few months of the implementation were rocky' (Cross 1995). Still, staff transfers went ahead as planned, with the majority of BP staff being laid off during the transfer. Only 49 per cent of the staff running BP's services at the time were actually integrated into the three suppliers. Since BP planned to outsource incrementally and learn by outsourcing in stages, the first country to be transitioned was the UK, which in any event had the most IT-intensive and diverse requirements. Early concerns arose with the negotiation of the site-specific contracts and service level agreements. As the contract had been signed for all of BPX, service level targets and price margins and other aspects still had to be localized, in accordance with the previously agreed Aston Clinton Principles. First-year activity frequently relapsed into defining and finalizing agreements at each of the business sites: 'So I think we spent a lot of short run time in the first years of the relationship actually just making certain that we glued down the services' (Head of IT, BP).

For each site transitioned, a vendor was appointed as the lead contractor to represent and take responsibility for the alliance's overall service performance for that site. As sites transitioned, the scope of services and geographic spread of service provisions increased. Eventually the transition turned into provision of services globally, bringing with it an increase in complexity, time zone and language differences, and also an increased demand for diverse and site specific services:

So I can be accessing services in Houston at 6 a.m. when nobody is there. So you suddenly find that actually I need someone servicing the computer system there at 6 a.m. in the morning. Well Houston local time didn't even allow for that in the beginning because they didn't come to work until 7 a.m. you see. So the service contracts were written around each local operating team. So you can see we were changing the demands on the nature of the service by beginning to become more global and the interaction of that placed quite a lot of continuing effort to try and keep the whole thing running as we kept modifying it. (Head of IT, BP)

The transition period saw a dramatic drop in service levels, as the suppliers attempted to acquire an understanding of the systems and requirements. This took quite some time and was not helped in any way by the fast changing IT strategy and structure of BP. BPX at the time was running numerous systems and was continuing to aim to operate at the forefront of technological developments:

there's always been a temporary deterioration even of services you outsource, that's my experience. A sort of sag as they take time to understand. I think the other thing is that we are actually also very complicated for our outsourcing partners because we were rapidly changing our own technology base and supporting a client server UNIX, Microsoft 95 and NT based world. They also lacked some of the advanced skills needed to support a rapidly changing environment. So I think they had some problems actually keeping up with us frankly, just keeping up with our operational service which pretty radically altered. (Head of IT, BP)

Indeed, suppliers found it difficult to keep up with BPX's intention to lead the market in terms of technological developments. This drive affected service performance negatively and almost resulted in the failure of relations. BPX had to seriously reconsider its options in the first year, and consider how to ensure suppliers could match their expectations:

BPX suffered by trying to move faster than the market could move. I think when we went to the suppliers they weren't ready to step up to where BPX wanted them to be. We got badly scorched the first 6 months of outsourcing. It then caused us to step back and we then got a real half-way house. The suppliers were then trying to step forward again and BPX was saying: 'I've been so badly burned, that's a bad place to be'. And it was at times like these that we came very close to cancelling the contracts in the first 6–9 months. (BP Partner Manager)

Additional problems vendors faced were with BP's culture and operational structure which was still changing towards a federalist or network-centric structure. One respondent noted about the suppliers' adjustment problems:

SAIC for instance had a horrendous job trying to adapt to a non-US culture, and that was just the UK which is not too different to the US. They had a horrendous time trying to fit into the UK. They just didn't understand where people were coming from. (BP Manager)

Sema, on the other hand, also faced the problem that they could not deliver services in America directly, because they were banned from doing business in the USA as 28 per cent of their shares were owned by a bank, and US legislation hinders any foreign company owned above a certain percentage by a bank to operate in North America. This caused a number of internal discussions. Nevertheless, in most other countries Sema was able to operate. In the first year Sema undertook an extensive rationalization programme of BP's data centres and processes, moving a number of them to their own premises in Birmingham and Glasgow. In addition, they consolidated BP's computer centre operations with their own facilities, decreasing operational costs substantially.

The operations structure implemented by BP initially was not as pervasive as intended. Although BPX had early on defined the role of the partner resource manager in the Aston Clinton Principles, at the regional, i.e. site level it was more a case of muddling through. In turn this caused some early problems, especially in the UK, where a direct result of the lack of clarity led to management conflicts. In some sites managers and staff were unprepared and lacked essential management skills, which led to heavy conflicts and almost a complete breakdown of relations:

It started off in the first 9 months of outsourcing in Aberdeen. That was a disaster because we were new to it, they were new to it, it was mainly all our old BP staff and they didn't have a clue how to run a commercial organization and what the relationship should be. And we came close to trashing the whole relationship deal. (Relationship Manager, BP)

With the realization that a more formal structure had to be implemented, additional managers at BPX were identified that were to take responsibility to oversee the vendor's performance for specific sites. In addition the central IT group at BP kept oversight of the whole relationship globally and held overall contract responsibility, which included being the last resort for conflict resolution. For the alliance, each BP site operated an integrated service management team consisting of representatives from all three partners. The service areas were split into different service lines and each partner took responsibility for their particular service area. For this to work, close cooperation and collaboration were fundamental:

whilst there are no formal contractual arrangements between the companies, everybody recognizes that for it to work people have to work very closely together and have to work in some alliance. [. . .] and increasingly we are being financially rewarded on the basis that we work well together. In other words a problem with any part of the service affects all of us, so on that basis a mixture of the fact that it's got to be teamwork to make it happen, and financial penalties or rewards for service across all the services, means that the relationships on a site level have to be very strong. (Senior Contract Manager, BP)

For the alliance, the vendor's account managers held ultimate control over the relationship both on a global and also regional level. Their responsibility was to oversee site performance, spot new business opportunities, and resolve any major problems. The account managers, however, had little impact on day-to-day interactions. The vendor's line or relationship managers were responsible for overseeing service performance regionally and interfaced with BP's regional partner resource manager (PRM) and business information managers (BIMs). Both specified and bought IT services, except that the former bought services for the whole site and the latter only for specific business units. By mid-1995 the following management structure had been developed (see Figure 5.1).

By 1995 each of BPX's eight (by 1997 it had grown to sixteen) key business sites globally had one supplier operating as the responsible 'primary' contractor for coordinating the services of all IT suppliers. This arrangement was found

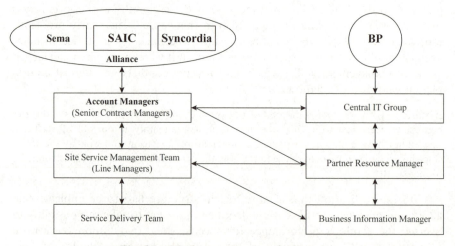

Fig. 5.1. *BPX's management infrastructure*
Source: Interviewees.

to be very effective, as it motivated the others to work closely together. Each vendor was appointed as primary contractor in some sites, and so was ultimately responsible somewhere in BPX for seamless service.

Operationalizing the service levels that BPX sites had agreed globally, these were to be measured and assessed site by site, the reason being that each site was made responsible for paying and buying services from the alliance. Similar to other deals, these service levels were expressed in technical measures, such as percentages of down and up time of servers, and response time to service requests. However, in early 1994, it became evident that, although vendors were performing according to agreed service levels, users remained dissatisfied with services:

our problem is that the contract probably doesn't reflect well enough our aspirations and the relationship which in some ways is and isn't strong enough to have them break out of the contract constraint to take it forward. So we ended up in a fascinating situation where what they are contracted to deliver is being met, but the customers were dissatisfied. (Deputy Head of IT, BP)

Consequently, BPX defined and implemented an important additional 'soft' measure that would evaluate user satisfaction levels. On a yearly basis key users were asked to rate the service performance on a scale of 1 (poor) to 5 (excellent). The minimum standard the alliance had to achieve was three, anything below that rating would be unsatisfactory performance not only for users but also for BP in general:

I think we draw a line at about 3 as the minimum required standard. Below that they can actually get a negative score, which can actually result in money being taken away. That really defines an unhappy customer. I think it's 2.5 is the base line, so 3 is beginning to get some positives, at 2 you can actually lose some points. So the scale goes from -1 to $+4$. So they could actually have 1% taken off their base margin, or they can have a total of 4% added to the margin. (Head of IT, BP)

That's why one of the service levels in any new contract is customer satisfaction. [. . .] Service levels are the technical means by which to achieve customer satisfaction. Still I'm much happier measuring it directly. (Relationship Manager, BPX)

It was to become an essential measure for gauging the services quality and also defined a critical variable in the risk/reward assessment. As agreed in the Aston Clinton Principles, quality penalties could be enforced if BPX's measures indicated continued failure to meet site service targets, which now included user satisfaction ratings. Conversely, if they exceeded expected levels then vendors were paid additional sums. This was on top of the baseline cost plus their margin:

The reason for the strictness of those measurements is the payment and reward process. What we've done is agree a base line deal that if they deliver this coming year's services they will be rewarded with $X million. What we've also put in is, if they meet a set of service criteria that exceed our expectations, i.e. this is about the quality of the service, then they can add an additional 4% onto their margin. [. . .] And that could be in two directions; if they improve the quality of the service, or if they take away more costs than anticipated. (Head of IT, BP)

Built into our contract is a risk-reward scenario, such that if we overspend on the financial budget we are penalized up to $300,000. Everything we overspend up to $300,000 per year on our budget this year we have to pay for. Conversely everything under that, we get a large share of it. So there's a financial stake to the relationship. (Senior Contract Manager, Syncordia)

We put questionnaires out to the percentage of the population and ask them several questions and on the basis of those returns the companies get awards. So it's hard measures, i.e. service level measures and customer satisfaction measures. (IT Director, BP)

Delivering services within BPX's expected cost boundary has not always been easy, especially as BPX has expanded globally. BPX set very high standards and expected to be provided with the same service levels at every site in every region of the world. This presented large challenges to the vendors, especially for Syncordia who had to provide the fundamental telecoms link from parts of the world that are not as technologically advanced as others:

They want to have the same quality of IT systems in China as they do in London and that means, because the IT systems are now so dependent on telecoms, that telecoms have to be as reliable in China as in London, which is very difficult to achieve at a cost effective price. So there's a pressure on us to ensure that that's the case and we are penalized or rewarded on the quality of the systems that we buy and manage. (Senior Contract Manager, Syncordia)

Further pressure on the alliance was the annual service levels and cost reviews and updates, which formed an important part of ensuring services and costs remained representative, especially in the context of BP's continuing technology changes:

We are contracted today that every year we sit down and describe the target, the budget that we are going to deliver. In there is also an understanding that we are given by each part of BP the performance targets of the IT management team. We then align our performance to delivering their performance. (BP Account Manager, SAIC)

What we do on an annual basis is set targets to be delivered the following year. So it could be quality targets, financial targets, customer targets, all sorts of things. (IT Director, BP)

The contract purely gives us the framework to define what we should be doing and it's good on both sides to have the discipline each year to say what is it you want us to provide this year, and we come back and say this is the cost to provide that. We agree that as a financial target and then it's our responsibility to deliver those services to that target or under for the year. (Senior Contract Manager, Syncordia)

To ensure costs and service competitiveness of the alliances provisions, BPX also agreed to independently benchmark vendor provisions regularly against the market place:

From time to time, BP will measure service provided by the Alliance against services of comparative quality and scope in the external marketplace. Where there is a significant differential between cost of provision of these services the Alliance will review with the view to resolving the matter within ninety days. (Aston Clinton Principles Agreement, BP 1992)

One benchmarking exercise and the push to offer best-in-class services led Syncordia in early 1994 to drop the existing subcontracted service supplier in Scotland—its parent company BT—because they were not cost effective enough, and instead subcontract a competitor that was already delivering services to other parts of BP. In general, to ensure BP gets the best in class services world-wide, Syncordia has had to subcontract services to numerous third parties:

What we've been doing has led the market place in that we've inherently gone out to the rest of the market place to select best-in-breed to integrate that together. For example on BP we manage up to 50 subcontractors which I think is relatively unusual. (Senior Contract Manager, Syncordia)

Formal reviews of the alliance performance on the regional, i.e. site basis, and any discussion regarding benchmark measurements were undertaken quarterly at management board meetings. Also, monthly service review meetings were held regionally between the service management team and BP managers, at which problems, requirement issues, or extra service requests were dealt with. The quarterly review meeting, however, was the most important and included BP representatives from business and IT and the various account managers and line managers from the alliance members:

And then once a quarter we sit down with the outsource companies and review their performance against the targets that were set. That is what we would say is the performance management process we put as 'trust me' around it to give us assurance that the delivery is going to happen. Again it's trust me isn't good enough. It's regular checking once a quarter on performance and delivery. (IT director, BP)

Overseeing the outsourcing venture and alliance was the outsourcing management board (OMB), which had the following function and remit:

- Providing global/strategic direction;
- Mechanism for resolving cross-site issues or issues outstanding from a site;
- One Board (BP and all Alliance members);
- Equal voting representation for BP and Sema, Syncordia, and SAIC; and
- Decisions will only be made on a unanimous basis unless the OMB wishes to change this arrangement (according to the Aston Clinton Principles, BP 1992).

In late 1994, BP decided to develop further a scorecard measurement tool to assess the suppliers' performance, the objective was to gauge each supplier's contribution to the overall value of the services delivered. John Cross explained:

With the balance scorecard, suppliers will receive points for innovation, business process improvements, financial management, customer focus, and organizational learning. The sum of the points will determine the margin that suppliers will earn on the direct costs for delivering services to us. We can weight the scorecard to suit prevailing business conditions at each site.

By early 1995, relations between the parties to the alliance were again put under serious strain, as Syncordia was asked to rebid for its service part. BPX had decided early on that due to telecommunications dynamism in terms of technology and price changes, Syncordia was initially only contracted for two years. During the rebidding the other two parties were also allowed to bid for Syncordia's business, even though they were unable to match Syncordia's resources. In the end Syncordia won the bid, and was recontracted for three years, but the undertaking had seriously strained relations between the alliance members:

They've [relations] gone through a tough patch, particularly with the rebidding, and I think they are pragmatic relationships built on the fact that if we all work together we will be successful. (Senior Contract Manager, Syncordia)

Relations were never to be the same again. Late 1995, the last site was to be contracted out in Alaska. The existing parties were approached, but Sema and Syncordia were not able to bid or deliver services for one reason or another. In the end SAIC was contracted and took responsibility for the data centre, helpdesk, and support functions, while GCI, a subsidiary of MCI, provided telecommunications services and CPG, a Buffalo, New Jersey-based company, provided application support. It operated on the same basis as the alliance scheme, with one vendor as the primary contractor. Due to the existing learning, it showed operational effectiveness early on.

MATURING RELATIONS (1996–1997)

By early 1996 all BPX sites worldwide had been transitioned and relations in those moved across first, like the UK, had settled down. Operationalizing the Alliance was not easy for the suppliers, and relations between the three, especially between Syncordia and the other two, had already been seriously strained by the rebidding phase. Also disputes tended to regularly erupt, especially between Sema and SAIC, the cause being the placement of new business, as their service portfolio and offerings were very similar in nature. However, relations between the suppliers continued, not least because BP required them to do so, but also because they had agreed to the Aston Clinton Principles of cooperating and collaborating to provide a seamless service.

In early 1996, one of the main criticisms voiced by the account managers concerned BPX's management infrastructure, which had no uniform interface. Offering global services site by site meant numerous regional contracts and interface responsibilities, and these were becoming increasingly difficult to manage. In effect, each account manager was having to interface with up to fifteen people or more, which implied having to develop multiple relationships at differing management levels and sites throughout BPX:

The problem I have at the moment is there are too many people for me to retain a relationship with. That list of names there are all the people I should be maintaining a relationship with—it's not possible to achieve that and do a job. So I'm trying to find some way of apportioning that. (Account Manager, Sema)

there's no one single point of accountability in BP [. . .]. They are very difficult to deal with because they present so many different faces. And what that means is that a company trying to deal and provide a consistent service has got a whole load of people to satisfy and that makes it very difficult to get an agreement across all those people because they've all got slightly different agendas and requirements. So that's the problem we've got, the hardest part I would say. (Senior Contract Manager, Syncordia)

You have to serve the group but you have to serve the individual business. One we have run up against in the past on the BP side is actually trying to get group perspective, not individual business unit perspective. It's one hell of a challenge. (Account Manager, SAIC)

BP's central IT managers were fully aware of this complexity, but could not find a solution to simplify this structural and management difficulty:

So they are now beginning to build up lots of little contracts and also they began to get involved with Sunbury as well. So now all of a sudden they've got 7 or 8 different contracts in the South East and BP doesn't talk to them in the same way. And this is the issue about the many different faces of BP. Their interfaces are making different demands of them and they couldn't view BP as a whole. (Partner Resource Manager, BP)

This complexity in part was due to BP's network structure, which gave each site autonomy and responsibility for their requirements and budget. Yet in order for the suppliers to maintain their economies of scale and control costs, they had to manage all of the sites with a single account manager. Of course this substantially increased the pressures on the managers appointed to handle the account. By having so many relations, it became increasingly difficult for them to develop the level of rapport and to be close enough to keep up-to-date on BP's strategic moves. Often the only source of information on BP's next moves was through internal reports, memos, and newsletters. Hence, over time, the multiple interface complexity hampered vital communication and information exchanges, resulting in unexpected surprises and resources pressures that drove suppliers to their resource limits: for example, the sudden push to roll out a new applications environment in October 1996:

BP isn't going to change its direction, it will go and do whatever its business strategy and John Browne (Group Chief Executive) declares. They are going to carry that through. We can support them in that but you can't, or at least it is difficult, to support them when you're not informed. For example they are planning to develop a common operating environment and implement this new product Windows '95 across the whole of BP, this dropped out of the sky. 7,000 installations by the middle of February, in 4.5 months, and it was achieved, but that's macho management, and isn't it wonderful when it's achieved, and everybody gets a buzz out of it. (Account Manager, BP)

However, the lack of information exchange and sharing of BP's strategy meant, ultimately, higher costs for BP. Although BP could always negotiate on price, a closer integration of the supplier and the planning of resources could have warranted considerable cost savings:

but if we would have known this [Windows roll-out], we could have planned it better, we could probably have done it cheaper, we could certainly have done it in a more structured way which will help the next iteration of it. So I have seen their strategy at the beginning of 9 months now I've seen, not once where BP sits down, not even once a week, once a month or once every six months, it does not sit down with the suppliers and say 'this is where we are trying to get to'. You can read it in the company newsletters, you can find things out and I'm finding out what they are doing in Algeria at the moment for example, but I've not seen any evidence where BP sits down and shares with its suppliers. (Account Manager, Sema)

In part, the lack of BPX's sharing reflected its perception of the IT suppliers. It was frequently argued that they are commodity suppliers, even though at the outset BPX was planning to use them as value-added providers and innovators. In most cases, however, this did not evolve, certainly not with Sema and Syncordia who in practice delivered mostly process and commodity type services. All the suppliers were aware of this development, and indeed it was accepted as being the case, because Sema's, and possibly Syncordia's, business services were technical and involved more easily definable commodity services. Even though this defined the vendors' core business for which they were considered best-in-class:

SEMA have shown tremendous responsiveness in the speed of which they can come into a new place to establish a service and that has been extremely impressive. Where things are very clearly defined they do deliver. So SEMA are very very good at what they do [but] the relationship with SEMA is manifesting itself as a purchase of commodity services and there is very little innovation and a lot of cost focus in the relationship. And frankly it doesn't feel like a strong partnership, it feels like a client–vendor relationship. [. . .] But their strengths really have grown from the mainframe environment where they are strong in facility management. But I would have to say that it always feels as if they are on the back foot. It's BP always trying to drive them forward and they almost have to be pulled with us forward into the relationship rather than what we would prefer, which is that they are taking us forward in IT innovation. (Deputy Head of IT, BP)

Of course Sema's managers were aware of this view and the account manager emphasized:

In Exploration we are a commodity totally. There is nothing on the strategic side yet, nothing at all. And by that I don't mean relationships at director level, I mean practical working with the company on the strategy. I don't actually believe that any of the suppliers are in that arena. Maybe that's in the nature of the company. Exploration treats all suppliers from the guys who drill, the guys who build the rigs, everything is a commodity to them in their quest for oil. They have a vision and you simply have to implement it. [. . .] Exploration speaks the words of partnership but actually it sees things as commodity, it counts every penny.

Syncordia, on the other hand, had very little visibility throughout BP because their service provisions were primarily handled off site. Also telecommunications for the most part is a relatively straightforward service and hence the most exposure an individual would get to this service is the telephone on a desk. Syncordia received a similar characterization:

Syncordia I can't say very much because frankly in 5 years I've had virtually no contact with them. That's interesting in itself. But how can I classify it, it would be the most commodity of all the services, telephone system, the wide area communications, video conferencing. My experience is very little direct customer contact with Syncordia staff. So it's fairly invisible and transparent and below the surface [. . .] Syncordia never seem to feature as a barrier. You will often find a bit of finger pointing when things go wrong and I don't ever hear that anybody points fingers at Syncordia. So to me my intuition says that their service just seems to run fairly stable, quite reliably, and below the surface in a commodity like fashion. (Deputy Head of IT, BP)

And again, Syncordia were fully aware of this perception, as the account manager explained:

I think that's to an extent the result of the fact that you don't see telecommunications on your desk, you see a phone and might realize that that's connected to a network, you see your PC, but you don't see the complexity behind it, particularly if it works well. Out of sight out of mind. One of our problems is that we don't have a dominant site presence anywhere because what we are providing is a very distributed service and that means that Syncordia as a name is not in people's faces.

Of the three suppliers SAIC was noted most often as providing services that go beyond the commodity type services. SAIC by 1997 had so many experts working in so many different areas in BPX, often giving BP access to an array of innovative technology, methodologies, and process. Yet SAIC's employee-owned organization structure did not exactly lend itself to distributing the latest developments. In fact, innovations sometimes seemed to appear sporadic and coincidental rather than planned in any way:

And there does not appear to be very much glue that glues the intelligence together. So you might find yourself lucky enough to speak to somebody in SAIC who's got a bright idea, in which case you get access to that. And we do find that. But we absolutely know that that company could treble its value to BP if it could access its own intelligence and share its own knowledge more effectively so that we didn't have to rely on luck to find somebody who might be able to show us a piece of innovative technology. But I would say they are the ones that have worked the hardest to develop a relationship with BP and to be flexible in respect of not worrying too much about the contract but thinking about how they can change the processes or structures to suit our needs [. . .] So there's a much richer source of value from SAIC in terms of a relationship and a journey that could create some new value. (Head of IT, BP)

However, although BP viewed SAIC as the most innovative, managers still found they were treated as a commodity service provider, except during particular projects and when they took the risk to invest SAIC's money for the benefit of BP:

In BP today we (SAIC) are seen as information technologists. A lot of people will actually still deal with us as a supplier, they still think of us as an information technology supplier. When they become aware of other things that we do for BP and that we have used our money to do them, they then become more aware of the fact that we do more than just that, that we are seen more as a partner. (Account Manager, SAIC, 1997)

These perceptions never changed the fact that BP keenly sought innovations from its Alliance suppliers, always hoping to gain from their experiences with other clients, and from their expertise, and knowledge of new technology and processes:

I was looking for process innovation. I was wanting to hear from the people doing the job that there are better ways of doing this. This cannot be right. Or we can bring more tools to the job that we are doing for you. And although there is a price these are the benefits. I was looking for those sorts of progress. I have to believe that there are other customers out there who are doing day-to-day things in a more effective way than we have done on this site. And that knowledge sharing they ought to have been offering to this contract. (Relationship Manager, BP)

I don't think any of the companies have really got into changing business processes as much as we would have liked. But I would say that SAIC is the nearest to it. And the vehicle, the access route to that is the advanced technologies that they help us with, such as the virtual team working technology. (Deputy Head of IT, BP)

I think the capacities of these companies to bring in innovation is clearly there, it's about actually making that happen. These companies need to be encouraged, they need to work hard at bringing innovation and creativity into BP. We probably need to pay a bit more for that. So that's something I think we need to focus on for 1997 and really bring out innovation. Because it's not happened to the extent that we would wish. (IT Director, BPX)

However, innovations and value-added benefits did not evolve to the degree expected and remained in many areas an area of underachievement. There were some exceptions. For example, SAIC substantially contributed to BPX's initiative to improve company-wide communication and knowledge transfer by helping to establish a virtual team infrastructure: 'Nurturing teamwork, promoting communication, and encouraging the transfer of knowledge—just some of the benefits that BP hopes to gain from the use of new information technology' (Frazer 1996: 46). Sema and Syncordia, on the other hand, implemented a number of operations management and process improvements, which were naturally not as far reaching and visible. Syncordia further introduced in 1996 remote telecoms access to sites around the world and in 1997 unitized its costs, to provide a detailed cost breakdown of all networks and operations.

Benefits were not one sided. From BPX's perspective, the Alliance had equally benefited from the improvements and the deal in many different ways:

We bring revenue and prestige and I think there is a reasonable return on their part for both of those things. (Relationship Manager, BP)

And I think all of them still regard the association with BP as having extraordinary business value. And importantly they have won some very substantial business based on their association with BP. So it has been clearly a good modelling piece of leverage from their own point of view. (Head of IT, BP)

SAIC in particular was able to use its experience with BPX to establish and formalize outsourcing businesses in areas of the world where no other company offered such services, giving them a market advantage. They used this advantage to subsequently procure contracts. For example:

We have done a deal with a company called Pedevasor. It is a state oil company in Venezuela. It is a very large company. Our revenues every year with Pedevasor would be in excess of $200 million, with an additional $200 million on core technology. We have used the BP template with Pedevasor and that deal we signed last year. (Account Manager, BP)

So to a certain extent mutual benefits were achieved. Of course prior to actually delivering benefits, a track record of services first needed to become apparent. In other words, the routine day-to-day interactions and processes needed to be in place before the value-added beyond the actual service agreement became evident. The track record not only shed favourable light on the suppliers' performance, but was also said to foster and develop relations. The impact was especially strong on the level of trust and confidence that developed between the parties.

Trust was repeatedly noted as essential for relations, but only when a track record existed to support it. This implied that trust from BPX's view could only evolve and indeed exist when the supplier had proven it could deliver the required services:

I'm reminded of old Ronald Reagan bless him—he said 'trust and verify'. That's the way it is here. It's trust and some assurance about the delivery is required. If only the supplier says, 'trust me it will turn out fine', that's not sufficient for me. (IT Director, BPX)

Confidence creates trust. If you believe that this person and the people who work for him in his company can be relied upon to achieve the things you want to achieve, if you have that confidence, then you will trust him. (Account Manager, Sema)

I have to feel confident enough in the other partners' ability to deliver to assure my management that we are not putting an unacceptable risk on our business. And that trust is brought about simply, in this case, through experience of their previous track record and delivery. (Senior Account Manager, Syncordia)

Indeed, once a proven track record evolved, relations seemingly became more open, and discussions began to focus on possible strategic issues, on value-added benefits and subsequent additional projects:

> there is no doubt you've got to have a quality dialogue, it has to be a very open one. And actually you share in some pretty important business insights that are probably not shared. So there is an element there which I call the trust basis. I would say one of the most interesting components of all of this is the requirement for trust. And clearly that has to be built on some degree of track record. (Head of IT, BP)

Of course trust could not be just one-sided but also needed to be reciprocated by BPX in some way to maintain both the relationship but also confidence:

> For the outsourcing partners I would say the manifestation of trust is their willingness to invest in process, relationship and quality without having to have every component of that resourced and remunerated as part of today's service delivery. [. . .] And quid pro quo, how does the trust manifest itself in us, our commitment to have them be a major player in every part of the BP empire and our commitment to promote them to other industries. (Deputy Head of IT, BP)

By late 1997 trust in the relationships manifested itself in the openness of BPX's managers about their particular requirements and problems. They trusted their IT partners by now to help them with any major concerns:

> I have been with BP where there have been turning points in our relationship in meetings where people have suddenly stood back and said—and we had one the other day on technology—'I only thought you actually wired computers. Why didn't you tell me you could do this. You've got 400 people sitting on my site delivering IT services, not one of them told me about all these skills. Why haven't you told me?' The chap was just overwhelmed. He said 'you've found an answer to a problem that I've been wrestling with for 4 years'. (Account Manager, SAIC)

This gave a clear impression of the state of the relationship between BP and the alliance.

Although trust indicated a good relationship at BPX, the contract always underpinned the relations. In fact, BPX ensured, through annual renegotiations of its service requirements and prices, that the contract was always kept up to date. Further signs that parties had a good working contractual relation were evident in these renegotiations, which initially were very arduous and lengthy and often taking months, yet by 1997 these would only take a matter of a day (Currie and Willcocks 1998). Although the contract did not explicitly filter into day-to-day relations, yet from BPX's perspective it governed interactions:

> They [contracts] are there as protective mechanisms, they are always in place, they are always active but latent if you see what I mean. I would like to get away from that and find some sort of contractual vehicle that says both parties need to switch these service levels on and if either party feels the need for protection then we'll bring the contract back into play. (Relationship Manager, BP)

I think there is a time and a place for the contract. Every now and again you have to amend the contract. You can end up with a contract with no relationship to the way you are actually operating it. So I think every now and again you need to play catch-up with the contract. (Partner Resource Manager, BP)

For the suppliers the contract equally guided their service performance, as non-fulfilment could result in possible penalty payments:

We tend to use the budget in the contract as the basis of being clear on the services that we provide. (Senior Contract Manager, Syncordia)

As they stand today we deliver everything we are contracted to deliver at a very good price. (Account Manager, Sema)

INSIDE THE ALLIANCE APPROACH AND NEW
CONTRACTING (1997–1998)

In the early months of 1997, BPX began to reconsider its future IT direction and how it would be organized. Critical to BPX's IT future was to be their out-sourcing strategy, since outsourcing by then was consuming 80 per cent of their annual IT budget and the contracts were coming to an end in March 1998. Additionally, there were a number of organizational challenges to be mastered.

During 1997 BP began a re-evaluation of its outsourcing arrangements. Changes in respect to technology and organizational requirements, but also their past experience with the alliance approach, were all factors that would inform the next outsourcing strategy. In particular, the demand for devising a corporate-wide common operating environment (COE) was a decisive influencing factor:

So we started to actually get a standard platform. But it was becoming obvious that we had a number of suppliers of service—3 or 4 major ones but also lots of others—and it was considered essential that if we wanted to have a commonality across the world (we are talking about 35,000 users) so that everything is common all the time, we had to think about reducing those suppliers down to one. [. . .] What happened was there was a central group effectively put together of what our common operating environment COE would look like, which I said is the hardware. It doesn't dictate the hardware necessarily by manufacturer, it might do it might not, but basic operating system, basic software we would normally use for all the packages and everything else. (Commercial Development Manager, BP)

Of growing interest to BPX was the end-to-end management of a number of services on a global basis. Although, BPX already had outsourcing partners providing the range of services, there were additional opportunities to be gained by using a single global supplier. A respondent commented on their future needs:

one of our biggest service needs is the end-to-end management of a particular service. For example, e-mail has many components from the desktop through telecom and so how do you structure an outsourcing framework, do you structure it by customer driven service like an e-mail service, or do you split out the wires from the desktop service and have those managed separately. (Deputy Head of IT, BP)

Of course, this implied a drastic change in their existing outsourcing strategy and hence it was becoming questionable what role Sema, SAIC, and Syncordia would have in 1998.

The approach taken to studying the options was similar to how BPX got into its alliance outsourcing venture in the first place in 1995. Managers began to spend increasing amounts of time studying the market opportunities and capabilities:

We spend a lot of time understanding the market and talking to it more generally so that you really need to be as informed a buyer of the market place as you can possibly equip yourself with. [. . .] So I just think if you look at the dynamics of the model, any organization that is a buyer in the information technology industry has got to go on remaining acutely tuned into what is going on. So I regard that—I probably haven't made enough of that point—but it is actually an important competency that I and my management team take away. You need to understand what the economic models are, what the strategic business models are being played out there, why and who are doing what. If you want to be informed enough about your own selection process. So this issue of the informed buyer is I think quite a challenging one. (Head of IT, BP)

An important lesson BPX had learnt from operating the Alliance approach over the past four years, however, was that it actually did not work as initially planned:

One thing we've learned, for instance, is that trying to broker any sort of alliance between direct competitors is almost impossible to keep together. (Relationship Manager, BP)

If they come with a genuine alliance they've already operated elsewhere and can demonstrate that it works then I think probably there's a chance. (Partner Resource Manager, BP)

The problem that has been there all along is that alliances don't work and we are rarely saving money on things. (Head of Business Information, BP)

Now you have to be careful because the danger is that each of them [suppliers] blames the other for a problem and things fall down between them. So it's not so straightforward. The experience is though that if you try and get people to work together where they are both basically doing the same thing, [. . .] it is difficult to manage and to develop the inter-link. (Commercial Manager, BP)

Even though the vendors had committed themselves to providing a seamless service by cooperating and collaborating, in many cases they found it increasingly difficult to work together. On occasions the effect on services was dramatic and performance suffered, forcing BP's managers to become directly involved in managing the vendors more often than initially intended. As a result, BPX had to allocate additional dedicated relationship managers to actively manage Alliance parties, even though one of BPX's objectives was to decrease the amount of time spent on actual management of IT and instead foster internal consultants concerned chiefly with planning and defining strategic requirements.

BPX's management role frequently involved adjudicating disputes about service provisions and responsibilities, especially between Sema and SAIC, as their service portfolio was actually very similar in many areas. In effect, vendors remained competitors, particularly in those instances where BPX placed additional business or asked for project bids. The following statements illustrate the position of the Alliance members:

We work with them in the alliance and we are positively excluded to the point where we have skills that can do the work that BP needs doing, we have people who are becoming available, and SAIC are going to the market place to recruit rather than to even look at the calibre of the people SEMA can provide. It's a business strategy. The outcome of it is that BPX is not getting the right result. BPX is getting consultants off the streets, whereas it has skilled people from its alliance partners that are not being made available to them. So the grand concept has not worked. (Account Manager, Sema)

As organizations we are surprisingly tolerant of each other. Syncordia is easy to work with. With SEMA and ourselves there have been instances where we've sat down and talked about where we thought we are better equipped and they thought they are better equipped and then BP have adjudicated. That adjudication though doesn't sit there as the parent; it tends to act as a facilitator or push it back to us to say go away and think about it because we don't know. Then you have to be mature about it and sit there and say well what are we really trying to do here, why is it of strategic interest to you SEMA, because this is why it's of strategic interest to us to do this. And again the people at SEMA, perhaps it's just the organization, very hard nosed, very straight, you know where they are coming from. (Account Manager, SAIC)

Syncordia did not figure in many of the disputes, as they generally had little visibility and their service remit was very different from what Sema and SAIC were providing. In fact, because of differences in the service area they were more complementary to SAIC's and Sema's portfolio and rated relations with the other two vendors as generally more positive:

I think relationships are brought about by reality and at BP's request, but also have been formed through the bidding process which brought us together on that basis. Because of their strength I would give them a 6 or 7 out of 10 at the moment. We've not tended to find the need to partner up outside the service delivery side of things. Having said that there are a number of projects we've done in collaboration where one of us might be a subcontractor to another, and that's worked well. So in specific projects we've partnered outside the site service delivery side of things. [. . .] The partnerships are strongest at the lower levels of the actual service delivery. (Senior Contract Manager, Syncordia)

BP's experience resulted in an IM model that no longer contains an Alliance outsourcing arrangement. A clear decision was made against such a construction to move to a more seamless single supplier, end-to-end management approach:

I think at the end of the day it was decided it becomes too complicated particularly at the interfaces, and too difficult. BP would have to put too much effort into managing that for not much of an advantage. Although you've got the advantage of having multiple suppliers for a particular area is that you've got some sort of competition, we felt we could get that through benchmarking and through the contract rather than having multiple suppliers. So it's really a change of thinking as we went through it and as we looked at it, as we tested it. [. . .] So we didn't feel that we would get benefit of economies of scale, of getting the innovation out of the suppliers. At the end of the day it was an option we decided not to go for. Instead we decided to go for the one vendor option. (Commercial Development Manager, BP)

By June 1997 BP had defined their future IT structure, and had presented their strategy to senior management and its suppliers. In terms of their outsourcing strategy it entailed one global strategic partner who would provide end-to-end service management of their infrastructure (including 35,000 desktop computers, client-servers, networks, and helpdesks). Additional vendors such as Sema, SAIC, and Syncordia would continue in the interim to deliver commodity services such as data centre management, application support, and telecommunications, but over time would be completely phased out. However, everything to do with the infrastructure would be single sourced:

It will be one company worldwide doing the infrastructure services. They will do all e-mail, desktop video conferencing, helpdesk, desktop, exchange, all that stuff. It's a big contract, so that's a lot of leverage. We'll keep different companies in different regions looking after the computer centre, and looking after the LAN and looking after applications. So we will keep multiple companies doing that. But all the stuff that glues and holds us together will be one company. And we will do it for one company in the UK first and then it will be transition over another year to 18 months to the rest of the globe. (Relationship Manager, BP)

In the following nine months BP undertook a major selection process to find the best-suited supplier to handle its infrastructure on a global level. The outsourcing team consisted of a corporate IT team in charge of the common operating environment, a senior manager with direct links to the board and a representative from each of the core business divisions, i.e. chemicals, exploration, and oil. To begin with SAIC, Sema, and Syncordia were asked to bid, along with a number of other large-scale suppliers including EDS and IBM. The front runners in the end were four vendors. The evaluation involved reference site visits of all bidders and proposals, which were assessed and scored according to preformulated criteria:

there was a pro-forma of how you would mark them, what you would tick off, what you would look for. So that effectively you came back with a score. [. . .] With that then there was a week's workshop where the whole week each of the suppliers was designated a lead person who presented to the evaluation team—which was at times up to 10 people—that particular supplier, what the good points were, what the weak point were, what was in the bid document, what they were promising, what they could deliver, what they'd shown they could deliver. [. . .] So we started to build up a picture. (Commercial Development Manager)

Four bidders remained, of which one was dismissed early on and one was a certain choice and two other suppliers designated as strong possibilities. EDS was chosen in the end as the preferred supplier and recommended to the BP board, which subsequently ratified the choice. EDS was chosen primarily for the following reasons:

- Track record of delivering against requirements;
- They seemed to be able to take control of complex situations by having well-defined processes and procedures;
- They were able to bring about a certain amount of innovation in reference sites visited;
- They had shown very stable, good, and high-level services across the globe; and
- They made a very cost-based offer, that include both lower transition and ongoing operation costs.

In August 1998, BP and EDS signed a $300 million, five-year contract for BP's IT infrastructure (Black 1998). Integral to this contract was the envisaged 30 per cent cost savings that EDS had to guarantee over the lifespan of the deal. EDS would, however, have to negotiate contracts with each division country-by-country to specify the exact service requirements. Regular benchmarking against best-in-class was designed to ensure cost and service competitiveness throughout the lifespan. Transitioning of the infrastructure including 35,000 desktop computers globally, would be undertaken incrementally, and was planned to take at least two years. BP UK's infrastructure was the first to be transitioned and this was expected to be completed by February 1999 (including 10,000 desktops). The deal also included the rationalization and consolidation of helpdesk service into one call-centre for the UK. This would eventually become Europe-wide and in future four help desks worldwide would provide a 24-hour service. EDS was also responsible for providing first level support on all problems or issues with technology; applications and their procurement would go to EDS. EDS would then deal with other suppliers in charge of applications to alleviate the problems, making EDS effectively the key interface and responsible for global service management. Additionally, BP would change their management infrastructure by appointing one global IT services director to coordinate the relationship and service provisions for a number of sites. This person's remit was explained as: 'He will have a group of people who will help him in each region, run and leverage the contracts and get the companies talking to each other. It's early days though' (Relationship Manager, BP). In August 1998 transition contracts were also signed with Syncordia for the provision of telecom services, with Sema to continue providing mini, midi, and mainframe legacy services, with SAIC also providing some of the former services and most of the technical application support. However, Sema's and SAIC's contracts were reduced considerably, and aspects recontracted with EDS. In effect, most services Syncordia, Sema, and SAIC now provided were commodity functions, except for the occasional application support. EDS was now in charge as lead supplier for all sites globally:

I don't think they are using much in terms of multiple alliances now because it's become much clearer what the lines are. [. . .] But it's mainly because with EDS now there are very clear lines. I think they will become even clearer. It's obvious that certain things are best done by global people and that's the way you get the best purchasing power, the best synergy, the best relationship. (Commercial Development Manager, BP)

ATTEMPTED GLOBAL SINGLE SUPPLIER DEAL AND UPCOMING CHALLENGES (1998–2001)

BP UK and its former Alliance parties were the first to transition their IT services to EDS, in late 1998. It was found to be a particularly testing time, as yet again a new IT service supplier came in that was culturally very different from BP. EDS in fact was noted as trying to enforce its own particular services provision style onto BP operations. For many this caused a serious conflict. Business units, in turn, were said to resist in their own particular way the transition, by withholding, for example, essential system and service specification information necessary for finalizing the post-contract due diligence process.

Key to finalizing EDS's contractual arrangements were local and regional negotiations to formalize service levels. One of the underlying reasons for this approach was the ongoing merger discussions between BP and Amoco Corporation. It was planned that eventually the group as a whole might contract with EDS for all of its IT infrastructure service requirements around the world. The key driver to single source with EDS was to acquire further economies of scale and drive down the overall costs by 30 per cent over five years.

Asking EDS to negotiate locally and regionally guaranteed operational closeness. What happened, though, over the 1999 transition period was that BP's and Amoco's divisions in the various regions and countries could not agree with EDS on their service contracts. By not achieving the contracts, the envisioned global deal basically fell apart in a big way:

the contract we had done with EDS was a global contract but actually it was to be negotiated region by region. In hindsight we realized that wasn't the right thing, because eventually everywhere except the UK fell apart. We tried to do a deal in the US and we couldn't come to a deal which both sides were happy with, the same in Europe, the same in Asia. The only other place besides the UK is South Africa (which is quite small). And partly it came at a time when we were looking to reduce costs, when we had the BP Amoco merger, for a period of time there was a big squeeze on costs, trying to get costs down. (Information Director, BP Amoco)

The differences in EDS's operations and its intention of enforcing a particular style were to be partly blamed later for why agreements could not be formalized. Moreover, EDS and BP pushed to specify service needs in one or two service levels. For most business units and divisions this was very difficult, and led to negotiation breakdowns:

EDS didn't really deliver what we were looking for and I think that was partly their processes, partly the way they'd organized various parts of the services. They didn't seem to be delivering the cost reductions we understood they were going to deliver. So we had a whole new process of looking at how we could improve it. We only had one service level, this is it. So we tried to introduce two or three different service levels which isn't always easy. (Information Director, BP Amoco)

These transition and negotiation difficulties were not helped by the merger between BP and Amoco running in parallel. Due to the size of the proposed undertaking, the merger was to affect every part of the business, especially in terms of IT. By November 1999, BP was forced to reassess its outsourcing objective with EDS, independent of its merger talks. Following difficult discussions both EDS and BP had to accept that the differences in working methods were irreconcilable, and more importantly, the lack of service agreements would not permit the global deal to take shape:

The knock-on effect of only getting a deal with EDS in the UK was that we then had to rethink everything else. Because we had wanted a global deal, we had wanted a consistent set of processes—and by the way what we found also with EDS is that when it came down to the detail, they were not able to offer a globally consistent set of processes quite in the way that we had thought. So it didn't quite go the way we wanted. (Information Director, BP Amoco)

A direct consequence of this experience was the resulting liberalization of outsourcing throughout the merged BPAmoco. It was decided that imposing centrally selected service providers would no longer work in such a diverse organization with differing operational processes. In the coming months, BP contracted in turn IT service suppliers by region that offered the best services at lowest costs. By mid-2000 the only global deal that BP negotiated and signed with a single supplier was its $650 million telecoms service deal with MCI Worldcom, signed in November 1999. Otherwise the USA, for example, had negotiated outsourcing deals with IBM for infrastructure services and SAIC for applications, while Europe was employing EDS, IBM, SAIC, Sema, and many others for its IT service requirements.

In parallel to these major changes in BP's IT strategy and outsourcing deal, a number of ongoing challenges had emerged, in particular, the Year 2000 and Euro compatibility issues starting in late 1997 and stretching all the way into 2001. These were of major concern throughout BP and were given special attention by senior management in 1997:

BP is taking steps to ensure that IT problems from the advent of the new millennium (the year 2000 problem) are dealt with. This will cost around $150 million [. . .] BP is modifying its processes and systems to be able to do business in the Euro when it is introduced, as well as in national currencies for as long as necessary. This work will cost around $100 million. (John Browne, Group Chief Executive, BP *Annual Review* 1997, p.12)

The complexity of these compatibility issues was worsened by the fact that BP used to have all the necessary skills, expertise, and capabilities to handle these issues, but was now highly reliant on the market to deal with these challenges. Furthermore, the pending merger did not improve the already costly and complex Y2K and Euro compatibility problem. By June 2000, most of the Y2K work had been successfully completed by using both existing outsourcing service providers and software firms:

The critical dates associated with Y2K are now officially behind us. [. . .] throughout the company, there have been only 70 minor incidents, and not one has impacted business operations. (Paul Davis, BPAmoco's group Y2K assurance director)

BPAmoco's three-year Y2K effort required 1,200 participants, 5,600 systems remediation projects, and, at a cost of $335m, was generally termed a big success for all parties involved. However, the upcoming Euro conversion issue still needed to be tackled, while efforts at integrating BP's and Amoco's IT services were ongoing. Foreseeable challenges were changing the oil business towards potential 'new economy' style operations, such as online market places, all with implications for how IT sourcing should proceed.

CASE ANALYSIS AND DISCUSSION

This case exemplies total IT outsourcing through the use of multiple suppliers working together as an Alliance. The approach taken gave BPX the benefits of selective outsourcing, and avoided the potential danger of contractual lock-in found in total outsourcing. Influenced by BP's previous experience with facilities management arrangements in the 1980s, which had highlighted the difficulties of obtaining value and true benefits, BPX decided that if they were to again outsource they would actively pursue partnering-based relations that integrate risk-reward sharing arrangements to attain real value. In addition, the sheer size of BPX's undertaking and the resulting requirements led managers to consider using more than just one supplier partner, more of a consortium-based arrangement.

BPX started its outsourcing venture from a strong position. It entered outsourcing with a very lean and operationally efficient organization, where many of the usual overheads one finds in large organizations had already been diminished. It had also gained invaluable knowledge from its prior experience of outsourcing. This experience clearly influenced the structure and management of the resulting multiple supplier venture, but also shaped management's belief that no single supplier possessed a monopoly on the best-in-class IT and service capabilities that BPX needed. Initial difficulties rested in ensuring that suppliers had complementary capabilities to be able to work with one another.

The downside of the alliance outsourcing arrangement was the increase in transaction or management costs of handling three and more suppliers. Although BPX had made early efforts to transfer the management responsibility to the alliance by appointing a lead contractor for each site and compelling them to deliver a seamless service for all areas contracted, but on many occasions ongoing competitiveness between vendors demanded adjudication and hence unanticipated management involvement. These coordination problems, and the way in which operational issues were often passed along the suppliers resulting in a 'finger pointing match', with nobody taking the blame, in the end, diminished overall service performance. The aftermath of these disputes about service competencies diminished the sharing of resources and commercial knowledge, and weakened the relationship advantage to be gained. Subsequent organizational changes in outsourcing arrangements ran into a number of challenges exacerbated by BP–Amoco merger activity, illustrating just how flexible outsourcing arrangements need to become in volatile business environments.

Risk Profile at BPX

Manifestly, BPX went into total outsourcing on a mature basis compared to Xerox (Chapter 3). Major risks lay in trying to total outsource in a fast-moving, highly competitive environment. BPX mitigated risks by using multiple suppliers on five-, rather than ten-year contracts, but at the same time did build in coordination and supplier motivation/behaviour risks. Supplier competitiveness, for example, to some extent did sharpen supplier performance, but in practice did not always benefit BPX. Ostensibly, BPX mitigated performance risks by choosing a 'best-in-class' supplier for each of three areas. Nevertheless, supplier-initiated innovation and the elusive 'value-added'—supposedly part of BPX's strategic intent for outsourcing—was often disappointing.

In building to contract, BPX took an innovative approach to relationship development, forcing the suppliers to choose partners, ostensibly reducing the workload and risks of attempting to choose suppliers who would be able to work together. The notion of reducing risk by ensuring seamless service and partnering by getting suppliers to manage themselves was continued into the actual operationalization of the contract. However, this innovative experiment failed, and required a lot more active BPX management involvement than originally thought necessary. In several ways BPX underestimated the amount of active in-house management outsourcing would need, and to that extent exposed itself to risks of underperformance, and more conflictual relations.

However, there were many positive risk-mitigating aspects to BPX's approach. IT was not treated as an undifferentiated commodity, and BPX remained clear on how IT would give them a business advantage. BPX were astute on the problem of incomplete contracting, and brought a lot of contractual and performance measurement experiences to play, and regularly updated and benchmarked performance criteria against the market. There were some weaknesses in retained capabilities and skills, and the processes and structures put in place to manage outsourcing. However, these particularly occurred in the technical, strategic consulting, and demand management areas, and this exposed BPX to a number of subsequent difficulties. Similarly, and with comparable consequences, BPX also underestimated the amount of management effort required to manage the relationship dimensions of the outsourcing. At the same time, BPX did not allow power asymmetries to develop in favour of the vendors, through its multi-supplier, short-term contracting approach, which was also adopted to ensure that BPX's outsourcing arrangements could keep up with business and technological changes. As events from 1998 showed, this has become increasingly more difficult for a company like BP to achieve, and the retention of core IT capabilities, and the ability to flex quickly and on a large scale have become critical enablers of risk mitigation in twenty-first-century IT outsourcing. At the same time, it is unlikely that BPX will ever rebuild its IT function to any significant degree; the switching costs would be prohibitive. In such circumstances the ongoing risk mitigation task is to ensure this does not result in power asymmetries slipping too much in favour of suppliers.

Strategic Intent

The '1990s Project' initiated the reorganization of a company that had become overly bureaucratic through its expansive diversification and growth in the 1970s and 1980s. The intention for the 1990s was to refocus the business on its core competencies of exploration and petroleum to ensure BP's competitiveness for the next century. Information technology as such did not directly filter into the core competencies, the implication of which was to reduce in-house IT considerably and eventually outsource it. In fact, BP's financial troubles and resulting push to restructure drove BPX to consider outsourcing IT on a grander scale, and as a catalyst for reorganizing how IT was perceived, planned for, and accomplished. BPX's IT section, in turn, was to see itself decrease in staff numbers from 1,400 in 1989 to 150 by 1995. In-house IT capabilities and skills were also to be refocused onto the business value-added areas. IT outsourcing was part of this restructuring and provided yet further savings. Additional motives of flexibility, and access to technology and expertise played a significant role, as did the need to reduce costs and restructure balance sheets and cash flow in the early 1990s business climate the whole of BP was facing.

Contract

With the objective of forming partnering relations with suppliers, BPX set out to negotiate a contract that would reflect this intention. EU regulations hindered BPX from integrating these ideals in a single contract. Therefore, BPX negotiated and agreed with all parties a separate framework document that outlined the principles and specifics of partnering to which all would adhere. This was to become the guiding informal agreement referred to as the Aston Clinton Principles, with the actual contracts arranged at each site providing the legally operationalizable elements. In principle, this built in a lot more (much needed) flexibility than was embodied in the more centralized—and problematic—Xerox-EDS contract (Chapter 3).

From the start, therefore, BPX had agreed that outsourcing would not operate merely on a contract-focused basis, but suppliers would be considered actual partners, and that their responsibility was to cooperate and collaborate to deliver a seamless service as a single entity. Although these Aston Clinton Principles were legally not enforceable, they set contractual relations in a different light where parties agreed to foster trustful relations, assure mutual benefits, enter into risk-reward arrangements, and provide incentives to develop and maintain relations. The Principles not only guided relations, but they provided the suppliers with the necessary incentives to cooperate and collaborate to deliver a seamless service for which they could reap additional reward payments. However, we have seen in the case that there were some flaws in this scenario when it came to be implemented.

At the same time, as in Xerox and BAe, BPX's intention was to contractually enforce most of the supplier performance, but also to ensure that contracts would be dynamic enough to always reflect the current situation of the venture, and how it could be leveraged. This was manifested every year in the renegotiation of service and price targets. It was also necessary to maintain the salience of risk-reward arrangement and to ensure vendors were fully cognizant of expectations via their new service performance targets. For the suppliers, contracting with BPX introduced significant additional costs as they had agreed to negotiate a separate contract with every site. This, of course, complicated matters and seriously influenced both the management processes and infrastructure, and eventually presented a number of points of contention. At the same time BPX proved good—unlike Xerox early on—at establishing and maintaining detailed contracts and measurement processes and targets that incentivized performance, while keeping the contracts flexible in the face of market pricing, technical, and business changes. So far as they were outside the legal contracts, the 'presentation' elements—embedding future requirements in the present agreements—were much less successful in driving the relationships towards increased business advantage from outsourcing, as evidenced by the disappointing levels of innovation forthcoming.

Structure

The management infrastructure was in part formalized in the beginning with the agreement of the Aston Client Principles. At a very high level parties had agreed to an oversight management board detailing roles and participants, but at the regional level the infrastructure was much more hazy. Although, BP had defined the role of a partner resource manager, who was to become BP's account manager, it was evident that many of these managers lacked essential capabilities and skills, and nearly brought relationships to a stalemate. Only with bringing in more experienced managers and muddling through the transition period did roles, responsibilities, and skill requirements become clear. In the end, although early steps had been made to develop a management infrastructure, more managers were needed to become actively involved in coordinating and building relations. This increased BP's overall coordination costs, and draws attention to the fact that multiple supplier arrangements are likely to increase management costs.

It is apparent that these management requirements were underestimated by BPX, and the management infrastructure actually had to evolve over several years. BPX initially had intended to decrease the amount of management time and effort they would have to invest in the venture by handing over most of the ongoing management to the Alliance, but since the suppliers essentially remained competitors, BPX's managers had to anticipate and frequently manage conflicts. This was identified as one of main arguments against the alliance approach.

For the suppliers, BPX also presented a management challenge. Due to the novelty of BPX's arrangements, the complexity of the management infrastructure needed was also underestimated by the suppliers, as happened also in the Xerox case. Although vendors had agreed to negotiate a separate service level agreement with every site, they were unprepared for what that meant in terms of management. By signing contracts with each regional site they also had to develop a separate relationship with each. Account managers responsible for BPX in turn were burdened by maintaining multiple relations and interfaces, dramatically increasing overall management costs. For vendors this was a common point of contention, and was put down to BPX's network-centric organization structure giving regional subsidiaries a lot of autonomy.

Interactions

Although BPX had taken the precaution that each site should negotiate their specific service requirements, it became evident that users could become easily dissatisfied with the services delivered. As in BAe, Xerox, and parts of ESSO, service levels did not correspond to the actual business users' needs. To alleviate the situation, BPX implemented, in parallel to the hard measures, a soft measure to determine to what extent services were actually meeting business users' needs. For suppliers this meant that performance would be measured not only on whether servers were up and running 99 per cent over the last month, but to what degree their services were actually satisfying users or not. It also gave BPX another measure on which to base the evaluation of reward payments.

The degree of measuring the suppliers' performance was taken a step further with the introduction of scorecards. These gave managers the means to assess suppliers on a range of dimensions, allowing them to differentiate between each supplier's individual performance. In summary, the interactions on exchange, normative, and communication content were quite well set up initially, but still needed a lot of development during the first three years before relationships could stabilize and be pursued efficiently.

Behaviour Dimensions

The Alliance approach was only going to work if suppliers truly cooperated and collaborated. By compelling and motivating suppliers to provide consortia bids, BPX was able to spark cooperative relations. This was then further strengthened by the negotiation and formulation of the principles of partnering, that not only formalized what it meant to cooperate and collaborate, but also addressed the importance of developing trusting and open relations. The preamble in turn was embodied not only in the Alliance approach, but also in the Aston Clinton Principles.

Moreover, by motivating vendors to manage themselves and by outlining that each supplier will be interchangeable site by site as the primary contractor, this ensured an environment of equality in which relations could be fostered to a partner level. Since all suppliers had a primary contractor role on a site, this made them interdependent and induced cooperation between the partners:

The relationship does have ups and downs, and again only works if we are open and honest with each other. Both parties understand their respective positions and there is an element of partnership—which is an abused term—that is, understanding that what's good for the other partner will be good for them. (Senior Contract Manager, Syncordia)

Clearly throughout, the suppliers were dependent on each other at regional levels, but in practice the arrangements made for little meta-regional collaboration. Moreover, within a region, there were often plenty of opportunities for conflict and uses of power by suppliers and BPX alike, mitigated initially by the mutual dependence and the monitoring systems enforcing performance. Over time, some mitigation also derived from the development of relations expressed in higher cooperation and trust behaviours. Where this occurred, such relations came from, but were also supportive of performance of obligations, the receipt of anticipated benefits and 'feel-fair', and from perceived advantages in continuing relationships.

Efficiency and Outcomes

Two critical contractual devices assured BP relational efficiency for the lifetime of the contracts. First, it had negotiated an annual update of prices and services, that guaranteed prices would always reflect the market situation and the demand cycle of the organization, and it could control on an annual basis the degree of cost reduction. Secondly, all parties agreed, even though only informally, that incentives would be available if they outperformed the annually agreed service levels, while underachievement meant penalties were due. By giving vendors a risk-reward option where they would be able to increase their margins by up to 40 per cent, BPX encouraged high service levels while costs were driven down. This put the burden of cost control on the suppliers, and in many instances resulted in vendors having to reassess their own internal operation efficiencies to ensure they would still make a margin. As noted by Syncordia's account manager, to ensure cost efficiency and service delivery, they were working with up to fifty subcontracted companies.

Although BPX put vendors under considerable cost pressures, the benefits for all suppliers were still substantial in terms of exposure to additional business within the whole of BP, and the resulting opportunities of working in the light of BP's reputation as a leading-edge technology user and 'blue chip' organization. For SAIC and Syncordia, the outsourcing venture actually helped to develop their business opportunities as outsourcing service providers: 'BP have been very helpful in acting as a reference customer for us, which enables us to grow our economies of scale which feeds back into better service and lower prices to BP' (Senior Contract Manager, Syncordia). Indeed, all three benefited from using BPX as a reference source. Additionally, all four divisions within BP over time placed outsourcing business with the vendors, increasing considerably their contract volume.

In terms of cost efficiency and driving down costs, the venture had been a success for BPX. It decreased the headcount and overhead costs and improved operational efficiency, but the actual business value-added was perceived as missing. BPX's cost-focused approach was blamed for initially hindering vendors from truly offering value-added. Managers realized they would have to pay extra for value-added and were prepared to do so, but only when the benefits were evident. The initial investment thus had to be made by vendors, which at times was perceived as too risky. Hence, it is possible that the risk-reward arrangement hampered vendors from actually presenting BP with value-added, because the arrangement already had a certain amount of improvement and overperformance ingrained in BPX's detailed requirements and tight price margins.

Overall, transaction costs of keeping the outsourcing tied to its goals were much higher than anticipated, suggesting that relationship costs were greatly underestimated initially. Still, the outsourcing deal certainly helped BPX to reduce uncertainty in terms of change, daily service delivery, and technology demand, for example moving to a 35,000-PC desktop environment under the suppliers' auspices. Customization of service was a more ambivalent outcome for there were weaknesses in the regional emphasis and lack of synergies, standardization, and sharing of best practice across the regions. As one respondent said: 'It often became a fashion show between sites.' In terms of satisfaction, it became pretty clear that BPX management ultimately saw the relationship approach as heavily flawed. Much had been accomplished on the strategic, financial, and technical fronts, but there was a question mark against whether the relationship arrangements—in terms of their fundamental structuring— were much of a contributor to this. Subsequent events with EDS and other suppliers also highlighted, however, how far BP's own structure, culture, and changes contributed to making supplier performance difficult, and contributed to suboptimal relationship structures and development in outsourcing.

CONCLUSIONS

Outsourcing at BPX presented a novel way of using multiple suppliers to deliver best-in-class services for all areas contracted out. The use of multiple suppliers in part was driven by BP's desire to keep control, yet at the same time seek benefits from their expertise and capabilities. BP's objectives of maintaining high global service and technology standards, while reducing the overall IT costs beyond what the internal IT group could possibly have achieved was accomplished. Vendors, on the other hand, benefited from the risk-reward arrangements, the new business projects and BPX's expansion globally, and of course from BP's prestige as a 'blue chip' company and leading-edge technology user.

However, the increased costs of coordination and the difficulties of making competitors work together as partners was found to be disadvantageous to the otherwise successful approach. Faced with recontracting as the Alliance neared its five-year contract completion point, BP decided against the approach as it had proven to be too management intensive and complex, especially in light of BP's upcoming endeavour of developing a global common operating environment. Instead, BP contracted a single supplier to take global control of its core infrastructure, and manage itself the other suppliers to deliver detailed commodity services. However, as in 1993–8, it maintained its five-year time horizon for outsourcing. The challenges of managing mergers, especially on a global level, made these newer arrangements even more difficult. There was, though, little chance that BP could have switched out of the large-scale outsourcing deal because, by 2001, the switching costs had become enormously prohibitive. This made active management of the suppliers perennially critical, as from 2000 onwards, and after two large mergers, the company positioned itself as a globally branded oil firm—BPAmoco.

REFERENCES

Black, G. (1998). 'Service Issues Fuel BP's $300m EDS Desktop Deal'. *Computer Weekly* (27 August), 6.

BP (1990). 'The World of BP'. BP April, pp. 20–1.

BP (1996). *The World of BP*. BP, London.

BP (1997). *Annual Review*. BP, London.

BPAmoco (1999). *BPAmoco Alive: Annual Report and Accounts 1999*. BPAmoco, London.

Cross, J. (1995). 'IT Outsourcing: British Petroleum's Competitive Approach'. *Harvard Business Review* (May–June), 94–102.

—— Earl, M., and Sampler, J. (1997). 'Transformation of the IT Function at British Petroleum'. *MIS Quarterly*, 21/4: 401–23.

Currie, W. L., and Willcocks, L. (1998). *New Strategies in IT Outsourcing*. Business Intelligence, London.

Frazer, F. (1996). 'IT's Virtual a Reality'. *Shield Magazine*, International Magazine of BP Group, Issue 1, 46–8.

Horizon (2000). 'ARCO: Deal Comes to a Close'. May, Issue 3, BPAmoco, London, 9.

Jones, G. (1991). 'British Petroleum Company Plc', in A. Hast (ed.) *International Directory of Company Histories*. St James Press, Chicago, iv. 378–80.

Keith, L. (1996). 'Technology Focus: Technically Speaking'. *R&E View*, 7–8.

Lorenz, A. (1998). 'BP Boss Drives Change through the Pipeline'. *Sunday Times* (26 April), 8.

Marsh, V. (1999). 'Combination Catapults Partners into Top League'. *Financial Times* (12 August), 19.

Mortished, C. (1998). 'Corporate Profile: BP'. *The Times*, Business News (29 June), 44.

—— and Durman, P. (1998). 'BP Pay Poised to Rise after Amoco Takeover'. *The Times*, Business News (17 August), 43.

Petrocompanies (1997). *BP*. PetroCompanies Plc., London, 63–70.

6

Relationship Management in Selective Outsourcing at ESSO-ITNet

INTRODUCTION

In 1994 ESSO UK signed a five-year, £1 million, selective IT outsourcing deal with ITNet for legacy application support services. ESSO's clarity about both objectives and type and detail of the contract focused the arrangements, but did not prove sufficient as a foundation to ensure relational effectiveness and success. Consequently, the first few years were riddled with operational difficulties, especially for the supplier, whose erroneous bid calculations caused serious service level problems and relational pressures, eventually leading to relational loggerheads and an over-reliance on the contract. Change was urgently needed as the supplier's losses mounted, relations remained adversarial, and service performance stayed mediocre.

In 1996, due to these ongoing difficulties, ESSO decided to renegotiate the contract with more favourable terms for ITNet to allow them to improve their margins. Only through these renegotiations and the appointment of two new relationship managers, was ESSO able to turn around the venture and prevent an early termination of the deal by the supplier. From then relations improved to such an extent that both parties decided to formulate in 1997 an informal partnership agreement. This consolidated their interests in cooperating to achieve operational success. Over seven consecutive months, ITNet delivered services that fully complied with ESSO's core service level expectations and agreements—something never achieved before. In return, ITNet was awarded considerable bonus payments, additional services, and was championed internally for additional work. In effect, it took almost three years to develop productive and functional outsourcing relations. But even then, relations were never truly considered to be anywhere near a 'partnering' arrangement: 'I don't believe we are anywhere near them, I don't think it fits our culture, a partnership. I think we work closely with people, but at the end of the day we do have contracted negotiations on rates, it's never a win : win situation. So I agree some of them are a little bit more than an SLA based relationship' (Supplier Manager B, ESSO). However, the satisfaction levels, and the operational success that resulted after the initial difficulties, led ESSO to extend its contract with ITNet, adding on another three-year period and an additional set of IT services.

Relationship Lessons

The case, on the one hand, describes the impact of a competitive bidding process on the post-contract management phase and how overlooked selection issues can seriously strain relations later on. In effect, the case analysis discovers two key factors which were probably the reason for early relationship problems and which subsequently were also identified as signs of a Winner's Curse[1] in outsourcing. These were, first, that ESSO's manager responsible for the deal at the time had a 'laissez-faire' approach to managing ITNet. Secondly, ITNet's lack of experience with diverse industry sectors, and assumptions about ESSO's requirements resulted in serious cost miscalculations, and put too much pressure on managers to deliver services strictly according to these cost calculations.

On the other hand, the case details how the pressure of incurring substantial switching costs, but also the client's willingness to save the deal led to early contract renegotiations which, together with introducing focused relationship managers, turned the venture around. The goodwill shown by the client and the resulting commitment and loyalty this generated in the supplier company saw relations move towards an informal partnership with significant value-added benefits for both parties. In fact, the successful turnaround of the contract and the continuous over-achievement on the adjusted service requirements saw the supplier become the premier supplier for the company in a multi-supplier site, and led to a contract extension.

CONTEXT AND OVERVIEW

ESSO UK Plc is an affiliate of EXXON Corporation, by the late 1990s the fifth largest petroleum company in the world. ESSO UK is an 'integrated' oil company combining the 'upstream' activities of oil exploration and production with the 'downstream' activities of refining, research, distribution, and sales (EXXON Corporation 1998). ESSO has been in operation in the UK for over 100 years and holds the largest market share for petroleum products.

ESSO-EXXON's History

ESSO's early history is traceable to Standard Oil, which emerged after the break-up of the Rockefeller oil empire in 1911 (PetroCompanies 1997).

---

[1] The winner's curse is said to occur if the winner of a deal systematically bids above the actual value of the objects and thereby systematically incurs losses. See also Kern, Willcocks, and van Heck 2000.

Following the break-up, Standard Oil entered a rapid acquisition phase, acquiring stakes in numerous organizations around the world and achieving a size of 156,000 employees (Standard Oil Company 1957).

As part of Standard Oil's acquisition phase it ventured into the European market, acquiring the Anglo-American Oil Company (founded 1888), which was later to be called ESSO Petroleum UK. Standard Oil's refining and marketing activities grew in Europe as the consumption growth started to gather pace in the region (Martin 1991). The Second World War effort, however, induced considerable losses, especially for its European affiliates. After reconstruction, the European affiliates recovered quickly, growing in turnover from $171 million in 1955 to $355 million in 1963. Europe became the fastest growing oil product outlet for Standard Oil globally. However, the European affiliates were very different, as they virtually defied anything more than the loosest control by Standard Oil corporation:

some of the affiliates had operated for almost as long as the time they first became part of the Jersey system [Standard Oil Company]. Distance and diversity tended to guarantee substantial autonomy to each of the European Affiliates. . . . And, of course, the same factors that hampered Jersey's exercise of control also tended to discourage anything more than limited, formal communications among the European companies. Cooperation was simply non-existent. (Wall 1988: 281)

The European affiliates' culture and identity intrinsically heralded independence, which continues to be an influential factor in any of the European affiliates' business dealings to date. It was thus decided in the 1960s, in line with Standard Oil's restructuring initiative, to devise a structure that would create regional groupings with local autonomy. The European operations became organized into a separate group referred to as ESSO Europe Inc. The reshaping of Standard Oil highlighted, however, its internal identity crisis, especially in North America, where retail outlets were either associated with ESSO, Enco, or Humble oil. In 1972 Standard Oil decided to standardize, and changed its principal American trading name to EXXON. Its foreign affiliates, however, kept their names, e.g. ESSO Imperial Oil Canada, ESSO UK Petroleum, and ESSO AG Germany.

In the 1980s EXXON continued its acquisition spree, with the its biggest acquisition to date being Texaco Canada for $4.1 billion dollars (1988). In the early 1990s EXXON again restructured across the globe, moving its headquarters from New York to Texas and generally downsizing its business. In addition, it centralized key management functions, making EXXON headquarters responsible for long-range planning and management oversight. It also reorganized its affiliates into divisions, making each essentially responsible for a particular geographic region or business area: 'we are a shrinking organization and therefore we have—in 10 years—have gone through several downsizing exercises' (Supplier Manager A, ESSO). In the 1990s the multinational Exxon Corporation engaged in all aspects of the oil and gas business, including petrochemicals, with interests in coal and minerals mining operations and electric power generation. Its affiliates operated and/or marketed products in more than 100 countries on six continents. In 1996 it sold more than 35 million gallons of fuels and speciality petroleum products every day, turning over $134 billion annually (Exxon Corporation 1996). Figure 6.1 depicts EXXON's organizational structure and the grey shading highlights ESSO UK's link.

Corporate Strategy and Operations

EXXON has been committed to improving profitability for all its operations and enhancing long-term shareholder value (EXXON *Annual Review* 1996). Thus its corporate strategy has been focused on enhancing productivity and efficiency, by reducing its operation costs especially in the more mature markets, such as the UK, where investments and growth opportunities have been limited. The company has been determined to maintain a strict cost control strategy for the future, particularly keeping operating costs at a minimum. During the 1992–6 period EXXON globally had been able to decrease its operating costs per business unit by an average of 8 per cent per annum (PetroCompanies 1997).

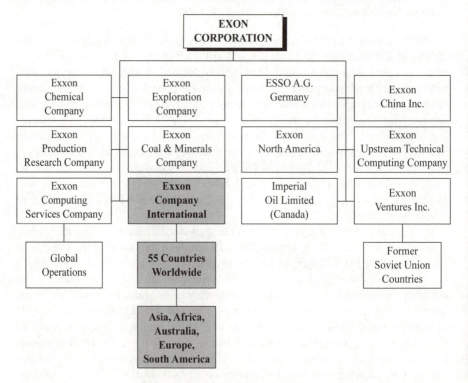

Fig. 6.1. *EXXON Corporation chart*

Lee Raymond, Chairman of EXXON, noted that 'reliable, efficient operations were key contributors to profitability across all business lines. Unit operating costs continued to decline, and we saw ongoing benefits of our Operations Integrity Management System in improving operating, safety and environmental performance' (EXXON *Annual Review* 1996). Subsequently, the organization's long-term investment strategy continued to focus on selective projects, whereby it only assigned capital to those projects that it believed would provide an acceptable rate of return, and make a significant contribution to future earnings growth. As a result, some projects were terminated early and their capital divested, especially to projects in regions where rapid economic growth was occurring, e.g. China, Eastern Europe, Central and South America (MacDonald 1997). In addition to its selective investment strategy, EXXON has been committed to extensive investments in technology: 'It expects to spend more than $500 million on technological research during 1997 to enhance its competitive strength in each of its business sectors' (PetroCompanies 1997: 142). The objective was to develop higher-quality products and improve its operating process, which would pay out by further increasing its return on its investments from selective projects and existing operating units.

Information Management at ESSO UK

In the early 1990s, ESSO's management—under the influence of EXXON's strategic operating efficiency imperative—refocused its efforts on the organization's core competencies:

we are clearly seen as an oil company at the end of the day. And Keith Taylor[2] would probably say we are not IT. We don't want to be bothered with that, it's not our business. (IT Manager, ESSO)

In addition to focusing on its core competencies, ESSO was finding its proprietary information systems increasingly inflexible, and adopting new technology costly. Thus EXXON decided, as part of the centralization process, to change its technology policy to off-the-shelf systems that would ensure future compatibility.

The information systems department (ISD), in turn, was downsized and restructured, through a process of centrally pooling IT services and IT outsourcing. Although no staff were made redundant or transferred to external suppliers, the headcount was cut from 250 people in 1994 to 39 managers in 1997 through lateral moves and early retirement initiatives:

we gradually reduced the numbers of our ESSO employees and transferred them and brought in contractors gradually. We deployed them, retired them, whatever we did. It took us 6 years to do that. Then we got to a point where we just couldn't rationalize

---

[2] Keith Taylor at this time was the Chairman of ESSO UK Plc. See also Essoview (1994).

any further, there were no ESSO people left and we just had several suppliers. (Supplier Manager B, ESSO)

The remaining staff of 39 had to take on a greater range of responsibilities. The majority were now in charge of managing service provisions and projects, rather than engaging in the delivery. In turn, there was a greater reliance on third parties, but only a number of IS people were actively involved in the management of external service providers. In fact half of the managers focused on managing specific projects:

the 39 people we now have do a mixture of things, we have programme managers who look after our development programmes portfolio, we have separate relationship managers, and we have people who run what we would call core business activities that we need like database design and things like that, which we still hold on to and budget. And then account management which is actually based in the business line, in individual departments which is the interface between the IS department, to make sure the IS department delivers the services to the other businesses. (Supplier Manager A, ESSO)

In parallel, Exxon established the 'Exxon Computing Services Company' (ECSC) to provide operations and management services and expertise on general purpose computing, networking and telecommunications for all its affiliates worldwide: 'the internal one with this regional operation is an organization called ECSE, Exxon Computer Services Europe they call it. What they are trying to do is produce standard desktops and standard tools and manage these on behalf of all the Exxon affiliates' (Supplier Manager B, ESSO). From ESSO's IS department, forty-five people moved to the European subsidiary as part of the downsizing initiative. The managers remaining at ESSO became primarily responsible for managing the IT outsourcing deals, strategy, service requirement issues, and new IT requests.

In addition to in-sourcing, ESSO also increased the amount of IT activities contracted out. ESSO had been procuring IT services from external suppliers since the mid-1980s and hence had been in a contract with CMG (an IT service specialist) for approximately ten years. The reason at the time was simply a lack of personnel to support existing systems and applications:

In the 1980s we had a lot of young graduates coming in. You had some older hands in place, the young graduates coming in doing their year there and saying I'm fed up with this I want to get out of support [. . .] We found it difficult to keep people. We started off in a very small way by out-sourcing just one area which was the general ledger corporate area, accounts payable, fixed assets, those sorts of things. (Supplier Manager B, ESSO)

However, with the operating efficiency drive by EXXON, ESSO had to diversify the amount of suppliers contracted, essentially in an effort to obtain expertise and specialized services while at the same time ensuring the greatest possible control and lowest dependency. ESSO's long-term experience with procurement led them to develop best practices guidelines for EXXON globally. Procurement at ESSO, in effect, was seen as an excellent means for achieving high returns (Newsline 1996).

ESSO's IT strategy

The long-term IT strategy was defined by EXXON and informed all affiliates strategies, but every affiliate in parallel developed a more localized version. Consequently, in some areas there was no actual alignment of the IT strategy to ESSO's local business strategy. There was only an indication that EXXON might endeavour, in the long run, to align it through ECSC. The centralization effort through ECSC aimed to diminish duplication of services and enforce a global IT strategy. The initiative was clearly sparked by desire to decrease the IT operating costs: 'the ECSC organization basically look after the operation itself in terms of running mainframes, looking after the local area networks, and managing the contract for all the hardware support, and looking after the network communications. All the physical bits and pieces' (Operations Support Manager, ESSO). However, as at 1997, the services delivered by the ECSC's European operation were not seen as very effective; in fact relations between ESSO's IS management and ECSC were strained.

ESSO's IT strategy covers a five-year time frame, and the overarching long-term strategy was informed by EXXON's strategy. Through EXXON's centralization push, ECSC had, over several years, accumulated more influence over ESSO's IT direction, and, by 1997, partially determined the strategy. However, there seemed to be a lack of communication about the long-term strategy between EXXON and ESSO's IS management. In fact, the only long-term strategy that had permeated through was the effort to continue reducing overall operating costs:

all the time our shareholder in the States is having more and more influence on where we are going. I don't feel comfortable when sitting down with our key suppliers now and saying in the year 2000 we are going to be here, because frankly I've got no clue where we will be in the year 2000. And I'm not too sure many other people, even in EXXON, know what we are going to be looking like. (Supplier Manager B, ESSO)

This uncertainty directly influenced ESSO's IT strategy planning, and in many cases caused confusion and unpredictability.

However, in terms of IT outsourcing the underlying strategic objectives have been cost cutting and access to technology and expertise. This clarity effectively informed ESSO's outsourcing strategy:

we've had an outsourcing strategy for a number of years now and we've always been fairly clear as to where we are going on that. We've always been fairly clear as to what we were going to hold, what we were going to control and what we were going to outsource, and why we were going to outsource. (Supplier Manager A, ESSO)

This has been particularly critical for operationalizing the contract, since all parties involved knew exactly what they intended and expected to achieve by outsourcing.

Table 6.1. *ESSO UK's outsourcing contracts 1998*

Vendor	Start	Outsourcing scope, i.e. service(s)	Size (per annum)
ESCE (insourcing)	>1980	Networking, telecommunications, and desktop computing	approx. £14 million
CMG	1986	Software development	£2–4 million
ITNet	1993	Legacy application support	£1 million
RIS	1991	Client-server development support	£0.5 million
REX software	1986	Process work	£0.5 million
PRINT	1996	Invoice production and mail	£0.5 million

IT OUTSOURCING

The pressure for operational efficiency drove ESSO to expand the number of areas outsourced, and by 1998, ESSO had contracts with five IT suppliers. ESSO adopted early on an incremental approach, essentially outsourcing commodity services, with contracts running for a predetermined five-year period: 'we talk about five suppliers, they are all key to us. We have chosen people who we believe can perform in those areas of the market that we want to use. I don't believe when you see all those wonderful FM deals I don't believe there are too many people out there who can do the whole show' (Supplier Manager, ESSO). Table 6.1 lists ESSO UK's outsourcing and insourcing arrangements as at 1998.

ESSO UK's selective outsourcing strategy was shaped and influenced by a number of factors. First, ESSO found that no single vendor could handle all requirements to the standard required. Secondly, careful selection of small niche suppliers ensured that ESSO's business was of strategic significance to the supplier, in effect assuring greater attention and control: 'with somebody like EDS a million or half a million contract is not big, they wouldn't be too interested in that. You are not going to get the best of them, you are not going to get the management attention when you need it' (Supplier Manager A, ESSO). Thirdly, they chose vendors with whom they could work and who closely matched ESSO UK's distinctive culture. In fact, the cultural aspect was often noted as a key parameter in the selection process.

Vendor Selection Process

ESSO's suppliers were carefully selected according to a formalized procurement procedure. Inherent to this procedure was the selection of specialist niche suppliers rather than large service suppliers: 'If you look at the sort of suppliers, we haven't got your big ones, we haven't got your Semas, we haven't got the EDSs, we are not talking about large amounts of business' (Supplier Manager B, ESSO). In fact, it was noted more than once that the head of IT would not enter into a contract with a third party without having the possibility to directly access the supplier's Managing Director at any point in time. He always wanted to have clear reassurance that ESSO would be a strategic customer to that supplier. These considerations underpinned the selection process.

ESSO's procurement procedure followed a standard protocol that was developed and monitored by the Contract and Materials (C&M) department. C&M provided guidance on planning, contracting, paying, and managing suppliers (Newsline 1996). However, since the IS group had formulated an outsourcing strategy earlier on, they already knew, without having to issue an open tender, to whom to send a 'request for information' (RFI). In line with C&M's protocol, they were then required to ask six different suppliers to bid. But before they actually issued the 'request for proposal' (RFP), each supplier was evaluated on a number of aspects:

What we do is a lot of work with those six suppliers up front before we actually go out to tender. There is only a certain amount we can do, though, because they haven't signed confidentiality agreements and things like that, [but] even if this is missing, you can try and work with them to see whether they've got the right culture. (Supplier Manager B, ESSO)

Part of this initial assessment also involved reference sites visits and in some cases, where available, working with the actual customer-facing personnel. The reference site visits were found to be the most telling, and it was a process of making sure the culture at least in some parts matched up:

We did actually take one of the suppliers off the list before we actually went to tender. And the reason we took them off, we had a reference site visit, things didn't go too well there, we met the senior people within the organization and we just didn't like them, we just couldn't get on with them. (Supplier Manager A, ESSO)

The resulting information gathered from the reference site visits and other sources, combined with the data from the bid offers, presented ESSO with sufficient data for an informed decision about who was the best suited supplier both culturally and operationally. One respondent further noted, in reference to the selection process:

What we would like to do is learn more, earlier. It's a lot like a development project as far as I can see this whole thing. The effort you put in up front rewards you later on. (Supplier Manager B, ESSO)

ITNet's Selection

In ITNet's particular case, the selection circumstances were different and hence did not coincide strictly with C&M's protocol. ITNet was specifically asked to present a competitive bid against the prices of CMG—at that time contracted to deliver the applications support service. CMG was the preferred supplier, as they had supplied ESSO with IT services for the previous seven years; nevertheless they were perceived as expensive. Consequently, ITNet was able to make a better priced offer, undercutting CMG to such an extent that it became worthwhile for ESSO to switch:

They [CMG] did it on a day rate basis and they were the company that moved us the furthest forward in terms of pro-actively showing us how to do applications support and development better. But, at a cost. This was a Rolls Royce service. (Supplier Manager A, ESSO)

ITNet's strong price offer and keenness to acquire business with a 'Blue Chip' company like ESSO, truly gave ITNet a strong impetus to outdo CMG: 'the reason we won the bid in the first place is because we were cheaper' (Customer Service Manager, ITNet). However, the low margin calculation ITNet made was to cause much strain in the subsequent years and subsequently was to raise questions in ESSO over whether cost-saving offers procured through a competitive benchmarking or tender process should not be scrutinized more closely before actually contracting with the competing bidder.

ITNet Overview

At the time ITNet was a UK-focused IT service organization, formed following a management buyout in 1995 from the former parent company Cadbury Schweppes Plc (Boarman 1997). ITNet in fact used to be the IT division of the former soft drinks and confectionery group. Since then ITNet's turnover soared to £82 million in 1997 with 1,600 employees. ITNet offered services in facility management, migration, application management, consultancy, PC and Unix support, and managed services (e.g. payroll, pensions, accounts receivable and payable, and pensions). Its customer base focused strongly on local government councils, although it had also signed a number of contracts with large private sector companies, e.g. BAA and BASF (ITNet Presentation 1997). In an effort to expand its resources and generate cash, ITNet intended, by 1998, to float on the London stock exchange, in a move likely to value the company at up to £200 million (Price 1998). Bridget Blow, managing director, emphasized that 'a listing will give us more flexibility to finance future growth' (Phillips 1998). ITNet's growth continued strongly in the late 1990s, with a range of new customers.

Outsourcing Scope and Objectives

ITNet provided key application support services for approximately 130 systems that were operating on ESSO's mainframes in 1998. These included functions like scheduling services, helpdesk services, and an operations and processing

Table 6.2. *Outsourcing expectations*

Outsourcing objectives

- Yearly cost savings
- Service levels
- Access to skills, expertise & technology

Source: Interviewees.

service from their data centre. The core service part of the contract demanded that these 130 systems were operational twenty-four hours a day. In addition, ITNet was contracted to supply ESSO with specific IT specialists as demand arose.

The objectives pursued were those of acquiring specific services, expertise, and technology for a good price. In more recent years, with EXXON's push to restructure, costs had become a greater issue for senior management (see Table 6.2). Every year management expected the operations costs to decrease. However, IS management were not slow to point out that cost and services had to be kept in balance:

Senior management's intention with outsourcing is to drive down the costs by a 5–10 per cent on IT services per annum. This has been the case for the department for the past 7 years. The problem with this being that new costs do arise, for example with issues such as the Year 2000 date change. (Supplier Manager B, ESSO)

Vendors were made aware of these expectations early on, as they had to agree and be prepared to renegotiate every year on price rates and services. If they were no longer able to deliver the price reductions, other suppliers could be asked to bid against an existing supplier; this was precisely how ITNet procured its ESSO contract. In line with these expectations, ESSO's particular objective with contracting ITNet was to move services and technology off-site in the long-term:

The aim obviously was to replace contractors from a cost point of view with permanent people over a short period of time. [And to] bring those permanent people into a good knowledge of the systems and then move long term off-site and support the systems off-site. That was ESSO's request because they wanted to cut costs. Obviously it's cheaper supporting it from Birmingham than from London. (Customer Service Manager, ITNet)

ESSO's objective was to collate the different service provisions of the contractors into one contract to simplify management and decrease operational costs. Therefore, the IT service manager's initial task was a customer service manager role which involved managing the different contractors at ESSO's site.

THE CONTRACT

In 1994 ESSO UK signed a five-year, fixed-cost contract with ITNet Ltd. for the provision of legacy application support services. The contract was structured into two core parts: on the one hand there was a core service which had to be supplied continuously according to service level agreements; on the other there was an enhancement service that would vary according to ESSO's requirements. A failure to provide the core services at any time, could diminish the potential bonus payments paid on the satisfactory delivery of services: 'We do have rewards based on performance, but it's a very low amount of money and it's not really that important in our profitability' (Customer Service Manager, ITNet). Pricing of the service provisions was also split into two parts. First, core services were priced on a fixed monthly call fee of £49,000 for all legacy application and system services. Secondly, all add-on change requests, i.e. Computer Work Control Forms (CWCF), varied according to agreed and accepted prices. However, on average ESSO spent an additional £45,000 a month on CFCWs: 'The changes we actually pay are fixed price amounts. They estimate and then they do those changes for a fixed price' (Operations Support Manager, ESSO). Overall ESSO was paying approximately £94,000 a month in total according to 1997 negotiated prices.

Generally, core service prices were calculated according to an agreed headcount number. In 1997 the core service fee was based on ten people providing the service every day of the week including holidays and sick leave. This flat fee was paid regardless of whether the work was carried out with eight or twelve people: 'If we provide that service with eight people that's good management on our behalf because we've provided the service with less people. If it takes us 12 people then we are making a loss because we can't do it, so we've got to manage it down' (Customer Service Manager, ITNet). On the CWCF side, if ITNet hoped to make a profit they had to perform better than their own cost estimates. Of course, ITNet could calculate its estimates to show they always performed better, and ESSO might find it difficult to countercheck these calculations, since no open book arrangement had been agreed: 'We don't actually tell them how long it took to do something because obviously that's giving away our profitability then and we don't do that as a company' (Customer Service Manager, ITNet). Nevertheless, the contract assured ESSO an annual cost reduction in the flat rate charges for the core services and CWCFs:

It's reduced by £20,000 per year next year and a further £10,000 the following year. [For] the CWCF work it is quite easy because the less work we get the less people we need. As the CWCF work comes down we just take people out of the team, but there's a minimum of £300,000 a year that ESSO guarantees us. So if the work dropped below that level then we would still get £300,000 a year from ESSO. (Customer Service Manager, ITNet)

The effect of shrinking the amount of work implied that the 1997/8 service provisions would become redundant at some point in the future. The planned time frame for phasing out the mainframe legacy system was 2004, at which point most applications should be operational on a client-server. Therefore the money ITNet was making in 1997–8 would tail off over the next seven years. As a result this put additional pressure on ITNet managers to identify new areas of business services they could provide ESSO with over the contracts life to ensure continuity: 'We need to manage ITNet into a position where the mainframe work shrinks but other areas of work increase' (Customer Service Manager, ITNet)

THE TRANSITION PERIOD: TAKING OVER FROM CMG (1994–1996)

The transition period for ITNet, starting in mid-1994, focused initially on taking over existing service arrangements from CMG and applying some of their own expertise to provide the promised reductions in costs. Cost savings defined the primary reason why ITNet won the business. This implied that ITNet would improve current operations to such a degree that it led to the promised savings, plus additional savings for a margin on top for themselves. Initial tasks concentrated on:

- Implementing and operationalizing the contract and its service levels;
- Introducing a customer perception rating system by ITNet;
- Consolidating and rationalizing of existing services and transferring of operations to ITNet's own site;
- Providing an appropriate operating environment that conformed to EXXON/ESSO's strict safety, security, and confidentiality requirements; and
- Developing a management infrastructure and procedures.

In mid-1994, ITNet took charge of CMG's service provision. Operationalization of the contract, according to ESSO respondents, was a straightforward matter of delivering what the service level agreement specified. Following ESSO managers' experience with other procurement arrangements, any deviation from the contract would raise questions and possible conflicts:

Originally when we took the contract on there was a take-on team at ESSO made up originally of quite a lot of strong characters who demanded and expected a service from ITNet. When that service wasn't provided they would want to know why, and not how can we help—it was why is this service not here. And it was very one way. (Customer Service Manager, ITNet)

One difficulty for ITNet was that they were taking over from an existing contractor, i.e. CMG, who had provided services to ESSO for the previous seven years and hence were used to ESSO's idiosyncrasies and expectations. For ITNet, it was a new environment and there was no one they could initially rely on to help operationalize the contract, especially not CMG, the competitor who had lost the business to ITNet. Interestingly, ESSO's managers initially were not aware of these difficulties. Only in retrospect did they recognize the correlation between their idiosyncrasies and ITNet's problems:

It was a difficult time because they didn't know how we worked, we weren't saying to them, 'here's five of our best people, they are going to sit and work with you', because we didn't have 5 people to work with them. Because the business had already been contracted. (Supplier Manager B, ESSO)

However, at the time, ESSO's strict adherence to the contract was informed by their policy and experience with procuring services. Conforming to its policy, in early 1994 ESSO had spent considerable time and effort on formulating a detailed contract and service level agreement, that then had to be delivered on:

There's nothing grey in our contracts, they are black and white, they are not open to interpretation. (Supplier Manager A, ESSO)

We've used it [the contract] as a base and we've often referred back to it in the past. (Customer Service Manager, ITNet)

The service level agreement is such that it is well known to everybody. [. . .] And the supplier knows what they are and we know exactly what they are. (Supplier Manager B, ESSO)

The actual specifics of the contract, however, were restricted according to the person's level of involvement in operationalizing the contract. Only a few managers were fully informed and aware of the totality of the contract:

I have a good understanding of the contract because I've been involved with the contract more than anyone else. But at lower levels, the normal analyst programmer really isn't aware of the contract that heavily. They are aware of certain areas which we've highlighted to them. The team leader is quite aware of the contract and they are aware of the particular areas that will affect them. But obviously at my level I need to be fully aware because I need to be able to sit in a meeting and not have to refer back to the statements in the contract. (Customer Service Manager, ITNet)

Yet all managers involved were aware of what ITNet was required to deliver and little additional clarification was necessary:

It's all laid down in here [contract]. The systems are all defined as being either critical, highly critical, or low criticality. They are graded according to how critical they are to ESSO and the business. And depending on whether they are critical or less critical it defines how many hours you can wait before you get a problem fixed. If you've got a critical problem and it's not fixed within so many hours it is escalated to higher levels within both companies. (Application Support Manager, ITNet)

The SLA detail simplified the payment system as well. All payments were effectively dependent on the achievement of the stipulated services. Nonaccomplishment inherently invoked conflict and more importantly resulted in the loss of any bonuses:

However, there are certain systems which are deemed critical to the operation. We've got certain on-line systems that must be kept running and we've got our batch schedule, of course, which runs overnight and we deem that to be critical. Within the contract there are certain bonuses that can be awarded if they manage to keep those on-line systems running and if the batch schedule is run to ESSO's satisfaction. (Operations Support Manager, ESSO)

ESSO offers a bonus scheme which essentially means if the service is running very well you are entitled to be paid a bonus. And various specific system bonuses as well. The converse is true, if there's been a problem on that system which is due to us being inept then they might say: no I'm sorry you've lost the chance to own your bonus this month. (Application Support Manager, ITNet)

The incentive scheme acted as a key motivator for ITNet to perform and deliver the specified services. Additionally, it also enabled close scrutiny of ITNet's performance to determine whether services had been delivered to ESSO's standard. In fact, ITNet's performance was monitored extensively:

First of all there are hundreds of jobs that run overnight—at the very base level—that run on our system. They have to work every night, 24 hours and if something goes wrong then they are fixed. And if something does go wrong even if it's a slight error it's recorded automatically on the computer system. And that's monitored very vigorously, and that's one of the major KPIs (key performance indicators). After that we monitor just how much work they do for us, number of hours they do for us. So we can actually see that the operational support is getting more and more efficient because they've got more time with the same number of people to do enhancements for us. We want them to do that, that is the market driver. (Supplier Manager A, ESSO)

We have a pie chart showing the 15 systems every month which have taken most core effort to support. And the core effort is an indication normally of how much work there has been to perhaps fix problems or address queries that have been raised by users on the system. [. . .]We in fact support about 130 odd systems. So those actually get listed out. There's a document that just prints out all the applications as to how much core we've actually used and that is monitored. [. . .] We also want to know how much CWCF work we get done because roughly half of that should be in delivering small changes. [. . .] And we monitor that flow of CWCF work through the system. The other things that important are the down times on the systems. (Application Support Manager, ITNet)

So, essentially, there were three main measures according to the contract: down time, the amount of change requests, and the amount of time spent on specific aspects of the core services. The core service levels and their prices were then annually renegotiated and updated, in an effort to ensure the costs were continually reduced, and the legacy services slowly phased out.

In late 1995 ITNet introduced a customer perception rating (CPR) method to additionally monitor the degree of customer satisfaction with their service performance and operations. CPR was in essence intended to provide the subjective perspective to the hard measures of the service performance reports. It was to be undertaken on a monthly basis and involved scoring the perceptions on a scale from 0 (lowest) to 6 (highest):

Something that we do regularly at our monthly meetings, each team leader will ask for a perception rating from the customer and that's scored between 0–6. Each score means something different. I have to report back to my management team every month on the average customer perception ratings. So obviously we've got to keep that perception up so it's very important to keep that perception up. (Customer Service Manager, ITNet)

They have a policy within ITNet where they ask for a customer perception rating. At the various monthly progress and prioritization meetings [. . .] each customer will be asked to provide a customer perception rating which is a gut feeling of what's going on. They are given some guidelines as to what goes with what gut feeling. (Operations Manager, ESSO)

Early measures using the CPR method revealed a very low average score—a reflection of ITNet's transition difficulties and an early sign of things to come:

When we started doing the perception rating about 18 months ago we scored 2.7 which was our average score, and that was taken from 6 or 7 business lines. Linda gives a score and also the operations manager at ESSO will give a score as well. (Customer Service Manager, ITNet)

In parallel to operationalizing the service provision of the contract, ITNet was to continue rationalizing and consolidating service delivery at ESSO's sites and eventually to move the complete service delivery and technology infrastructure off-site to their headquarters in the UK.

We actually started the contract based on the London site. My job title has changed over the 3 years since I started there. Initially I was the customer services manager when taking over from the manager actually on site. [In addition on-site there were] . . . a number of contractors hired to cover the existing systems. The aim obviously was to replace the contractors from a cost point-of-view with permanent people over a short period of time. Bring those permanent people into a good knowledge of the systems and then move and support the systems off site in the long term. That was ESSO's request because they wanted to cut costs. Obviously it's cheaper to support it from our HQs than from London. (Customer Service Manager, ITNet)

Rationalization also involved changing the paper-based change request system to an on-line-based system. This was a fundamental improvement to the otherwise lengthy authorization process of collecting signatures. Other rationalization and consolidation changes included moving a number of key systems to ITNet's building.

The transition period also illustrated ESSO's strong corporate culture, to which ITNet would need to adjust. ESSO in fact had the tendency to impose its thinking, for example of security and safety, on its suppliers. ESSO's culture indeed has a strong element of security, safety, and control consciousness. In part this was traceable to ESSO's parent company EXXON, a strong proponent of these factors. In fact, security, safety, and control was found to characterize the nature of ESSO's business. The customer service manager explained how ITNet experienced this culture:

ESSO are very, very safety conscious. Obviously with them being a multinational company with a number of environmental and safety issues in the past like the EXXON Valdez oil disaster, they are extremely safety conscious. In their public face and to all their suppliers they put safety above everything else, [. . .] even off site on our own site, we have to do things in our office that the rest of ITNet don't have to adhere to. For example, we've got a key pad on the front door that's for every active employee to get through. I also have restricted access into the block that we work in and then only ITNet-ESSO employees are allowed to go into our office. Even the managing director of ITNet couldn't go into our office without knocking on the door and signing in. And that was ESSO's decree when we took the contract on.

Working with ESSO was thus seriously complicated by their security, safety, and control-driven culture. This culture not only influenced the selection of individuals, but also affected all operations in or with ESSO. In many situations the key perceivable influencing factor of ESSO's culture was the concern for control:

We are not a very hands-off organization. We like to influence everything, we want to be involved. We [also] have very stringent controls. [. . .] It costs us without a doubt because of our controls. But they are an EXXON driven thing, so we aren't going to change them overnight. We've got piles of this stuff on controls. We spend a fortune every year with different departments being audited and things like that. [. . .] It doesn't matter what we buy, we say we are buying a managed service and we've got to influence it, we want to get in there and control it. And we are fairly demanding. (Supplier Manager B, ESSO)

And these controls, of course, cost ESSO considerable additional monies:

We've had a number of suppliers tell us that our controls potentially add 25% to the cost. (Supplier Manager A, ESSO)

Even more discernible was the impact of ESSO's culture on ITNet's operation. Indeed, during the transition period (late 1994) it put a serious strain on both the relationship and operations:

We had an original room that we earmarked for the ESSO office and it was rejected by ESSO because there were wells in the roof and the floor for the heating which someone could crawl under. [. . .] Obviously as a supplier we have to stick to that and get involved in the safety and security issues. (Customer Service Manager, ITNet)

Of course, these early problems of operationalizing the contract complicated matters. And to late 1998 in some cases ITNet's managers working on the ESSO account were still affected by the cultural impact; they continued to be perceived as outsiders in their own offices:

Other ITNet employees perceive us as quite different because we are locked behind a door. As you can see the office is all open plan, it's not like that in our office, there's a door and it's all sealed off and we only have access by a swipe card. (Account Manager, ITNet)

By early 1995 some of the operational and cultural problems had been alleviated, but overall service levels had hit at an all time low, and relations were not developing as had been expected:

Trust was at a low because the service wasn't being provided to an adequate level and it just spiralled down really. . . . we had bring the trust back up by providing a good service. (Customer Service Manager, ITNet)

The effects of poor service performance were widespread, and hampered the development of the relationship. In accordance with ESSO's control culture, managers were seeking to find the source of these difficulties. Blame was later to be apportioned to both ESSO's and ITNet's operation managers handling the deal, and these were subsequently replaced.

The arrangements ESSO had put in place to manage ITNet corresponded largely to the management infrastructure that existed while CMG was the contractor. The 'take on team' comprised a number of managers who expected service performance according to contract. As it stood, the account on ESSO's side was handled by the operations manager, who previously had been running the CMG deal. Figure 6.2 displays the management structure as of 1994.

On the other hand, ITNet's IOR structure consisted of a number of carefully selected individuals, who, following ESSO's strict scrutiny and security

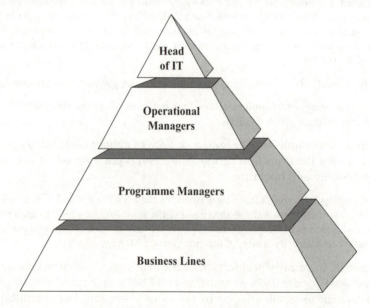

Fig. 6.2. *ESSO's structure 1994–1995*

vetting, became eligible to access and work on the ESSO account. Security clearance defined an important part of ESSO's practice and hence culture, but also implied managers had to be culturally matched:

It does state in the contract that they can stop us taking on staff they are not happy with because they have to vet all of our staff. They are allowed to have control over how many staff, the type of staff and mix of staff we have. (Application Support Manager, ITNet)

The main person who is managing the contract has to be right, and I can say I've personally kicked several out. [. . .] if you don't get that right, that fulcrum person right, who is the customer facing person who is going to do the communications; the sort of person if a problem happens they know they've got to talk to that person and that person in that order, immediately to tell them those things otherwise they will give them a problem 100 times bigger to manage further down to the road. (Supplier Manager A, ESSO)

Cultural match did not, however, imply that the management structures implemented would mirror ESSO's infrastructure arrangements initially. Rather, this would have to evolve over time.

ESSO managers relied on structures established during the CMG account, and these had been operational for some seven years. Indeed, relying on his previous experience with CMG, the ESSO operations manager went about his business as usual, managing the ITNet relationship as a procurement arrangement, as with CMG, in which services were to be delivered exactly according to agreements. The manager's strict contractual adherence left little room for flexibility and actual management of the relationship. Internally, he was held responsible for the account and its operations, which meant handling day-to-day enquiries, requests, and problems.

The early operational and cultural difficulties ITNet encountered led on their side to a decline in service performance, which on ESSO's side resulted in an increase in pressure on the operations manager to ensure improvements and resolution of the difficulties. ESSO's culture demanded problem ownership and resolution and this is likely to have been responsible for overwhelming the operations manager in light of continuing difficulties. Respondents indicated that he lacked the competencies to manage and cope with the ongoing pressure for improvements, relationship management, and day-to-day issues:

At the beginning it was probably his position that he was trying to manage it all. I don't think it's possible to get involved day to day and try and sort out the relationship type issues as well. (Operations Manager, ESSO)

The individual that we had managing [ITNet] didn't have the right competencies to manage the relationship. [He] was very much a hands-off individual, and felt that the supplier had won the business, so therefore the supplier is big enough—they are out there doing a lot of work with other people—that they should just come in and do the job. [But] what he actually did was refer to the contract constantly. (Supplier Manager B, ESSO)

On ITNet's side the divisional manager in charge was equally not able to turn around their performance and the relationship. Eventually, the continuous strain on the relationship and the managers in charge ended in loggerheads in late 1995.

Realizing these difficulties, the Head of IT at ESSO responded first by completely revising the existing management structure and appointing two extra relationship managers (called Supplier Managers) in late 1995. Their remit was to oversee the account and actively develop the relationship on a day-to-day basis:

[the Head of IT] view was that as the department became more dependent on third parties then what we needed to do was have a strong vendor management to make sure that those third parties were delivering to us, and that we were delivering to those third parties. So it's a two-way street. So he asked me to come down and have a look at it. I sat down there probably 3–6 months doing some work around putting together best practices [. . .] And we had some particular problems with one of our suppliers in particular, most of those problems were I guess of our own making. And we needed somebody with the necessary skills to come in and work that relationship, so [Supplier Manager B] joined to work that particular relationship. (Supplier Manager A, ESSO)

In addition, both parties removed the managers responsible for handling the ESSO account and two new account managers were brought on board:

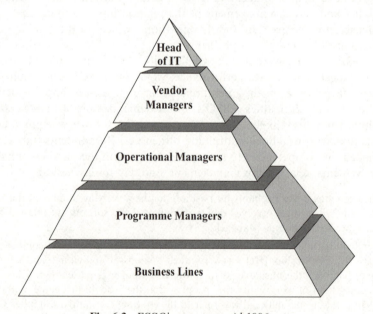

Fig. 6.3. *ESSO's structure mid-1996*

ITNet have been fairly open and fairly helpful with us in that as soon as we got in there and said we don't like this individual, that individual was then out of their account. Because what we had to do was build up that two-way thing. And likewise when they turned around to us and said that they had a problem with one of our individuals, we moved that individual sideways. (Supplier Manager A, ESSO)

The original account manager who shall remain nameless, that was when we were making a large loss. Around 18 months ago a lady called Jane took over the team and she was my previous manager and she managed the team from making a large loss to making quite a heavy return on sales. (Application Support Manager, ITNet)

These changes were very costly for both ITNet and ESSO in terms of having to allocate additional resources. However, this change in structure was critical for continuation and, later on, was claimed to be a defining moment in the turnaround of the relationship. Figure 6.3 depicts ESSO's revised management structure (mid-1996).

Part of the relationship managers' remit was to ensure that ITNet's structure and hence managers closely matched their expectations of a good interface and contact point. In this respect, they became much more involved in the personnel arrangements and the alignment of ITNet's structure with ESSO's:

We are fairly proactive in working with our suppliers. We have a fairly tight conduit, if you like, between each of our suppliers at all levels. She [Supplier Manager B] would have a way into ITNet, [the Head of IT] would have a way into ITNet [. . .] And we've got support on both sides of the organizations. Likewise where we are we've got a conduit in and even further down we've set things in place to enable the business lines to be able to talk directly to people. And communications goes all ways. (Supplier Manager A, ESSO)

I would go as far as to say that we've actively encouraged them to have their organization aligned to our structure so that we've got these parallel routes. And also escalation routes. (Supplier Manager B, ESSO)

The decision to formalize the structure was also influenced by the growing amount of time managers spent on the relationship rather than just focusing on businesses' requirements. It became obvious that IT outsourcing service success was directly correlated with an effective relationship and hence its management: 'The contract takes up 25% of our time and the rest of it takes 75%' (Supplier Manager A, ESSO). Effective relationship management depends on well-working management processes. It soon became evident, though, that the management processes used with CMG did not work with ITNet. Consequently, during the far-reaching changes to the management structure in 1995–6, some of the management processes also had to be addressed. In fact, ITNet managers at different levels raised a number issues that were causing problems in the management of the account:

we had a list of problems, like the procedures that ESSO have are extremely tight. If it's for rerunning a job that has failed, for example, or a piece of work to be written,

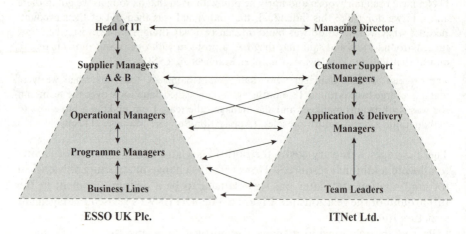

Fig. 6.4. *ESSO and ITNet's interface structure*

Source: Interviewees.

they are very very controlled and most people haven't been used to that environment before they worked on the ESSO contract. So in order to get the ITNet people happy we had to make the procedures slicker. So we looked at that initially as a partnership between ESSO and ourselves and how can we improve it. [. . .] And what we did we sat down as a team and brainstormed the issues and wrote them on a chart and identified them in a priority order and how to tackle them. [. . .] And by doing that we've really turned things around. It was a large turning point. (Customer Service Manager, ITNet)

The brainstorming sessions revealed a number of problems. For example, ESSO managers were redesigning parts of the databases and essentially preventing ITNet from supporting those applications. As another example:

The reports we were producing weren't satisfactory and we hadn't been told that, so it was an identification of reporting what they actually wanted. And we tailored monthly reporting to what the business line actually wanted. That was obviously an improvement. (Account Manager, ITNet)

The improvements that came from revamping the management infrastructure and by addressing a number of the management problems included a greater clarity in the interactions and contact pattern between the parties. By 1996 a new structure had been developed for ESSO-ITNet (see Figure 6.4). The advantage of having a defined interaction structure then enabled ESSO to formalize its management process, outlining particular meetings at which ITNet's performance would be reviewed and according to which payments were made and bonuses granted. These meetings were key to ESSO's control agenda, and gave both senior, operations, and functional managers an opportunity to closely monitor ITNet's performance. In addition, they provided the possibility for voicing any concerns or problems that had arisen and drawing, senior

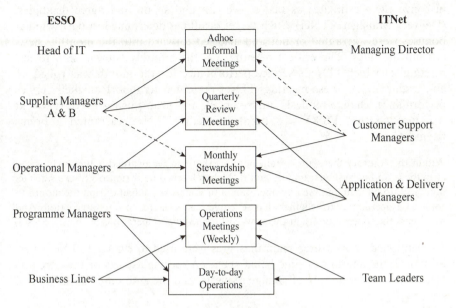

Fig. 6.5. *ESSO's management process 1996*

Source: Interviewees.

management's attention to them. The evolving management process included ad hoc meetings, quarterly, monthly, and weekly meetings at different levels. Figure 6.5 depicts the management process that evolved over 1995–6.

Key were the ongoing operational meetings and the day-to-day operation reviews. For this, ITNet's team leaders interacted with the five different business lines on a daily basis to monitor their satisfaction and problems. The programme managers oversaw ITNet's daily performance across the business lines through an on-line reporting facility. Operations began with a routine daily meeting at which any issues or problems that emerged in the past twenty-four hours are discussed:

Every day there is a 10-minute telephone conference call to make sure everything is running smoothly. Every day between our computer centre and our delivery people within ESSO. And if there are problems that goes straight back into ITNet. (Supplier Manager B, ESSO)

More serious problems were instantly brought to the attention of the operation and supplier managers.

At the weekly operation meetings problems, issues, and extra work requests were rolled up and discussed. In particular at these meetings the business lines would inform ITNet of the urgency of specific work, which was then prioritized for completion: 'They list that work which is really urgent, and then we just give them estimates as fast as we can and so on and agree deadlines' (Delivery Manager, ITNet). Such target deadlines determined in part whether bonuses were warranted or not and also fed forward into the monthly stewardship meetings. The critical meeting was the monthly 'stewardship review meeting' at which ITNet's service performance for the month was rolled up and evaluated. At these meetings ITNet presented its report on their service performance, change requests implemented, and problems resolved. It was at this meeting that ESSO also decided whether ITNet warranted a bonus payment:

Within the contract there are certain bonuses that can be awarded if they manage to keep those on-line systems running and if the batch schedule is run to ESSO's satisfaction. So I do have to analyse any operational problems we've had during the month to come to a decision as to whether that schedule has been run to our satisfaction. And we discuss that once a month at the stewardship meeting. (Operations Manager, ESSO)

As mentioned above, three main measures were used to evaluate ITNet's performance: the amount of time being spent on specific aspects of the core services, the completion rate of change requests, and the amount of down time of systems.

The quarterly review meetings had a similar agenda to the stewardship meeting, except this time services 'trends' were discussed with senior management in both firms: 'It's very much like the stewardship meeting except the information is rolled up and presented in the major trends in the quarter and so on' (Application Support Manager, ITNet). Senior management became involved at this stage to monitor the general performance of the account. Major problems or change requests could be addressed at this meeting: 'We go and if we only have lunch that's the way I want it. There is a set agenda for all the quarterly stewardships and we discuss certain points always' (Supplier Manager A, ESSO). The meeting was not as rigorous and formal as the monthly review meetings, and tended to focus more on building and/or maintaining the relationship. Likewise, the ad hoc meetings arranged between ESSO's Head of IT and ITNet's Managing Director: these meetings were very informal and few details of the actual account were discussed:

What they are discussing is not day to day, what they are discussing is strategy, what's coming up in the future, what is resourcing going to be like next year, what are the problems going to be next year on resourcing, how much money ESSO Petroleum has got that we can spend next year. (Supplier Manager B, ESSO)

These meetings ensured senior management involvement in the outsourcing account, and ensured both sides' awareness of any dramatic future plans and changes.

In summary, the transition period was a difficult, often testing time for both parties, especially for ITNet who had made a number of wrong assumptions about ESSO's operations. In the coming months ITNet would be faced with no other alternative but to ask ESSO for contract renegotiations or face early termination. Additionally, ITNet encountered difficulties with ESSO's strong corporate culture and lack of support in developing the relationship. ESSO started the venture with insufficient management processes and managers, believing it could continue to operate the service arrangements as it had with its former supplier. These management and operational difficulties contributed to the eventual breakdown and need for introducing additional management resources to improve relations and services.

CONTRACT RENEGOTIATION (1996)

Towards the end of 1995 it had become clear to ITNet that they were no longer able to deliver the services as originally priced and agreed. For the first one and half years they had only made losses, and the contract was in fact costing them significant amounts of money. As a consequence services were also suffering, and both sides were highly dissatisfied with the arrangements. One respondent noted, referring to the initial set-up:

When we very first started with the contract with ESSO, ITNet wasn't making much money, and in fact we lost a lot of money initially. Working down at Leatherhead and paying enormous amounts in travel costs, that was a main issue. And also we weren't delivering the service very well so other issues came into it. A bleak time and we weren't making money either. (Applications Support Manager, ITNet)

As a result, ITNet were forced to re-evaluate the contract and their business with ESSO. In part, they had to admit to themselves that some of the problems they were encountering, especially the lack of profit, was a result of their erroneous calculations and assumptions about ESSO's business. However this only became apparent to ITNet during the actual operationalization of the contract:

When ITNet first came in the frame with us they were very much used to dealing with public utilities and councils and things like that and they found us very strange. They came in, they took our business and they made some assumptions that we were organized like a council or a utility. We had high overheads all those sorts of things. We had excess resource working in that area. But we didn't. We'd already done all that work. They were a little bit naive to start off with. (Supplier Manager A, ESSO)

Consequently, in mid-1996 ITNet was left with few options but to confront ESSO with their partially self-inflicted problem and request an early contract renegotiation. Essentially they had two real options for resolving the situation—either renegotiate or terminate the contract early: 'ITNet came to us a couple of years ago and said look we've got a problem here, [. . .] we cannot provide that resource any longer at that price' (Supplier Manager B, ESSO). ESSO's response was favourable. They were sympathetic and understanding of ITNet's situation. They were not interested in causing ITNet a loss and wanted both parties to mutually benefit from the deal. Hence ESSO's management agreed to revisit and evaluate the contract in light of ITNet's specific problems: 'ESSO didn't want ITNet to find themselves financially embarrassed and unable to carry on with the work, so they agreed to sit down and look at what was going on and try to help address it' (Applications Support Manager, ITNet). Interestingly, when ESSO revisited the originally negotiated contract they were not surprised to find terms and prices scales that essentially prohibited ITNet from making an adequate return on their costs. Reflecting on the original state of the contract one of the supplier managers (B) from ESSO emphasized:

> The contract that was put together was appalling. It did not take into account the avail-ability of additional programmers as needed, and the very significant price rises in the market. This thing wasn't tied to KPIs [Key Performance Indicators], it wasn't fair, they just couldn't deliver the services for us on it, so we had to go in and make some changes.

The procedures adopted for the renegotiation cycle was simple. Whilst the ongoing service delivery was continuing as specified in the initial contract, a team on ITNet's side was formed which negotiated the specifics of the changes with ESSO's Contracts and Materials department and the ESSO Supplier Managers:

> We recently went through a contract negotiation with ESSO which was a renegotiation of the original contract—a difficult time but it was mainly done out of the delivery area. So we were continuing to provide the same service but our salesmen negotiated with ESSO, the contracts negotiation department, to improve the contract that we had with ESSO because we were making a substantial loss at the beginning. (Account Manager, ITNet)

The ensuing review and renegotiation realigned, for example, the contract to the present and actual service demands and also uncovered a number of stip-ulated terms that were unenforceable in business terms:

> There was a review on how much they were paying for core services because we were doing a lot more core work than we were being paid for at the beginning [. . .] but also there just seemed to be a lot of unnecessary stuff in the contract which we were never going to try and do. It didn't seem to make business sense to do it. So that was taken out. (Applications Support Manager, ITNet)

Another example of the fundamental realignment was the change request procedure:

> In the beginning [. . .] we had to give them an estimate within X days, I think it was about 7–10 days of receiving the request to make sure we didn't just sit on it and doing nothing with it. And then once we'd given them an estimate we were then meant to complete that work, assuming it was authorized, within the number of days times two. And it was all rushed out in the end and if it didn't meet those target times we were penalized, and they didn't pay quite so much for the work. Or if we beat them we got paid more. But that was unworkable because we very rarely could get enough infor-mation back from the business lines. They are very good at filling out the CWCF form

to say they wanted something done, but it often wasn't very clear what was needed. And once you started looking at it and had queries on exactly what they meant, by the time you got an answer to those queries there was no way you were ever going to meet the delivery target of giving them an estimate in seven days. We did review the contract about a year or so ago. And one of the things we did agree to take out was these forms. (Application Support Manager, ITNet)

Once a section had been renegotiated and finalized, the changes were then taken on board straightaway by ITNet's account team and ESSO's operational managers. This meant direct implementation and operationalization of the new terms. At times, the renegotiation phase was a trying time and relations suffered, but it was an essential process for ITNet to be able to continue with the outsourcing venture.

The outcomes of the renegotiation were found to be a very positive experience for both parties. At least it ensured a mutual benefit from the deal for the future:

I think to a certain extent we've both ended up walking away from that saying hey yes we are happy with the result. They are not getting everything they wanted, and we are not getting everything that we wanted. (Supplier Manager A, ESSO)

Now we have actually got the contract negotiations through and we've got a better understanding of the contract. We are actually making a satisfactory return on sales. It's not as good as a lot of customers that we have, but it's satisfactory. (Customer Service Manager, ITNet)

ESSO weren't trying to make a lot of money out of the deal they had with us and perhaps risk bankrupting IT Net, the agreement we ought to all work to. So we both worked together to come up with a better and comfortable contract on both sides. ESSO win, we win, there's a win/win situation. (Application Support Manager, ITNet)

Since the renegotiation core service levels went to par, and then above. The high level of contentment with the resulting arrangements led both parties to formulate an additional informal partnership agreement in early 1997.

POST-CONTRACT RENEGOTIATION (1997–1999)

The successful outcome of the renegotiation phase and the changes in management structure and processes put the relationship back on track and generally facilitated a dramatic improvement in ITNet's performance. In the months following the renegotiation a number of changes and improvements were made in the relationship and the operations. In particular the following aspects received significant attention by both parties:

● Agreeing to an informal partnership;
● Development of a trusting and open relationship;
● Value-added benefits for both ITNet and ESSO;

- Continuing contract governance; and
- Upcoming challenges.

In line with developments in the relationship and the service performance improvements, both parties agreed to formulate an informal, yet novel partnership agreement. This agreement would spell out a number of principles about working together to achieve a win/win situation. It embodied however, no legal commitments whatsoever and in essence was primarily rhetorical:

It's an informal thing but it's been written by both sides. We have a partnership agreement with them rather than just do this only and only this [contract]. But I don't think it's actually officially recorded anywhere. It's one of those things that ITNet and ESSO do mention a few times, we are trying very hard to work with ESSO not against them. (Application Support Manager, ITNet)

The underlying objective of the informal partnership was one of fostering commitment that ITNet's managers would, in any event, inform ESSO, for example, of any planned changes that may affect the relationship. In a sense, it was an extended promise to cooperate and collaborate more closely:

I think it's just ITNet liked to build relationships with their main customers and relationship does mean that there might be a contract that we have to deliver, but it means we will try to be more helpful and open with our customers, so they know what we are doing. Really it comes with the ideas of if I want to change the team size or restructure the team in any way or move the team, or even equipment which is really in some ways outside of what the contract requires us to let ESSO know about, we will involve ESSO and make sure they are happy with what we are doing. [. . .] But ESSO also say that they are happy with this, they want to work in a partnership with ITNet. (Application Support Manager, ITNet)

The impact of this informal agreement was manifold. Respondents indicated that it basically opened up the relationship and resulted in a more cooperative and trusting relationship. ESSO's managers have consciously worked on fostering such an operating environment because they wanted to ensure (as agreed to in the partnership approach) that they were always aware of any difficulties or problems ITNet faced:

I trust them to speak to me if ever they need anything or want to tell me anything. I think I've more or less achieved, that they will phone if they've got the slightest need to talk. I also want to make sure it's a very informal relationship. That's developed quite nicely, they don't feel inhibited, they will call if they need to. (Operations Manager, ESSO)

If you haven't got the right people in the right positions then you are never going to get an open and trusting relationship to start off with. I think you've got to demonstrate as you work through it a willingness to be open. You've got to demonstrate a manner of handling things. It's taken us some time to get there with a number of our suppliers. (Supplier Manager B, ESSO)

What I did initially with ITNet was just go in, hear what their problems were and sort a few of the quick wins out, so that they start to trust you a little bit. And demonstrate also that I had credibility within our organization and that I could make things happen. So I just made sure that I chose those scenarios that I could fix quite quickly, deliver some real benefit to demonstrate that we were serious [. . .]. And that meant a lot to them. (Supplier Manager A, ESSO)

The impact of ESSO's efforts to foster such an environment improved relations considerably and also stirred a strong sense of loyalty on ITNet's side. The application support manager from ITNet explained the impact on their operations and their relations with ESSO as:

We do tend to feel that we are in a way ESSO employees. The team is very dedicated to ESSO as it should be. [. . .] In fact, we feel really very beholden to ESSO and we have a lot of loyalty to them. Which is perhaps unusual. [. . .] But we do all feel very committed to making sure that we do a very good job and fair job. (Application Support Manager, ITNet)

In fact, ITNet's strong loyalty eventually evolved to a state where operations with ESSO became pervaded by an almost ethical undertone and characterized by fairness:

We do not want to overcharge for the work we do, we want to deliver good work. And I think we do. We all have this. When the new [renegotiated] contract started off and people like team leaders were checking through estimates and so on we did get quite a few queries in the beginning in the early ones, whether these estimates really were valid or not. There was a bit of discomfort that perhaps we were trying to get too much money for doing a piece of work. (Delivery Manager, ITNet)

To maintain the positive behaviours and attitudes that have evolved between ITNet and ESSO, managers from both parties took a step further to develop a team spirit and unity. Senior managers from ESSO were particularly keen to initiate such a unity:

we encourage team building exercises, not at our sorts of level, but across the piece. One of the things that we hope to do this year, we did a little bit last year, was some cross team building kind of stuff, so that we can get the likes of CMG and ITNet and whatever playing basketball together or go-karting together or whatever. (Supplier Manager B, ESSO)

The reason being, clearly, that it was hoped that these activities would contribute to the successful operation of the account, by furthering openness and bridging any remaining culture gap. However, as so often noted before, one has to draw a line somewhere:

you've got to be careful it doesn't become too personal. You've got a line to draw there. At the end of the day you are for better or worse you are still representing the company that employs you. So you've got to remember that at all times. (Supplier Managers A, ESSO)

Nevertheless, the benefits of this new openness and closer cooperation were found by all involved to be of mutual advantage. For example, in ITNet's case the developments not only provided new opportunities for business with the IS department but also with other customers in ESSO:

They were asked recently to bid for a piece of work for another company, our Chemicals company, and they bid for that. To have it included as part of the main contract. (Supplier Manager A, ESSO)

Another benefit for ITNet was ESSO's IS group's willingness and openness to discuss with them their future developments and long-term strategy:

This company has shared, adapted and reinforced its vision. I think that's one of the things we found most important. We've got a meeting in a month's time where we will get all our suppliers around the same table in the same room and share what we want to do. We did it last year for the first time, and they were very uncomfortable with that. But they welcomed it this year and without question they are all coming at very senior levels. Yes it was important, it was worth doing. Ian will stand up and say this is where we are going, how can you help us, what are your problems, how can we help you. (Supplier Manager A, ESSO)

In a sense ESSO was giving ITNet an early opportunity to not only bid for new and upcoming business, but also outline possible innovations that would differentiate their bid to competitors:

So the open relationship is quite good from our point of view as it gives us an opportunity to know in advance what we are going to bid for and to do preparation for that. So the partnership thing is an excellent idea. And only by being open can we provide the best service to ESSO anyway and provide those opportunities and see what else we can do. There are other things that we can do that were mentioned in the past that they've looked into like printing services. We've put a bid in for printing services which we weren't successful in, but there are other areas that we are looking at doing. (Account Manager, ITNet)

On the other hand, the benefits for ESSO were those of access to advanced and leading-edge technology, expertise, and skill resources, enabling them to implement projects faster, support existing projects and operations, and generally help to move their business forward:

There have been occasions where I can say I've allowed the supplier to move us forward faster because it's their business because they understand it. And that's what we saw them as. And they moved us forward in certain areas that we potentially recognized or wanted to do. And it's achieved faster results especially when we were moving between the half and half situation when we had ESSO employees and contracts to perform FM outsourced type projects. And that's all great and that's the benefit. (Supplier Manager A, ESSO)

More importantly, ESSO began actively to seek value-added by offering a bonus award if ITNet could show they had implemented any new processes or innovations that directly added value or benefited ESSO's operations:

We try and implement ideas and innovation that is one of the things that IT NET division are looking at, at the moment. And we are being rewarded for coming up with ideas and things. So it's something we have to report on monthly on our new innovations and ideas we've put forward to ESSO. It's value added is the term we use in the company. (Customer Service Manager, ITNet)

The clearest signs that the relationship and hence operations had improved to a stage of adding value became apparent in early 1997. By this time ITNet had adapted to ESSO's management procedures and requirements and the relationship was working well. Service levels were in line with ESSO's demands and in most cases above stipulated service levels. ITNet's achievements above requirements in return were duly rewarded with substantial bonus payments and additional rewards:

If they manage to achieve that bonus to be awarded for a certain number of consecutive months in one period there are bonuses as well that are added. It's quite an incentive to be given that bonus for consecutive months. And just recently I think they went for 7 consecutive months where the batch bonus was paid which was quite an achievement. Because that's a long time to go, a whole month without anything happening. (Operations Manager, ESSO)

ITNet's customer perception rating also reflected the overall improvement of the services and the relationship. By mid-1997 they were achieving a customer rating of 4.5 on a scale of 6:

we are currently on 4.5 which is really good. It's higher than the average of ITNet so the perception has gone up. (Customer Service Manager, ITNet)

Independent of the partnership agreement and the successful development of a well-working relationship, the contract continued to define the governance structure in 1998. Although the contract no longer got referred to as regularly as it did during 1994–6, it still defined the foundation of relations and outsourcing operations. In fact, the contract received, by nature of the agreement, a yearly renegotiation attention on price rates and services. In addition, on a monthly basis, parties would refer to it to clarify payments and bonuses:

I only refer to the contract really once a month when I'm preparing for my stewardship meeting with ITNet. And that's mainly because there are certain clauses where they can earn bonuses within the contract and so I analyse the performance during the month and then refer to the contract to understand exactly how that bonus can be awarded. (Operations Manager, ESSO)

The parts of the contract which we refer to are—for example we get bonuses every month and they are defined in the contract. There are certain things defined in the contract where we refer back regularly [. . .] (Customer Service Manager, ITNet)

The contract was also regularly used to clarify particular terms and payments for change requests, i.e. CWCFs:

There are certain things defined in the contract where we refer back regularly, e.g. whether work is a standard piece or negotiable. [. . .] the main area of contention is: 'what is call work—which ESSO pay a flat fee for—and what is CWCF work which is their change requests?' And where do you draw the line? (Delivery Manager, ITNet)

Another regular use of the contract was to check the criticality level of services:

Occasionally if there is a problem and I feel that maybe ITNet should have responded quicker, more readily than they did then I will refer to the contract just to remind myself of the criticality of systems. Because they've been classified within the contract. (Operations Manager, ESSO)

Finally, the contract was used to seek clarification as and when escalated disputes needed resolving: 'Only if we have occasional disputes as to whether I need to give them extra money or not, then I'll seek clarification from the contract to remind myself as to whether that's applicable or not' (Operations Manager, ESSO). The contract by 1998 had become very much an operational tool. It would remain to be used throughout the venture and was clearly integrated in operations and management processes not in a negative way, but as the underlying support structure and reference basis. Interactions and the relationship were often said, and were thus perceived, to operate in the 'spirit of the contract'.

In 1998, ESSO-ITNet were confronted with a major business extension to existing services that was likely to affect significantly the relationship and the existing pricing and service arrangements. ESSO was faced with ensuring that all its systems would be Year 2000 compliant by the millennium. This entailed placing a range of additional services with ITNet, positively boosting the relations and profit margins of ITNet:

The biggest thing we've got going at the moment (1997/8) is our year 2000 programme and we've got 3 or 4 ESSO people actually involved in that, running it. (Supplier Manager A, ESSO)

Now clearly where we are in this market now, which is exploding to a certain extent with the year 2000 problems, is we have to try to minimize our exposure to huge rate increases. And we've got our contracts that run through to past the year 2000. [However] we recognize that our suppliers are going to have a problem. [. . .] we have to recognize what's happening in the industry. If the industry suddenly demands a 15–20% per year increase because of the year 2000 and legacy system programmers that we are using to support our legacy systems, and we then can't expect to see a year on year reduction on the small base that we've got in our costs. We are going to have to expect to see some growth in our charges. (Supplier Manager A, ESSO)

A related issue here was the planned switchover from the mainframe and legacy system services to a client/server, i.e. Sapphire III system over the following three years. Although the legacy system would eventually be phased it out, it had to operate beyond the year 2000.

Of course, the phasing out of ITNet's current services eventually would imply losing its contract with ESSO. ITNet in turn was facing considerable pressure in identifying new areas of potential business that they could offer to ESSO and which would allow them to continue doing business with ESSO:

We are providing mainframe services, and they will not be needed extensively in the future so the company ITNet needs to prolong their contract with ESSO by providing other services. Now currently we are not being considered for client server work but we've got to look towards getting involved somehow into the future with ESSO. [. . .] So as the work dips, as systems are being decommissioned, I've got to keep our level of return on sales high by looking at other areas to develop and only by keeping the customer perception up can I do that or will they look at us to provide that service. Because there's quite a lot of competition within ESSO with suppliers. There is CMG and ISS are the two main ones [. . .]. But there is competition for work like the year 2000 work. We've got to remain competitive, and obviously by being quite cheap. And by providing the service off site that's one of the ways we can stay cheap. (Delivery Manager, ITNet)

For the 1998 and 1999 period these two concerns would pervade and influence operations. Nevertheless, the developments up to this point had seen considerable strengthening of the relationship through the informal agreement to a partnership, that entailed openness, closer cooperation, collaboration, and trust. The improvements presented benefits and advantages beyond the contract for both parties. However, throughout the developments and changes the contract continued to define the governance structure.

CONTRACT END AND UPCOMING CHALLENGES (1999–2001)

By early 1999, ITNet had merely one more year before the contract would reach its agreed end. The timing was very problematic as ESSO was under pressure to ensure ITNet would continue with making them Y2K ready. ESSO's managers took an early decision in 1999 to recontract ITNet for an additional three-year period. ITNet's success in turning around the account and performing up to service specifications had seen all parties involved become increasingly happy with the existing contractual, relationship, and operational arrangements. In fact, ITNet's account team had become very dedicated to ESSO's needs. The supplier managers summed up the key reasons for extending the contract:

[A] It's quite a big risk actually because you are in danger, if you go into a tender process right at the end of 1999, when nobody knew what the outcome of the year 2000 would be. Trying to keep their people motivated could be tricky. (Supplier Manager B, ESSO)

[B] We were fairly comfortable with the rate we had on the contract, the structure of the contract, ITNet's performance, as we've said. It would

have taken us a lot of effort to have beaten it with another supplier—
we felt anyway. (Supplier Manager A, ESSO)

[C] It was good for us because I think it was the right time to do it. I think
it was good for ITNet because you've got 30–40 people working on our
work. It wasn't at the forefront of their mind that this contract is going
to be up for renewal in 3 months' time are we going to get this business,
am I going to have a job. (Supplier B, ESSO)

A crucial task throughout was maintaining a high degree of ongoing
commitment by ITNet's staff; so much so that ESSO often tried to increase
commitment by generating loyalty and a sense of team spirit. Rewards for major
achievements and extra-curricular activities were found a particularly useful
option for generating and maintaining close ties. In fact, in late 1998 when
ITNet achieved a record one year service delivery without falling below agreed
performance levels, ESSO awarded ITNet publicly as its premier supplier:

And in 1998 we award them our premier supplier award—and in fact last year because
there was no outstanding contender for it, no one had done something really special,
all been very very good, all of our suppliers, but you couldn't say that one is excep-
tionally good, and head and shoulders above the others. So we chose not to award it.
So the last people that won it were ITNet. (Supplier Manager B, ESSO)

By mid-1999 loyalty had very much become a vital issue for ESSO as the
amount of business they did and would do with ITNet in the future was relatively small in comparison to their other clients and would further decrease,
yet ESSO expected top-rate experts that would normally work on ITNet's larger
accounts. In addition, ESSO had always put high security and cultural adaptability demands on ITNet's team, introducing additional pressures and
demands on ITNet. In turn, they were pushed to maintain the closeness and
loyalty of key individuals:

The A team if you like, and still keep their management focus on us, things like that.
The only thing we felt we had that we could use was our name. A very strong name in
the industry. And that's one of the reasons why we devised the premier supplier award
because we were able to give them a nice piece of glass which they put in their foyer
which had the name ESSO on it and them as premier IS supplier [. . .]. It's one way of
us saying thank you back to them for the efforts they put into turning the contract
around. (Supplier Manager A, ESSO)

Another example of how they maintained their closeness with ITNet's account
team, was by their caring approach to people's safety:

Small things but fairly significant, the ITNet people spent a lot of time on the road
travelling backwards and forwards between [various offices and refineries]. One of the
things we recognized was that it might be useful to get them some driving type of tui-
tion. So we got the police along to tell them about safe driving. (Supplier Manager A,
ESSO)

Having successfully maintained the relationship at this level of closeness ensured that the Y2K transition was mastered without any significant problems. More importantly, it also ensured that the upcoming challenges of the STRIPES global systems standardization project (initiated in 1997 and piloted in Switzerland)—to be rolled out and running by late 2000 in the UK—remained on target, and that the current merger of EXXON and Mobil's IT services could be supported.

The STRIPES project would eventually replace, with global standardized applications, the existing legacy services ITNet was supporting. Yet for the time being ITNet was in the best place to develop and integrate it with the existing systems:

We've made some strategic changes in as much as we have a strategic direction to replace all the company's financial and accounting systems with one system for the world that's being rolled out inexorably, which is SAP R3. We are calling that the STRIPES programme. It's basically re-engineering the business as well as putting the system in. So it's not just purely rolling out an R3 application, it's taking the business and building the business. (Supplier Manager B, ESSO)

The integration of such a far-reaching system would require extensive knowledge of existing systems and processes supported. ITNet's extensive knowledge of ESSO IT systems in turn put them in a good place to undertake some of the STRIPES work for ESSO. In parallel, ESSO faced an additional challenge of the merger between EXXON, its US mother firm, and Mobil in late 1999. The resulting demands on integrating Mobil's IT services in the UK presented a number of challenges, especially as Mobil had most of its IT infrastructure still in-house:

[Mobil are mainly into] body shop contracting. It's not so much odd, if you look at the organization across Europe it looks to me like 20–30% of their applications people are body shop contractors. Just picked out of the market, you've got the necessary skills so we'd like you to come in on a 6 month to a 1 year contract. So they haven't looked at the market as we did and developed a strategy of how they are going to meet these shortfalls. (Supplier Manager A, ESSO)

For ESSO and ITNet this posed the challenge of not only integrating systems, but also working with another IT service group. The adjustments to the differences in IT service operations, but also the necessary global standardization of structures, operational process and hence systems would pose considerable challenges for all parties involved:

What's going to happen in the future? I don't think we know yet. I don't think we actually have a strategy [due to the merger] which we can all buy into as to which way we are going. So there's some uncertainty there as to what we are going to be doing. And this is going to be the test as to what happens over the next year. Over the next year we are going to be building something which says this is what we are going to be doing. (Supplier Manager A, ESSO)

Of course, for ITNet, the merger may also identify potentially new avenues for business and further contracts with an enlarged IT services group. In turn, efforts on ITNet's side were made to keep experienced ESSO account managers in place that could identify business opportunities during the ongoing integration of Mobil in 2000. It inherently also ensured that the currently effective relationship would continue further into the contract's life.

CASE ANALYSIS AND DISCUSSION

The ESSO case provides a detailed illustration of how more traditional cost-focused, contract-based, adversarial relationships can undermine—and open to unexpected risks—the very performance requirements they are supposedly designed to pursue. The case is also interesting for the lessons it provides on how to develop and flex relationship arrangements, in the light of the inevitable, unanticipated difficulties experienced even in selective outsourcing. Finally, it underlines the importance of active relationship management, staffing properly, and allowing the client company to lead the deal in the pursuit of winning performance. Using the main constructs of our two conceptual models, the following presents a more detailed analysis of ESSO's selective outsourcing venture with ITNet.

ESSO-ITNet: A Risk Perspective

Esso sought to mitigate risks inherent in using the IT services market by going down a selective, multi-supplier route, each on three- to five-year contracts. The case only focuses on one of these. The strategic intent was to pick the most appropriate supplier for each discrete activity, to redirect internal effort into management and business focus, and to contain costs while driving up service levels where possible. In principle, in a highly competitive, changing business context, this represented fairly robust risk mitigation tactics, especially as ESSO was careful to select 'commodity'-type IT activities as outsourcing candidates. From a supplier perspective, ESSO represented a prestige account for an aspiring company, and the work fitted its capability profile, though the degree of cultural fit was overestimated, causing some subsequent difficulties.

These factors led to ESSO driving a very hard bargain which, partly due to genuine miscalculations and partly due to the desire for the account, saw ITNet accept a deal from which it was basically very difficult to extract a reasonable margin. This situation was exacerbated by the tightness and detail of the contract, and the ESSO culture of controlling suppliers very closely according to a formal contract. While much of this appears good practice, the irony in this case was that this combination of factors actually contributed to heightening the risk of ITNet *not* delivering required performance. The contract and style of management gave little leeway for ITNet to find additional work it could charge for. Ironically, the problems stemmed not from incomplete contracting lackadaisically enforced, but from complete contracting, and strong policing of the original agreement. Clearly, risk mitigation here is about finding the right balance in specific contexts and circumstances.

However, ESSO initially failed to build the requisite relationship-oriented in-house capabilities and skills that, in their practice, would have helped to mitigate these risks. The strong fixed-cost element in the contract also created difficulties in the first few years, and, over time power asymmetries moved so much in favour of ESSO, that ITNet's final resort of terminating the agreement seemed, at one point, a likely outcome. From a risk perspective, this 'Winner's Curse' (see Chapter 9) could only be dealt with by building a relationship management capability within ESSO—in particular informed buying, contract facilitation, and monitoring (see Chapter 1)—to help flex and transition the contract and relationship to more productive ways of working. In identifying this selective outsourcing as a traditional, contract-led, commodity-based arrangement, and not thinking of it in terms of a relationship (unlike Xerox in Chapter 3, and Inland Revenue in Chapter 7), ESSO went too much the other way, clearly greatly underestimating the importance of the relationship dimensions for achieving required performance.

Strategic Intent

Although ESSO has a high degree of autonomy from its parent company EXXON, in the case of outsourcing it was given little choice—a 'voluntary necessity' indeed. In line with EXXON's global policy of decreasing costs and improving operational efficiency, the IS department, which was not widely perceived as part of the organization's core competence, had few options outside outsourcing when it was confronted with dramatic staff reductions. Pressure to provide ongoing reductions in costs and headcount left little room for developing internal capabilities and competencies. Outsourcing, in turn, had to provide a two-headed solution. On the one, it had to ensure continuing reductions in costs. One respondent explained:

The Chairman of our company is looking to CMG to deliver savings. [. . .] What he wants to see is a 5% reduction year on year. What we have to do, because as a department we have been actively looking every year to drive down our costs by between 5–10% for the last 7 years. (Supplier Manager, ESSO)

On the other, it needed to present new innovations and get access to resources and expertise to improve and ensure operational efficiency. In the long term it becomes questionable to what extent the IS department would be able to continue with the cost reduction drive and still guarantee high service levels to its customers—a similar dilemma found at Xerox-EDS, for example. At ESSO, one result was to pass this dilemma to the supplier, and expect a deepening of 'reciprocity', without ESSO actually contributing to that deepening. The result was a false 'efficiency' in the costs of running the relationship dimension, because the poor relationship arrangements fed into a deepening of service problems.

Contract

The contract ESSO had negotiated was strongly weighted in their favour, giving ITNet few possibilities for recovering their bidding expenses and negotiation costs. In fact, as negotiated, ITNet found the contract would only cost money to operationalize. The learning point from the subsequent experience? Allow the supplier a reasonable profit, by contract. It is interesting to speculate how ITNet could make such erroneous cost calculations when competitively bidding for ESSO's business. Managers at ESSO suggested that ITNet had made assumptions at the outset about ESSO's high resource base costs and operational inefficiencies and was unprepared to find that ESSO for the past years had been on a drive to minimize costs and downsize operations where possible. However, there is another plausible explanation, which in other cases such as BAe-CSC (Chapter 4) is also evident, that ITNet needed to contract with ESSO to gain credibility and references by working with a Blue Chip organization. To ITNet, essentially a small niche supplier, such a contract can hold widespread benefits when bidding elsewhere.

Nevertheless, the consequence of the miscalculations cost ITNet dearly in the initial one and half years; they were left with no option but to ask for an early renegotiation. At this stage, ESSO could also have responded by emphasizing that ITNet needed to honour the contract or pay a termination fee, but they were not interested in going down a track of high publicity, especially in light of other negative publicity at that time, for example from the *EXXON Valdez* disaster, and instead decided to renegotiate the contract. This renegotiation proved to be beneficial for both parties, as services improved considerably and ITNet began to make a return. It is clear that a balance needs to be struck here between service levels and costs, and ensuring the vendor makes a return. In a one-sided situation, the vendor has to try to cover its costs in any way possible, which is likely to affect services adversely. In addition, in situations of competitive bids the client has to ensure that the vendor is fully aware of the exact requirements, and the client might have to spend more time on evaluating the bid proposals to avoid having to invest in costly renegotiations after such a short period of operation. A further point is the degree to which even in very contract-focused deals, the non-promissory accompaniments to the contract, and their management, must play an integral part.

Structure

Early on it became evident that neither party had really given the management infrastructure much attention prior to contracting. Ostensibly, this was because the size and complexity of the deal was not great, and so it was assumed that the structural issues would not be significant either. Furthermore, ESSO felt it could rely on an inherited structure that had worked with its previous contractor CMG for the previous seven years. They failed to anticipate that this structure could not be migrated to their venture with ITNet. The early structure of having a single manager responsible for day-to-day operations and relationship development was impractical, especially in face of the ongoing service delivery problems ITNet ran into, and ESSO's cultural demands on managers to take ownership and resolve any problems. In addition, ESSO's operation manager seemingly lacked the competencies to foster a relationship, and instead relied all too heavily on the contract. As research has shown, managers in charge of an account, especially when also responsible for developing the relationship side, need three critical skill sets: technical, business, and interpersonal skills (Feeny and Willcocks 1998).

However, in ESSO's case, too much was expected from a single manager, especially in this situation where a new supplier took over with no previous dealings with ESSO and little experience of working with large private sector organizations. Selective outsourcing has not really been much associated with relationship management, due to the contractual clarity typical of such arrangements. However, a clear learning point for other deals is that, in ESSO's case relationship management had to be handled much more actively. ESSO's response in implementing two 'relationships', i.e. Supplier Managers was a decisive step to saving and turning around the venture. Two respondents noted, in reference to the structural changes:

In fact at the very beginning I don't think Linda and Mac were in place. I know Linda worked very hard to build up the relationship. That was probably the turning point actually when we decided that vendor management was a critical aspect of the thing. (Operations Manager, ESSO)

And then a new team was put in and that involved Linda Smith in order to help the relationship grow and that was a very distinct change of direction from ESSO. They saw that we couldn't provide the service at that level because we weren't getting any help from ESSO and there was a one-way argument really. By changing the management team, and it was quite a big sweeping change of the management team [. . .]. And since then the contract has gone from strength to strength and the relationship has gone from strength to strength. (Customer Service Manager, ITNet)

For ITNet these changes meant improved cooperation and support to adjust to ESSO's idiosyncrasies. In fact, the cultural and operational differences between the two parties had presented quite a number of difficulties for ITNet. This underlines that switching contractors to do the same work is often much more problematic than is assumed, and has all manner of implications for the 'relational diligence' issues we spell out in our conceptual framework (see Figure 2.3).

Interactions

ESSO had spent considerable efforts on specifying at great lengths its service requirements. In turn, the high degree of contractual clarity inferred few, if any, misunderstandings on what ITNet's service delivery requirements were. Indeed, the specificity even revealed the criticality of every system and hence service. This explicitness also applied to the price and payment arrangements. Moreover, to ensure these remained as accurate as possible throughout the contract's life, ESSO incorporated an annual alignment clause.

Surprisingly, looking at 'exchange content', service levels plummeted in the transition period and remained below target for a number of months. In retrospect, and looking at the other cases in this book, service levels invariably seem to dip during the transition period as the vendor adjusts to the specifics of the systems and applications. One ITNet respondent explained in reference to the initial adjustment period:

The specific stage when the trust went down is when we started and it's extremely hard to provide a service whatever the level of personnel is when you don't understand the systems. Obviously systems are very different within different companies. Technology is the same and ideas of how systems work are the same but the actual specifics are very different. So when you come in cold and start to provide the service from nothing then the user will see a dip in their service from the previous supplier to you. (Customer Service Manager, ITNet)

However, since ITNet had made a number of assumptions about ESSO's operations and requirements, it is also plausible to assume that they were not fully aware of the systems and applications, and very likely lacked some of the competencies and resources to actually deliver ESSO's service levels. ITNet's miscalculations on cost/service seemed to corroborate this fact as did the lengthy period for the actual consolidation and eventual transfer of the systems to ITNet's headquarters in Birmingham.

Matters were made more difficult by ESSO's managers' initial strict adherence to the contract and the restricted cooperative processes, ESSO's strong control, security and safety culture, and problems with the management infrastructure. Together they presented a combination of factors that gave ITNet little opportunity to ask for some support and guidance in operationalizing the service requirements. In practice, interaction was formal, and infrequent, communication between managers was one-sided, and eventually the relationship dimension was proving counter-productive. This interaction dimension received an immense amount of attention subsequently and proved to be an important support to both realigning the contract and then its subsequent delivery.

Behavioural Dimensions

The case seemed to highlight a relational development from a strict contract- and measurement-controlled environment to a more trusting and cooperative environment. It was in the nature of the way EXXON/ESSO operated that they generally endeavoured to control closely operations with a supplier. One respondent explained, referring to ESSO's culture for managing suppliers:

We do have a difficulty with our lords and masters, or shareholder in the States and the people that are actually part of this organization, because we are now the European operations or regional operations department [. . .]. I guess their view very much is real men don't get involved in these sorts of vendor management type issues. As far as they are concerned a supplier is a supplier, and we've gone out and asked them to provide X and if they don't provide X then we are going to hit them over the head until they do provide X. (Supplier Manager, ESSO)

This was clearly influenced by their previous extensive experiences with procurement arrangements where they adopted a power wielding approach. However, in this situation the control approach failed and led to the breakdown of relations. What ITNet needed, initially, was some guidance in understanding ESSO's operations. It was important that parties worked together to clarify the requirements and idiosyncrasies of ESSO; but this was clearly missing. The result was evident in the amount of conflict, which led to the eventual loggerhead of the account managers. Effects were disastrous for both parties. Service levels were low and ITNet was losing money.

Improvements came with the introduction of the Supplier Manager role, and a person who seemed to be interested in helping and cooperating to ensure both parties mutually benefited from the venture. In fact, ESSO's managers then quite deliberately focused their initial efforts on resolving ITNet's problems with ESSO and began to rebuild trust. Cooperation between the parties was to become fundamental and it is plausible that only in this kind of context did ITNet gather sufficient momentum to actually approach ESSO to request an early contract renegotiation. The developments following the renegotiation were remarkable considering that the relations had broken down, yet literally eighteen months later parties had informally agreed to a partnership, and managers from all levels were engaged in team building exercises. The environment fostered by cooperation and working through problem issues was one of greater openness and trust, yet the contract was still governing the relationship. Throughout these developments what seemed to matter was ESSO's realization that both parties had to mutually benefit from the venture and hence their willingness to change the contract and replace people on their side to foster and maintain the relationship. The impact of such fairness stirred a loyalty in ITNet's managers to ESSO, that subsequently saw them achieve in consecutive months service delivery beyond stipulated terms.

Efficiency and Outcomes

The key objective underlying ESSO's outsourcing initiative was operational efficiency, and hence cost reduction, balanced with maintaining existing service levels. From the beginning, ESSO had been able to achieve its annual cost savings through the continuous phasing-out of the legacy systems and applications. This was contractually anchored, and assured ESSO an annual cost reduction of 5–10 per cent. Furthermore, ESSO made sure this would continue for the lifetime of the contract by integrating an annual renegotiation process on price rates and services.

However, the lack of a reciprocal profit for ITNet contributed to deficient services levels. Only through early renegotiation in 1996 was this alleviated, which of course introduced considerable extra costs for both parties and raises questions over whether ESSO truly made a cost saving that year. Nevertheless, the renegotiation process assured that both parties made a return on the venture and saved ITNet from having to terminate the contract which undoubtedly would have been disastrous in terms of costs for both parties. As a matter of fact, the renegotiation helped improve relations to such an extent that other value-added benefits have emerged since from the venture not only for ESSO, but also for ITNet, and in the long-term may even improve ESSO's operational efficiency.

Finally, the case illustrates the false economy of seemingly reducing IT costs by leaving behind a much reduced and inappropriately skilled in-house management capability. Only with the outlay on populating this capability with high performers, along the lines of the Feeny and Willcocks (1998) model, did the contract and relationship dimension begin to come right and feed through into the performance levels required in the original strategic intent.

CONCLUSION

The case illustrated ESSO's IS department's initiative to deliver on the mandated request by its parent organization EXXON to improve its operational efficiency, including cost cutting, and downsizing the number of staff. Selective IT outsourcing did contribute to meeting these requests, although making outsourcing work in favour of ESSO's operation was shown to be problematic at times, especially in its dealings with ITNet. The ITNet venture highlighted the difficulties of a competitive takeover bid and the resulting complexities the vendor faces when picking up services provision where a long-term deal left off. It also emphasized the lack of attention both parties had given to the post-contract management structure, and the resulting breakdown of the relationship. However, the greatest impact on the relationship were ITNet's false assumptions and hence erroneous calculations concerning ESSO's operations, which forced them to request an early renegotiation.

The ESSO-ITNet experience illustrates that even where there is a high level of contractual clarity outlining explicitly the supplier's responsibilities, relationship management remains absolutely critical to ensure successful service delivery. Only through active relationship management and ensuring both parties mutually benefit from the relationship was ESSO-ITNet able to save and turn around this relationship—to a point where parties found value in agreeing informally to what they regarded as a 'partnership' approach. The ESSO-ITNet experience demonstrates that even in small-scale, selective, commodity-based outsourcing contracts, there is a significant relationship advantage to be had, if only the participants can perceive this in time.

REFERENCES

Boarman, C. (1997). 'Blow Recognised for Job Well Done'. *ComputerWeekly* (10 April), 7.
Essoview (1994). 'Why ESSO Has a Code of Conduct—Interview with Keith Taylor'. *ESSOVIEW*, 19: 1–3.
EXXON Corporation (1996). *Annual Review*. EXXON USA.
—— (1998). *Annual Review*. EXXON USA.
Feeny, D., and Willcocks, L. (1998). 'Core IS Capabilities for Exploiting IT'. *Sloan Management Review*, 39/3: 1–26.
ITNet Presentation (1997). 'Tim Fowler—Company Overview Presentation'. ITNet, Laburnum Road, Birmingham.
Kern, T., Willcocks, L., and van Heck, E. (2000). 'Relational Trauma: Evidence of Winner's Curse in IT Outsourcing. Erasmus Universiteit Working Paper, Erasmus, Rotterdam.
MacDonald, J. (1997). *Global Oil Company Profiles*. Financial Times Energy Publishing, London, 362.
Martin, J. (1991). 'Petroleum: EXXON Corporation', in Adele Hast (ed.), *International Directory of Company Histories Volume IV*, St James Press, Chicago, 426–30.
Newsline (1996). 'Saving while we're Spending'. *ESSO Magazine* (May), 16.
PetroCompanies (1997). *EXXON*. PetroCompanies, London, 141–8.
Phillips, S. (1998). 'ITNet Seeks Listing to Fund Expansion'. *ComputerWeekly* (30 April), 4.
Price, C. (1998). 'Cadbury's: ITNet Seeks UK listing'. *Financial Times*, Industries, 27 April.
Standard Oil Company (1957). 'The Jersey Standard Story', Report.
Wall, B. H. (1988). *Growth in a Changing Environment: A History of Standard Oil Company (New Jersey) 1950–1970 and Exxon 1972–1975*. McGraw Hill Book Co., New York, 1020.

7

Strategic Partnering in Public Sector IT Outsourcing

INTRODUCTION

In line with the UK government's policy changes in the early 1990s, the Inland Revenue (IR) was pushed to market test the cost-efficiency of 25 per cent of all of its activities, including Information Technology (IT) services, against external suppliers' prices. The outcome, as apparent from this case study, revealed the private sector to be more efficient in operating IT services, as a result of which the Revenue decided by mid-1992 to outsource its whole IT operations. Due to the size, time frame, and uncertainty surrounding the proposed venture, the Inland Revenue was not just looking to procure services and suppliers, but instead was seeking a 'strategic partner'.

In November 1993 the UK government awarded a £1 billion, ten-year, contract to the US-based supplier EDS. At the time this represented the biggest outsourcing contract ever awarded in Europe. The extent of the deal that the IR was to undertake was previously thought unimaginable, particularly in the public sector: 'In addition to being a daring, innovative, dangerous exercise it could also be labelled huge, unmanageable, overwhelming or influential' (Senior IT Executive). The estimated cost savings from handing over IT assets, staff, and management activities were calculated at £225 million over the life of the contract. In addition, EDS was to make a one-off payment of £70 million for the IR's technology assets. Both parties also agreed that IT staff would be transferred in two tranches, rather than one: 1,200 computer operations staff at the commencement of the contract in mid-1994, and the remaining 800 key development people eighteen months later in early 1996. This was part of IR's risk mitigation plan, giving it the opportunity to assess whether the venture was achieving the expected targets.

The outsourcing deal was signed in light of a complex challenge. During contract negotiations the UK government had announced the biggest tax reform in fifty years that entailed the introduction of a £200 million computerized self-assessment tax scheme that had to be up and running by April 1997 (Collins 1995). Irrespective of this challenge the venture went ahead, yet this shift in government policy was to introduce a number of pressures on the venture right from the beginning, which included putting EDS's commercial reputation at stake.

The case details events and developments across the 1992–2000 period and provides further insights into large-scale outsourcing in the specific context of the UK public sector.

RELATIONSHIP LESSONS

The IR case provides us with an opportunity to gain an in-depth understanding of public sector IT outsourcing practice, and the degree to which there are common practices that can be applied across 'total' outsourcing deals. The decision to outsource was based on the UK government's view that privatization in light of market opportunities is likely to offer superior cost savings, services, and benefits. Yet outsourcing in the public sector tends to be confronted by substantial uncertainties due to the frequent regulatory changes that emerge with new legislation. The resulting demand for flexibility in service, contract, and relationship management from both parties put high pressures on IT capabilities and resources.

Moreover, in an environment of strict accountability and audibility, strategic partnering runs into issues of 'public good' and the need for as much transparency as possible. Constant accountability created even more need for detailed planning of service requirements, operational processes, and management structures. Up-front thinking also entailed careful risk mapping of those factors that could possibly impede the development of strategic partnering. Actually, risk mitigation and management became an integral part of relationship as with the introduction of new pieces of work a number of risks arose and reoccurred. Introducing a partnership manager early on ensured the relationship operated in a cooperative and communicative style even when problems arose due to particular risk issues.

The case reveals the fundamental importance of the relationship dimensions for keeping outsourcing performance tied to a complex combination of base work and constantly shifting demands in a volatile legislative and political context.

CONTEXT AND OVERVIEW

The 1980s saw the United Kingdom (UK) spiral into a deep economic recession, which unavoidably and substantially minimized the tax intake in the following years. In response, the Conservative government initiated extensive public sector reforms in an effort to ensure that taxpayer money was spent just as efficiently and for similar quality work as in the private sector. Civil service reforms saw significant staff cuts from 732,000 in 1979 to 594,000 by 1986 (Drewry and Butcher 1988). These reforms continued far into the 1990s, subsequently leading to a range of market-testing initiatives including the Inland Revenue's total IT outsourcing venture.

United Kingdom Public Sector and The Inland Revenue (IR)

In early 1991 the government issued the White Paper *Competing for Quality* that formalized its intention to bring private sector disciplines to bear on public services operations, in an effort to ensure accountability and operational efficiency. The quest to improve the 'value for money' of the services called for extensive reviews of departments and agencies. In common with all central government departments and agencies, the Revenue similarly had to test the cost efficiency of 25 per cent of all of its activities against external suppliers' prices. The result of the government's revised public management approach ensured that all government functions were systematically reviewed and categorized as follows:

- inappropriate for government—should be abolished or privatized;
- inappropriate for government delivery—should be contracted out to private sector organizations;
- appropriate for government—decentralize to specific or local government. Subject to private sector disciplines, especially competition.

In cases where services stayed in the hands of a public agency or department, it became mandatory to continuously market test these against private sector practices, to establish whether in-house services remained competitive. An amendment to the *Competing for Quality* (CfQ) programme in 1992 enshrined these latter revised principles of market competition. Between April 1992 and March 1995 public sector agencies and departments reviewed £2.6 billion pounds worth of activities, resulting in numerous activities being market placed (British Council 1997). The estimated annual saving of these changes were £544 million, with a reduction in civil servant staff numbers of approximately 20,000 (British Council 1997). In all, 50 per cent of those services market tested were eventually awarded to the private sector. According to a special report by the government, 937 activities in total had been reviewed by various government institutions. The outcome, according to the British Council (1997), resulted in the changes shown in Table 7.1.

Table 7.1. *UK 'Competing for Quality' review outcome*

Outcome of review	No. of changes
Abolition	47
Privatization	4
Contracting out (no in-house bid)	241
Market tested: outside suppliers	153
Market tested: in-house team	345
Internal restructuring	147

The general focus of these changes embodied an operational efficiency drive: 'There is a point beyond which you cannot make changes as the private sector can in order to be as efficient and effective and deliver value for money as the private sector equivalent' (Senior Executive, IR). In addition to the CfQ programme, departments and agencies had to introduce a set of *Efficiency Plans*. In these plans, organizations had to show how they intended to deliver key outputs within tight running costs over a three-year period. The British Council's (1997) briefing elaborated the following as the main elements of these plans:

- Total cash spending on running departments imply a cut in real terms of 10 per cent. The working assumption is that any pay and price increases will be offset by efficiency savings.
- Continued delegation of responsibility for budgets and attribution of costs to specific cost programmes is required in these plans. Managers are responsible for planning the work, controlling administrative and financial resources, and achieving savings.
- There is a push for greater use of information technology.
- Ongoing reviews of working practices, paperwork, procurement, accommodation, service delivery processes, office services, printing, and reprographic services.

In general, the CfQ initiative highlighted that the private sector offered better value for the taxpayer's money than the IR department could achieve. As a result, in May 1994 the Inland Revenue decided, following a market test, to contract out its information technology office. In June 1995 the Information Technology Services Agency contracted out its service delivery, and many more departments and agencies were to follow. What were perceived as positive results led the central government to open up an additional £1 billion of government work to competition in 1996. In parallel, the government had also launched similar privatization programmes, such as the 'Private Finance Initiative' for local councils and other public sector institutions.

Inland Revenue's Information Technology Office

The Inland Revenue's information technology office (ITO) over the years had earned itself a sound reputation for providing IT services and for successfully developing and running large-scale computer systems. Its experience of managing technology services involved extensive IT procurement experiences to compensate for lacking capabilities:

We've always operated buyer–supplier contracts in the past of a fairly standard nature. We buy up big bits of IT and if they don't work we are giving the supplier a hard time. (Senior Customer Service Manager, IR)

The easy way of managing this contract is the way we've always managed our contracts, and that is in terms of ticking, stamping and not varying from a fairly hard-nosed approach to our suppliers. (Senior Partnership Executive, IR)

The economic recession and the resulting policy changes in the 1980s seriously diminished the level of access the ITO had to IT funds. The responsibility for budgetary requirements and monies were generally handled by the Treasury department, which was forced by government policy to cut costs where possible:

Within the public sector the whole question of funding for an IT business is arguably more difficult than the private sector. One is constrained by the limits that are set by the Treasury, to begin with, and those limits can be affected as they are today very much by the government's view of the importance of constraining public spending. (Senior IT Executive)

Over time the lack of funds resulted in outdated computer systems, compatibility problems, and system breakdowns:

We couldn't understand how we would be able to keep abreast of the fast moving world of technology if we stayed with our in-house division, which I think had been seen publicly as reasonably successful. The problem was that it was an ICL VME shop, people had got a lot of credibility and high reputation coming out of the COP project, but in fact we weren't keeping up with developments as fast as we should [. . .] And at the same time the government was saying all the time that it wasn't prepared to allow the civil service to invest any money to buy CASE tools or whatever it might be that you needed. (Senior IT Director)

Another example of the state of technology at the IR was reported by Leslie Yazel (1994) in *Computing*. He noted, 'the current electronic mail system the Revenue uses does not allow on-screen messages; instead messages have to be printed out and treated in the same way as any other piece of post,' which raises serious questions about its actual usefulness.

Consequently, any service or process change at the Revenue would most likely be hindered by the lack of sophistication of its ageing computer systems— some dating back to the early 1980s. The IR recognized that fundamental improvements were necessary to ensure the ITO could put systems in place that would support the Revenue's operations in the next decade. One interviewee elaborated: 'They were beautifully equipped for the 1980s, but not for facing the challenges of the 1990s. And so that then argued for some kind of external intervention' (Consultant). In a report commissioned by the Revenue in September 1991, CSC Index consultants identified that a number of problems— including poor development processes, lack of key IT skills, high costs due to duplication of services and significant overstaffing—would induce considerable costs for any internal change initiative (National Audit Office 1995).

Following the issue of the government's White Paper *Competing for Quality* in November 1991, the department was pushed to market test its services against the private sector. As an IR respondent noted: 'The general view is that we got into all of this because we were pressured by Ministers under the Competing for Quality initiative. Actually that was the catalyst which enabled us to get the support' (Senior IT Director). At this stage Lucidus, an outsourcing consultancy, became involved and investigated the scope for involving the private sector in delivering the ITO's services. Lucidus confirmed CSC Index's previous findings, and further suggested that by private sector standards the department could operate with between 650 and 880 fewer staff (NAO 1995). In light of the government's pressure and the two consultants' reports, the ITO was given little choice but to market test its services. By 1994 the IR had embarked on a radical change programme, with the ambition of cutting the department's costs by up to 25 per cent within three years. As part of this programme the Revenue had decided to contract out most of the IT function:

The basic motivation for going all out was that we thought that we needed access to the whole corporation with whoever it was that we went out with. We wanted something more than just a straightforward customer/supplier relationship and one of the ways of getting that was actually to do that strategically—we totally needed to run the business and they totally needed to provide the IT—so that you could engineer out of that a win: win situation. (Senior IT Director)

Market Testing—IT Outsourcing

The market-testing exercise for the IR's information technology office (ITO) was of considerable complexity due to its size and overall value. Conscious of this complexity, the Revenue implemented a number of arrangements that ensured effective management of, and integrity in, the exercise. This included, for example, detailed risk management plans and the appointment of Marshal Resources (management and IS consultancy), KPMG Peat Marwick (accountants and management consultants), and Denton Hall (solicitors) to audit and oversee the market testing. The ITO completed the vendor selection process in an estimated eighteen months following the formal authorization by the government. A delay of six months was incurred due to the complexity of the exercise and a general reluctance to cut corners and reduce standards (NAO 1995). By the time EDS had been selected as the preferred supplier the department had spent approximately £4 million on the process, including £2.1 million on consultancy fees (NAO 1995).

Vendor Selection

In October 1992, the Revenue was given ministerial authorization to test the benefit of IT outsourcing, with the specific objective of finding a vendor with whom the Inland Revenue could form a strategic IT partnership:

The department judged that a strategic partnership—involving the transfer of most of the Office to one company, subject to a market test against in-house costs (but no in-house bid)—was the route most likely to provide the flexibility and resources needed to achieve the market test objectives. (NAO, 1995: 8)

Early on the IR had decided not to consider an in-house bid for the following reasons:

- The regulations of the civil service constrained change, for example it did not allow the redeployment of surplus capacity, and the civil service pay rates hindered access to expert skills.
- The ITO would have to compete against world-class IT specialists, whereas earlier reports already indicated in-house performance is not comparable to private sector standards.
- The department would be unable to free the significant investment of some £50 million in the initial years that was needed to buy new skills and technology.
- Fewer staff were needed in the ITO and a private sector employer would undoubtedly have better opportunities to provide new employment.

Authorized by the government, the Revenue issued their 'Expressions of Interest' (similar to the private sector's 'request for information') in December 1992. Eight suppliers responded with bids, but due to the size of the undertaking a number of them had to form consortia to be able to provide the required services, thus leaving in effect only six bidders:

1. Cap Gemini Sogeti;
2. CSC and IBM UK;
3. Digital Equipment Corporation, Logica, and Barclays Bank;
4. EDS;
5. ICL and Andersen Consulting; and
6. Sema Group.

The shortlisted bidders were then scrutinized for their commercial stability, customer relations, and service quality. EDS, and CSC and IBM UK, were chosen as the front runners of the six bidders (Green-Armytage 1993), and were invited to tender for the contract in May 1993. The resulting bids were then compared and assessed against the set of criteria detailed in Table 7.2.

As part of this assessment the IR's IT Director at the time, Geoffrey Bush, visited two reference sites in the USA that signed outsourcing deals of similar size—General Dynamics and Eastman Kodak—to acquire an understanding

Table 7.2. *IR selection criteria*

- cost of each tender against in-house costs
- commercial stability
- customer relations
- ability to maintain the security and confidentiality of taxpayer data
- outsourcing and technical strengths
- ability to sustain the partnership relationship and
- the impact of an innovative bid

Source: NAO 1995.

of how such large-scale undertakings could be rendered effective. According to the National Audit Office's report (1995), cost benefits and comparison criteria were calculated by the ITO by taking into account the existing costs and modifying these by the expected efficiency savings over the life of the contract. This provided a proxy for an in-house bid and a baseline against which savings could be compared to the vendor bids. These projected baseline costs were then verified both by KPMG Peat Marwick and the National Audit Office.

The contract management team responsible for the assessment varied in size from six to twenty people at different times. The team was a mixed group of professionals with expertise drawn from legal, human resource, procurement, IT, civil service, property, and contract management areas as needed. A senior IR manager worked full time at making the high-level decisions, providing the resources, protecting the team and its progress, and managing the relationship with other senior IR managers and government ministers. There was also administrative support to establish a critical audit trail. At a later stage in market testing, the person who was going to manage the contract for the IR also joined the team and took part in the 1994 contract negotiating phase. The role of the contract team was to make a market that would attract bidders and also vet the bids. Respondents stressed that how this was handled had implications for the relationship with the eventual vendor. As one respondent stated:

People thinking of outsourcing rarely take into account the cost of actually responding to their requirements. If the potential customer is not thinking laterally, and does not see the issue, they are already doing something to the relationship [. . .] because that cost has got to be recovered and there's only one place it comes from [but] if you are minimizing the bid cost, you really are doing something really rather helpful to the potential deal down stream. (Senior IT Executive)

In practice bidding for the IR contract probably cost a company like EDS in excess of £2 million. The team also used ex-vendor consultants to predict with great accuracy the information the vendors would need to make a bid. This included, for example, details of current performance measurement, costs, budgets, human resource policies, and pension arrangements. Coupling this with an analysis of the slack in the systems in terms of IT performance and cost also enabled the team to calculate a price at which a vendor could agree the deal, while still making a reasonable profit. This again was felt to have relationship implications: 'It's terribly hard to get across this notion that the supplier absolutely has to make a reasonable return if your objective is to have some kind of strategic relationship, and some real power being pushed into your business by the vendor to achieve your business objectives' (Consultant). Following a lengthy evaluation period, EDS was selected in November 1993 as the preferred supplier over CSC and IBM. Although both bidders had presented very competitive bids on grounds of quality and costs, EDS's bid proposed substantially more net savings of about 17 per cent on the projected in-house costs which CSC and IBM could not match. Aided by Denton Hall (solicitors), lengthy contract negotiations followed, which on 23 May 1994 led to the contract signing.

Electronic Data Systems (EDS) Limited

EDS was (and still is) an IT services company offering IT services for every industry sector. EDS was founded in 1962 by Ross Perot in Texas, USA. Its first major contract was Blue Shield Insurance in 1969. In 1973, within four years, EDS was turning over annually $100 million. In the coming years EDS became a major global service supplier, which was eventually sold to General Motors in 1984 by Ross Perot. In 1987 EDS separated from GM through a management buy-out and has since then grown to be the largest single IT outsourcing service supplier worldwide.

EDS's service portfolio includes systems and technology services, management consulting, business process management, and electronic business, i.e. electronic commerce. EDS's traditional base of business has been systems and technology services with which, in 2000, it was still generating its greatest revenues. In 1997 it had a turnover of $15.3 billion and was able to sign a record $US 16.3 billion in new and future business (EDS 1998). As at 1998, it employed approximately 110,000 people in forty-four countries worldwide, but only 35 per cent of its revenues came from outside of the United States. EDS's general strategy for procuring new contracts has been termed quite aggressive by competitors. Sharon Smith (1997) reported: 'Its approach is straight in at the top, promising good value for money because it can afford to take the long-term view when relatively poor returns and high costs in the short-term will be rewarded by a big pay-back later on' (p. 41). Nevertheless, over the years EDS has negotiated contracts with approximately 9,000 key clients and by 1999 held some of the largest outsourcing contracts in the world, including Xerox, American Express, UK Inland Revenue, Commonwealth Bank, and South Australian government.

Outsourcing Scope

The IR contracted EDS for the totality of its information technology assets, including the infrastructure and its applications. The annual budget was estimated at £250 million, with thirteen major data centres, sixteen different functional areas of IT, and approximately 60,000 desktop computers. The department had decided to keep a number of information technology (IT) functions in-house because they were critical to its operations. It kept control of its IT strategy, planning, finance, and telecommunications. The total cost of the retained functions was estimated at £18 million annually. Of the 2,500 people, 500 were retained to carry out various functions, including monitoring of the contract and EDS's service performance. The IR did expect, though, that 200 people would leave through natural wastage over the life of the contract.

Outsourcing Expectations and Objectives

In line with the government's policy, the key outsourcing objectives were according to Geoff Bush, the IT Director in 1993:

- value for money
- to gain rapid access to new technologies;
- to enhance the capability of IT to meet business needs, and to reduce development time;
- to optimize IT staff career opportunities; and
- to achieve step improvements in the Revenue's efficiency.

Clearly efficiency was to be an underlying driver, as early cost calculations by Lucidus consultants had indicated significant saving opportunities:

So we then looked at this position of their technology department, did some sums that said there's about typically 20% cost improvement to be made in most of these organizations, some as much as 30%. (Consultant)

Yet managers also noted privatization would increase flexibility within IT—in terms of pay, conditions, and promotion policies, in terms of escaping public spending constraints, and also increasing the capability to respond to change by re-engineering activities or re-equipping staff as needed. Taking control of existing resources would further open up the opportunity to possibly sell any spare computing capacity—not previously an option in the public sector—thereby freeing extra funds for investments.

Other key objectives were to improve services through investment in new tools and technologies, but also to gain access to expert skill resources and know-how:

Ours was to do with reducing the time scale from design through to implementation, to do with reducing costs where a lot of reduction of cost was already written into the contract anyway. It was to do with access to 1990s technology and was to do with developing our people, career prospects of the people who were transferring to EDS. Some of those objectives were similar in EDS. (Senior Partnership Executive)

Access to IT specialists with expert skills would, it was hoped, provide substantial improvements in the Revenue's development time of new applications—urgently needed for the Self-Assessment project to be delivered in April 1997, for example (see below): 'Because one of the objectives was to reduce the development cycle time from 6 years to 2 years. Another objective was to achieve greater responsiveness' (Consultant).

THE CONTRACT

The Inland Revenue (IR) estimated the value of the contract at £1,033 million over the ten-year period, which, compared to the projected baseline cost of services in-house of £1,286 million, meant a gross saving of £225 million. That implied a saving of 17.5 per cent on the IT costs, but these were of course calculated on the basis of the IR's current volume of work over the ten-year life of the contract: 'In practice, the actual volume will depend on changes in tax regimes and legislation and on technological change' (NAO 1995: 11). It was decided early on that a fixed contract could not be developed. The IR thus pursued fostering a close relationship hoping that this would minimize control concerns. This notion was ingrained in the contract in subtle ways, and in some areas more explicitly. A senior executive explained: 'We have full partnership objectives that are actually written in the contract. Not as obligations, it's written in the contract as something that we desire from this arrangement. We didn't write in any equivalent for EDS, but we do know what their partnership objectives are. And the concept of shared objectives is a fundamental for this partnership.' It was found that a number of objectives EDS had corresponded in part to the IR's, thus defining some mutual objectives: 'EDS's would be able to make an honest return, to have referenceability, they wanted this to be a successful contract. And to develop their people' (Customer Service Executive). It was widely recognized amongst the outsourcing team that with 134 risks of varying severity, risk mitigation was to be critical throughout. It was to be part of quality assurance in terms of what one respondent termed the 'up-front thinking'. The contract was to mirror this thinking, embedded in particular clauses such as:

- safeguarding the confidentiality and security of taxpayers' information;
- protecting the public assets and the interests of staff transferred; and
- defining adequate provisions to ensure and monitor the quality, improvement, cost-effectiveness, and continuity of services to the taxpayer.

In terms of confidentiality and security, the contract placed specific obligations on EDS to ensure all its employees, subcontractors, and agents signed a standardized document acknowledging their statutory obligation not to disclose any information concerning the Inland Revenue deal. These were to be monitored and reviewed at least once every six months. Any breaches that occurred during this period had to be reported to the Revenue immediately:

In substance, the law that applies to civil servants who make an unauthorized disclosure of what we call taxpayer confidential information, is exactly the same law that applies to non-civil servants and third party suppliers of services, and that provides for a fine, imprisonment or both on conviction. Hence a contract with any supplier will provide them with broadly the same raft of sanctions. (Senior IT Executive)

In essence, security at the Revenue was to be handled in the same way as prior to contracting EDS. This was, essentially, according to the Department's Security Manual, except that all EDS personnel are vetted for security clearance and the IR has had a veto to reject any appointments. In addition, all data handling was initially UK restricted (this changed later): 'EDS must not process, handle or store any taxpayer information outside the United Kingdom, or take any taxpayer information out of the country without prior consent of the Department' (NAO 1995: 14). To ensure adequate control and an audit trail, the contract provided full access to EDS's books and records relating to any part of the services provision to the Inland Revenue:

We've got open access to all their books—not something that they particular invite—but it's a fundamental plank to us. All being the sort of open relationship that we can rely on without having to spend a lot of time needlessly ticking and stamping everything, and checking everything. (Senior Partnership Executive)

Open book audits had to cover not only the current operations and costs, but also the economic efficiency and effectiveness with which EDS have used the IR's resources.

For the hardware assets transferred, EDS was expected to pay a lump sum of £68 million in addition to £1.3 million for the proprietary software. The assets transferred were localized, so that EDS also had to lease and/or license sixteen properties from the central government. With this transfer the IR also transferred all responsibility to EDS for purchasing any new equipment needed to deliver the services formerly provided by the ITO and regional processing centres.

Of course, this gave EDS the flexibility to eliminate any surplus capacity of assets, in addition to recovering the transfer investments through its service charges. However, if EDS intended to dispose of any equipment the contract required prior consent, and in those instances where the sale price exceeded the unamortized transfer value, EDS would have to pay to the IR the larger share of the profit made on the disposal. The latter arrangements also applied in those cases where EDS used the Inland Revenue's facilities to provide services to third parties. According to the National Audit Office (1995) report, benefit sharing was agreed for:

- computer facilities—the IR received a fixed percentage rate and a share of the balance depending on the level of the ITO's efforts in generating the income; and
- buildings— for any use of buildings the IR received an agreed percentage and a split of the balance.

Integral to the contract negotiations was the issue of contract management processes. In part these were to be reflected in service level agreements, but additional processes were needed. The IR consulted Lucidus to help develop a contract management scheme:

So they invited us to create the contract management arena and we devised this four-tier model, which has at the bottom the basic telemetry [SLA] that says how are you performing, let's pay you some money, right up to the top level that says this agreement is predicated upon delivery of some objectives. Let's maintain a focus on those objectives to make sure that we are delivering them. And part of that top level is about

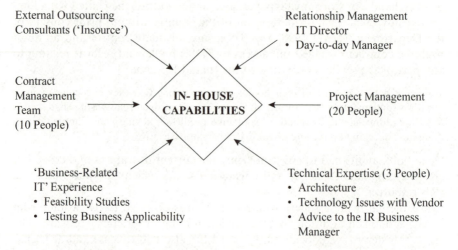

External Outsourcing
Consultants ('Insource')

Relationship Management
• IT Director
• Day-to-day Manager

Contract
Management
Team
(10 People)

**IN- HOUSE
CAPABILITIES**

Project Management
(20 People)

'Business-Related
IT' Experience
• Feasibility Studies
• Testing Business Applicability

Technical Expertise (3 People)
• Architecture
• Technology Issues with Vendor
• Advice to the IR Business
  Manager

Fig. 7.1. *Retained skills and capabilities at the Inland Revenue*

Source: Interviewees and secondary documentation.

relationships. So it will have all kinds of detailed grief lower down, but up here we will maintain the big picture, we will keep the relationship good and any problems can be escalated and we can deal with them in a sensible way and that will be fine. We designed the basic contract management processes that have subsequently been refined. (Consultant)

To ensure adequate provision of services, the contract integrated 170 separate service level agreements that defined the service dimensions and requirements for the Inland Revenue and the Information Technology Office (ITO). However, these were not arrived at during the general contract negotiations. Instead, they were to be formalized during the initial six months of post-contract management: 'The department decided it would not be cost-effective to renegotiate the agreements—170 in all—before contract signature, because it would have tied up considerable resources and delayed the strategic partnership and the benefits expected to flow from it' (NAO 1995: 25). Finally, the retention and development of certain in-house skills, involving about forty people, was also decided during contract negotiations, in order to mitigate risk (see Figure 7.1).

The central group here was the contract management team, described as 'the guardians of the contract'. The contract management processes were deliberately over-engineered at first to ensure tight control, that could be loosened subsequently. The leader of the ten-person team had an understanding of IT at the IR, of the IR business, together with experience of negotiation. The team also contained expertise in resource procurement, commercial accounting, productivity monitoring and planning, and covered fourteen different disciplines and/or tasks in all. The IR also retained three people with technical expertise to look after the overall architecture of IR systems, to understand the technical issues the vendor was grappling with, to work with them at a high technical level, and to provide advice to IR business project directors. About twenty of the latter were also retained in-house to lead all projects and work with the relevant vendor project managers:

We retained a number of project managers when we moved this across to help strengthen our plan to drive these projects out. And the business was, and is, in the driving seat and EDS are one of the cost accounts within that project. Again, we find it very important that accountability and responsibility are driven and owned by, and seen to be owned by, EDS for IT deliverables. We want to know what they are doing, and want to understand it. (IT Director, 1997)

Additionally there were several IT staff working in the IR business with what was called 'business-related IT' experience. These would work on feasibility studies with EDS, on developing business requirements, and in testing systems for business applicability. Clearly all these retained staff would need to work closely with relevant vendor staff in order to perform their mutual roles. Additionally, external outsourcing consultants from the original contract team were regularly used to review progress and developments.

Financial Arrangements

The contract specified detailed penalty clauses, which included financial remedies. For development and future work, a charging mechanism was developed that combined pricing certainty with flexibility, in order to avoid price escalations typically found in long-term deals. This worked on the basis of a set work unit price, with discounts offered where volumes of work were ordered sufficiently in advance:

The basis on which prices would be calculated is essentially as I said earlier: 'this is an input deal so we work with EDS to understand the resources needed to do something, we order those resources, and if we can give them 12 months notice, we get them at a cheaper rate, and the rate effectively drops year on year.' That's EDS's challenge that they've got to be able to deliver more, but we pay them less each year. So each resource has got to become more productive. (Senior IT Director)

However, for the base workload and related manpower resources EDS had agreed a fixed standing charge. Charging was expected to vary, to take account of the changes in volume work and resources. Two main elements define the charging rate:

- infrastructure costs—hardware and software utilities, and maintenance including rent plus a mark-up management fee; and
- manpower costs—defined by different skill rates plus a mark-up management fee.

These charges were annually reviewed and compared against market prices. For example, labour costs have been benchmarked against the Average Earnings Index for Services Industries published by the Department of Employment. Infrastructure and technology, on the other hand, were competitively market tested and benchmarked. If lower prices for services were available, EDS needed to reduce its prices accordingly. The contract further stipulated that the supplier could not bind the Revenue to technology not available from a third party, and had to allow the comparison of any prices raised for new technology in the market at any time. In terms of the contract, the IR can in fact market test any activity, with the possibility of another supplier taking over that activity if it could do it more cost-effectively.

Additionally, the contract provides a mechanism for profit sharing. An internal report noted 'where the gross margin exceeds a percentage target level calculated in accordance with the contract formula, the Department and EDS share the excess equally'. In practice this worked as follows:

We agree within the contract the target margins for all the areas of work that we give to EDS, and that's a different percentage for the different areas of work, manpower or hardware or infrastructure whatever it turns out to be. And if EDS make a greater margin than that average margin, we have a 50:50 split of the excess profits. [. . .] And we have had profit sharing for the opening 3 years of the contract. (Senior Partnership Executive, 1997)

Conversely, if there was a shortfall in profits then EDS alone had to bear the loss of its targeted margin, the general underlying objective being to improve the Revenue's cost-effectiveness by reducing the costs of the original volume of work transferred by about 35 per cent over the life of the contract.

POST-CONTRACT MANAGEMENT

Senior managers from both EDS and the Inland Revenue were very aware of the high-profile nature of what some participants had termed the 'strategic partnership' between the two organizations. They were in turn understandably anxious to make it work.

Emerging Issues: 1994–1995

As part of mitigating risks it was decided during contracting that IT assets and/or work would be transferred in stages. Initially four separate stages were planned by the Revenue, but it was changed to two following EDS's proposal to increase the net present savings by 20 per cent by splitting it into two tranches; with the standard services and processing tranche being transferred first, and the major development work transferred over later—provided the first tranche was working out:

It went in two tranches. The reasoning behind that was really risk mitigation [. . .] The basis was that EDS should take the first tranche, if that doesn't work out then we could delay the second tranche for 6 months, and if it still wasn't working out we could say well we won't go any further. (IT Director)

A total of eighteen months was allocated for transfer completion. Before authorizing the second tranche in January 1996, a detailed evaluation of EDS's performance was to be undertaken before any part of the second tranche was transferred.

The transition period in essence concentrated on:

- the transfer of the first tranche and post-contract verification of services and technology by EDS;
- continuation of the Revenue's consolidation, rationalization and standardization programmes;
- implementing management processes and structures to build the relationship; and
- monitoring and controlling service levels in parallel to negotiating the Master Service Level Agreement (MSLA) and the departmental SLAs.

The transfer of the first tranche presented a number of difficulties for both parties. Post-contract verification of the service levels, technology, and some of the clauses led to a range of misunderstandings and resulted in an extended due diligence process. In the end resolution was only achieved through a mutual give-and-take stance on a number of issues. As one IR respondent explained:

We had an issue in post-contract verification where there was a genuine misunderstanding on both sides of what was intended by a series of clauses in the ITT, in the bid, in the contract. We ended up getting advice from lawyers and barristers saying, actually there's a view to be had on both sides and we are not absolutely clear. Eventually, we had to take the people out who were involved in the initial negotiations and contract implementation because they could not get away from the fact that they had fought so hard for the contract. So we took those people out of it, so we could resolve the issues and come to some accommodation. (Assistant Director Partnership Group)

Because of the early complexities and lengthy due diligence process, a number of business streams had proceeded to implement the contract by mutually agreeing a separate interpretation. However, due to the complexity and their restricted access to the complete contract, some business streams' interpretations turned out to conflict with the actual contractual arrangements. Consequently these business streams were advised by the contract management group to change these:

And there have been occasions where they've [the business streams and EDS managers] made what they thought was a convenient arrangement and when the contract was submitted to frank it and to make a commitment, they've had to say, 'well hang on a minute, this should actually be treated in a different way'. (Customer Service Manager)

Another area requiring resolution early on was pricing. In practice the original savings on running the base service remained protected by the contract. However, after the contract was signed, EDS was given a further £100,000 because it was discovered that IR did not have licences for all the software being transferred. By mid-1995 EDS and IR were negotiating over a further £200 million addition to the original bid price over the life of the contract. Inaccuracies in the original tender documents led to an increase of £5 million a year, while additional hardware maintenance was to be charged at another £15 million a year. A senior executive further explained:

We signed that contract in 1994 and there was then a trial 12-month period where they could verify what they had actually inherited from us aligned to the ITT, and of course it had changed. The net arrangement was that there would be a pound for pound adjustment for anything up or down that was inherited by EDS over what was said in the ITT. And that pound for pound adjustment did bring something in the region of about £100 million adjustment to the contract as a result. That was the one component, I think there was another about £100 million of inflation in there as well making up the £200 million.

The IR was also finding it difficult to keep to some of the contractual terms which EDS legitimately demanded. For example, to get the lowest labour rates, IR needed to forecast its staff requirements thirteen months in advance. This was difficult to do, as was the categorization of skills needed into forty-eight types, and the definition of where all the equipment was.

Upon transfer of the first tranche, EDS picked up some of the consolidation and rationalization programmes the Revenue had started before outsourcing. For example, the IR had planned to rationalize its printing facilities between the fifteen processing centres, into one main centre. EDS closed down three of these processing centres immediately upon takeover of the first tranche (Macintyre 1994). In May 1995 some questions were raised about the fragmentation of the IR Worthing computer bureau, identified by an external benchmarking firm as more efficient, taking into account its output, than any private sector datacentre operation. In the case of Worthing, EDS people argued that they could run things even more efficiently by redeploying half of the staff and relocating the mainframe equipment to EDS's headquarters. At the same time the Revenue was running into problems with the development of its 'Pay and File' system for handling Corporation Tax. The system collected billions of pounds annually in company taxes. Problems emerged with EDS's handling of the system, though these stemmed mainly from inadequacies in what was handed over to EDS. Flaws in the system resulted in late or non-paying companies not being reported to senior IR management for follow-up action. In practice because of the staff transfers taking place the IR found itself short of resources to develop the 'Pay and File' system.

After initial contractual adjustment problems on both sides it also became clear in late 1995 that relationship management required more comprehensive attention. Indeed, relationship management structures and processes had to be addressed more explicitly. Two IR managers elaborated the reason for this demand:

We did actually, at the beginning of this contract, have to change both of the contract managers to get a more reasonable basis for the relationship because the two of them had continued the negotiations in a way and they were locking horns day in day out. We had to take both of those individuals out and try to recover that relationship. (Senior Partnership Executive)

It became clear that we couldn't manage the relationship on this basis because it was sending out incredible signals—these guys aren't interested in a partnership they are just interested in beating each other up. (IT Executive)

In practice, outsourcing induced the IR to two new sets of skills in addition to those they already had available in-house: contract and relationship management (see Figure 7.1 above). The Inland Revenue's IT Director assumed responsibility for relationship management, initially spending most of his time on this set of issues, though this reduced to 30 per cent by late 1996. Another IT manager was made responsible full-time for relationship management on a day-to-day basis. Partnering operated at several levels. At the highest level there has been a six-monthly board-to-board meeting between EDS and IR:

One is that we have every 6 months what we call a board to board meeting at which Les Alberthal (EDS CEO) meets either our Chairman and Deputy Chairman and in fact the whole board, and he's here in a fortnight's time [. . .] And that's a meeting at which we talk at the highest level about the pressures on the partnership, plans for the partnership particularly with the focus over the next 6 months and beyond. (Senior Partnership Executive)

At the operational level there have been joint partnership meetings every four weeks to pick up on issues that emerged during day-to-day operation:

We've just had our internal monthly partnership review board [where] we've had a discussion about progress and our partnership goals. What we actually do here is look at the totality of the service, and this is a 3-monthly report, where here are the Inland Revenue's four main objectives, customer service, compliance, cost effectiveness, caring for staff, and a number of measures associated with the IT service that are attributable to those. [. . .] It's done jointly by ourselves and EDS, and these are EDS's objectives here, customers, business and their people. And we are actually bringing these reports together on a quarterly basis and saying how are we doing. So we are assessing the effectiveness of the partnership overall in this sort of way. (Partnership Executive)

Through this jointly staffed partnership development group issues were identified that required special attention in the future and that would not get dealt with through the normal contract management mechanisms:

Each activity was given an EDS owner and an Inland Revenue owner. Each was charged with setting out plans and would report monthly to me and my EDS counterpart [. . .] settlement of the issue was included in their performance agreements and pay structure. [. . .] none could say that the reason an issue is not settled is because my counterpart won't agree. (IT Director)

For the above purpose, the central contract management group was thus assigned to the partnership development group. It comprised four legal specialists, five managers monitoring the contract, and a senior contract manager overseeing the group:

We've got a contract team which is part of my group, and they check on anything that we are being asked for from EDS that has to be fed through the contract management team so they have direct control on all the commitments the department is making. So we've got very firm control in the centre of what this contract is providing. (Senior Partnership Executive)

We rely on our contract managers to have a very subtle role. One of being able to say absolutely objectively what the contract says about this particular issue, but secondly to be able to suggest what might be a fair minded movement from that. That's quite difficult because on one front it's easy to be a hard nosed negotiator and say, 'this is what it says exactly in black and white'. It's more difficult to not get locked into that and not get wedded to that at all costs, but to be able to move the process forward. (Customer Service Manager)

As Figure 7.2 illustrates, these mechanisms and processes led to an oversight structure which was clearly designed to enhance the working relationships. The

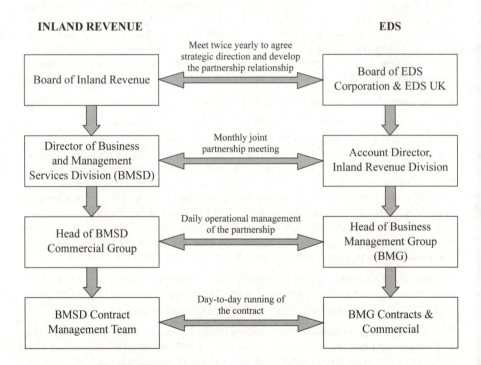

Fig. 7.2. *Inland Revenue/EDS partnership structure*

Source: NAO 2000: 60.

structure also allowed focus on developing mutual understandings, perceptions, and goals. The objectives here were to achieve the wider goals of both parties. As one respondent put it: 'The management here is about the totality of what you get for your money, not just from the micro-level' (EDS Managing Executive). In addition to these mechanisms and processes, a consensus amongst senior managers was developed around over a dozen guiding principles to regulate the relationship. According to one respondent, over 1995 these became a code of behaviour: 'When people do not behave in line with them it's not uncommon for them to be challenged' (IT Director). In parallel, Revenue managers began to carefully monitor EDS's service quality, timeliness and performance, and enforced the annually negotiated cost reductions. The service levels EDS was initially contracted to provide for the first months were actually the existing levels of service as indicated in the Information Technology Office's past performance records. The parties had agreed that, within the first six months of the transition period, a Master Service Level Agreement (MSLA) defining the quality and quantity of the service would be provided, and how these will be measured and reported over the life of the contract would be formalized. Up until the agreement, EDS had to maintain the existing performance, monitoring and reporting arrangements. In early 1995 the MSLA negotiations were completed and the framework within which each business stream would then develop a separate service level agreement (SLA) was set:

The MSLA sets out the global range of services that the business is acquiring from EDS, and the general framework within which those services are acquired. So it tends to set the tone and the structure for individual business needs. EDS's service delivery philosophy is centred on doing business on a one-to-one basis with the business stream. As a partnership we are very supportive of that. So what we then expect is the individual business stream, the individual IT function of the department—of which there are broadly about 35 in the case of this contract today—to then negotiate within the realms of that master service level agreement their own agreement with EDS. Now that sets out some very specific terms of what the services are that they are seeking to acquire, what levels of service they require, negotiating targets and improvements that they envisage. Clearly setting out both parties' obligations and therefore creating a basis on which objective measurement and evaluation of service can be made. That's fundamental for the resolution of issues and other aspects of the contract. (Customer Service Executive)

The eventual SLAs negotiated by the departments specified their objective measures and essential baseline services. EDS's performance was then to be monitored against these SLAs on a monthly, quarterly, and annual basis:

Once EDS sits down with the business counterpart and says legally this is a reasonable level of service that we can deliver, we are prepared to contract to deliver this. Then the business can reasonably expect to have that level of service and to complain and seek some form of redress if it doesn't get that. [The] business streams are encouraged to review month by month, based on formal performance reports logged by EDS—and that's a feature of the contract—what levels of service have been achieved and what issues have occurred in the quarter. (Customer Service Executive)

In addition to the objective service performance measures, both parties formalized a subjective evaluation measure using a colour scheme of red (serious problem), amber (heading in the wrong direction), and green (perfectly acceptable). This allowed IR and EDS managers to gauge the service perceptions of the end-user population:

Where we've got a flag rather than a box, that's more a subjective measure, that's a result of a report where a group or an individual is actually saying that's green, red, or amber. It tends to be actually that the flags are all green, but this one isn't [looking at the report]. But generally when you've got subjective judgements they tend to be a bit more generous. When we've got hard facts it's more clinical. That probably says something about the psychology and the state of the partnership at any one point in time, that if people are feeling relatively comfortable we'll give the partner the benefit of the doubt. (Partnership Executive)

In addition, it helped with managing the overall relationship:

The value of this [subjective evaluation scheme] as a mechanism has forced us to sit down periodically and ask where this relationship is taking us. (Customer Service Executive)

Both the hard and soft measures combined were then integrated into a monthly report, which was exchanged and then discussed at the monthly review meeting. The resulting trends of service performance were then evaluated quarterly. One respondent noted:

In this focus of work there are something like over 1,000 different measures that we are tracking on a monthly basis. The trends for that come into this quarterly report. (Customer Service Executive)

However, should the service level performance fall short of the agreed performance level, then the business streams and IR's IT managers had the opportunity to enforce penalties as a means of restitution:

There are some caveats within the contract that allow penalties to apply if levels of service fall short. It is not intended to be a compensation scheme, it is intended to actually identify in very clear terms those aspects of service which are paramount to the business operation. And it in effect clearly signals that this is an area where we really can't collectively afford to fail. (Senior Partnership Executive)

Finally, a yearly review of the EDS-IR venture has been undertaken by the government's independent National Audit Office. This selects at random parts it wishes to review. Additionally, there was to be an extensive review of the overall success of the venture at mid-term of the contract, in 1998–9:

They have an annual report to do with the integrity of the way the IR operates in terms of the relationship with the taxpayer. And of course the EDS component of that is important. So there are parts of the EDS area that are examined by the National Audit Office every year just to make sure those processes are working properly. But the assessment of the 'value for money' from this contract is one that they would intend to do at around year 5 or 6 of this contract. (Partnership Executive)

In summary, the venture started off on a difficult footing as the service requirements had not been formalized and the complexity of the contract still had to be operationalized and interpreted for the end-user community. The management infrastructure and processes helped to bridge the early difficulties by guiding interactions. The eventual negotiation of the MSLA provided the foundation for the relationship.

THE SELF-ASSESSMENT TAX PROJECT AND TRANCHE TWO TRANSFER (1995–1996)

One of the objectives of relationship-building was to sharpen mutual responsiveness and access to resources. By mid-1995 a fundamental time-constrained development tended to be attracting all of the available resources. This was related to the UK government's announcement in 1995 of its intention to save some 3,000 jobs amongst tax staff by formalizing the self-assessment tax scheme, which had to be operational from April 1997. When the IR first drew up its outsourcing plans it was not aware of the exact details of this project. It represented probably the biggest single reform of UK tax administration for fifty years (Collins 1995). To make it work was highly dependent on the supporting information systems being in place. Not surprisingly, these system development requirements created considerable anxiety amongst EDS's and IR's senior IT staff. Neither wished to be seen to fail on such a high-profile development project, now called the Computerized Environment for Self-Assessment (CESA) project.

Senior EDS managers believed that the system should be kept as simple as possible. Off-the-shelf packages could provide the capability to record who should receive the forms and the payment history of each taxpayer. The difficulty was that two systems would have to be maintained, because the new system would not interface immediately with the existing Cop/Coda systems holding all current records. Moreover the new 'simple' system would not facilitate spot-checks on the accuracy of taxpayers' returns. IR management therefore wanted a tailored package to meet its specific requirements, but this in turn greatly increased the risk of failing to deliver a robust system on time. In addition, development was shot through with technological, requirement, and specification uncertainties. The cost of the project was unknown as at mid-1995. An estimate that the system would have to handle 90 million transactions annually was not that dependable and could be significantly more. EDS managers questioned whether the chosen technology was sufficiently expandable. The proposed system—ICL VME mainframes linked to servers and several thousands of terminals—was dependent on ICL Goldrush super-servers that had never before been used on such a large project. EDS also worried that the ICL equipment seemed to cost more than twice as much to buy and run as equivalent IBM hardware.

For EDS managers the project represented high risk in terms of short time scales, technical complexity, and a major change in the way business would be conducted. Furthermore, the project was only to come under EDS control when the remaining 800 IR development staff were transferred to them in early 1996. This added a significant risk as senior managers in both organizations conceded, with management of the project being transferred in mid-flight to an outside supplier. In his special report on the IR, Collins (1995: 33) noted: 'EDS is not happy about the fact that it will be contractually responsible for delivering the self-assessment system by April 1997, but as yet does not have control over the project.' By mid-1995 EDS managers were asking for control of the project to be handed over earlier than the planned transfer date for tranche two. They felt that they could not give a guarantee of delivery before they had control, and had arrived at an agreement over the choice of systems. IR senior managers were willing to concede this control to maintain the 'strategic' relationship, but more importantly to give EDS an improved opportunity to deliver the CESA project on time in full. Thus, in parallel to the CESA project, the IR initiated evaluation procedures of EDS's past performance to determine whether to authorize transfer of the development tranche. The IR evaluated EDS for:

- the progress towards the strategic partnership objectives;
- the quality of the work carried out and its plans for managing the transfer of the next stage (considering the pressure of the CESA project);
- the strength of the relationship between managers at the different levels;
- the value for money of the services to date and the benefits of transferring the development tranche; and
- the ongoing commercial stability of EDS.

The evaluation was detailed, but rushed, as EDS pushed for control to ensure timely delivery of CESA:

Tranche two in January 1996 was about the development services. And for almost all of 1996 we were trying to establish what it was the IR were capable of providing in terms of output to the development area. And our records were not complete, they were open to conjecture and yet we had to try and establish some productivity base lines around the development area. And that was a very hard time. And we had some very difficult meetings in that and at the end of it we had to make the thing work. In a sense it's been a real test of the relationship because we've both had to take some pain on that in order to get through it. (Senior Partnership Executive)

Eventually, despite the lack of clear productivity measures, the Revenue authorized the transfer: 'The decision was made despite the fact that the Revenue has not yet completed its formal evaluation of EDS to see whether Tranche 2, the transfer of the development staff should take place in January 1996' (Collins 1995: 35). The decision was clearly made in favour of avoiding a possible failure of CESA, which would not only reflect badly on the management, but also on the whole outsourcing contract. A number of managers so far had been promoted because of the success of the contract and a sudden failure of such a critical project could possibly raise doubts over the adequacy of these promotions. In these circumstances, the cost of the project was also becoming less of an issue than the actual on-time delivery of a robust system. In fact by late 1996 the cost of the outsourcing venture over the ten years had already increased by a total of £600 million (i.e. 60%). The CESA project alone had gone over budget by 20 per cent and additional requirements and projects pointed towards even more costs: 'The costs of self-assessment have been much higher than anticipated. This had led to the Revenue revising downwards by about 10% its projected £225 million 10-year savings from the £1.2bn privatisation contract with EDS' (Collins 1996*b*). Unforeseen requirements indicated a need for additional resources, i.e. staff, that had to be either diverted from other IR projects, or bought from EDS directly at an additional cost. These were, of course, above the original contract price, though developments in the partnership were making price and quality of resources increasingly an uncontentious issue. Collins (1995: 35) noted: 'Understandably, neither EDS nor the Revenue wants money to get in the way of the successful delivery of a system that has the highest political priority and which, if it failed, would undoubtedly damage EDS's reputation.' In November 1996 the first CESA release went live with a number of serious problems. The second release, however, was supposedly still on track to go live in early 1997. Early on both parties had agreed to develop and go live with only the essential functions. In turn, the compliance system checks for the first release were said to have been reduced from about 700 to 400, essentially to assure on-time delivery. As a result of the rush and pressure to deliver on a time, a number of problems crept in: 'The network rehearsal was trying to test the whole system allowing 15,000 users to sign on: 3,000 could not log on and many of those who could, were faced with very slow response times or blank screens' (Smith 1996: 48). The Revenue expected 9 million taxpayers to be using the system by 1997. In March 1997 the Revenue reported yet more teething problems with the system, but were assured that by April the system would be fully functional:

The Inland Revenue has admitted to mismanaging the computer-generated mailing to the first wave of self-assessing taxpayers. The department failed to tell taxpayers that their tax bills were due several days before the deadline date of 31 January, to allow time for cheques to clear. Thousands of customers whose payments arrived late subsequently were told that they owed small amounts of interest. ('Revenue confesses to systems blunder', *Computing* (8 March 1997), 10)

The third and final compliance element release was planned to go live in March 1998.

MATURING RELATIONS: IN PARALLEL TO THE CESA PROJECT (1996–1998)

In parallel to the CESA project, relations were steadily progressing towards strategic integration. With the handover of Tranche 2, the actual transition, i.e. transfer period had been completed, giving EDS full control over the Revenue's IT infrastructure and applications. It was now up to both parties to ensure the relationship succeeded. The focus of relationships revolved predominantly around the CESA project, but, in parallel, relations matured and a number of issues were receiving and becoming of greater interest to the IR and EDS:

- closer integration of EDS as a strategic partner;
- relationship development through a joint perceptions exercise;
- value-added focus;
- fostering an open and trusting operating environment;
- contract alignment and changes; and
- up-coming challenges for the relationship.

As a result of the takeover of the second tranche in mid-1996, EDS became much more involved in the strategic planning level of the Revenue's information technology direction. In fact, by late 1996 EDS was integrated in a number of the IR's specific planning meetings that furnished them open access to the Revenue's future objectives, financial commitments, and possible changes:

In terms of the partnership, we have full involvement of EDS in our strategic planning forums. So we have a big departmental implementation committee which is chaired by the Deputy Chairman of the investment committee, and includes another Deputy Chairmen from the board and EDS sit on that. And that's a monthly meeting which is actually agreeing what projects are within the departmental priority, what isn't. And they are overseeing the commitments that we are making to EDS. With EDS party to all that. So we've got them as fully paid up members of departmental commitment, and behind all that is our resource ordering process, and all our contractual arrangements are meshed in with that. So we are providing information about our long range plans for the coming two years of manpower plans, and 10 years of capital and infrastructure plans. We construct these and we feed this information up to the departmental planning investment committee, and EDS again is party to all of that. (Partnership Executive)

As a partner, EDS reciprocated by giving Revenue managers full access to their quarterly financial review meeting. At these meetings EDS unveiled the importance of the Revenue's and other clients' business to their overall profit margin and future:

Our director goes along to their quarterly finance meetings, so he sees what their projections are for their income stream over the year, and the contributions being expected from EDS at the Inland Revenue. And it's not unknown for anything that's causing pressure to be brought to our joint partnership meeting, where we will be talking about how we are going to get over that as a joint venture. (Senior Partnership Executive)

Relations between the senior levels were in accordance with the Revenue's intention of developing strategic partnering. Still, the tough negotiations of tranche two and the pressure of the CESA project gave rise to a number of tensions at the operational levels. In late 1996 both parties took stock of the relationships at the operational management levels through an innovative joint perceptions exercise. Both client and vendor managers were asked separately to disclose their grievances and perceptions of the other party, after which they were compared to elicit where they overlapped and defined commonality and where they diverged. The consultant facilitating the exercise noted:

And they [perceptions] were as far apart as you could imagine. Absolutely astonishing. So what we did was to present each other's models and perceptions to the other party, and there were some tensions in there as you can imagine—real head banging stuff. We then said let's unify the models because if it's going to be one relationship you'd better be working off one model or the two models together. We eventually got a joint understanding of what all this was about. (Consultant)

That exercise identified sixty-eight different strands of activity, specifically designed to make the relationship work better, and needed to achieve the higher objectives of EDS-IR. For example, EDS found that IR managers only ever wanted to talk and never wanted to make decisions. So one strand of action was to improve decision making at the Revenue. To undertake the root cause analysis and changes, a client and vendor managerial pair responsible for delivering results from each was assigned. Their progress would be reviewed at a monthly partnership meeting:

We assigned a pairing from the joint partnership meeting to get to the bottom of the way we regarded those issues. We analysed those issues, put them into certain categories and we tasked them to examine them and to set out a work-plan of how they would solve those particular issues—each one of them. (Senior Partnership Executive)

The strands of actions were split into three separate categories and aimed at long-term improvements:

1. *Relationship enablers*—actions that benefited the relationship and its development;
2. *Mechanical issues*—actions to improve, maintain, develop processes; and
3. *Value added factors*—actions that would develop real value-added for both parties.

To further develop the relationship, both parties had agreed at this stage to undertake actions to assure closer integration of EDS. This depended on EDS achieving continuously the Revenue's service requirements, to then move relations beyond the arms-length service supplier perception that many end-users still had of EDS. Although institutionalization of routine exchanges had to precede any new developments, both the Revenue and customers were seeking to benefit from EDS's expertise early on:

The nature of the relationship we are encouraging was for EDS to work intrinsically with the business and not be seen as an arms length IT supplier, and really take specifications of IT products and deliver those products overall. Actually getting them there and understanding how IS could be used to best advantage by the business. (Customer Service Executive)

Certainly over the three years of the contract the service has improved in many areas and it's developed considerably. (Senior Partnership Executive)

EDS's track record of service improvements and the successful development of CESA contributed to the IR managers' general view that EDS was truly endeavouring to achieve their objectives. Combined with the interest in sharing mutual goals, managers found EDS to be a trustworthy partner. The IR managers' response was to reciprocate through openness and honesty, establishing a working environment where issues could be discussed and frankly addressed:

Openness and honesty and respect, those sorts of things which are easy enough to say but a bit more difficult to operate on a day-to-day basis. But it actually means that if I'm having a debate about something in particular I can lay out to my EDS counterpart how this particular thing is affecting me, how I have perceived to be affecting them so I can see their side of the story and they can tell me whether that's true or not and tell me how they think it's affecting my side. And we can get on the same wavelength as to what the effect of this is and what's the best result from this particular issue that we are toiling with. Generally we use that sort of technique. It's not highly structured, it's a natural style of being able to discuss openly and look at both sides of the problem. But I think that's fundamental. (Partnership Executive)

The push to increased cooperation and collaboration had been initiated by the perception exercise. However, additional actions were to be undertaken to standardize and simplify some of the mechanics, i.e. processes of the relationship, that affected both parties. An example of a conjoint action to improve the management processes was the initiative to move away from resource types to work types, providing a broader approach to service requests. Another example was elaborated by an IR respondent:

One of the ones I had was for process improvement, improving bureaucracy of how we were ordering our manpower, how we were clearing invoices, etc. So we jointly applied the efforts of myself and counterpart on the EDS side and our two teams to sort that out. That was a programme that took 12 months to make any real impression in terms of improved process, and is an ongoing programme. (Customer Service Executive)

Simplifying the mechanics helped EDS to understand the IR's business and requirements, illuminating potential areas where EDS could apply their skills and capabilities. As with CESA, the Revenue was seeking extra benefits and value-added. EDS in turn was able to present innovations through, for example, the controversial merger of the Department of Social Security (DSS) and the Inland Revenue's (IR) management of the computer functions (see Figure 7.3).

In January 1997, Alan Stevens (Managing Director of EDS UK) announced the formation of a new strategic business unit (SBU) that combined EDS's

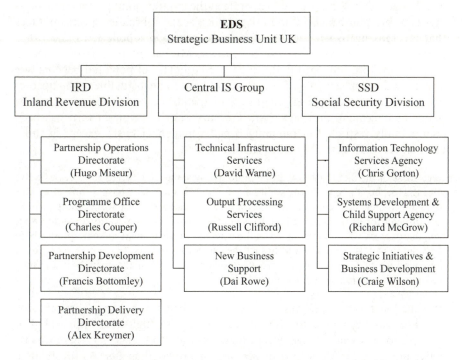

Fig. 7.3. *EDS's strategic business unit structure for the IR and SSD*

Source: Interviews and Collins 1997: 14.

Department of Social Security (DSS) and IR technical and production services groups (Collins 1997). This merger was to free up money for investments in improvements and provide EDS with savings, but the merger would not impinge on the legal data protection requirements. EDS intended to diminish duplication, streamline management, and improve account coordination and its management infrastructure. The changes led to the formation of a newly dedicated business support group with the sole responsibility of technical consultancy and the provision of new business support services. EDS's restructuring dedicated part of its SBU to delivering solely value-added benefits.

By mid-1997, following EDS's reorganization, discussions once again centred on the potential cost savings. The Revenue was still seeking to achieve the targeted cost savings of £225 million. These renewed discussions seemed feasible now since EDS had acquired an understanding, and was aware of where the cost drivers were at the Revenue, and could structure any additional service requests and costings accordingly. The renewed awareness, however, was not intended to restrict any value-added benefits EDS could provide. Indeed, the Revenue was very much looking for value-added benefits. At monthly review meetings managers discussed keenly a number of possible initiatives that EDS

Strategic Partnering in the Public Sector

could undertake: 'What we try to operate at the monthly joint partnership meetings is to bring in beneficial initiatives which are of a broader spectrum. Ones that are looking to get the best approach from our suppliers, to encourage them to use their creativity' (IT Executive). Mutual interests were vested in these discussions, but, for the Revenue, the boundary of potential benefits was drawn by the contract. Any changes would have to be justifiable in the upcoming audit, and of course any additional expenditure had to be approved by senior management, and hence the Treasury. The Revenue in turn has been contractually restricted in pursuing benefits that incur costs, except in those cases where EDS actually makes the investment:

Regardless of the fact that it might be inhibited by some of the control processes we've got in place, but to actually say we'll have a go at this and let's have a look after how we might change those control processes to take advantage of those sort of things. That's very difficult for us because we've always got the prospect of our National Audit Office hanging over us who are bound to make a report to Parliament at some point about the validity of this contract. And in fact they start that big audit later this year. So we are conscious that we've got to have a reasonable account of the changes in the relationship that we are making. (Senior IT Executive)

In some instances, however, where critical benefits became apparent the Revenue has been able to alter the contract with high-level approval. For example, one crucial change was to take account of the fact that there was no active incentive for EDS to over-perform or provide benefits. As formulated, the contract did not incentivize EDS to reduce costs, instead they would only take the risk and gain no reward:

We have changed the contract over the course of the opening three years where we thought it would be mutually beneficial. And one particular area is where we've introduced an incentive for EDS to reduce the capital costs of IT. Prior to that they had an active disincentive in the contract because they got an agreed mark-up on any capital item they buy for the provision of our service. And if it costs less they got less mark-up, just in total terms. So we introduced some arrangement within the contract that meant that it was worth their while to drive some harder bargains and deals. We would then share the benefit of those decreased costs. (Senior Partnership Executive)

Other changes have been made to the underlying procedures that the contract implicitly addresses. These have been adapted according to changes and became more streamlined than before. For example:

If you looked at the way our central resource ordering process worked and compared it over the three years to the contract it's significantly simplified now. We now run it with about 25 resource types rather than over 50, we run it on a quarterly basis rather than monthly, so we've come to an accommodation jointly as to how we handle that. We've also got quite a lot of flexibility about the provision of resources and when, for reasons not within our control, some of those things don't come to fruition, how we deal with that. (IT Director)

These changes have helped both parties' flexibility. However, in those circumstances where minor changes may be beneficial, informal arrangements have been agreed. This was critical to the relationship and in terms of preserving the legality of the contract, because the contract at the end of day had to be seen to govern the relationship. As one respondent noted:

We are always looking at what the clauses in the contract are saying about this area, we are looking to whether we believe that the contract was comprehensive in that area, whether it needs to have some changes because we are quite open to changes in the contract if they are beneficial. But we always view that in the context of what is the contract saying about this area of work. (Customer Service Executive)

In order to ensure the contract's representativeness of technological, business, and government changes it has had to be updated and aligned regularly. This meant the relationship continued to be governed by the contract:

No, we have the contract out where there's any clarification needed. And we try to keep it up to date as well. So that's something we can refer to and set the basis for an ongoing discussion. (Partnership Executive).

And that's why we are constantly reappraising how well these processes and structures are serving our business community. If we were to find that there was something fundamentally blocking the provision of service or the exploitation of the technology, we will change it. And that's a prominent feature of this contract. (Customer Service Executive)

By late 1997, initial performance and cost evaluations indicated that the Revenue was on target to achieve their predicted costs saving of £225 million pounds. In part, some of the early extra costs not accounted for were being recovered through the sharing of risks and rewards: 'We are sharing the rewards of the venture. We are getting cheaper IT than we started with, and if there is excess profits we are sharing in those, but I think we are taking opportunities along the way to lay off some of the risks within the IR' (Assistant Director Partnership Group). However, the unpredictability of two up-coming challenges in late 1997 and early 1998 were of particular concern, with potential significant repercussion for the relationship and for achieving the anticipated costs savings. First, the relationship had to face and adapt to the challenge of policy changes, in, for example, the tax system, following the election of the new government:

We are expected to be able to provide a certain element of policy change and adaptation to our tax systems. In fact, at the moment, because we've just had a change in government, we've got some far more significant policy changes being considered, announced through the House [of Commons] and some of which will no doubt be announced in the upcoming Budget. Which are significantly more than we've had. (Senior Partnership Executive)

We are facing more change than we've seen before, so we are concerned as a partnership whether we can cope with the amount of change that is being pushed our way. (IT Executive)

The impact of potential policy changes on the relationship required a joint re-evaluation and prioritization of system implementations and technology changes. In addition, in many cases these demanded renewed cost calculations and budgetary assessment, and quite possibly placing requests for further funds to compensate for the additional services.

What we have to do is assess how we can cope with the existing funds and how we prioritize the money we spend on IT within the IR and whether we can get other funds from within the Revenue budget and apply them to IT. And we have a big prioritization process, it's a committee chaired by one of the Deputy Chairmen, and actually we have representation from EDS on that committee. [. . .] and when we are providing estimates of what certain policy changes would cost they are coming out of the EDS camp. We've got people that are collaborating with our feasibility appraisal people in what those estimates would be and what the costs would be. And the partnership is central to all of that. And where we can't cope, where we've got something that's far too big, we have to make special representation right through to the Treasury and to the Chancellor [of the Exchequer] himself if necessary to get extra funds. (IT Director)

Secondly, the relationship was facing a challenge in relation to the changes in technology undertaken at the Revenue over the past months. Particularly significant were the issues of compatibility and the Year 2000 computer compliance problem:

We've got changes in technology that we've become alert to in the last six months or so which is to do with the impact of the move of the desktop support services from a 16 to 32 bit architecture. And we've got some heavy dependency in some intricate interim software that we've created ourselves on specific products that are associated with the 16 bit architecture. And how we move our desktop terminals, of which there are 50,000, from 16 bit to 32—because the market place is not supporting 16 bit any more. (Technology Adviser)

And there was the Year 2000 issue:

Over the last year we've faced up to the year 2000 problems and we've come to an arrangement with EDS to do that as a big fixed price deal. (IT Executive)

In summary, the relationship by early 1998 had achieved a high degree of maturity and revealed clear signs of strategic partnering. Both parties had engaged in risk-reward sharing scenarios, had gone through testing times of improving the relationship (e.g. the perceptions exercise), and EDS and the Revenue had been integrated at high strategic levels. Of course, the increase in costs of 60 per cent of the contract value presented EDS with significant incentives to invest substantial resources to ensure success. Upcoming challenges in 1998/1999 were to present new testing grounds for the workings of the relationship, especially in a context of a tighter budget and the looming mid-term government audit.

MID-CONTRACT AUDIT ON NEW WORK PLACED (1998–1999)

With the onset of the mid-term audit of the contract after five years, a testing time was to arise for both parties for the next year. Of particular concern was the significant increase in the overall expenditure. Given the government's requirement for IR's accountability, this posed a significant concern, especially since none of the additional services that the Revenue was now receiving from EDS had been market tested. As it stood, by March 1999 the Revenue had paid £874 million for services and an additional £163 million for the use of capital equipment. According to the National Audit Office (NAO) Report in 2000, the mix of these services by value was split into 62 per cent operations, 23 per cent development work, 8 per cent maintenance, 6 per cent enhancements, and 1 per cent other. This implied that, after five years, the Revenue had already covered the initial estimate of the overall contract value of £1,033 billion. In fact, the projected contract value was now estimated to be £2.01 billion for the ten years. Table 7.3 breaks down the updated cost projections.

Clearly, most of the expenditure over the said time period was on new work. Nearly 400 new projects had been authorized since the start of the contract, fifty of which accounted for 95 per cent of the increase in costs. In particular, the introduction of CESA and the Department's infrastructure 2000 initiative each accounted for over a quarter of EDS's development effort. In securing the optimum value from EDS for the £533 million spend increase on new work, it was crucial that the IR ensured that the technical solutions procured from EDS would offer the most efficient, effective, and economic means for supporting its business requirements. This also defined the basis for the ensuing NAO investigation into some of the main projects listed in Table 7.4. The focus in particular was on how the following issues were handled (see NAO 2000: 15):

- identification of the requirements;
- investigation of the requirement, definition of the information technology element, and development of solutions;

Table 7.3. *Updated projected spend on outsourcing contract with EDS*

Projected value at contract award (1994)	£1,033 billion
Post-contract verification adjustment	£203 million
Workload increases, including new work completed, ongoing, and projected	£533 million
Inflation	£248 million
Current projected revenue spend	£2.01 billion

Source: Inland Revenue, NAO Report 2000.

Table 7.4. *Projects and new work placed with EDS since 1994*

Project name and description	Estimated EDS life-cycle cost (£m)	Estimated total life-cycle cost (£m)	Status in Dec. 1999
Computerized environment for self-assessment (CESA)—Release 2 *This was the second stage of the IT project designed to support the implementation of the income tax self-assessment initiative and related to the development of software to enable taxpayer returns to be entered and processed. Separate costs for this element were not available*	N/A	N/A	Completed
Infrastructure 2000 (I2K) *Department-wide programme to upgrade desktop IT systems*	122	203	In development
Construction industry scheme *Development of new system to support reform of tax collection in the construction industry*	55	102	In development
Collection of student loan repayments *To enable the Department to assume responsibility for the collection of student loan repayments, and to pay over and pass details of payments to the Student Loans Company*	8	32	In development
Payroll and personnel management information system *To develop an integrated payroll and personnel management information system*	8	28	Completed
Individual savings accounts *To support introduction of individual savings accounts from April 1999*	9	21	In development
Integrated debt management system *To develop a fully integrated debt management environment*	1	16	In development

Table 7.4. *Continued*

Project name and description	Estimated EDS life-cycle cost (£m)	Estimated total life-cycle cost (£m)	Status in Dec. 1999
Call centre experiment *To set up a fully functional executive call centre to assess the viability of a national call centre network*	2	13	In development
Business continuity implementation *To provide a disaster recovery facility for critical mainframe services*	2	12	Completed
Integrated repayment system *To develop an integrated repayments system for the Financial Intermediaries and Claims Office*	N/A	4	Completed
Repayment of interest on PAYE *Enhancements to BROCS system (Business Review of the Collection Service) to introduce a cost-effective and efficient means of repaying interest in cases of PAYE overpayments*	0.6	0.7	Completed
Regional processing centre rationalization *EDS performance improvement programme involving the closure of three regional processing centres*	N/A	N/A	Completed

Source: Adapted from NAO Report (2000: 67).

- evaluation of proposed solutions received from EDS and approval of the project concept and of the funds to proceed;
- project management of the overall development; and
- project evaluation and handover to live running.

As a side effect, the relationship suffered from the strain of having NAO investigators monitoring daily operations and interviewing managers about their perceptions concerning the relationship and the business of placing new work. The pressure on EDS, but also on the residual outsourcing relationship management team, was to ensure that a true reflection of the partnership was transmitted to the investigators. This was difficult as many operations had become implicit, rather than being explicitly described. As one senior executive noted:

They did have a couple, two or three of their investigators involved, which took about a year in research and a fair amount of effort from ourselves in making sure that it was a true reflection of what had been achieved and what was in place. They were particularly concentrating on 'how in a contract of this nature a series of rewards of new work over a 10 year period is placed'. And were they always guaranteeing good value for money for the department. There were some recommendations in it, but generally it confirmed that the relationship was robust and the contract controls were operating properly.

The NAO's probing was based on trying to determine whether the contract was representing true value for money and whether the anticipated benefits were being achieved. In response the IR together with EDS spent substantial time on calculating the financial benefits to give not only an insight into the savings, but also to have a better means of forecasting the overall contract value:

And we developed a big—what we call a unit cost—model to actually establish what all the outputs were, and how the unit costs were reducing year on year. And we were able to say that for the actual volumes we'd signed up to we were at around £300 million savings already on the equivalent rate at the start of the contract in March 2000. So we are comfortable that we are ahead of the target savings and at the end of the contract we will be able to report that we have made more than the £225 million on the base undertakings. (Senior Partnership Executive)

The outcome of the contract audit was extremely positive. Not only had the investigators found a well-working strategic partnership that had led to extensive value-added benefits in terms of technology, services, new development, and cost savings, but also the underlying operational processes in terms of new work placement, contract management, and relationship management were extremely robust and effective. Nevertheless, a number of recommendations concerning software development were made, especially in relation to procuring software development productivity rates comparable to the private sector.

POST-AUDIT AND UPCOMING CHALLENGES
(2000 AND BEYOND)

Following the positive outcomes of the audit, both parties felt much more secure and reassured about the strength of their relationship, and about their under-lying operational processes. In fact their sense of operational comfortableness led managers, in accordance with the contract specialists, to minimize the amount of regular service level measures that parties were performing. They found that the extensive degree of measurements being regularly performed provided little useful insights, as the technology infrastructure had changed so much over the last few years. In addition, it was consuming too much time and was incurring significant administrative costs. A senior manager further explained:

At one point we were measuring something like against 1,000 measures a month to see all the intricate parts of the service. We are looking to reduce that to the more signifi-cant ones at the moment because it's a lot of data. Some of it is not valuable and we can get rid of that. So we are looking to focus.

The impetus for this change in monitoring practice came, in part, from the desktop 'refresh' project that entailed the complete changeover of the existing mainframe-based computing infrastructure to one that operates essentially on a client-server, desktop computer basis. The change would involve a major roll-out of new machines to enable the IR to run Windows NT. This Infrastructure 2000 (I2K) project posed quite a short-term challenge:

The thing that's happened along with what we call our desktop refresh, we call I2K (infrastructure 2000) and the new software controls around that service, we are able to get some insight in service from the terminal end rather than from the mainframe. [. . .] Now we are able to get statistics for the desktop itself. And we are having a more sophisticated debate with the user community about what sort of level of service they can anticipate. EDS broke all records to roll out 55,000 terminals over less than a year. It was a big undertaking, and the roll-out went generally very smoothly. (Senior Partnership Executive)

The integration of this new infrastructure was to take at least ten months, due to the size and complexity of the system, the compatibility problems, and the adoption of the system/computers by staff. In many instances, the intro-duction did cause considerable dissatisfaction as an October 1999 article en-titled 'End of the EDS Dream' noted (Collins 1999*a*). End-users had become so dissatisfied with poor services, computers going down, bad response times to requests, being unable to print and access vital programs, that they called for the early termination of the contract. John Yard,[1] the IR's IT director, explained that EDS was not to blame for the difficulties in many cases as 'with the increasing complexity of IT we need to recognise that it takes time to con-

---

[1] Quoted by Collins (1999*b*: 22).

solidate and bed down systems of great complexity. [. . .] we are having a concentrated attack to put the problems right and make the service more robust.'

In the longer term, for the coming years up to the end of contract, three
developments posed a major concern for the outsourcing relationship. The first
challenge was going to put the most pressure on the relationship, as it focused
on the upcoming re-tendering of the overall contract which would start in
earnest in 2002. The pressure would be on EDS to ensure continuity of services
at a very high level, but also maintain the relationship at a strategic level. In
any event, if the relationship was working well and service levels were being
achieved EDS may have an advantage:

Because we will be obliged to compete this contract at the end, and that process will
start from about the two-year mark. The end of the contract is July 2004, so from July
2002 we will be starting to look at how we create real market competition. From EDS's
point of view, if they are delivering they are clearly going to be in a powerful position,
but we do want to go to market competition, so that we can get the best value from the
market place. And that will be difficult for us and also for EDS because that will bring
pressure on them and no doubt there will be some tensions as we go into that. (Senior
Partnership Executive)

The second challenge would be the move of the IR to the Euro currency.
This implied substantial programming changes to ensure conversion, which
would affect every system currently operating in some way. As managers noted,
this would very likely occupy them for a number of years until all systems had
been altered. The third challenge would be the increasing focus of the government on the Revenue to take over additional services from other departments
due to its successful track record of delivering high-quality services. For
example, this had, in 2000, led the government to decide to transfer the national
insurance recording system (NIRS) being developed by Andersen Consulting,
from the Department of Social Security (DSS) to the Revenue. The reason was,
first, that it phased its output directly into the IR's systems anyway, but secondly, extensive development problems had occurred, which needed careful
project management attention to see it through to completion. A senior IT executive further explained the upcoming NIRS challenge:

We've got this big national insurance recording system which is with Andersen
Consulting. And it is a system that interfaces with ours because the basic return that
comes from an employer that says how much I've been paid, how much tax and national
insurance I've paid as a result of that, is required for both the tax systems and the
national insurance and pensions systems. So there is a natural interface between
Andersen's and EDS. [. . .] The NIRSII programme had a very bad reputation. It was
late going live, it wasn't fully functional, it's still not absolutely fully functional. It probably is fully functional at the moment but just in the last couple of months it's become
fully functional, but we've got backlogs of work that need to be recovered.

The difficulty with integrating and operationalizing this NIRS system would
be fostering cooperation between Andersen Consulting and EDS, the general
requirement being that they provided a seamless service. In light of the BPX

experience in Chapter 5, and them being essentially competitors, this could turn out to be extremely problematic.

CASE ANALYSIS AND DISCUSSION

The Inland Revenue–EDS case portrays a reasonably effective outsourcing arrangement in the 1994–2000 period, given how high risk the venture was as a total outsourcing, long-term single supplier deal in a complex public sector context. There always remain cost issues in such large deals in the public sector—as has been witnessed since the mid-1990s not just at the IR but also in several other deals in the UK, USA, Australia, New Zealand, and mainland Europe. The IR argument would seem to be that the original cost savings would be achieved, but they were always for a restricted range of operational services. EDS was prepared to take a loss on mainframe operations, for example, in order to get access to the wider IR market place for additional services and development work. In fact EDS made no profit on its mainframe service until the DSS and IR consolidation took place some halfway into the contract. The reality was that the total cost of the ten-year arrangement would be closer to £2.4 billion than to the £1.2 billion originally cited. At the same time much was being achieved, and EDS and IR, after a problematic start, had certainly developed relationship dimensions that ensured risk mitigation, focus, and delivery.

Risk Profile at Inland Revenue–EDS

The case demonstrates some successes with 'total' or 'strategic' outsourcing. As indicated above, ostensibly the risk profile was not promising. At the same time, the fact that the IR was in many ways *the* central government department—dependent on it as the UK government was for tax revenue—meant that the IR-EDS deal was always going to be very high profile, and had to be demonstrably successful from the point of view of all parties involved. This in itself was a significant risk mitigation factor. For EDS, the IR could be a significant reference site for other potential large-scale deals it could chase in public sectors in the UK, Europe, and elsewhere. After all, every government has a tax revenue function. EDS could also concentrate its effort, unlike in the Xerox case, which was on a more geographically dispersed and global basis, and would prioritize its best skills to work at the IR, or make sure the skills were obtained from subcontractors, as occurred in the CESA project.

The IR invested much time and effort in building to contract, and this helped to stabilize its control of events:

I think they [EDS] were surprised about the preparation we'd done. I think in a sense that was a big advantage to us because we were able to drive, and I think that a key for us was to stay very much in the driving seat about what we want from them. (IT Director)

Table 7.5. *Risk factors in the IR-EDS venture*

Decision factors and objectives	Inland Revenue's application	Comments by participants on risks at Inland Revenue
Leading competitive advantage or commodity IT	Both outsourced	Staff could be transferred to other contracts. Break-up of leading competence advantage over time.
Critical or useful IT	Both outsourced	Risk of long-term loss of control of critical systems
Degree of business political and technical uncertainty	All high	High risks for both IR and EDS
Degree of in-house technology maturity	Operations: high Development: low	Dangers if business user not committed to IT projects and in-house technical capability is not maintained
Level of IT integration with other systems/users	Mixed	Risks in vendor relations with business
In-house capability relative to market	High in some areas, but time and number pressures	Needed external assistance given government deadlines. Reduced functionality as a result.
Economic rationale	Cost savings on base service of £225 million	Economies of scale achievable. Development costs higher than anticipated. Some superior management practices introduced.
Rate of technological change across 10-year contract	Predicted to be high	Could be locked into vendor's IT strategy
Suitable vendor available	Few capable vendors	Likely high switching costs
In-house management capability to deliver outsourcing	Adequate at the start but needed development	Some danger of losing control of IT destiny
Handling of human resources issues	Resolved after initial difficulties	Not a significant issue

Source: Adapted from Willcocks and Kern 1998.

A number of significant risks remained latent within the outsourcing arrangement over its first four years, and subsequently. These are summarized in Table 7.5 which compares the decision-making factors and objectives detailed in the earlier part of the case against 1994–2000 events at the Revenue.

The problems of incomplete contracting and 'presentiation' became notorious in some similar long-term deals signed in the early 1990s. However, on the whole, IR's contracting arrangements made a lot of sense, though it found it difficult to achieve discounts for early notification of future work, due to difficulties in actually predicting resources required. The IR also retained a strong contract management group, though it had some weaknesses in the technical knowledge, project management, and relationship management areas, which put it in a less strong position relative to the vendor. Certainly, a risk factor initially was the lack of experience the IR management had with managing total outsourcing. By 2000, an interesting question was: how far had asymmetries of power developed in favour of the vendor? Certainly switching costs had become so prohibitive that it seemed unlikely that anyone other than EDS could be chosen when the contract came up for renewal in 2004. Had the IR retained and developed enough countervailing power? Where such power rested was in the high-profile nature of the deal, its closeness to the UK government, in the contractual and measurement arrangements, in the retained management capabilities, and in the relationship management arrangements. Certainly by 2000 these were well developed and continuously maintained.

Strategic Intent

Outsourcing at the Revenue was a government-mandated necessity once a comparative review of external suppliers' prices revealed that the external market could perform some of the IR's IT activities at a lower cost. A worrying aspect was that the government mandate was informed as much by ideology as by a strong economic rationale, and this could have put the success of business, technical, and economic objectives in danger. The resulting argument in favour of total outsourcing was stated as the intent to access the eventual supplier's complete organization and expertise, with the specific objective of forming a strategic relationship. The true debate for not selectively outsourcing did not become evident in the research, though it seems plausible that the costs of revamping the technology, infrastructure, and application would have generally increased the overall costs of IT at the Revenue and exceeded those offered through outsourcing.

In addition, the CESA project, announced by the government at relatively short notice, benefited from having a totally committed and risk-involved supplier right from the start, even though the government's exact intentions prior to signing the contract were not completely apparent. Still the Revenue has benefited from total outsourcing, as it meant sharing the risks with a highly resourced and competent vendor.

The case points, however, to the political and technical uncertainties that can plague public sector projects. The government-mandated introduction of the self-assessment scheme by April 1997 represents merely a large-scale high-profile example of the additional risks engendered when having to develop new systems during an outsourcing contract. Even a 'strategic partnership' arrangement seems to come under considerable strain in such circumstances as prevailing in the Inland Revenue deal. In previous work carried out by Willcocks (1994) examples are provided of senior government ministers developing government policy without a real understanding of the IT implications, and the difficulties involved in providing information systems support. In the Inland Revenue case this factor would seem to have a bearing both on the government commitment to tight deadlines for the delivery of the self-assessment scheme, but also to its predilection for privatizing IT services wholesale. In the Inland Revenue case it may well have been looking for a domino effect, with the Inland Revenue deal having managers and a supplier committed to making it a high-profile success, so leading the way for other government departments, and perhaps also for local governments and the National Health System.

Contract Isssues

Both parties were very secure on establishing the relationship on the basis of the contract. With the help of internal and external lawyers, the resulting contract was highly detailed and designed specifically to reduce negotiations on price to a minimum, not only at the bid stage but across the lifetime of the contract. 'The contract is a bit like a nuclear deterrent, you need one and you've got to have a framework, but actually if you've got to use it you are probably in trouble' (John Yard, IT Director). The IR realized early on that a ten-year contract presented considerable risks and uncertainties, especially in terms of completeness and representativeness of the contractual arrangements over time:

But it [the contract] never gets around the problem that you cannot tie your supplier down to the projects that you are going to undertake in the long term. You don't know what they are. The Internet for example, I think I'm right in saying it was hardly talked about in 1993, but now it's big business. (IT Director)

Mainly because we knew that we couldn't possibly predict what our requirements would be and how they would change from day one through the life of a ten-year contract. So we were quite clear that we needed a lot more flexibility than that traditional relationship would bring us. (Partnership Executive)

There was, in turn, to be a real threat of opportunism as the dependency on EDS and the relationship grew over time and the contract's updatedness eroded. Although the Revenue had invested in external experts to draw up detailed contractual safeguards against any such opportunism, it became apparent that these were more theoretical than realistically enforceable, since the Revenue could not afford to fall out with EDS, especially in light of the high-profile CESA project. For EDS, on the other hand, it became clear that they could only meet the contractual promises if they had the level of control they desired. In fact this seemed the overarching reason why EDS was given control of the self-assessment project six months earlier than contractually planned.

The Structural Dimension

After initial staff problems, assets and staff transfers were managed well by both EDS and the Revenue. Very tight performance assessment criteria and procedures were put in place and a well-staffed contract management team monitored EDS's performance closely and exchanged information on a regular basis with vendor counterparts. The management process developed over the years integrated and hence permeated every management level, up to the board level of both organizations. As one respondent noted, in explaining the efforts put into developing a management infrastructure:

The skills you need to put in, the time you need to put in, the money you need to put into deciding what you are going to do and then carrying it through are considerable. It's got to be managed properly and that will stay the case for a long time until there are some templates which people can follow much more easily. (Director General, Revenue)

In fact, EDS for its part, over the first three years, established suitable complementary management staffing arrangements, and service ethics, to deliver the contract. Informal social adaptations necessarily developed over time between the parties as a result of communication and contact. One comment here is that both vendor and client managers in the first eighteen months were used to operating on a strict contractual basis, but this created modes of exchange that hindered further cooperative developments, and both had to be replaced. People were more important than structures, as we also found in, for example, the BPX case in Chapter 5. However, as also found in Chapter 6, the case emphasized that it is important to operate both at a contractual and cooperative level. As one respondent said, in referring to the need to go beyond contract micro-management: 'The management is to do with the totality of what you get for your money, not just at the micro-level' (Director General, Revenue). As evident in the case, IR and EDS managers operated closely on cost/performance and service issues, and on eliciting business requirements and getting these translated into EDS objectives. But none of this focused on the larger picture, and over time none of it could be guaranteed to translate into the 'totality' of joint benefits intended from the overall outsourcing arrangement. Both parties came to realize that this required additional mechanisms and management effort, particularly in the area of relationship development and maintenance. The 'exception review' determined just some of the activities and actions that needed attention, and efforts undertaken by both parties were designed to respond to some of the perceived relationship needs over the coming months of 1997 and 1998. In addition, EDS's structural amalgamation in 1997 of the Social Security and Inland Revenue divisions into a single SBU, presented EDS with economies of scale, improved relationship management arrangements, and for the IR improved the potential to benefit from cross fertilization of ideas and value-added benefits.

Interactions

The formal mechanisms and management arrangements defined right from the start by the Revenue were essential to IR-EDS's relationship development. The management structure initially defined part of the Revenue's risk mitigation plan and identified early on the essential interactions between the parties. This was to pay off for both parties as it simplified the interaction process by defining explicitly the exchanges. In particular, it determined vital information exchanges. Indeed, communication helped to facilitate the development of mutual objectives and social and cultural adaptation. In many instances throughout the case it identified a critical part that assured continuation and a well-working relationship.

Even though the formal service levels and requirements were only specified during the initial six months of post-contract management, most service exchanges had continued as defined by the IR's previous performance records. In fact, few problems were mentioned by interviewees concerning service level problems. The operational task involved running the inherited systems, largely with the same staff. Furthermore it is plausible to assume that, due to the high profile of the CESA project, EDS and the IR also focused undue attention, and in fact most resources on its successful achievement. These two factors in combination might explain in part why so few service level and request problems arose in the 1994–7 post-contract period. Subsequently, in years 4–7 of the contract, the relationship dimension had entered what Lacity and Willcocks (2000) have called a Middle phase. What is noticeable in the EDS-IR case is how the interactions became much smoother and had stabilized into much more productive relations.

Behavioural Issues

The case presents an interesting conflict scenario in the first eighteen months of its operation, which effectively hindered the operationalization of the contract, because both the account manager and the Revenue's manager were still battling over terms as they had done in the contract negotiations. Only once this conflict situation had been resolved through their replacement, did the relationship begin to take form. This emphasized the criticality of mutually resolving conflicts early on in the relationship, or else the relationships as such will grind to a halt. It also gave a flavour of the importance that active relationship management was to have in keeping on track and leveraging the outsourcing deal.

The case also raises some concerns about asymmetries of dependence developing over time. As one example, contractually, if IR senior managers were unhappy with EDS performance, they could have decided not to transfer the development staff in 1996. The contract was specifically set up to transfer staff over at different times in order to give IR some leverage over the supplier. However, one can already see that by mid-1995, the Inland Revenue could hardly switch supplier; it was already highly dependent on EDS. It has also been clearly in the interest of the 'strategic supplier' to increase this dependence. As reported by Collins (1994):

EDS has become the back-room controller of some of the nation's most important tax assets. It 'owns' 1,200 of the Revenue's computer operations staff, 800 of its development specialists and business analysts, much of its hardware and software and even its buildings. In short it controls the skills and software that have been built up over 30 years which have a vital function in the collection of the nation's tax revenues. (p. 6)

One particularly worrying feature in other long-term outsourcing deals Willcocks et al. (1995, 1996) researched was the extent to which in-house technical capability became eroded over time. Some elements of this are present in the IR case. It is possible for an in-house IT function to lose control of its IT destiny over time as a supplier actively penetrates the business as well as the technical management of the client organization. Such dependence on a single supplier also means that switching costs at any point would be very prohibitive.

Finally, in terms of behaviours, the IR case highlights that in practice both client and vendor organizations found considerable difficulty in moving to a cooperative stance and developing trust. On the one hand, this might be due to the Revenue's strict confidentiality, accountability, and audibility pressures, which hinder the development of cooperation and trust in an external organization whose culture and mode of operation does not resonate with that of the Revenue, or indeed with public sector practice generally. On the other, the deal's complexity, size, and the time pressures for delivery ensured there was an understandable focus on the contract. Both parties subsequently recognized that additional mechanisms for the development of cooperation and trust needed to be facilitated and implemented. Once again, these needed to be such that they took into account—as they eventually did—the fact that the relationship between the IR and EDS parties could be cooperative, collaborative, or adversarial, depending on the task and issue at hand (Lacity and Willcocks 2000).

Efficiency and Outcomes

In retrospect, one can begin to question the original economic rationale, though the real issue is whether, without using the market extensively, the IR could have carried out many of the projects, like CESA in the time frames required. Also it is necessary to assess the economic rationale as part of the multiple objectives, rather than in isolation. In the light of rising costs over the 1994–2000 period it is not clear that in-house service costs were out of line with what the market would charge either. On the other hand, it was clear that the outsourcing evaluation enabled the identification of ways in which in-house IT could be run more efficiently:

The contract helps to drive out [. . .] a lot of the questions of cost and origin of costs, which seemed less important. They weren't necessarily less important, they just seemed less important at the time. I think one of the things that the contract does drive out is a much better understanding of costs within individual business streams. What it is they are acquiring, they are forced to consider what it is they need and what their relative priorities are in the first place. And they have to accept, like any commercial undertaking, that there is a price to pay. (Customer Service Manager)

The two most economically viable options were to achieve these in-house, or point them out to the vendor and let this be reflected in the price charged. The IR chose the latter course of action.

The reasons cited for outsourcing make sense but the overall mandate from the government would seem to have been the dominant influence. An important driver was the desire for cost savings and the assumption that private sector suppliers could deliver IT more efficiently than public sector departments, even while making a profit. The 20 per cent cost savings regularly touted at the beginning of the project would seem to have been partly offset by the unanticipated £200 million extra cost incurred within a year of project commencement. When the self-assessment development project is then taken into account, it becomes clear that cost savings were, even by 1996/7, becoming a much lower priority, though the original operational cost savings of £225 million were still protected by contract.

Were the other original objectives being achieved after seven years? The deal did enhance IT staff career opportunities, reduce development time, allow the IR to gain access to new technologies, and improve IT efficiency. The NAO 2000 report suggested that there was value for money in the arrangement, though the measures for evaluating this were not always found to be in place. As in the BAe case in Chapter 4, it is actually quite difficult to make a judgement on this issue. Ostensibly there are efficiency improvements in IT operations, and EDS are providing a lot of development, but at the same time IT costs have risen significantly beyond those cited at the beginning. At the same time, control and relationship management seemed to be in place, and the relationship had developed considerably and, given the understandably complex business of delivering service, seemed to be a productive one.

CONCLUSION

The case study reveals a complicated set of issues being managed through a strategic relationship in a difficult public service context. The case raises the issue whether the UK public sector environment in the early and mid-1990s was actually appropriate for anything other than relatively short-term contracts on a selective basis. At the Inland Revenue it became clear that volatility in government policy added a high-risk project to an already complicated large-scale outsourcing arrangement in 'start-up' mode. The fact that this cut across attempts to develop several major new systems using new technologies that the supplier as well as the in-house IT staff were not clear on, only heightened the uncertainty, risks, and difficulties for developing a relationship. However, the high-profile nature of the deal, and the importance of the IR as the tax raising department for the government has probably served to counterbalance many of the uncertainties that would not be so easily offset in other strategic partnering cases.

Upcoming for the Inland Revenue, by 2001, were two major issues. The first related to the dangers inherent in allowing EDS to develop a 'natural monopoly' on IT work at both the Inland Revenue and Department of Social Security. A settled down supplier invariably has advantages over potential competitors, including knowledge of the client systems and ways of working, strong relationships with client managers and staff, an insider understanding of requirements and likely future directions. To maintain its position a company such as EDS would be eager to underbid any competitor if the contract was put up to competition in 2004, and could manifestly demonstrate superior client-specific skills and know-how. The problem always remains to develop enough countervailing power and leverage to ensure supplier performance remains sharp. In the IR's case much will depend on the ability to create appropriate contracts and relationship mechanisms, and retaining key in-house capabilities to actively manage the supplier(s). But we would suggest that by 2004 switching costs out of the large-scale outsourcing deal would be prohibitive. One move might be to give EDS a more limited contract and introduce a level of competition in certain types of IT work. Some organizations, after worse experiences than that of the IR, have actually started rebuilding parts of their in-house development capability e.g. at East Midlands Electricity-Perot in the mid-1990s, and MLC-ISSC (Australia) in the late 1990s—which remains a possible option at the IR.

The second related issue was how to manage the final three years of the contract to ensure continuity of service, whatever choices are made about IT sourcing direction post-2004. In what Lacity and Willcocks (2000) call this Mature phase, the IR needs to recalibrate its investment criteria and determine if the relationship will be extended or terminated. But it also needs to manage the arrangement productively from day to day, in such a way that a range of IT sourcing options will still be possible in 2004. This really does require very careful relationship management, and is another point at which a relationship advantage can be achieved.

REFERENCES

British Council (1997). 'Governance and Law: Briefing issue 1'. UK government.

Collins, T. (1994). 'Is EDS Worthy of the Lion's Share of the Tax System?'. *Computer Weekly* (June), 6.

—— (1995). 'Special Report Inland Revenue: Many Happy Returns?'. *Computer Weekly* (22 June), 32–5.

—— (1996*a*) 'About-Turn As Tax Data Goes Abroad'. *Computer Weekly* (24 October), 16.

—— (1996*b*) 'Is EDS Overtaxed?'. *Computer Weekly* (11 April), 20.

—— (1997). 'How EDS will Merge the Revenue and DSS'. *Computer Weekly* (16 January), 20.

—— (1999*a*). 'End of the EDS Dream'. News Analysis, *Computer Weekly* (28 October), 22.

—— (1999*b*) 'Addressing the Problem'. *Computer Weekly* (28 October), p. 22.

—— (2000). 'Report Shows Lack of Revenue Testing'. *Computer Weekly* (30 March), 6.

Drewry, T., and Butcher, T. (1988). *The Civil Service Today*. Civil Service Statistics, UK.

EDS (1998). 'Financial Highlights'. http://www.eds.com

Green-Armytage, R. (1993). 'Six Firms in Battle for Inland Revenue Deal'. *Computer Weekly* (28 January).

Lacity, M., and Willcocks, L. (2000). *Global Information Technology Outsourcing: In Search of Business Advantage*. Wiley, Chichester.

Macintyre, M. (1994). 'Case Study: New Face of the Taxman'. *Business & Technology Magazine* (January), 25.

National Audit Office (NAO) (1995). *Inland Revenue: Market Testing the Information Technology Office*. HMSO, HC 245, London.

—— (2000). *Inland Revenue/EDS Strategic Partnership: Award of New Work*. HMSO, HC 351, London.

Smith, S. (1996). 'Systems: Taxed to the limit'. *Computer Weekly* (31 October), 48.

—— (1997). 'Government IT-EDS: Playing the monopoly game'. *Computer Weekly* (17 April), 40–2.

Willcocks, L. (1994). 'Managing Information Systems in UK Public Administration: Issues and Prospects'. *Public Administration*, 72/1: 13–32.

—— Fitzgerald, G., and Lacity, M. (1996). 'To Outsource IT or not? Recent Research on Economics and Evaluation Practice'. *European Journal of Information Systems*, 5: 143–60.

—— and Kern, T. (1998). 'IT Outsourcing as Strategic Partnering: The Case of the UK Inland Revenue'. *European Jouranal of Information Systems*, 7: 29–45.

—— Lacity, M., and Fitzgerald, G. (1995). 'IT Outsourcing in Europe and the USA: Assessment Issues'. *International Journal of Information Management*, 15/5: 333–51.

Yazel, L. (1994). 'Audit Office damns Revenue', *Computing* (16 June), 3.

8

Relationship Management:
A Cross-Case Perspective

INTRODUCTION

In the previous five chapters we have learned a great deal about how IT out-sourcing has been conducted in a range of contexts, what risks were under-gone, what relationship management practices were adopted, and with what outcomes. At this point we ask the question: what more can we learn from revisiting the case histories and looking at events and findings across them? The answer is: a great deal. While a case study provides a specific context, the experiences and the findings on risks and relationship management practices—for example what works and what does not—are not necessarily unique and ungeneralizable.

A case history is interesting for its explanatory power. It is frequently assumed, incorrectly, that one can only generalize by a process of statistical inference from a statistically valid sample. However, an important distinction can be made between statistical inference on the one hand and causal inference on the other. More accurately, causal inference refers to the logic of analytical induction, or logical inference. Logical inference is the process by which an analyst draws conclusions about the essential linkage between two or more characteristics in terms of some explanatory schema—some set of theoretical propositions. In our study the theoretical propositions reside in our two ana-lytical frameworks arrived at by a study of relevant theory and prior research. We have been very careful about how we have arrived at these frameworks (see Appendix 2) because, as Mitchell (1983) puts it, 'the extent to which general-ization may be made from case studies depends on the adequacy of the under-lying theory and the whole corpus of related knowledge of which the case is analysed rather than on the particular instance itself.' The claim that a case study's findings have validity, therefore, derives not from the case study's rep-resentativeness as such, but from the fact that an infallible logic has been applied in the analysis. Applying our theoretical frameworks to each case history has enabled two things: first a focus on and a making sense of events that relate to relationship management, broadly conceived; and, secondly, some assessment of the adequacy of these frameworks themselves, that is their explanatory, sense-making power.

In this chapter we wish to take the analysis further. A cross-case analysis enables us to achieve further insights into the relevance and strength of factors in any causal scheme—something of which the analytical frameworks could only provide limited prior understandings. This process also enables a further testing of the relevance, and a potential deepening, of the analytical frameworks themselves and the insights they can bring to bear in future studies of the phenomena. From this further analysis we are also able to draw out further implications for management practices that can support the gain of what we have termed in this book 'the relationship advantage' in IT outsourcing. We begin with the issue of risk and its mitigation.

RISK PROFILES AND THE ROLE OF RELATIONSHIPS: A COMPARISON

What prior evidence we had on risks in IT outsourcing has been documented in the first two chapters of this book, and captured in the risk profile framework (see Figure 2.1). This classification of major risk areas turns out to be fairly robust across the new evidence provided by the five case studies in Chapters 3–7. However, the cases allow us to look in closer detail at additional micro-risk scenarios, and also how risks can combine in specific circumstances, to create compounded, exacerbated risk.

Total Outsourcing

Three of our cases—Xerox-EDS, BAe-CSC, and Inland Revenue-EDS shared a high-risk large-scale, long-term, single supplier outsourcing route. Of the three, Xerox-EDS, the largest, most global, and, in terms of multiple strategic objectives, the most ambitious has been the most disappointing. This is unsurprising given the in-built risks related to large scale and high ambition in IT outsourcing. It is also fairly clear that even the largest IT services provider in the world at that time could not provide Xerox with all its services to the required standard. The subcontracting of telecoms was symptomatic of this, but it is probable, and several respondents explicitly stated this, that more suppliers, more regionally based, on a more selective, rather than 'total' basis, would have been the lower risk option. But once again, the supplier seemed much better at selling its services, than the client at buying them. One aspect of this was overestimating the power of having a 'strategic relationship' and the 'spirit of the contract', whilst underestimating the importance of the contract detail, the relationship processes and the staffing, which were all found essential for the relationship and for building it to mutual advantage. It is undoubtedly the case that in many areas Xerox did do many things right. But these weaknesses in 'contextual' and 'building to contract' features, nevertheless, had significant impacts, leading, for example, to a quite early restructuring of the contract and management arrangements.

Contract

On contract, a particularly interesting risk—of inflexibility—rested in having a centralized contract to be applied with very few degrees of freedom throughout the Xerox regions. Service and management issues meant this had to be remedied subsequently. But compare BP Exploration (BPX) where a framework agreement arrived at by the centre received its significant detail at the regional level. Here, the unanticipated consequence was that diverse arrangements eroded sharing of best practice, developing common systems and standards, and achieving synergies e.g. shared helpdesks across the regions. Different contractual strategies with differing micro-risk scenarios. The difficulties Xerox experienced once again demonstrated that despite the considerable time, effort, and cost invested in preparation, a lack of maturity and experience in managing total outsourcing did make it difficult to anticipate and mitigate certain outcomes.

Both BAe and Inland Revenue (IR) put into place much more detailed contracts than Xerox, and this supported greater control over the initial phases of their arrangements. One learning point is the importance for risk mitigation of applying tight control at the beginning of outsourcing, allowing subsequent loosening only as the relationship becomes more mature, and flexibility becomes more important in the face of business and technical change. BAe presents an interesting contrast with Xerox and IR in several respects. There were several distinctive 'contextual' risk mitigation features needed, given that BAe signed in times of a financial crisis, was for several years very cost conscious, and there were risks of supplier opportunistic behaviour stemming from early difficulties in making profit margins. One risk-mitigation factor was the supplier's own experience in aerospace and defence, and the second in BAe staff's long experience of strategic contracting and procurement with external allies and suppliers. This fed into more realistic expectations and goals for its IT outsourcing venture. Contractual adjustments, benchmarking, and reviews in price and service parameters also helped to keep the arrangement on track, supported as these were by a large spread of retained core IT skills and capabilities. This is not to say that the deal has not run into difficulties; more that risk mitigation features ensured that the deal never foundered, while the relationship dimensions described below ensured that business leverage continued to be gained over the arrangement's lifetime.

Both the IR and BAe gained significantly from their deals, which were regarded as prestige, high profile, and references sites by the suppliers they engaged. This was much less the case in the case of Xerox-EDS, though BPX also reaped similar risk mitigation benefit from their 1993–8 multi-supplier deal. For CSC, the BAe account was a major catch for developing its European operations; for EDS, the UK Inland Revenue was high profile and opened up other central government department possibilities, both in the UK and globally. Neither CSC nor EDS could be seen to fail. BAe and the IR also both went down a detailed contracting route, retained a lot of contract management skill in particular, and both actively managed their outsourcing, and consciously developed the relationship mechanisms, processes, behaviours, and structures. This became expressed in the stability and productivity of their relationships entering into the second half of their contract terms. Difficulties arose, large and small, operational and significant in both cases, but they were managed through the relationship dimension, which proved extremely robust.

But in all three cases an interesting question is: have asymmetries of power developed in the vendor's favour to such an extent that switching costs are prohibitive, and the supplier can dictate too much the basis of the cost-benefit equation? Certainly all three would see switching costs as stopping an early termination unless the deals really went seriously wrong. In the case of the IR and BAe it is probable that senior managers would argue that they would not want to switch anyway at the end of the contract term, though in each case, as a risk mitigating exercise a competitive tendering process might be operated before this could be confirmed. In the case of Xerox a more likely scenario is that the company would move to a more selective sourcing pattern; the risks that materialized with a single supplier might push them in this direction.

Selective Multi-sourcing

BP Exploration (BPX) and ESSO-ITNet provide interesting risk mitigation contrasts to these three cases. Both went for selective multi-supplier sourcing on shorter contracts, as a conscious exercise in managing structural risk. BPX achieved most of its transformation objectives, but less on its cost saving and innovation objectives. The selection of 'best-in-class' suppliers worked out in some cases, but less so with others. One 'problem child' with BPX was the underestimation of technical capabilities and skills needed to run a 'total' outsourcing deal, and the appointment of a number of existing staff to new roles for which they were not necessarily equipped, especially in the demand management and strategic, 'high-impact' consulting areas. Given the requirement for fewer, but high-performing skilled staff, when these are not present in sufficient numbers the adverse impact on risk, problem identification, and resolution can be disproportionate. Likewise with the wrong contract managers in place initially at ITNet-ESSO and IR-EDS.

A further BPX 'problem child' turned out to be its novel experiment with getting suppliers to manage themselves—an attempt actually to mitigate risk by making the suppliers co-dependent and forced into cooperative behaviours. In fact the experiment caused BPX to do a lot of refereeing and management they thought had been outsourced. However, a root-cause risk factor lay in the behaviours of the regions themselves, that continued 'local' behaviours when 'global' cooperative behaviours were required. These behaviours tended to reinforce the latent competitiveness of the suppliers, certainly between sites. The significance of this risk factor can be seen when, after April 1998, EDS was given global responsibility for supporting the desktop and had a direct relationship with BP. EDS still ran into serious problems trying to get agreement on standardization of technology, requirements, and practice. That said, BPX exhibited a lot of good risk mitigation practice on its contracting, measurement systems, and continual updating of the price, service levels, and benchmarks for performance.

In principle, ESSO-ITNet should have been the least risky IT outsourcing deal. ESSO represented a prestige site for ITNet. ESSO went in for selective multi-supplier outsourcing, on relatively short-term contracts, and was outsourcing commodity IT. ESSO also had considerable experience in managing outsourcing: in fact ITNet was taking over from a previous supplier. So why did the deal almost founder? ITNet had a strategic intent in getting the contract, but, in its over-eagerness, miscalculated on the profit margin it could achieve, and the tightness and cost consciousness with which ESSO would keep to the contract, and run the arrangement.

A 'Winner's Curse' operated (see Chapter 9); the arrangement proved to be something of a poisoned chalice for the supplier with adverse impacts also on service and the client. This is an interesting case of the micro-risks that can occur even if everything in the risk profile framework presented in Chapter 2 looks largely like a low-risk scenario. What rescued the deal for both parties was ESSO putting in place the right relationship building capabilities and skills for managing external supply. The appropriate contractual details, service parameters, effort-reward arrangements, and management processes followed on. Here was a stark example of the difference the relationship advantage can make.

In summary, the risk profile framework of Figure 2.1 really does highlight the major generic risk factors in outsourcing. In the light of our research, however, we develop it further and the result is discussed in the next chapter, and shown in Figure 9.6. However, we also found that each outsourcing experience has distinctive characteristics and dynamics, and this makes micro-risks a key additional area needing analysis. Only then will stakeholders get the detailed risk profile required as a basis for implementing risk mitigation management practices.

SHAPING THE ADVANTAGE: STRATEGIC INTENTS IN IT OUTSOURCING

Let us look in more detail across the five cases to see evidence for this relationship advantage, and how it can be built. Getting the strategic intent right has a considerable contextual influence on the levels of risk, how well relationships are founded, and how far the other relationship dimensions need to come into play to correct for unsuitable strategic intents by either or both client and supplier(s). You will recall that the Relationship framework in Chapter 2 saw strategic intent as having four aspects: necessity, reciprocity, legitimacy, and efficiency.

Necessity

Outsourcing at the Inland Revenue was a government-mandated necessity once benchmarking revealed that significant operational savings could be obtained in the private sector. Operational efficiency measured through cost comparisons was a major, but not the only, underlying objective. ESSO, for example, also looked towards outsourcing as a means to improve its operational efficiency in terms of costs, although no direct pressure was put on the IT function. However in ESSO's case, EXXON indirectly applied pressure by introducing a group-wide, and in parts centrally coordinated, effort at finding ways of improving operational efficiency globally. A similar situation existed in BPX, yet outsourcing became a direct necessity to continue its internal restructuring initiative as the organization looked to the IT function for further cost reductions in the long term.

Necessity in all cases was financially linked. BPX, BAe, and Xerox in particular looked towards outsourcing partly as a 'cash cow'. Their necessity to outsource was a direct consequence of prolonged business problems, financial difficulties, and declining markets. Outsourcing thus freed necessary funds and financed the essential restructuring of the IT infrastructure. In terms of necessity, the framework thus proved useful in eliciting the different pressures that guided the client organizations into outsourcing. The cases pointed towards three types of necessity: externally mandated, internal direct pressure, and indirect internal pressure. Necessity and the direction it takes—cost focus, broader financial pressures, need to catalyse the IT function etc.—greatly influences the need to form a relationship with an external IT services company, and the form that the relationship will take. ESSO-ITNet, for example, had a cost focus, and this pushed the relationship initially into adversarial forms, before more productive arrangements emerged. At BPX the corporate necessity to outsource on a large scale led to the creative alliance approach as a way to mitigate risk, but the experience led to different forms. At Xerox large-scale outsourcing led to an overriding belief in a single supplier relationship, but the contractual dimensions, and relationship processes required a lot more work.

Reciprocity

The framework prescribes outsourcing as being pursued by organizations with an intent of reciprocity to benefit from the vendor's technical competencies. This is also what the case studies suggest. All five organizations acknowledged that outsourcing was expected to be a source of business benefits and improvements. Benefits focused on vendors' technical expertise, resources, and experiences with other customers, but BAe, BPX, IR, and Xerox also sought organizational and operational improvements. The case examples showed that the expected benefits informed the degree of reciprocity clients anticipated to invest in operationalizing the venture. Xerox, BPX, and IR intended to develop the deal to a strategic partnering arrangement and thus expected benefits beyond the technical outsourcing scope. In fact for Xerox and IR, reciprocity was to entail the necessary flexibility to develop and implement major new infrastructures that undoubtedly involved organizational and operational changes. Flexibility for them implied extensive collaboration, as both relied on EDS to formalize their particular requirements. Despite the different degrees of reciprocity, all five cases are unanimous in viewing reciprocity as an essential part of outsourcing. This position seems independent of the type of outsourcing arrangement and length of the deal pursued. Reciprocity thus characterized the anticipated degree of collaboration in the cases which ranged from low, medium, to high depending on the case. Initially ESSO had a much lower reciprocity objective than, for example, BPX as the focus was primarily on legacy systems, whereas BPX expected benefits on all levels of information technology operations. BAe, Xerox, IR are classified as high reciprocity due to the scope and wide objectives of these deals. In all cases a higher degree of relationship work than anticipated was needed to secure the reciprocity expected.

Legitimacy
The framework prescribes political motivations as a strong driving force to outsource. BPX, BAe, IR, and Xerox all confirm this to be the case. The motivations are commonly associated with the IT department's quest to legitimize their IT operations and prove their team player credibility by outsourcing their 'kingdom' (Lacity and Hirschheim 1993). For example, senior civil servants in the IR did not argue much against outsourcing, and were fully inclined to take the route once the opportunity arose:

We couldn't understand how we would be able to keep abreast of the fast moving world of technology if we stayed with our in-house division. [. . .] So we made a conscious management decision, that it was right for us in business terms to see whether or not we could outsource our activity, because we felt if we could do that we could get access to expertise whenever and wherever we needed it. (John Yard, IT Director, 1997)

For BAe's and Xerox's senior IT managers, outsourcing presented a bridging strategy to revamp the infrastructure without incurring considerable outlays for an already cash-hampered organization. Yet managers at Xerox, IR, BAe, and BPX also used outsourcing to legitimize a major reduction in the workforce through a much needed restructuring of the IT infrastructure. Indeed, in all four cases staff transfers, including redundancies, ranged from 1,900 to 140 people. Outsourcing in turn legitimizes staff cuts to employees, the unions, the industry, and/or shareholders. Therefore, legitimacy in the framework focuses our attention on the political motivations behind outsourcing, which included legitimizing operations, overhaul of the infrastructure and staff reductions.

Legitimacy emerged as an important influencer of relationships, not just those between client and supplier(s) but also in terms of in-house staff morale, response to supplier staff, and supplier staff motivations.

Efficiency
The cases were unanimous about efficiency being the strongest outsourcing intent. All five organizations had cost reduction amongst their primary reasons for outsourcing. As noted in Chapter 1 and by numerous other researchers, the cost benefits touted by vendors, in the 1990s, presented the most powerful lure to outsource. The Inland Revenue, for example, was promised a potential saving of £225 million over the contract's ten-year lifespan, Xerox received a cash payment of $170 million, and BPX was said to have saved some £150 million. The case companies unanimously sought to reap these touted savings. In fact for BAe and Xerox, business conditions required them to liquify their assets in order to generate cash to finance the overhaul of their IT infrastructure. In spite of the differences across the cases, vendors unanimously suggested they were able to outperform internal operations, offer savings, and still make a return. As long as such offers can be made and seem feasible, outsourcing will continue to attract organizations. Thus efficiency in the framework prescribes the savings offered by the vendor and identifies a primary outsourcing intent. Surveys in the USA and Europe in 2000 also show that cost savings remained a major client expectation, going into the new decade. We found the strategic intent of efficiency influencing how relationships were set up and conducted, with senior managers in all cases finding that detailed, regularly updated measurement processes were a key, but all having to work hard at the softer side of interactions and behaviours for the efficiencies to come through.

Summary: Strategic Intent in the Relationship

The underlying outsourcing intentions that guided the relationship in the case study organizations are summarized in Table 8.1. The summary suggests two patterns: (*a*) where the necessity to outsource was internally directed or mandated, major infrastructure changes were at stake that legitimized large-scale staff redundancies, and a high degree of reciprocity was anticipated, and (*b*) where the necessity is indirect and/or independent of any pressure, a low degree of reciprocity is anticipated and the focus is primarily on reducing operational costs. These two patterns seem to generally reflect large-scale or 'total' and 'selective' outsourcing arrangements respectively. It also suggests the conceptual framework sufficiently covers the range of outsourcing forms.

The case studies validate the four elements as appropriately delineating the outsourcing intent, yet they are all clearly influenced by other external and/or internal factors. The conceptual framework at present does not support the two latter dimensions, although, instinctively, the framework was never assumed to

Table 8.1. *Summary of outsourcing intent*

	BAe-CSC	Xerox-EDS	ESSO-ITNet	BPX-Alliance	IR-EDS
Necessity	Direct pressure	Direct pressure	Indirect	Direct pressure	Mandated
Reciprocity	High	High	Low	High	High
Legitimacy	Staff reductions	Staff reductions	None	Staff reductions	Staff reductions
	Overhaul of IT operations	Overhaul of IT operations		Overhaul of IT operations	Overhaul of IT operations
Efficiency	Reduce costs +	Reduce costs +	Reduce costs	Reduce costs +	Reduce costs +

exist in a vacuum. Still, the importance of considering intent and indeed the relationship in this larger context is essential as any external and/or internal change may need to be reflected in the relationship. Disregard of these can be potentially very costly. Hence the endogenous and exogenous factors need to be addressed more directly in the framework and entail an important amendment. We look at this in Chapter 9.

Reflecting on the findings and existing research on outsourcing intent (DiRomualdo and Gurbaxani 1998; Lacity, Hirschheim, and Willcocks 1994), it is clear that the 'interorganizational approach' (see Chapter 2) has much value to add in terms of identifying reasons for forming relationships. In essence, the cross-case analysis findings corroborate DiRomualdo and Gurbaxani's (1998) and Lacity et al.'s (1994) core reasons for outsourcing as being financial, technical, business-based and/or political. However, applying the framework revealed two additional insights over and above these contributions. The first is that outsourcing becomes a 'voluntary necessity' because of a complex mixture of mandated demands, and direct and indirect internal and external pressures. The cases help to illustrate the richness of such mixtures. Secondly, there are varying degrees of reciprocity. Previous work has not delved deeply into this area, whereas the case histories illustrate how the objectives of reciprocity are espoused in strategic intents, but also how the issue is played out post-contract, and what the influences are on the outcomes. In Chapter 9 we will deal further with this issue of types of relationship and the levels of reciprocity they imply.

THE RELEVANCE OF THE CONTRACT IN RELATIONSHIPS

The cases unanimously emphasize that IT outsourcing is largely, in practice, a contractual 'fee for service' arrangement. The role of the contract was shown to be one of guidance and governance over the lifespan of the deal. In practice we found contracts were generally perceived very positively, as forming an integral part, indeed a foundation stone, for the outsourcing process. It was also time and again described as a 'necessary but insufficient' condition of success. Our analytical framework in Chapter 2 posited that the contract structures and impacts relationships in at least three distinctive ways—through its inherent promises, its non-promissory accompaniments, and through how the issue of 'presentation' is dealt with. This was supported strongly in all five cases.

Promise
The five case histories illustrate that promise refers primarily to the cost-service trade-off, embodied typically in service level agreements (SLAs). Organizations rely heavily on the promises outlined in these, as a representation of the supplier's delivery requirements (Kern and Willcocks 2000). Yet Xerox was technically unable to define its requirements at the point of contracting. In the absence of detailed SLAs, Xerox formulated novel promissory frameworks to state its general technological objectives. These 'evergreen frameworks' proved too vague for operations. BAe, ESSO, and BPX, on the other hand, were able to achieve a high degree of promissory clarity. Relational operations benefited from a high degree of clarity although in the short term promissory clarification was found to be time intensive and costly. For BAe, their detailed contract was so complex that it required a separate document to distil its meaning for operational use. Still, respondents were unanimous in their emphasis on the importance of promissory clarity; the higher the better. Xerox's experience in particular corroborated this fact, while for ESSO and BPX promissory clarity was a necessary precondition to implement their risk-reward arrangements. The IR also put much work into gaining this clarity at the front end of the deal. For a range of reasons, including the level of clarity and realism embodied in the contracts, delivery on these promises seemed to work best in the IR and BPX cases, followed by BAe.

The case examples reveal four distinct ways to achieve a high degree of clarity. BAe documented all promises made during bidding and then integrated those that would be of benefit. In addition, it ensured all relevant business unit managers were involved in negotiations; it also formulated unit specific SLAs. Secondly, BPX made each division responsible for formalizing SLAs, but imposed the use of industry-standard terminology to ensure company-wide pervasiveness and clarity of promises. Thirdly, ESSO had the benefit of existing SLAs and merely adapted them to their new deal with ITNet. The IR also relied on existing SLAs, but spent a lot of careful effort developing them before and during the transition period. Xerox failed to achieve the clarity needed initially, and inherited relationship and measurement problems as a result. ESSO ran into problems, partly because the cost-service trade-off was clear, but not an equitable one for the supplier.

Non-Promissory Accompaniments

To compensate for contractual ambiguity the conceptual framework in Chapter 2 prescribes non-promissory accompaniments as 'gap-fillers' (Barnett 1992*a*, 1992*b*; Macneil 1981). All the organizations we studied needed these as an integral part of their arrangement. Except in BAe, these accompaniments provided the necessary flexibility to operationalize the contract and develop the relationship. Of importance to note here was that non-promissory accompaniments in each of the four cases were not restricted to limited time periods but spanned the whole venture.

Accompaniments took three distinctive forms: one was through a mutually agreed and fostered strategic relationship, as in Xerox and IR. From the outset both Xerox and IR were unable to define explicitly their technology demands and service requirements for a major infrastructure changeover; yet the strategic relationship provided some compensation (not always satisfactorily acted upon) for the inherent contractual ambiguity, and hence uncertainty. The second was through internalized practices (i.e. corporate culture), as in ESSO. ESSO's strong ethical business approach gave ITNet the opportunity to make a case for early contract renegotiations to ensure a mutually fair return on the deal. This accompaniment not only prevented early termination, but entailed unexpected additional benefits. The third was through a mutually developed and agreed approach to partnering, as in BPX. BPX's non-legal 'principles of partnering' provided an agreement framework for operationalizing the contract and the multiple relationships.

BPX, ESSO, Xerox, and IR's arrangements facilitated a high degree of flexibility in operationalizing the contract. In contrast, BAe had no such arrangement. Managers instead pursued a strict procurement approach that operated along stipulated terms. This meant that the contract would have to cater for all possibilities, making it intrinsically complex due to the size and complexity of BAe's undertaking. It is interesting to speculate whether the consideration of non-promissory accompaniments from the outset could have prevented the extensive clarification work and subsequent formal realignment of the contract. It is fundamental to take note at this stage that any formal early renegotiation or realignment phase that was not planned for from the outset will inherently raise costs and in most cases will disrupt and even strain relations. Thus avoidance of such a procedure, or a mutually agreed regularizing, as occurred at BAe eventually, must be of the utmost priority.

'Presentation'

Contractual incompleteness was a fundamental issue in all five case exemplars, the main reason being that internal dynamism prevents long-term representativeness of service levels. Interestingly, the cases showed incompleteness to be less related just to whether organizations operated within a 'stable' or a 'dynamic' business environment (Duncan 1972), although it seems quite plausible to assume that the environment generally affects presentation (Kern and

Willcocks 1996). Rather, they all seemed to operate in dynamic business and technical conditions, but this was expressed in differently paced and sized internal responses to those changes, making 'presentation' a different level of problem at different times. But one exceptional and overriding factor that needs highlighting is the volatility of market rates for skilled labour, for which all organizations found it difficult to legislate in ways that were in the interests of all parties. The danger was that the position of either party or both parties could deteriorate quite markedly, if effective 'presentation' mechanisms were not in place.

The dangers of contractual incompleteness are highlighted by Xerox's case. In fact in both Xerox and IR the low degree of presentation substantially increased costs in terms of coordination. Nevertheless, client organizations attempting to presentiate service requirements and payments for much longer than two years (e.g. BAe) tended to waste valuable resources, time and effort as alignment and renewal became necessary following a maximum period of two and a half years. BPX and ESSO took the precaution of renegotiating service levels and payments annually to ensure a higher degree of presentation. This seems a logical strategy to guarantee contractual representativeness over a venture's lifespan. It also improved BPX's and ESSO's control over costs and any opportunistic behaviour that may have arisen with an increasing level of incompleteness.

The Advantage, Value, and Impact of the Contract for Relationships

Table 8.2 summarizes the three areas of impact and value that contracts provide to outsourcing relations. The findings suggest that the impacts of contracts on relationships can be classified along a range: from functional to dysfunctional. Relations that operated contractual arrangements with high degrees of promissory clarity and 'presentation', and had access to non-promissory accompaniments, encountered less functional problems in relations than others. In addition they proved to have a higher level of control over their outsourcing destiny. The cases with other arrangements encountered considerable problems, including substantial additional coordination costs because of their contractual arrangements. The most dysfunctional proved to be those of BAe and Xerox.

BAe's contract experience emphasized that a contract needs to be developed and formulated in a way that allows for easy implementation. Otherwise the complexity and legalese of the document hampers operationalization and will foster clarification conflicts that, combined, introduce significant additional time and coordination costs. In light of BAe's experience of formulating a contract that supposedly caters for every eventuality, and Xerox's opposing experience of having a very loose contract framework, it is clear there needs to be a balance between complexity, completeness, and clarity. In terms of the conceptual framework in Chapter 2, this suggests another element needs to be

Table 8.2. *Summary of contract*

	BAe-CSC	Xerox-EDS	ESSO-ITNet	BPX-Alliance	IR-EDS
Promise	High clarity	Low clarity	High clarity	High clarity	Med. clarity
Non-promissory accompaniments	Low flexibility	High flexibility	High flexibility	High flexibility	High flexibility
Presentation	High	Low	High	High	Low

incorporated that specifically addresses the contract's complexity and its effects on the relationship.

Given the limited research into contracts in IT outsourcing relationships, the findings here make an important contribution to identifying vital areas of impact. The findings generally corroborate the importance of a well-documented contract, especially in the start-up of the relationship. Lacity and Hirschheim (1993) and Kern and Wilcocks (2000) in particular argue for highly formalized contracts. However, the case findings clearly suggest that promissory clarity in relationships needs to be balanced between complexity, completeness, and clarity to ensure operability. In turn, formalizing all-encompassing discrete contracts may be self-defeating. Another argument often put forward, for example by Richmond, Seidmann, and Whinston (1992), is the importance of a high degree of contractual completeness. The case exemplars strongly endorse this proposition, highlighting that the contract will continue to govern relationships. However, its representativeness is severely time-constrained in outsourcing, thus requiring organizations to plan ahead for regular realignment phases in intervals of between one and a maximum of two years.

Finally, a main area of contribution are the findings surrounding non-promissory accompaniments in relationships. They identify what others have always noted as the flexibility that allows outsourcing to continue, even when there are no contractual obligations. Their importance was highlighted in the operation of relationships, especially in those where there was a high degree of promissory uncertainty.

GETTING THE STRUCTURAL DIMENSIONS RIGHT

The case studies unanimously showed that organizations underrate significantly the importance of the structural dimension. All case organizations had to redress their management structures to alleviate serious deficiencies. In addition, most organizations experienced an increase in coordination costs, raising concern over the efficiency of the relationship. In particular, complexity, and the vertical and occupational management structure were areas of considerable impact. Thus the heuristic power of the analytical framework, and the findings, identify structural issues and ways forward that make a major contribution to our understanding of outsourcing relationships.

Size

The macro-view of the relationship in terms of structure is identified by the number of parties and size of the arrangement. The amount of money involved and the extent of outsourcing both provide a good indication of how important the deal is to the client, but also the vendor. Thus size has not only a number of implications for the structural arrangements, but also for the whole venture. For instance, in the BAe, Xerox, and IR cases, the size of the deal limited the choice of partner to a select number of suppliers. This 'small number problem' (Williamson 1975) defines a situation with few or no alternative exchange partners, thus effectively diminishing the possibility of choice and switching in the future, and inviting opportunistic vendor behaviour. In such deals the relationship also increases in importance, as any serious breakdown can jeopardize the operations of the whole organization. ESSO and BPX tried to circumvent a lock-in situation through their selective and multiple partner outsourcing approach. Generally, this proved to be a good short-term strategy, but developments in the relationships still tend to lock partners in over time (see BPX's experience with Syncordia). Heavy prior investments in organizational arrangements to handle the relationship make subsequent switching too costly and traumatic.

In terms of structural impact, the size of the deal will influence the complexity of the venture in terms of service provisions, operations, and organizational arrangements. The case studies emphasize what is unsurprising—that, as the size increases, the need for management resourcing to handle the deal needs to increase proportionately. BPX in particular had not taken this into account and had to redress this with additional managers. However, BPX never resourced its management team sufficiently to handle the size and complexity of the deal. Communication thus seriously suffered, which on a number of occasions raised concerns over the efficiency of the relationship arrangements.

Complexity

Child's (1973) assumption that an increase in complexity will entail an increase in hierarchical levels, standardization of procedures, specialist functions, and centralization of procedures was used as the basis for determining the degree of complexity inherent in the ventures. BAe, Xerox, and IR all had outsourcing arrangements that have very complex technical and operational requirements. BAe and the IR accordingly formalized structures and standardized procedures as much as possible prior to outsourcing. In contrast Xerox did not, and yet encountered no serious problems subsequently. The complexity perspective provides, in fact, another angle through which to explore Xerox's problems. Moreover, both IR's and Xerox's arrangements were likely to increase in complexity as infrastructure projects were completed. Xerox realized, that with increasing complexity, and already lacking sufficient structural and procedural arrangements, it needed to begin formalizing and standardizing operations. Thus, in terms of increasing complexity, even when already starting with a high degree of complexity, further increases in management and procedures will become necessary, or else problems will arise. BPX exemplifies this scenario. BPX's complexity increased incrementally, whereas their management structure and procedures did not. Realizing they were failing to manage the alliance, they had to bring in additional managers and invest more time in managing their suppliers. Hence the alliance approach may work in circumstances where the complexity is at a manageable level, but once it increases exponentially as in BPX with increasing number of sites around the world, complexity defeats the alliance approach as it takes up a lot of management time.

Complexity, however, varies throughout the different components of an out-sourcing venture and across time, and will put changing resource and operational pressures on the relationship. Micro-risks can develop, and become real issues. Although ESSO had a low complexity level, it experienced a build-up of operational problems that substantially increased operational complexity. To alleviate the situation, ESSO had to invest additional management resources. Complexity thus needs to be seen as a dynamic issue that requires access to flexible resources to alleviate pressures as they arise. If these are not available, pressures on management structures and the relationship may lead to serious problems.

Vertical and Occupational Management Structure
The framework prescribes the importance of having multiple stakeholders with the right mix of competencies for managing the relationship. This is also what the cases revealed. Using Willcocks and Fitzgerald's (1994) typology of business and IT strategy, business development, informed buyer, systems integrator, contract intermediary, contract monitoring, and exploiting vendor relations to classify the client management team's main competencies, the cross-case analysis identifies the vertical and occupational density of the client's management structures. The importance of distinguishing the management structure is emphasized by the case organizations' experiences of relational problems due to inadequate vertical and occupational arrangements. Table 8.3 below presents the results of the cross-case analysis.

The findings revealed that case organizations in general, except for the IR, had spent very little time and resources prior to outsourcing to define a management structure for the operational level. Some had defined a structure but it was at a too high level. Xerox for example, had an overview of the X*EDS structure, but little else. In turn, all case organizations had to readdress their vertical-occupational arrangements during the initial years of operation.

The most common problem was finding the right mix of competencies. The most crucial—but also the most neglected—skill set was relationship management. Xerox, ESSO, and the IR encountered serious problems because they

Table 8.3. *Cross-case analysis of vertical and occupational management structure*

Management level	Management positions		Competencies[a]
Senior management	Global IT Director (Xerox) Corporate IT Director (BAe) Head of IT (ESSO) Group Head of IT (BPX) Chairman of Board (IR)		• Business & IT Strategy (Direction) • Informed Buyer • Exploiting vendor relations (at the highest level) • Oversight of venture
Senior managers	IT & Finance Director (Xerox) IT Director (BAe) Vendor Manager (ESSO) IT Director (BPX) IT Director (IR)		• Business & IT Strategy (Control) • Contract Oversight • Exploiting & developing vendor relations • Oversight of account • Cost control • Dispute resolution
Operational managers	**Strategy managers**	IM Strategy Mgr. (Xerox) Strategic Mgr. (BAe) ESSO BPX } Domain of Senior IR } Mgrs.	• Business Development • Managing technology strategy • New technology • Alignment of IT with business strategy
* Denotes multiple roles	**Contract managers**	IM Controller (Xerox) Central contract group (BAe) Operations Mgr. (ESSO)* Partner Resource Mgr. (BPX) Contract Management Team (IR)	• Informed Buyer • Contract Monitoring • Management of costs • Management of service levels • Overall performance measuring
	Technical managers	Telecoms, Process Area Support & Infrastructure Mgr. (Xerox) Technology Mgr. (BAe) Operations Mgr. (ESSO)* Business Information Mgr. (BPX) Technical experts (IR)	• System integrators • Monitoring and oversight • In charge of particular IT functions • Technology integrators • New technical requirements
Technology managers	N/A (Xerox)—handled by operations mgrs. Business Line Manager (BAe) Programme Manager (ESSO) N/A (BPX)—vendor in charge Project Managers (IR)		• Contract Intermediary • Technology integrators • Customer facing managers

[a] Integrates Willcocks and Fitzgerald's (1994) suggestion of the management tasks needed to handle the remaining in-house IT function.

lacked this competency in their structure. Relationship management for the whole account needs to be handled at senior levels, as ongoing day-to-day operations will give rise to too much friction that inhibits operation managers from developing relations. As in the other cases, in BAe relationship development at the business unit, i.e. operations level was primarily part of the IT Director's and vendor account manager's responsibility. The relevant managers may be distinguished as strategically, contractually, or technically focused. Of key importance here are the contract and technical managers. Integral to Xerox and ESSO was the role of contract management and monitoring to ensure achievement of stipulated terms according to agreed prices. Similarly the technical manager carried responsibility for the technical function including technology management, requests for new technology and services, and monitoring of technology integration. Finally, technology managers identified the crucial links with customers in the organization. They are primarily in charge of overseeing systems integration, systems use, and problems. In ESSO, for example, the programme manager checked on a daily basis with her key customers for problems and any additional service demands.

It is evident that the bare minimum in terms of vertical density for handling the outsourcing relationship has to include a senior manager overseeing the venture, senior operations manager, operations manager, and technology manager (see ESSO for example). However, more important is that the management structure covers the occupational density in terms of competencies outlined in Table 8.3. The density in general in terms of amount of managers involved in managing the relationship ranged across the cases from high (Xerox, BAe, and IR), medium (BPX), to low (ESSO).

But the structure in which these people operated was found, in the cases, to also play an important part in how productive relationships could be. Centrality in terms of structure alludes to the flow of information between the parties. Transaction cost theory notes that one-sided control over information may lead to opportunistic behaviour, whereas the interorganizational paradigm suggests that information is power. In either circumstance asymmetry in favour of the client or vendor has a negative effect on operations and the relationship. Xerox presents the extreme case where centrality was, ironically, in favour of the vendor. The lack of information flow at the operational level decreased Xerox managers' control over EDS's performance and their service requirements. Similar developments were evolving at the IR. The handover of the second tranche and EDS's complete control over the CESA project implied EDS also acquired control over the information flows. Both cases invited the vendor's opportunistic behaviour in terms of cost increases. Although in the IR information flow by late 1998 seemed relatively balanced, indications of changes to come were evident in EDS's internal structure changes.

Conversely, structural arrangements where centrality is in favour of the client were found to hamper the vendor from providing value-added benefits such as cost savings and technical expertise. ITNet managers noted that ESSO managers initially were not sharing information about their particular operational needs and methods, which caused considerable relational friction as ITNet took over from the former vendor. ESSO's close control over information essentially hindered ITNet from adapting to ESSO's idiosyncrasies. In BPX, vendor managers noted that the centrality of information prevented them from planning and resourcing ahead when particular projects came along, which meant they could not really apply their expertise and create savings. BPX managers recognized this problem as partly due to the insufficiently resourced management structure. In effect BPX's centrality increased costs as information concerning developments often reached vendors too late, if at all.

Stability

On a macro level, stability is identified by the length of the contract. Clearly the longer the contract period, the more important it will be to have well-functioning and efficient relationships—as in the cases of Xerox, BAe, and IR. To ensure vendors do not become disinterested, close relations were sought by Xerox and IR that entailed 'carrots' of more business. Any disruption of the stability of the relationship at the micro level in turn can have macro consequences in jeopardizing the efficiency, and even the stability, of the overall arrangement. In Xerox's case, because of the problems at the operational level, senior managers began to question the whole outsourcing concept. It can be seen that there were a number of operational developments across the case studies that strengthened stability or led to instability.

A key factor often noted as destabilizing operations and relations was the changes in key managers on either side. These occurred more frequently in the vendor organization. In ESSO, for example, the change of ITNet's account manager was seen to disrupt operations, in particular in terms of trust and communication. On the other hand, the secondment of CSC's account manager to BAe to take on a dual role of IT manager/account manager was found to have a stabilizing effect. It increased the level of trust in terms of confidence and openness. Other key destabilizing factors for relationships are realignment, renegotiation, or rebidding of contracts. Respondents emphasized how operations were disrupted in BAe, Xerox, BPX, and ESSO. Particularly severe was Syncordia's rebidding experience, which left managers disillusioned and demotivated and seriously disrupted their relations with the other two suppliers, SAIC and Sema. In Xerox, the renegotiation meant relationships became more formalized, and relations were restructured in terms of focusing exchanges more on what was contractually agreed. It did, however, also stabilize operations at Xerox as parties now knew their operational targets. The difficult task for managers is to differentiate between what can be stabilizing and destabilizing, aiming to avoid those factors that can destabilize and potentially cause relational inefficiency.

Table 8.4. *Summary of cross-case analysis of structure*

	BAe-CSC	Xerox-EDS	ESSO-ITNet	BPX-Alliance	IR-EDS
Size[a]	£900m	£2bn	£5m	£525m	£1bn
Complexity	High	High	Low	Incremental increase	High
V&O density	High	High	Low	Medium	High
Stability	10yrs	10yrs	5yrs	5yrs	10yrs

[a] According to initially negotiated costs over the lifespan of the contract.

Structure in Relationships

Table 8.4 summarizes the findings for the structural dimension across the case studies. There seem to be two generalizable patterns. First, organizations entering into long-term ventures with an outlook beyond five years, with substantial costs and complexity, need to ensure their vertical occupational density is high in numbers, competencies, and hierarchical levels and that centrality is balanced between the parties to ensure free flow of information. Secondly, organizations entering into ventures with a five-year or shorter time frame, with low to medium costs and complexity need to make sure the vertical and occupational density involves all hierarchical levels, and is sufficiently resourced to interface with customers and supplier(s). Centrality in such ventures is likely to be in favour of the client, as the nature of the deals will be more procurement focused.

The findings also illustrate that structural dimensions in the framework need to distinguish between macro and micro issues. Size, complexity, and stability, in particular, characterized the relationship at the macro level identifying the number of parties, the likely overall complexity, and its length. Conversely, at the micro level the vertical and occupational density, and stability issues are most critical in terms of impact on the operations of the relationship.

Structure has received very little attention in the outsourcing literature. Existing research primarily offers normative management suggestions about competencies and the importance of interface points at different management levels (Feeny and Willcocks 1998; Klepper and Jones 1998; McFarlan and Nolan 1995; White and James 1996; Willcocks and Fitzgerald 1994). This research generally corroborates the existing normative management suggestions, in particular Willcocks and Fitzgerald's (1994) findings of the management competencies that residual client management teams need to have. But this study makes a number of further important contributions to defining crucial structural management competencies for the relational advantage.

First, it identifies the fundamental vertical management levels a management structure needs to integrate in outsourcing relationships (see Table 8.3).

Secondly, it reveals that relationship management and development is primarily handled by senior management and senior operations managers, emphasizing the importance of having very competent managers in terms of interpersonal, technical, and business skills in these positions. Thirdly, it finds that management density will have to vary substantially according to the size, complexity, and stability of the undertaking. In addition, in terms of relational stability, it is evident that management changes and contract alterations in terms of realignment, renegotiation, and rebidding can have both destabilizing and stabilizing effects. Moreover in terms of centrality, information asymmetry in favour of the vendor was shown to invite opportunistic behaviour, whereas asymmetry in favour of the client was revealed as preventing vendors from applying their expertise. Finally, the cases highlighted that the greater the complexity, the more important it will be to formalize procedures, structure, and contracts.

INTERACTIONS: THE PROCESS SIDE OF RELATIONSHIPS

The analytical framework (Chapter 2) prescribes the interaction dimension as the process dimension of outsourcing. This is also what the case studies suggest. All management actions, tasks, and efforts in the five cases concentrated on the exchange of services, technology, money, and/or information. This exchange-based nature of outsourcing has strong parallels to the process dimension of the 'Nordic school' conceptualization of buyer–supplier relationships (Hakansson 1982). This suggests that the Nordic school's conceptualization has much to offer for those carrying out further studies into IT outsourcing (Kern and Willcocks 2001).

Exchange Content

Van de Ven and Ring's (1994) taxonomy of perceptive ratings of exchange impact on relationships was used to analyse and classify the case-study data on exchange. Findings illustrated the exchange process to have a positive, neutral, or negative effect on relations. The effect was dependent on, and a result of, the level of exchange clarity in the case organizations. Xerox and IR managers complained about not having sufficient knowledge about agreed service exchanges. It became difficult, and at times impossible, to monitor, control, and oversee EDS's performance. The attempt of operation managers to bring about local clarity by imposing additional exchange content detail failed on numerous occasions as it conflicted with the general thrust of the agreement. Disputes, especially at Xerox, negatively impacted relations, which continued as long as uncertainty about the exchange content remained. A change in these perceptions only came with the formulation of tighter SLAs. On the other hand, BPX, BAe, and ESSO's relational perceptions ranged from neutral to positive.

The reasons were that managers had a clearer understanding of the exchange content. However, BAe managers did suffer initially from the complexity of the service levels.

Exchange content clarity needs to be ensured throughout the venture's operations. Therefore operating updates need to be planned to ensure all parties remain satisfied with the exchanges. The impact of negative exchange perceptions is far-reaching and becomes particularly evident in the normative exchange content, i.e. satisfaction ratings.

Normative Content
Generally integrated into the framework is Bagozzi's (1975) argument that exchanges are intertwined with 'psychological, social and other intangible entities' that affect managerial and user perceptions of the process dimension. 'Satisfaction' was noted as a good overall indicator of these perceptions. The difficulty with using satisfaction in a cross-case analysis was that definitions varied substantially and also changed over time. Indeed, all cases began on high expectations and satisfaction, which however soon diminished as operations began to unfold. Unsurprisingly, the general non-fulfilment of exchange expectations tended to negatively affect relations. Over time, though, satisfaction levels did improve where track records of consistent service delivery emerged. In ESSO's case, for example, ITNet was able to outperform expectations over consecutive months, and this boosted satisfaction. The effect was increased confidence (psychological), trust (intangible benefit), greater openness, and loyalty (social), all of which together substantially improved the interactions and the relationship. Similar developments occurred in BAe-Airbus where rising levels of satisfaction with exchanges increased managers' confidence and trust, improving interactions and giving CSC the opportunity to apply their expertise. Conversely, in Xerox the exchange process was affected negatively. Managers became more critical and sceptical (psychological), operations increased in formality (intangible benefit), and managers became uncooperative and more contract-focused (social). These findings summarize two examples of the polar extremes. They highlight how the normative content, and performance, can influence the process dimension, at least on a perceptual level.

Communication Content
The framework prescribes the importance of communication in the relationship, yet the findings generally illustrated that case organizations had given this aspect very little consideration (see Table 8.5). The communication process provides the necessary information for client managers to monitor the vendor's performance and to determine the adequacy of payments. The lack of any regular information exchange can cause severe operational problems. Xerox's operational managers, for example, were unable to monitor EDS's services, coordinate operations, and plan for future requirements as no management process existed that guaranteed regular information feedback from EDS. Only

Table 8.5. *Communication content (by 2000)*

Information exchanges	Type of information	Management relevance
Day-to-day	Technical	• Operational issues over the past 24 hours
Weekly	Technical	• Change requests are prioritized and followed up • Problems are rolled up
Monthly	Technical & financial	• Operational problems • Service performance and progress • Payments and bonuses • Relationship management
Quarterly	Technical, financial, organizational	• Service performance and cost effectiveness • Relationship maintenance • Objectives achieved
Half-yearly & annual	Strategic, technical, & financial	• Strategy and future issues • IT requirements • Resourcing forecast • Budget

the IR, ESSO, and BPX had put some detail around the communication process prior to outsourcing by identifying at least one key strategic management meeting at which long-term issues were discussed. Generally though, case organizations expected these processes to evolve by themselves, and this proved to be an ineffective approach.

By 2000 all ventures had formalized a management process that consisted of at least five routine information exchanges: daily, monthly, quarterly, and half yearly and/or annually. These are summarized in Table 8.5.

These processes are core to relationship management, as at each meeting different information sets are exchanged that are essential to operating the venture. For example, ESSO's daily interactions focused on technical issues or problems that arose over the past twenty-four hours. The exchange of up-to-date technical information is fundamental to prevent any major long-term service problems. The monthly meeting received the most emphasis in all five case organizations. Information exchanged at this meeting provides key insights on the vendor's performance, costs, problems, potential areas of problems, and future developments. It presents sufficient information to assess whether payments or penalties are warranted. For ESSO and BPX in particular, it provided necessary information to determine whether bonuses should be paid. Respondents noted that the quarterly meeting gives an overview of the vendor's track record and consistency. It also elicits any particular problem area that may require closer management attention. Finally, the half yearly or annual meeting focuses on strategic issues such as resourcing and technology implementation for the next six months or year. For the IR it identified particular pressures that might affect CESA and service levels, whereas for BPX and ESSO it defined the annual renegotiation phase of costs and service levels.

Interestingly, before 1998, BPX never truly formalized its communication process, even though the members of the alliance complained about the lack of information exchange. Operations continued to focus primarily on two meetings, the monthly and annual renegotiations. Respondents said that this arrangement prevented relational and operational effectiveness. It is interesting to speculate in turn whether a more structured approach covering the above five information exchange points would have benefited BPX in its 1993–8 IT outsourcing relationships.

Types of Interaction

Case organizations identified formality and standardization of interactions as most relevant and significant for exchange and communication content in relationships. These findings corroborate and overlap with our findings on the 'structural' dimension above. Table 8.6 summarizes the cross-case analysis findings.

In BAe, ESSO, and BPX exchanges had the highest degree of formality. Operations were strictly according to stipulated terms. In these cases the exchange process seemed to work very effectively, thus suggesting the greater the formality of exchanges the better. Xerox's experience corroborates this argument. Formality of interactions generally need to become institutionalized over time. Thus as formality surrounding exchanges becomes ambiguous they

Table 8.6. *Summary of types of interaction*

Type of interaction	Exchange content		Communication content	
			Pre-contract	Post-contract
Formality	BAe	● High	● Low	● High
	Xerox	● Low	● Low	● Low
	ESSO	● High	● Low	● High
	BPX	● High	● Low	● Low
	IR	● Medium	● High	● High
Standardization	BAe	● High		
	Xerox	● Low		
	ESSO	● High	N/A	N/A
	BPX	● High		
	IR	● Medium		

need to be renewed, as Xerox and IR had to do initially. This eventually also entails realigning or renegotiating the contract as BAe, ESSO, Xerox, and BPX did in order to achieve exchange clarity. This is further supported by IR's experience. The IR normally depends on formality in all its dealings with third parties to ensure audibility and impartiality. However, IR respondents seemed to suggest that in the CESA project, and before the master SLA was signed, little formality existed. As in Xerox, this had to be changed subsequently.

In terms of communication, formality was low in all cases except the IR prior to signing the contract. In accordance with the IR's public sector idiosyncrasies, information exchanges had to be detailed. In the other case organizations' communication content was formalized in subsequent operations, and by 1998 all except BPX had specified these exchanges.

Standardization primarily applies to exchange content and was found to be linked to formality. BPX, BAe, and ESSO enforced a high degree of standardization through carefully formulated contracts. BPX further imposed the use of industry standard terminology to describe service requirements to ensure replication, ease of renegotiation, and general management oversight across all its units. Generally speaking, formality and standardization in interactions determine the degree to which clients are in control of the exchange process.

Summary: The Process Dimension of Relations

The findings suggest the 'black box' of process in outsourcing consists of two core parts: one is the exchange content that encapsulates the service, technology and monetary exchanges. Second is the communication content that defines the information type and regularity of exchanges. These processes will be pervaded by 'psychological, intangible benefits and social' factors, which describe the subjective degree of satisfaction of individuals with the interactions in the relationship. Moreover, processes were found to be positively influenced by formality and standardization. The higher the degree of the former the more effective exchanges and communication were in the relationships. Management, in turn, needs to focus on a high exchange-content clarity throughout the deal and on implementing early on an effective communication process that incorporates routine daily, weekly, monthly, quarterly, and half-yearly, or yearly information exchange points. Enforcing these arrangements was shown by ESSO to have significant operational and normative benefits.

The process dimension identifies a major contribution of this study, as few studies have actually addressed this issue. Only Klepper (1995) and Davis (1996) pointed towards such a dimension in outsourcing relationships. However, Klepper focuses mainly on the evolutionary development processes of outsourcing relationships and disregards the operational perspective of relations. Only Davis (1996) in turn refers to the operating processes of relations which he explains as consisting of core processes, product/process technical system, and task/job design. The latter two make little sense in terms of process, but Davis's core process dimension does corroborate the importance of the exchange content element in the conceptual framework. This research study's contribution in turn lies in, first, identifying the characteristics of the operating process—exchange, communication, and normative content. Secondly, it illustrates empirically the importance of exchange content clarity and its perceptual (in terms of negative, neutral, and positive) impact on outsourcing relationships. Thirdly, it determines that inherent to exchange content is a normative content dimension that affects the exchanges in terms of 'psychological, intangible benefits and social' factors. Fourthly, it reveals the criticality of information exchanges in outsourcing relationships and identifies some 'best practice' in terms of regularity and type of information to be exchanged. Finally, it determines that process, exchanges, and interactions generally have a positive influence on relations when they have a high degree of formality and standardization.

Behaviours: From Dependency to Trust

The framework's behavioural dimension prescribes how individuals relate to the outsourcing venture and the other party through their conduct, perceptions, and intentions (Bennett 1991). In line with the framework, the dominant behaviours identified in the case studies were dependency, power, conflict, cooperation, and trust. An unexpected, but revealing finding was that these also characterized the nature of the overall relationship from the client's perspective. So in this respect the clients could discern the relationship, at different times, with the vendor as dependent, control (i.e. power) oriented, adversarial (i.e. conflictual), cooperative, and/or trusting.

Dependency

The case findings emphasize that outsourcing by nature places the client organization into a dependency relationship. De Looff (1997) noted that this is unavoidable as the vendor takes control of people, technology, and/or services that are otherwise fundamental to the operations of the client. Of primary concern here is the extent to which suppliers are the single source of services and/or products. The cases showed that on a continuum of dependency towards vendor lock-in, individuals or companies adopted a cooperative or control-oriented stance that varied according to the overall degree of dependency. For example, a high degree of dependence, as in Xerox and IR, diminished client control and increased cooperation. Operational managers in both organizations had to rely on EDS to define, implement, and provide them with a service that was being formalized as the new infrastructure was rolled out. Managers in both organizations, in turn, had to be highly cooperative and flexible. Yet in Xerox dependency at times caused serious frustration for managers, who lacked control and influence over developments and service delivery. This dependency, on occasions, led to heavy arguments, and generally invited the risk of opportunistic vendor behaviour. In Xerox's case this over-dependency contributed to the relational breakdown.

In contrast BAe, BPX, and ESSO attempted to balance their dependency from the outset. The strategy they took was one of a very detailed, all-encompassing contract. In BAe, managers explicitly and implicitly looked to the contract to handle the dependency, but it soon became evident that the nature of the deal inherently entails further dependency as the contract became outdated. Conversely, ESSO and BPX took the conscious choice of an outsourcing arrangement that minimized the degree of dependency through the multiple supplier and selective outsourcing approach (Currie and Willcocks 1998; Lacity, Willcocks, and Feeny 1996). BPX stood out initially as having a balanced approach, which proved essential to operationalizing the Alliance arrangement. Despite the attempts made to minimize dependency, all proved ineffectual over time as high switching costs sooner or later prevent any dramatic changes in suppliers. BPX exemplified the drastic effects such an attempt might entail in the rebidding of BT Syncordia's business. ESSO also experienced unanticipated difficulties in switching from its previous supplier to ITNet. Difficulties had not been envisaged because service measures were in place and ITNet was to fulfil the same set of commodity tasks. Generally a lock-in evolved over time as a supplier's service provision addressed more successfully the specific requirements of the client, the reason being that switching costs out of a supplier then increased.

Power
Power arises with dependence in outsourcing, a generalization supported in the case histories. This interplay influences relations in different ways, depending on the degree of asymmetry. All five client organizations strived for power, yet some had more control over their ventures than others. ESSO, BAe, and BPX's relations, for example, were strongly asymmetric in their favour. BPX, BAe, and ESSO managers had close control over the amount of information their suppliers were given concerning developments, allowing them to control their involvement. All three also used contractual mechanisms such as benchmarking, annual renegotiations, open book accounting, security vetting, and others to enforce control in their relationships. ESSO revealed, though, that power (through control mechanisms) can introduce up to 25 per cent additional coordination costs. A particular situation in BPX exemplified the adverse and costly dimension of asymmetry during the introduction of new software. In this context closer involvement of the supplier could have saved BPX money. Similarly, ESSO's control-driven culture diminished the amount of flexibility that could have prevented the early relational breakdown.

IR operations in terms of power seemed more symmetrical. IR managers preferred to work very closely with EDS managers, as the success of the venture and the CESA project was under the close scrutiny of government ministers.

Collaboration was essential, as the success of tax reforms depended on the successful development and implementation of CESA. Although there were many control mechanisms idiosyncratic to the Inland Revenue—because of its public sector position—there were strong indicators that relations were becoming more asymmetrical in EDS's favour, especially following the transfer of the second tranche of IT personnel. Xerox's case, on the other hand, exhibits the dangers of asymmetry in the supplier's favour. Early on, EDS had sufficient power to self-determine tasks, services, and even technology to develop the new infrastructure.

Conflict

With the 'interorganizational relationship approach' as a central element of the analytical framework, Robiecheaux and El-Ansary's (1976) taxonomy of functional and dysfunctional conflicts was used to analyse and classify the case study data on conflict. Respondents found conflict primarily dysfunctional in relations. Conflicts in Xerox, ESSO, BPX, and IR all attained sufficient severity at the operational level in the initial years that relations became stalemated and managers had to be replaced. BAe encountered similar problems in the early stages, requiring frequent interventions from head offices to clarify contract meaning. All five experienced considerable disruptions through conflicts.

However, time mediated the severity of conflicts at BAe, ESSO, and IR. Conflicts became more a routine part of 'clearing the air'. They became functional as conflicts identified problem areas that both parties needed to address. For example, IR-EDS undertook a 'perceptions exercise' to flag particularly severe problem areas in the relationship. By working through these cooperatively it strengthened overall cooperation:

We assigned a pairing from the joint partnership meeting to get to the bottom of the way we regarded those issues. We analysed those issues, put them into certain categories and we tasked them to examine them and to set out a work-plan of how they would solve those particular issues—each one of them. (Assistant Director Partnership Group)

ESSO went one step further, by appointing a relationship manager whose primary remit was to address some of the key conflict areas in their deal with ITNet. Subsequent resolution of these strengthened cooperation substantially.

Ongoing dysfunctional conflicts were very debilitating. In addition to a general increase of coordination costs, operations and relationships suffered. Xerox, for example, formalized its relations with EDS, with an emphasis on operating the venture in future as a procurement arrangement. At BPX they decided to drop the Alliance approach altogether, as ongoing conflicts between suppliers demanded too many management resources. Thus dysfunctional conflicts will foster dramatic changes to both relational operations and can impact on the whole venture, as ESSO found.

Cooperation

Our framework prescribes cooperation as inherent to outsourcing, which all five case studies corroborated. Table 8.7 summarizes the primary areas of cooperation across the case studies.

Cooperation in terms of working together to achieve the outsourcing goals is indicative of mutuality in the relationship. Although there are different objectives that each party pursues, it is fundamental for the client organization to foster this type of cooperation. The vendor will generally cooperate to ensure maximum remuneration (e.g. BPX), whereas clients cooperate to achieve their outsourcing intentions. Managers in Xerox and IR, for example, worked closely together with EDS to ensure their infrastructure project is successful. In ESSO, senior managers agreed to renegotiate the contract to ensure ITNet made a return on the deal and to avoid early termination. By cooperating in this way ESSO was eventually able to reap significant benefits from the strengthened relationship.

Table 8.7. *Summary of cooperation in the case studies*

Main areas of cooperation	Key examples of cooperation in the case studies
Working together to achieve goals	• BAe-CSC initial contract clarification to operationalize deal • Xerox-EDS overhaul and revamping of existing infrastructure • ESSO-ITNet willingness of ESSO to renegotiate on behalf and in favour of ITNet • BPX-Alliance suppliers have to cooperate closely to deliver a seamless service • IR-EDS handover of development staff to achieve CESA on time in full
Conflict minimization & cooperation maximization	• Xerox-EDS mutually agreeing to replace operational managers in the UK and the 'perception exercise' to progress relationship • ESSO-ITNet mutually agreeing to replace operational managers and the contract renegotiation on behalf and in favour of ITNet • IR-EDS mutually agreeing to replace operational managers and the 'exception review' to develop a relationship • BAe-CSC contract clarification and development of contract interpretation and the secondment of CSC account manager to be both IT Director and Account Manager
Ideological agreement	• ESSO-ITNet agreed to an informal partnership late 1997 • BPX-Alliance agree to non-legal partnering principles (Aston Clinton Principles Appendix III) • IR-EDS agreed and included informal partnership objectives in their contract

The most prominent area of cooperation was related to conflict minimization. Particularly strong examples were the mutual replacement of operational managers to cooperatively alleviate serious problem situations in Xerox, ESSO, and the IR. However, when conflicts could not be resolved cooperatively, as in Xerox, including into 1999/2000 where one issue went to a court case, relationships as a whole tended to suffer. Generally this dichotomy advocates that managers need to approach relationship management with a give-and-take stance. Careful judgement is often needed here with an outlook that marries with the overall outsourcing objectives (see ESSO's approach).

Finally, ideological agreement is posited to portray a particular high degree of cooperation. ESSO, BPX, and the IR case corroborate this suggestion. Two different approaches were evident, though, in these three cases. First, in ESSO the ideological agreement evolved over time as a response to service improvements beyond expectations, whereas in BPX and the IR the agreement formed part of the initial contract. For BPX and the IR, a high degree of cooperation was essential to their outsourcing deal. Openly discussing this fact with the supplier managers made sure everybody started with a similar mind set. In ESSO, the overwhelming developments from severe relational problems to seven consecutive months of faultless service delivery was to be strengthened ideologically by an informal partnering agreement.

Trust

Trust receives much attention in declarations of intent in outsourcing. Our case experiences suggest that there is no such thing as an instant relationship, or instant trust; trust is earned over time, but can become a fundamental building block for subsequently achieving a relationship advantage. Similar to Ring and Van de Ven's (1992) proposition, case findings suggested that trust can exist both at an informal and formal level in outsourcing. Formally, trust exists in terms of confidence in the vendor. All clients chose their vendors because they felt sufficiently confident in the supplier's integrity and capabilities to handle and deliver service requirements. BPX even integrated the notion of trust into its 'partnering principles' agreement to affirm its confidence. Formal confidence can also be explained as calculative-based trust (Williamson 1993). Trust, on this level, might be termed inherent to operations.

Findings illustrate that relations in outsourcing start on a formal trust basis and evolve towards relational-based trust (Child and Faulkner, 1998; Rousseau et al. 1998). Our analysis revealed that informal trust can be compared to relational trust, to the extent that respondents noted relations evolved towards relative openness and honesty. Dependability and reliability were the preconditions for relational trust. The emotive feelings trust gave rise to in the relations led ESSO to agree, for example, to an informal partnership. In the BAe case it gave senior managers the necessary sense of security to approach CSC for strategic advice on technical innovation and organizational matters. For both cases, relational trust entailed significant benefits as a result of the close ties.

IR and Xerox managers rarely experienced relational trust. For the IR, public sector idiosyncrasies clearly prohibit the evolution of this form of trust, in order to ensure impartiality and accountability. However, one can see some forms developing in the second half of the contract. Xerox, on the other hand, experienced too many operational difficulties, and conflicts which prevented EDS from developing a track record of problem-free performance. Trust between Xerox and EDS degraded to mistrust with a consequence that Xerox's senior managers kept EDS managers at arm's length: 'I have EDS people less involved in my management meetings than I did in the early days. We now are much more inclined to give them the output of that meeting and say this is what we want you to do, rather than have them involved with us in trying to decide what to do' (Global IT manager, Xerox). The case studies generally revealed that relational trust only evolves in situations where key individuals were able to develop a rapport. The backdrop tended to be a good track record. Indeed, not every case achieved a relational level of trust; most relations tend to operate more at a formal level of trust, based on service performance that had to be re-proven every day.

Summary: Behavioural Issues in Outsourcing Relationships

The findings (see Table 8.8) generally corroborate the literature's suggestion that dependency, power, conflict, and cooperation are systemically interrelated. The argument being that, for example, a change in conflict or cooperation will influence the other. A number of interesting empirical patterns emerged. In terms of dependency power, low to medium dependency meant relations were asymmetrically in favour of the client and implied the client was in control. Conversely, in those where dependency was high, power tended to be asymmetrically in favour of the vendor and implied the client had little control. The latter presents considerable concern over whether vendors will behave opportunistically, and generally such arrangements should be avoided (Lacity and Hirschheim 1993).

Table 8.8. *Behavioural dimension findings*

	BAe-CSC	Xerox-EDS	ESSO-ITNet	BPX-Alliance	IR-EDS
Dependency	Medium	High	Low	Low	High
Power	Asymmetric in client's favour	Asymmetric in vendor's favour	Asymmetric in client's favour	Asymmetric in client's favour	Symmetric to asymmetric in vendor's favour
Conflict	Functional	Dysfunctional	Functional	Dysfunctional	Functional
Cooperation	Medium	Low	High	High	High
Trust	Formal & informal	Formal	Formal & informal	Formal	Formal

Conflict cooperation revealed a variety of patterns. In those situations where conflict is functional, parties' cooperation was found to be either medium or high, whereas in those cases where conflict is dysfunctional cooperation can either be low or high. The pattern dysfunctional-low points to operations that are generally failing. Organizations that encounter such situations may have to bring in arbitration (e.g. Xerox-EDS). Generally dysfunctional situations need to be counterbalanced by high cooperation. Such situations proved operationally beneficial as they allow parties to 'clear the air' and progress relations, but frequent dysfunctional conflicts will increase management efforts (e.g. BPX's arrangements and IR's and Xerox's 'perception and exception exercises'). In contrast, those relational situations where conflict is functional and cooperation is medium or high display an environment where conflicts are more routine problems of relations, and cooperating to resolve them amicably may bring considerable added value.

The framework proved useful in suggesting that trust does exist at different levels in outsourcing. Trust exists, though, primarily at a formal level and is characterized as confidence in the operational processes and service performance of the vendor. In line with Williamson's (1993) and Rousseau, Sitkin, Burt, and Camerer's (1998) suggestion, trust in outsourcing does evolve on occasions towards a relational form that can hold significant operational benefits, but much depends on labour stability, that is retaining good personnel over time. This is not a noticeable feature in IT outsourcing, and the IT labour market generally, and is always an important issue to take into account before assuming that a relationship advantage and high trust can be achieved.

The findings above are in many ways confirmatory of existing research. However, there are a number of areas that extend existing research. First, Lacity and Hirschheim (1993a) looked at dependency and power in terms of effects on outsourcing evaluations and operations; this research identified a number of dependency-power patterns that define relational operations. Secondly, Klepper (1994) theoretically elaborated the interplay between conflict and cooperation, which this research extends by identifying empirically a number of patterns that emerge in relational operations in outsourcing. Thirdly, both Klepper (1994) and Willcocks and Choi (1995) explore the importance of cooperation, but present either only theoretical or empirical examples of cooperation. This research actually identifies three areas of where and how cooperation might arise. Fourthly, Klepper (1994) and Davis (1996) partly focus on trust, allowing them to reveal many formal aspects of trust in outsourcing, but they do not acknowledge nor identify explicitly the possibility of relational trust. Conversely, this research presents clear data showing that at times trust may actually take this form in outsourcing.

EFFICIENCY AND OUTCOMES: A RELATIONSHIP ADVANTAGE?

Relational efficiency refers to how far, and how efficiently, relationships support a client's objectives—including, typically the minimization of its IT operation costs while achieving improvements in service and technology quality, and getting access to innovations. With the transaction cost approach guiding the framework, relational efficiency from the client's perspective was evaluated through transaction costs; uncertainty reduction; the customization of service and attention it experiences from the supplier; and the degree of satisfaction with the relationship on contract, structure, interaction, and behaviour dimensions. The findings indicate strongly that relational issues and development, as we have defined them, are actually fundamental to all kinds of IT outsourcing of any significant size, but that they are significantly overlooked and underestimated, making outsourcing relationships inefficient, and much less supportive of the IT outsourcing objectives than they could be.

The second set of measures relate to overall outcomes and these provide an additional means for assessing, in retrospect, whether contracts, operational practices, and objectives are being delivered as originally expected. Generally, the case findings support a less optimistic view of relationship management and overall outsourcing effectiveness than that portrayed at the beginning of the ventures. Let us look first at relationship arrangements and their efficiency across the cases.

Relationship Efficiency: (a) Transaction Costs

The focus of transaction costs in outsourcing relationships is mainly on operating, monitoring, and maintenance of operations. Hence, respondents frequently talked about transaction costs as coordination issues. Table 8.9 summarizes the findings for the main areas where transaction costs arose, and provides a perceptual indication of the costs according to the respondents. Interestingly, very few transaction costs could be quantified, because the organizations did not focus on collecting this type of information.

Contract management costs were particularly high at BAe, Xerox, and the IR due to the complexity of the undertaking and the impact of bounded rationality. Lengthy localization and clarification phases were necessary, increasing transaction costs (see for example BAe's case). In Xerox, the lack of detail entailed frequent operational debates about what was in and out, which were often only resolved with the involvement of central management. Operational problems were often down to haggling with EDS about contract terms. Similarly, IR managers had to develop operational agreements, for as long as the service level agreements were still being negotiated and finalized.

Table 8.9. *Summary of transaction costs*

Transaction costs	BAe-CSC	Xerox-EDS	ESSO-ITNet	BPX-Alliance	IR-EDS
Contract management	High	High	Low	Low	Medium to high
Contract renewal	High	High	High	High	N/A
Management structures	Medium to high	High	Medium to high	Medium to high	High
Communication management	Low	High	Low to medium	Medium to high	Low

The problem was that these operational interpretations were later found to be inconsistent with the SLAs and thus had to be amended, wasting valuable time and resources. Conversely, ESSO and BPX experienced few of these problems as they had demarcated finite operational areas for suppliers.

Contract renewal in BAe, Xerox, ESSO, and BPX was also noted to increase transaction costs substantially. Influencing factors were opportunistic behaviour and 'moral hazard' issues (Blois 1996). ESSO and BPX highlight that renegotiations take up considerable management resources and time. In addition, they disrupt operations and relationships, and can cause animosity. For example, respondents at the IR explained that both sides' managers who had been involved in negotiations were unable to work together. In ESSO the subsequent renegotiation of the contract in ITNet's favour was found not only to have strained relations, but to suggest potential opportunistic behaviour and moral hazards. Blois (1996) suggests that if it is possible for a party to take actions that are of benefit to it and adversely affect the other, after a contract has been signed, then a 'moral hazard' is said to exist. Although ESSO managers agreed to renegotiate, ITNet's actions can be interpreted as opportunistic behaviour and raising moral hazards, as some assets were already specific to the relationship and switching was really out of the question. A similar set of circumstances can be identified in BAe's case.

The cases also showed that any changes to the management structure will increase transaction costs, as often operations will be disrupted. Costs arose in three ways. First, in all the cases senior operation managers had to be replaced due to ongoing operational problems, lack of skills, or having fallen out with the opposing supplier manager. Replacing managers often involved senior management mutually agreeing and coordinating to remove, search for, and appoint new senior operation managers. Secondly, in Xerox's case, managers were confronted with 'information impactedness' and coordination bottlenecks because the EDS management structure did not mirror Xerox's structure. The third situation is related to the former, but this time ESSO, BPX, and the IR found their operations to be suffering because they lacked essential relationship managers. Management structure in turn raised considerable coordination, agreement, search, and information costs.

Communication management difficulties were often found related to issues with management structure (see above). Hence, most costs that arose in this context were due to lack of information or 'information impactedness'. Blois (1996) terms these types of costs as 'motivation costs'.

In summary, the findings clearly show that there are significant additional transaction costs that arise with contract management and contract renewal, management structures and communication management across the cases. In part they corroborate Earl's (1996) suggestion that companies significantly underestimate set-up and management costs. Particularly worrying are those areas that were identified as high levels in Table 8.9, as they would suggest serious operational and relational inefficiencies. Contract renegotiation/renewal on a large scale, especially, is something that needs to be avoided. Other areas can be carefully planned for and can be managed down to low cost levels. In this context, BAe, Xerox, and BPX's arrangements proved particularly costly in terms of relationship management and raised serious doubts over whether operational cost benefits could be achieved. In BPX's case the subsequent decision to drop the 'Alliance' approach substantiates this post-analysis concern over its operational efficiency.

Relationship Efficiency: (b) Uncertainty Reduction

Relationship efficiency is equally affected by uncertainty factors. Uncertainty may introduce additional costs and require resourcing and service changes. In line with the 'transaction cost and interorganizational relationship' approach that undergirds our analytical framework, environmental and task uncertainty is of primary concern here. In turn an organization's market (environment) can be described as being 'stable' or 'dynamic' (Duncan, 1972). A stable environment is predictable and its market remains largely unchanged over time. A dynamic environment is one which is in a constant state of flux and is characterized by strong competition. The organizational market situation will in turn inform the tasks in organizations. Tasks in outsourcing relationships are distinguished as services and technology, and transactions. Table 8.10 summarizes the cross-case analysis findings for uncertainty reduction.

BAe operates in an environment that is very dynamic, that frequently changes with political decisions around the world. It has often little influence in turn on business demands, and thus volumes in BAe's business can vary dramatically with new orders. Since new orders often comprise major investments its environment is very competitive, thus requiring a lot of flexibility in its operations. The IR equally is confronted with a very dynamic environment, although there is no competition to deal with. It is primarily dependent on the government and political decisions and new legislation. On a yearly basis with the

Table 8.10. *Summary of uncertainty reduction*

Uncertainty	BAe-CSC	Xerox-EDS	ESSO-ITNet	BPX-Alliance	IR-EDS
Market	Dynamic	Stable	Stable	Stable	Dynamic
Service & technology[a]	High	High	Low	Low to medium	High
Transaction[a]	High to medium	High	Low	Medium	High

[a] denotes task uncertainty

roll-out of the new Budget, taxation requirements change, which implies operational changes and at times far-reaching changes like CESA. Relatively speaking, BPX, Xerox, and ESSO have been operating in more stable environments where developments were more predictable.

The impact of a dynamic market on the outsourcing relationship can cause service volumes to fluctuate and make transactions unpredictable. In BAe's Military Defence unit for example the placement of an order for Nimrod transport planes demanded resourcing of an additional forty programmers. In the IR and Xerox the real uncertainty surrounding the service, technology, and transactions evolves from the major technology infrastructure changes that undergird the outsourcing venture. In many ways service provisions and transactions are thus very unpredictable as parts of the infrastructure come on line during operations. Conversely, ESSO's relationship experienced no such uncertainties as services, technology (i.e. legacy) and transactions were being phased out. BPX on the other hand did experience some task uncertainties as it expanded its operations globally, as it achieved mergers, and as new technology and service requirements arose.

In summary, a dynamic market environment will entail considerable uncertainties for an outsourcing relationship in terms of service and technology requirements and transactions. These uncertainties will imply fluctuations in costs as resources, services, and technology are redefined. Additionally, major infrastructure projects also make it very difficult to predict service, technology, and transaction requirements and inherently increase operational costs. In all these cases our empirical evidence supports what many would term the 'logic of the situation', that it is robust contractual arrangements, relationship structures, interactions, and behavioural management that considerably reduce/manage these uncertainties.

Relationship Efficiency: (c) Customization

The framework highlights that customization refers the degree to which particular investments are idiosyncratic, mixed, or non-specific to the relationship

Table 8.11. *Summary of customization*

Customization	BAe-CSC	Xerox-EDS	ESSO-ITNet	BPX-Alliance	IR-EDS
Service & technology	Mixed to idiosyncratic	Idiosyncratic	Non-specific	Non-specific to mixed	Idiosyncratic
Organizational[a]	Idiosyncratic to non-specific	Idiosyncratic	Idiosyncratic	Idiosyncratic	Idiosyncratic

[a] framework includes it as part of transaction specificity

and the venture. Although it is evident that vendors need to tailor most of their services and processes to each individual customer, the analysis is more concerned with the effects of customization on services and technology and the extent of idiosyncratic investments clients had to make into the relationship. Table 8.11 summarizes the findings for customization.

The idiosyncratic specificity of service and technology assets Xerox, the IR and, in part, BAe were looking to receive from their suppliers, not only implied the commitment of significant funds, but also inferred vendor lock-in. This is potentially a high-risk strategy. In Xerox and the IR, EDS was developing and implementing major technological infrastructure changes and innovations that effectively meant they were locked in at least until the main parts of projects were complete. Yet even then once the infrastructure is in place EDS's intricate know-how about the technological developments and organizational procedures will make it very difficult for Xerox and IR to change suppliers. To ensure operational efficiency and to mitigate risks, respondents explained they have to prevent their suppliers from taking control, behaving opportunistically, and neglecting stipulated terms. In contrast, ESSO and BPX carefully controlled their degree of asset specificity, giving them the benefit of being able to switch suppliers if need be. The level of risk in turn was much lower. BPX, for example, was able to ensure it received 'best-in-class' service by benchmarking and if need be by rebidding service frameworks against other suppliers (see the rebid of BT Syncordia in BPX).

Although BPX, ESSO, and BAe (in part) were in control of their service and technology specificity, the relationship-specific procedures and management structures (see above) introduced a high degree of organizational specificity across all case organizations. The organizational specificity implied not only committing considerable funds (in terms of people, resources, and time), it also entailed eventual lock-in. Indeed, the investments clients had made into relationship management even three years into their deals, effectively prevented them from switching/terminating, let alone returning to in-house delivery. BPX highlighted that even after the contracts had expired, managers explained they would not drop their existing suppliers because the idiosyncratic assets that had evolved between the parties in terms of structures and procedures would have been lost investments outside the relationships.

Table 8.12. *Summary of relational efficiency elements*

Efficiency	BAe-CSC	Xerox-EDS	ESSO-ITNet	BPX-Alliance	IR-EDS
Transaction costs	Medium to high	High	Medium to low	Medium	Medium to high
Uncertainty reduction (market uncertainty)	High (dynamic)	High (stable)	Low (stable)	Medium (stable)	High (dynamic)
Customization[a]	Mixed to idiosyncratic	Idiosyncratic	Non-specific	Non-specific to mixed	Idiosyncratic

[a] disregards organizational specificity

Outcomes: Satisfaction

Outcomes focus on the venture's overall success in terms of achieving the client's outsourcing intentions and/or expectations. One way of assessing outcome is the degree to which client organizations were satisfied with their relationship arrangements taking into account transaction costs, uncertainty, customization, and overall outcomes achieved. In summary, we would say that all experienced hidden costs and unexpected difficulties in setting up and rendering their relationship arrangements efficient (see Table 8.12). All participants highlighted how important these relationship dimensions and activities were to keeping the IT outsourcing objectives in the realms of feasibility. ESSO eventually ended up with efficient relationships, and the IR and BAe expressed satisfaction with their relationship arrangements after some five years into the contracts. Despite considerable investments in relationships, Xerox was still experiencing very mixed results from its IT outsourcing during 2001. And as we saw, while BPX achieved a lot of its objectives from 1993 to 1998, it also made the judgement that its relationship arrangements needed to be reconstructed.

On outcomes generally, a summary is shown in Table 8.13. Except for ESSO, the case organizations reveal that outcomes generally do not match clients' intentions and expectations. Innovation and operational satisfaction are the two areas that vendors commonly failed to deliver on. Conversely, the area vendors unanimously delivered on across the case exemplars were the financial benefits, including some, rarely all, cost savings. Still in BAe, ESSO, BPX, and IR savings of significant size were made available, essentially deriving from the base operational costs, rather than new technology, or new development work. Of concern, though, were the touted savings in the IR case, where extra costs of implementing the contract and CESA had already exceeded the overall savings threefold. A similar situation unfolded at Xerox.

All client organizations associated value-added in essence with innovation in terms of service, technical, financial, or operational improvements that fed

Table 8.13. *Summary of outcomes*

Outcomes	BAe-CSC	Xerox-EDS	ESSO-ITNet	BPX-Alliance	IR-EDS
Outcomes vs. intentions	Low	Low	Achieved	Low	Low
Financial benefits	30% (overall)	$170m (cash payment)	5–10% (annually)	3–5% (annually)	£225m (over 10yrs)
Innovation	Low	High	Low	Low	High
Operational satisfaction	Low	Low	High	Mixed	Mixed

through into business advantage. BAe, for example, defined its expectations of innovation as business, capacity, and utility value-added. It explicated these for CSC because no identifiable improvements were being proposed, developed, or implemented. Across the cases innovations were generally found missing, even in BPX and ESSO, who offered additional rewards for them. Only respondents in Xerox and IR indicated they were receiving innovations with their extensive infrastructure changes. Innovations, it would seem, need to be considered as additional costs for vendors who need to be able to recuperate the costs of these somehow. In Xerox and IR these costs were integrated or charged as extras with the roll-out of the project. Some of these costs were, for example, ingrained in the extra £400 million that arose with CESA. In the BPX and ESSO cases, although they offered rewards, they often did not sufficiently cover the costs of developing, transferring, formalizing, and implementing benefits. Furthermore vendors often had to take the full risks and hence cover the costs for failures, thus making it too risky and costly for them to undertake.

The reason why clients generally were expecting to receive innovations and value-added goes back to notions of economies-of-scale and 'world-class' technical and management expertise. Because vendors have large resources, a range of expertise and capabilities, and benefit from the intrinsic knowledge transfer that comes with outsourcing and providing services to numerous customers, clients expected knowledge transfers in terms of improved practices and technologies that translated into business value-added. However, in many instances the differences in technology and operations across the various customers prevents a one-to-one transfer. Additionally vendors needed more guidance on the areas of innovation. In ESSO, BAe, BPX, and IR conjoint reviews and request issues often had to identify the actual areas for innovations.

Disregarding the general degree of variation in operational satisfaction over the lifespan of the contract, only ESSO was truly satisfied with its outsourcing venture. Four areas were evident that circumscribed outsourcing satisfaction as a measure in ESSO. First, general end-user satisfaction had dramatically improved since the deal's inception. Secondly, service levels were being met and delivered above expectations. Thirdly, operationally relations were working well, few disputes disrupted operations, and managers found themselves agreeing informally to being 'partners' (see above—normative content). Fourthly, the bonus and recognition rewards encouraged ITNet to be responsive and attentive, which paid out mutually. In the other cases, disputes, low service performance, operational problems, and non-achievement of outcome expectations all diminished operational satisfaction in varying degrees. At the same time, given the complexity and scale of these other deals, it should be remembered also how much was being achieved in situations of considerable difficulty.

CONCLUSION

Three patterns emerge that characterize relationship arrangements as inefficient, adequate, or efficient. Xerox, BAe, and IR's arrangements were found generally to be inefficient in the first few years, raising serious doubts over whether the relationship arrangements offered operational advantages or benefits over the previous in-house operations. Subsequently, all three sets of arrangements were improved to a more than adequate level, with less positive impact at Xerox, where there were a number of more deep-seated problems. BPX's arrangements described an overall adequate arrangement in terms of relational efficiency, even though the Alliance approach generally proved operationally ineffective. Finally, after a bad start, ESSO's arrangement showed the nearest to what could be termed relationally efficient, although certain practices (e.g. contract renewal) do introduce considerable transaction costs. The ideal scenario in terms of efficiency would be low results on all three accounts.

Relational efficiency in general has not yet been addressed by researchers in outsourcing due to the little understanding that is available concerning relationships. The contribution the framework makes in this area may be a decisive influencing factor in the future approach of organizations to planning and managing outsourcing relationships. Three particular contributions were made. First, the findings illustrate the critical importance of planning for and achieving 'relationship efficiency' through transaction costs minimization, uncertainty reduction, and customization in IT outsourcing, and presented case data of how these will influence risks, efficiency of operations, and the business value-added achievable. Secondly, it showed that most organizations will become locked into their outsourcing deal, not least because idiosyncratic investment in terms of organizational specificity eventually hinders early termination and switching. Finally, contract restructuring/renewal and management structures emerged as responsible for raising most of the transaction costs in outsourcing relationships.

In respect of outcomes, four factors emerged as of primary concern, those being outcomes vs. intentions, financial benefits, innovations, and operational satisfaction. Four out of the five case organizations did not achieve their anticipated outsourcing intentions and hence expectations, emphasizing that the delivery of outcomes requires closer management. It is interesting to note that those cases identified as relationally inefficient also revealed that their outcomes were not being achieved (e.g. Xerox), whereas the one case found nearest to relational efficiency was shown to be most successful in its outsourcing arrangement. Consequently, this research study verifies what so many researchers have assumed—that relational efficiency can make the difference between a successful and less successful outsourcing venture.

REFERENCES

Bagozzi, R. P. (1975). 'Marketing as Exchange'. *Journal of Marketing*, 39 (October): 32–9.

Barnett, R. E. (1992*a*). 'Some Problems with Contract as Promise'. *Cornell Law Review*, 77/5: 1022–33.

—— (1992*b*). 'Conflicting Visions: A Critique of Ian Macneil's Relational Theory of Contract'. *Virginia Law Review*, 78/5: 1175–206.

Bennett, R. (1991). *Organisational Behaviour*. Pitman Publishing, London.

Blois, K. J. (1996). 'Relationship Marketing in Organizational Markets: When is it Appropriate?' *Journal of Marketing Management*, 12: 161–73.

Child, J. (1973). 'Predicting and Understanding Organization Structure'. *Administrative Science Quarterly*, 18: 1–17.

—— and Faulkner, D. (1998). *Strategies of Co-operation: Managing Alliances, Networks, and Joint Ventures*. Oxford University Press, Oxford.

Currie, W. L., and Willcocks, L. (1998). *New Strategies in IT Outsourcing*. Business Intelligence Ltd., London.

Davis, K. J. (1996). 'IT Outsourcing Relationships: An Exploratory Study of Inter-organizational Control Mechanisms'. DBA thesis, Graduate School of Business Administration. Harvard University, Boston, 310.

De Looff, L. A. (1997). *Information Systems Outsourcing Decision Making: A Managerial Approach*. IDEA Group Publishing, Hershey, Pa.

DiRomualdo, A., and Gurbaxani, V. (1998). 'Strategic Intent for IT Outsourcing'. *Sloan Management Review*, 39/4: 67–80.

Duncan, R. B. (1972). 'Characteristics of Organizational Environments and Perceived Environmental Uncertainty'. *American Scientific Quarterly*, 17/3: 313–27.

Earl, M. J. (1996). 'The Risks of Outsourcing IT'. *Sloan Management Review*, 37/3: 26–32.

Feeny, D., and Willcocks, L. (1998). 'Core IS Capabilities for Exploiting IT'. *Sloan Management Review*, 39/3: 1–26.

Hakansson, H. (1982). *International Marketing and Purchasing of Industrial Goods: An Interaction Approach*. John Wiley & Sons, Chichester.

Kern, T., and Willcocks, L. (1996). 'The Enabling and Determining Environment: Neglected Issues in an IT/IS Outsourcing Strategy', in *Proceedings of the European Conference of Information Systems*, Lisbon.

—— —— (2000). 'Contracts, Control, and Presentiation in IT Outsourcing: Research in Thirteen UK Organisations'. *Journal of Global Information Management*, 8/4: 20–35.

—— —— (2001). 'The Client–Supplier Outsourcing Relationship: An Exploratory Study', Rotterdam School of Management, Erasmus University Rotterdam, Working Paper 00/19.

Klepper, R. (1994). 'Outsourcing Relationships', in M. Khosrowpour (ed.), *Managing Information Technology with Outsourcing*, Idea Group Publishing, Harrisbury, Pa., 218–43.

—— (1995). 'The Management of Partnering Development in IS Outsourcing'. *Journal of Information Technology*, 10/4: 249–58.

—— and Jones, W. (1998). *Outsourcing Information Technology, Systems & Services.* Prentice Hall PTR, Englewood Cliffs, NJ.

Lacity, M. C., and Hirschheim, R. (1993). *Information Systems Outsourcing: Myths, Metaphors and Realities.* John Wiley & Sons Ltd., Chichester.

—— —— and Willcocks, L. (1994). 'Realizing Outsourcing Expectations: Incredible Expectations, Credible Outcomes'. *Information Systems Management* (Fall), 7–18.

—— Willcocks, L., and Feeny, D. (1996). 'The Value of Selective IT Sourcing'. *Sloan Management Review*, 37/3 (Spring), 13–25.

Macneil, I. R. (1981). 'Economic Analysis of Contractual Relations: Its Shortfalls and the Need for a Rich Classificatory Apparatus'. *Northwestern University Law Review*, 75/6: 1018–63.

McFarlan, F. W., and Nolan, R. (1995). 'How to Manage an IT Outsourcing Alliance'. *Sloan Management Review* (Winter), 9–23.

Mitchell, J. (1983). 'Case and Situation Analysis'. *Sociological Review*, 31: 187–211.

Richmond, W. B., Seidmann, A., and Whinston, A. B. (1992). 'Incomplete Contracting Issue in Information Systems Development Outsourcing'. *Decision Support System*, 5/8: 459–77.

Ring, P. S., and Van de Ven, A. (1992). 'Structuring Cooperative Relationships between Organizations'. *Strategic Management Journal* 13: 483–98.

Robiecheaux, R. A., and El-Ansary, A. (1976). 'A General Model for Understanding Channel Member Behaviour'. *Journal of Retailing* 52/4: 13–30.

Rousseau, D. M., Sitkin, S. Burt, R. and Camerer, C. (1998). 'Introduction to Special Topic Forum: Not so Different after all—Cross Discipline View of Trust'. *Academy of Management Review* 23/3: 393–404.

Van de Ven, A. H., and Ring, P. (1994). 'Developmental Processes of Cooperative Interorganizational Relationships'. *Academy of Management Review,* 19/1: 90–118.

White, R., and James, B. (1996). *The Outsourcing Manual.* Gower Publishing Limited, Aldershot.

Willcocks, L., and Choi, C. (1995). 'Co-operative Partnership and Total IT Outsourcing: From Contractual Obligation to Strategic Alliance'. *European Management Journal*, 13/1: 67–78.

—— and Fitzgerald, G. (1994). 'Toward the Residual IS Organization? Research on IT Outsourcing Experiences in the United Kingdom', in R. Baskerville, S. Smithson,

O. Ngwenyama, and J. DeGross (eds.), *Transforming Organizations with Information Technology*, Elsevier Science BV, Amsterdam, 129–52.

Williamson, O. E. (1975). *Markets and Hierarchies: Analysis and Antitrust Implications. A Study in the Economics of Internal Organization.* The Free Press, New York.

—— (1993). 'Calculativeness, Trust, and Economic Organization'. *Journal of Law & Economics*, 36 (April), 453–86.

9

The Relationship Advantage as Practice: Reflections

INTRODUCTION

The cross-case analysis in the previous chapter illustrated the adequacy of our framework in characterizing IT outsourcing relationships. Prior to that, the individual case analyses in Chapters 3–7 elicited a number of strong links between the dimensions which, combined with Chapter 8's detailed analysis, provide a number of important pointers for outsourcing relationship management. This section makes use of the framework in a normative sense to determine a number of critical propositions for relationship management practice. We also suggest some small but important revisions of the framework, for future use by practitioners.The discussion below follows closely the main dimensions of the framework, and, for coherence in the discussion, some repetition here of findings from the previous chapter is inevitable.

Based on the comprehensive analysis we carried out in this book on IT outsourcing, and the relationship dimension, we will now reflect further on the evidence and elicit key learning points and relationship management pointers. In the second part of this chapter we identify three ways of thinking about, and striving for understanding of the possible relationship advantages to be gained. We structure these discussions by way of three additional frameworks that can be used by practitioners as they debate, move towards, or are heavily involved in IT outsourcing. The first issue is the nature of the Winner's Curse in IT outsourcing, and how its risk can be minimized. The second issue is diagnosing the type of IT outsourcing arrangement you might be involved in, and the implications this will have for the relationship dimensions. The third relates to the six phases of an IT outsourcing arrangement identified by earlier research in which we participated. The evidence in this book strongly corroborates the usefulness of thinking in these terms. Therefore we describe here the framework, and use the case histories to pull out the implications for managing relationships across the six phases of our relationship framework.

RELATIONSHIP MANAGEMENT: PRACTICAL IMPLICATIONS

Although the analytical framework (see Chapter 2) depicts relationship management as static and systematic, in actuality it has to be very iterative and dynamic. Van de Ven and Ring (1994) argued—correctly—that relationship management is cyclical rather than sequential, and suggested that relationships are maintained 'not because they achieve stability, but because they maintain balance between formal and informal processes'. Our framework actually acknowledges this aspect and addresses it indirectly through the 'time element'. A constant interplay between the relationship dimensions occurs over the life-span of the venture. In practice, the unidirectional flow of the diagram is deceiving, as it only refers to the passing of time.

As part of this dynamism, it is clear that the relationship dimensions we isolated for analytical purposes have an intrinsic dynamism. They interpenetrate and have mutual effects on each other, and in combination affect other factors in the IT outsourcing arrangement. The five figures in the sections below summarize the cross-case analysis findings of the strongest cause and effect links, and present an indicative value judgement of their positive and/or negative impacts. Since these links identify the main relationship management issues that client and vendor organizations were confronted with, the authors point to an understanding of these as being critical for developing robust relationship management practices.

Outsourcing Intentions in Relationships

Unlike the framework's suggestion, Figure 9.1 shows that outsourcing intent primarily affects the contract, the structure, and the efficiency outcome of the venture. Still these findings corroborate the position of intent as an input dimension of the relationship, and as the measure against which to evaluate its efficiency outcome. Since managers' tasks and actions tend to be directed by outsourcing intentions, it seems paramount that these are pervasive. Financial, business, and technical intentions can be readily communicated to managers across the organization for they can be formalized. However, those intentions that focus on 'reciprocity' or partnering can only be stated as a directive, as the transfer of 'soft' intentions, behaviours, and established relations is infeasible (as we saw in Xerox's case). This needs to be taken into account when planning intentions and for managing organizational expectations.

Outsourcing intent affects the contract as the promises agreed to, in essence, should reflect the client's objectives. All cases illustrated that the core objectives pursued were ingrained into the shape, structure, and nature of the contractual arrangements. Decisive for relationship management here is the 'tightness and looseness' of the requirements specified in the contract. This determines, in respect of relationship management, the degree to which

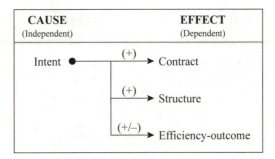

Fig. 9.1. *Intent links*

managers can depend on the contract as a guide to effectuating the arrangement.

In terms of structure, strategic intent prescribes the size, complexity, and stability of the venture. These are decisive factors influencing relationship management, defining for example the extent and costs of the deal, the number of suppliers, and the length of the venture. Hence, strategic intent will also inform the resources to commit to the management structure for handling the relationship. The findings generally suggest that for any deal resourcing should span four groups of management that include senior oversight managers, senior operational managers, operations managers, and technical managers. The number of managers involved depends in part on the organization's management culture, the size, and the complexity of the undertaking. For example IR started with a team of forty managers, whereas ESSO had only four managers.

Strategic intent also affects the outcome of the outsourcing venture in terms of outlining the client's objectives. This implies that depending on the outsourcing intent, procedures need to be put in place that ensure achieving the objectives and managing the expectations. The negative effect of intent on outcome occurs when the objectives are not clear. In their study of fifty deals, DiRomualdo and Gurbaxani (1998) found poor outcomes are often due to unclear intentions and goals, and not aligning these with the contract and relationship. Xerox and the IR case illustrate such circumstances, where intent is so dynamic and uncertain that few clear goals can be pursued. In turn, relationships also suffer when strategic goals are at a too high level to inform local operations, or be influenced by local intents and conditions.

Contract Management in Relationships

The contract not only outlines the 'bare bones' of the deal, it assumes a much more active role in relationship management. Indeed, the contract governs relationships over their lifespan. The framework, therefore, argues that the contract is implicit to most interorganizational operations—be they strategic,

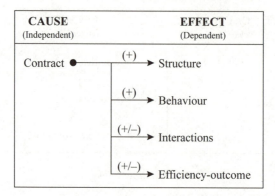

Fig. 9.2. *Contract links*

technical, or operational in nature. It often delineates the area of operation, circumscribes the tasks and activities, and identifies key deliverables for the short and long term. Therefore, it should not be perceived just as a 'shield and sword' as lawyers so often emphasize, but as an integral means to clarify, guide, and aid managers in achieving the outsourcing intentions. In line with Macneil's (1974*a*, 1974*b*) and Macaulay's (1963) suggestions, the cases illustrate that contracts are essentially vehicles for 'relational development'. Managers on both sides, especially during the transition period, look to the contract to provide structure to their operations and to describe their roles and tasks. Contract management in this respect was found to have a positive and negative impact on structure, interactions, behaviour, and efficiency outcome of relations (see Figure 9.2).

In terms of delineating the relationship, the contract incorporates a macro-structural overview of the deal. This comes back to the 'bare bones' notion identifying the parties involved (i.e. size), outlining to a certain degree the complexity, specifying the length (i.e. stability) of the venture, and giving some indication of key individuals and processes (as for example in the IR). The case findings suggest all of these should be integrated into the contract, as well as details of the management structure. The cases highlighted the problems that emerge when they are not. In terms of managing structural issues, the contract managers or contract group will then assume an important oversight and control function of the relationship. They will become a key reference point for problem adjudication and performance monitoring at the operational level.

The contract, and particularly the degree of promissory clarity, has a strong impact on the exchange content, i.e. service levels. In terms of management this link determines whether client managers are able to monitor and oversee the vendor's performance, and generally control their outsourcing destiny, or not. The importance of this causal link emphasizes the criticality of short-term clarity and long-term requirement transparency. Presentation of services in turn needs careful planning and regular review to ensure interactions remain accurate. Good practice according to the findings suggests that contracts should be realigned and updated to ensure representativeness either on an annual or at least on a two-year basis.

The contract also sparks a particular set of behaviours in managers with both positive and negative effects. Most commonly, it gives rise to a sense of power or dependency (Lacity and Hirschheim 1993; Kern and Silva 1998). Operation managers should be particularly aware that this will affect their attitudes in terms of being cooperative or in control.

Finally, contract management influences relational efficiency and outcome. It is evident that contractual uncertainty in terms of promissory clarity and presentiation will increase transaction costs, as it raises coordination efforts. The issue of bounded rationality will undoubtedly arise as it is impossible for managers to foresee and unambiguously define every contingency that could possibly be relevant (Blois 1996). This will in turn invite vendors to behave opportunistically. The contract plays an important part in compensating for uncertainties, while it may equally introduce uncertainties. In terms of outcomes it is important that contracts state explicitly what is expected from the supplier. Only by carefully stipulating the requirements and managing the contract will clients achieve their outcomes. However, bounded rationality always needs to be taken into account—a key role, indeed, of relationship management.

Structure in Relationships

Structure was shown to be a surprisingly overlooked aspect in relationship management. In fact, mismanaged structure was responsible for the greatest relational problems. The most common issues were misalignment of either party's management structure resulting in operational and/or management

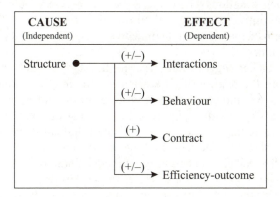

Fig. 9.3. *Structure links*

'bottlenecks' and asymmetric centrality of information. Structure in general has a wide impact, but at the micro (i.e. relationship) level it particularly affects interactions, behaviour, contract, and the efficiency outcome of relations (Figure 9.3).

A well-functioning management infrastructure that is sufficiently resourced in terms of vertical and occupational density had a positive impact on managerial behaviour. It increased willingness to cooperate and allowed relational trust to evolve. The impact further gives rise to what Uzzi (1997) calls 'embeddedness' of relationships, which becomes particularly explicit with the arrival of joint problem-solving, trust, and rich information sharing. The effects of embeddedness can lead to substantial economic and relational benefits (as ESSO and BAe experienced). However, structure can also have negative behavioural effects, particularly when management resourcing problems persist over time or when the centrality of information is one-sided (e.g. in the Xerox-EDS case).

An appropriately resourced management structure is critical for effective communication in the relationship. This raises the stakes of having an appropriately resourced structure in terms of its vertical-occupational density. Successful relationship management has been shown to depend on the 'sharing of rich information' at all levels of the management structure. The findings suggest management representation needs to include senior management, a senior operations manager, an operations manager (multiple tasks of strategy, contract, and technical oversight) and technology managers. The work by Feeny and Willcocks (1998) as outlined in Chapter 1, receives further endorsement here. Effective communication becomes particularly important if the objective is to access value-added benefits. Structure has also been found to influence negatively the contract in situations of considerable complexity and size; the reason is that both size and complexity make promissory clarity and presentiation difficult to achieve (cf. Xerox, IR, and BAe). In turn, management should be prepared to encounter significant relational inefficiencies and difficulties in such situations where a sizeable proportion is outsourced and/or those functions contracted out entail substantial complexities. Therefore, an adequately resourced management team with expertise in contract management seems fundamental.

The findings further suggest that structure has a significant positive and/or negative effect on the relationship's efficiency outcome. Its primary impact is on transaction costs, and the degree of customization and uncertainty reduction experienced. Coordination, i.e. transaction costs escalated in those cases where an inadequate management team operated that subsequently had to be revamped and enlarged. The case findings also revealed that as complexity increases, so will specificity, uncertainty, and coordination costs. BPX's incremental outsourcing approach is a prime example. However, complexity costs can be controlled through formalizing requirements early on (diminishing uncertainty), updating service levels regularly, and closely overseeing the vendor's performance. These tasks become particularly important since an increase in complexity proportionally increases transaction specificity. As the need for customization increases, so also does the pressure on the relationship and the venture to be efficient. The relationship management task, in turn, becomes one of handling this tension.

Interactions—Process Management in Relationships

Process management in outsourcing is a relatively uncharted area and this study makes a positive contribution to its understanding. The framework prescribes processes as exchange, normative, and communication, and characterizes these along the lines of formal, informal, and/or standardized (i.e. institutional). Figure 9.4 depicts how interactions primarily affect contract, behaviour, and efficiency outcome. The study's findings revealed that the core focus of process management is on exchange and communication. Operational managers thus need to concentrate their activities on planning, monitoring, and controlling these aspects in relationships.

One interesting finding is that interactions tend to negatively influence contracts. How does this happen? After all, some would argue, as we sometimes found, that interactions are positive in that they can fill in for incomplete, ambiguous contracts. But through interactions, exchange content changes and adapts over time to requirements, and as these change, contracts become unrepresentative and incomplete. New norms may develop as customs and practice render the contracts less representative. This may have a positive side, but what happens if a large discrepancy develops between the contract and informal custom and practice about acceptability of what is delivered and how? To reduce the negative impacts this can have, it is important to ensure that any changes are documented so that they can be integrated at a future contract alignment or update stage. Regular formal updates are fundamental. If they are neglected and dispute situations arise, parties will not have too few secure reference points for adjudication.

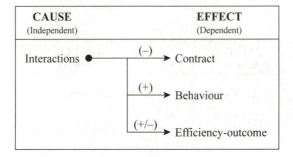

Fig. 9.4. *Interaction links*

Moreover, interactions were found to have a positive and negative behavioural impact in terms of exchanges and communication. Clarity in terms of exchanges can help to balance the degree of dependency. Exchange content clarity gives operations managers the means to control vendors' performance. A similar situation was evident for communication. Information generally gave managers power to monitor, enforce, and reward vendors. Asymmetry in either of them towards the vendor was found to put serious strains on the relationship, which stresses the importance of ensuring control over processes.

Most critical for the efficiency of the relationship was the exchange content's impact on the degree of uncertainty in the venture. Clearly, the uncertainty surrounding the core process of exchange in the relationship causes operational difficulties for managers, often giving rise to increased coordination costs and potential threats of opportunistic behaviour. Conversely, a high degree of clarity has a positive mediating affect on uncertainty and will minimize coordination costs and opportunism. This again implies careful management of exchange content in terms of clarity, completeness, and comprehensiveness.

Behavioural Impacts on Relationship Management

As noted in Chapter 8, outsourcing relationships emerged as being dependent, control (i.e. power) oriented, adversarial (i.e. conflict based), cooperative, and/or trusting, following closely our framework's delineation of behavioural dimensions. Over time these varied, even in the same outsourcing arrangement. Behaviours affect relational operations in many ways, and are integral to operations; but in this study behaviours were found to particularly influence interactions and the efficiency outcome of the venture (see Figure 9.5).

Behaviours were found to have a positive and/or negative impact on interactions in terms of improving communication (e.g. BAe and ESSO cases). Cooperation and trust in particular were found to affect the kind of information that was shared between the parties. The cases illustrated that as individuals grew more accustomed to each other and confidence increased, parties began to share 'rich information' (Uzzi 1997) about particular pressures and/or difficulties. The achievement of 'relational trust' in this form proved extremely

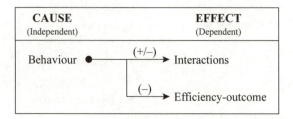

Fig. 9.5. *Behaviour links*

useful as, through the sharing of information, suppliers could apply their expertise and resources to add value or improve services.

Conversely, conflict and power and/or dependency asymmetries were shown to seriously diminish managers' willingness to communicate. In some cases communication was restricted, for example, to the transfer of information concerning only operational matters. Behaviours thus constrained one of the core processes, which in turn had a negative impact on the efficiency outcome of the venture (see for example ESSO and BPX). Curtailing the information flow will hamper operations and is likely to increase coordination costs to balance the lack of information. Relations in this way are likely to become inefficient and endangered by vendors' opportunistic behaviour. Awareness of these impacts can help managers anticipate and avoid inefficiencies.

Planning for Relational Efficiency and Outcomes

The case findings highlighted that clients and vendors have a strong tendency not to plan and resource sufficiently their relationship management arrangements prior to outsourcing. As a result, relational operations were often inefficient and prevented clients from achieving their goals. Three areas in particular suffered from this planning neglect—contract management, structure, and process management. All three had to be subsequently addressed, and this required significant investments in time, expertise, and resources. These areas were shown generally to be prone to transaction, i.e. coordination, costs due additionally to the factors of uncertainty, and increasing specificity.

In terms of preparation, the findings suggest that for, contract management, clients should shorten their promissory, i.e. service level planning horizon to a length that allows them to clearly presentiate their requirements. The cases suggest an annual renegotiation phase as best practice (see BPX and ESSO). In addition management should be prepared for unexpected promissory gaps, and may want to plan for procedures that provide adequate flexibility to compensate for such occasions. One suggestion might be to formalize an oversight board. This brings us to the second planning issue, namely structure. Client organizations should formalize a relationship management structure that comprises at least adequate competencies and skills to handle the relationship at the strategic and operational level, the technical requirements, and the contract in terms of service levels and legal matters (see Feeny and Willcocks 1998; Fitzgerald and Willcocks 1994). Once a structure has been formalized, vendors should be asked to present a formal management structure that identifies clearly the interface points, which at best should mirror the customer's structure. Of particular importance here is to check the contact points, i.e. information flows to avoid potential 'bottlenecks' (see Xerox case).

This brings us to the final issue of process planning. The cases emphasized the importance of regular information exchanges to ensure measurability of the vendor's performance. In terms of payments these exchanges are fundamental.

Thus formalizing the processes that ensure these exchanges seems good practice. Again, this requires cooperation between the parties to be able to define an appropriate management process. The case findings suggest at least weekly, monthly, and half-yearly or yearly management meetings should be established.

Careful planning of these issues contributes to ensuring an operationally efficient relationship and achieving outsourcing intentions. The value of being aware of the 'efficiency' dimension in terms of transaction costs, uncertainty, and specificity will help a client identify costs that it may need to anticipate and manage. Relationship efficiency does affect outcomes. But outcomes themselves need managing as much as any other part of the relationship—witness BPX's use of the balanced scorecard, for example. Early clarification of the expected outcomes, such as the areas, for example, where innovation is expected will improve the possibilities of actually achieving them. In turn the framework provides a helpful overview for the purpose of planning, offering practitioners some valuable insights into how to conduct post-contract management and relationships.

REVISITING THE ANALYTICAL FRAMEWORK

The findings largely support the analytical framework's characterization of the main dimensions of outsourcing relationships. However, a review of the evidence highlights for us four significant issues that could be usefully incorporated into the framework (see Figure 9.6).

1. *Endogenous and exogenous factors* were shown in the case studies to have a significant influence on outsourcing and the subsequent relationship. Endogenous factors that need consideration in this respect are the client's overarching long-term vision, the business strategy, including the short-term organizational goals and objectives, and the IT strategy. In regard to the business and IT strategy, the outsourcing venture and hence relationship will have to be aligned to ensure the relationship provides the required services, technology, and benefits to achieve both the long- and short-term goals. Disregarding alignment may introduce inflexibility and additional cost factors. Conversely, exogenous factors were equally shown to influence operations as legislative, market dynamism, technological, competitive and economic factors affect the organization. A 'systems theory' perspective might be useful here to emphasize the 'interactional' impact exogenous factors may have on the organization and the outsourcing relationship.

2. *Contract complexity* was revealed as a significant factor to consider, especially in terms of operability. The findings showed that a too complex contract can hinder operations and relationship development, and introduce significant additional costs. A balance needs to be achieved by yearly contract revisits that help to maintain the up-to-dateness of the contract and service levels.

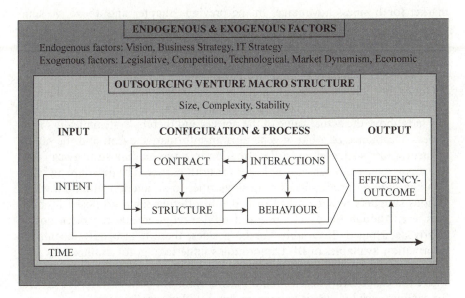

Fig. 9.6. *Revised framework of outsourcing relationships*

3. *Structure* in outsourcing needs to be considered in terms of both a macro and micro level. At the macro level, structure defines the overall shape and structure of the outsourcing venture. Findings show this to include size (e.g. number of parties and costs involved), complexity and overall length (i.e. stability). At the micro level or relationship level, structure focuses on the vertical and occupational density of the management infrastructure, the operational complexity, and the overall stability.

4. Finally, the rich case histories revealed that the relationship dimensions are *linked* in a number of ways that differ from, and could not really be incorporated into the initial assumptions. These are integrated into the revised framework, which now clarifies further how these dimensions and their elements are connected.

From the research undertaken for this book we are able to make three further reflections useful to improving relationship management practice, and achieving relationship advantage.

AVOIDING THE WINNER'S CURSE

IT outsourcing emerges from this study as mostly a high-risk, hidden-cost process. Explicit risk mitigation and relationship management practices are needed, as delineated in this book, if IT outsourcing is to leverage the IT services market for business advantage. In the previous chapter and above we summarized many of these practices. However, here we would like to draw attention to a particular risk that seems to go to the heart of managing the cost-benefit trade-off and that can affect either or both client and supplier adversely (Kern, Willcocks, and van Heck 2000).

One of the more intriguing phenomena in auctioning/tendering is the winner's curse. The winner's curse occurs if the winner of an auction/tender systematically bids above the actual value of the objects and thereby systematically incurs losses. Acceptance of a bid in general is an informative event, and the failure to incorporate such contingent information into the bidding strategy can lead to excessive bids and subsequent losses for both parties. The outsourcing selection and bidding process has strong similarities to an auction situation, where various suppliers may be asked to make an offering for a proposed IT business, even though the exact value and service requirements can often not be clearly determined. Invariably, for both sides, there is also only incomplete information available. In BP Exploration's undertaking, for example, six suppliers were eventually asked to bid for the offered services in circumstances where the exact future service requirements were not certain. Decisive criteria for winning such bids tends to be costs, value-added benefits, technology, expertise, capabilities and reputation or prestige of bidders. The difficulty in such bidding circumstances is to select those supplier partners that offer the best deal, and here the focus tends to be not least on what cost efficiencies suppliers can deliver (Ang and Straub 1998; Lacity and Willcocks 1998, 2000*b*). The assumption here is that suppliers have sufficient economies of scale, and improved IT management practices, to be able to deliver improved services for a cheaper price, and that the resulting savings are those that the client will benefit from.

Two dangers have become more apparent over the years to researchers studying IT outsourcing experiences, and from this study. One is the often large disparity between what suppliers initially tout in their proposals and what at the end of the day is delivered. In fact, some companies and government institutions have found outsourcing services to provide few measurable improvements or additional benefits (Kern 1999; Lacity and Willcocks 1998); and in the late 1990s some have even subsequently terminated contracts early (for example American Express, East Midlands Electricity, Sears UK). These and similar cases seem to suggest that suppliers can be overly keen to win a particular deal for possible reasons of prestige, size, partnering, costs, and long-term business opportunities.

The second, related danger lies, as this study shows, in the general lure of ridding oneself selectively or totally of the 'bottomless IT investment pit' and instead paying a fixed monthly sum for IT services. This remains a major comparison measure for selecting a supplier (see also Ang and Straub 1998; Lacity and Willcocks 1998, 2000b), though we do not fail to recognize that organizations typically outsource for a mix of reasons.

However, a client's focus on cost savings can drive supplier organizations into the corner of making service delivery promises that are initially calculated on a slim or even nil profit margin (Willcocks, Lacity, and Kern 2000). They may do so, for example, because they are short of business due to recession, decreased competitiveness, or are a new entrant into the IT services market; they are keen to enter a new market segment; they want to shut out competitors; they have a strategic intent to dominate certain market segments; and/or they believe that they can recoup the investment and broaden margins later. It is precisely in such circumstances that the danger of a 'Winner's Curse' arises, as suppliers make bidding promises to ensure they win the contract, but inherently already know, or subsequently discover, that they are unable to recover their tendering, business, and operational costs, at least in the near future.

Instead they hope, as research has shown (Lacity and Willcocks 2000a, 2000b) that they can recover their costs by, for example, identifying service areas that are in need of particular attention and responsible for low service performance, and/or areas of immediate service provision excluded from the contract but needed operationally, so meriting excess fees. In addition, suppliers will attempt to offer additional services from their portfolio of technology capabilities, service management, and consultancy services over the life of the contract. Since supplier account management will need to concentrate disproportionately on recovering costs, and may well be under pressure from its senior managers to make stipulated margins in unfavourable circumstances, it is more than likely that trade-offs will occur that disadvantage the client. For example, case studies demonstrate that decreasing costs to the supplier can result in decreases in service quality and additional costs for the client (Kern 1999; Lacity and Hirschheim 1993). A supplier's disproportionate concern for containment of its costs can lead to inflexibility in the interpretation of the letter and spirit of the contract, which can also lead to adversarial relationships (Currie and Willcocks 1998). Thus operational performance and the client–supplier relationship will receive less attention and suffer (Kern 1999). As a consequence, we suggest that in 'Winner's Curse' situations suppliers may risk the success and effectiveness of the operations and outsourcing relationship as their focus settles primarily on recovering their costs, rather than on developing and maintaining the relationship and mutual objectives. A supplier would thus undertake opportunistic behaviour, seeking to reduce its own operational costs, often at the expense of the client.

We provide Figure 9.7 to dramatize the main possibilities in IT outsourcing. The Figure should be read as an indicator of the main extreme outcomes. In practice the experiences of many organizations will fall between these extremes. Furthermore organizations, through behaviours and actions of the interested parties, may well change positions, as was the case, for example, in the IT outsourcing arrangement at ESSO-ITNet.

Amongst our cases, the ESSO-ITNet case is the most obvious example of a winner's curse. Here ITNet over-bid and subsequently could not make its

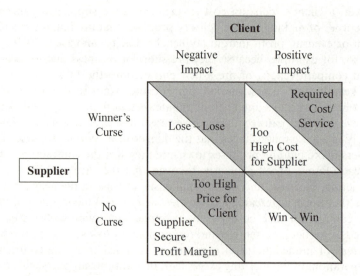

Fig. 9.7. *The winner's curse and other scenarios in IT outsourcing*
Source: Kern, Willcocks, and Van Heck 2000.

margins. The client contributed to making this a winner's curse for the supplier by tightly controlling price and service levels. But the supplier became so disadvantaged that service levels deteriorated and in fact both moved to the Lose–Lose quadrant in Figure 9.7—in other words a 'winner's curse' for the client also became an outcome. As we saw in Chapter 6, this was only changed when a relationship dimension was brought to bear, and when the contract was mutually reconstructed to move both parties to the Win–Win quadrant of Figure 9.7.

The bottom left quadrant is also a danger area for the client. As our case studies showed, it is quite possible for a supplier to disguise the fact that the deal is actually in this quadrant, by offering for example cost savings on parts—usually the more visible and front-end parts—of the deal. Thus at both Xerox and the IR EDS felt able to guarantee cost savings on operations and present requirements because it calculated that it could make much larger profit margins on future work. Xerox reacted against aspects of this subsequently, while BAe and the IR both experienced rising costs in the overall IT budget without always knowing exactly how to attribute these costs and how far the developing cost-service trade-off represented value for money.

Of course, such circumstances are rarely publicized and made explicit, but other evidence of them does exist (Lacity and Hirschheim 1993; Lacity and Willcocks 1998, 2000*b*). Indeed the possibility of these more adverse outcomes arising may well be increasing, if the growing competitive pressures on suppliers push them to compete increasingly on prices and service deliverables (Willcocks and Sauer 2001). There emerges from our study the importance of negotiating contracts that allow a supplier a reasonable profit. But more than this the relationship management practices delineated in this study become a critical influence on how far the more adverse outcomes can be anticipated and mitigated.

TYPES OF RELATIONSHIP: IMPLICATIONS FOR MANAGEMENT

Distilling our findings, there emerged from our cases a strong relationship between the strategic intent a client organization chose to pursue, the kind of technical capability it needed to employ, and the type of relationship needed to match intent and supplier capability, and achieve expectations. A strong finding from this, and complementary research (Lacity and Willcocks 2000*b*), is that there are frequent misperceptions on the part of all parties as to the nature of the relationship, and what can be expected from each other as a result. Let us, first, classify the types of relationship we have observed, then illustrate, through examples, the importance of getting strategic intent, technical capability, and relationship definitions aligned.

The main types of IT outsourcing relationships are classified in Figure 9.8. Here strategic intent, in terms of expectations from outsourcing, is divided into whether the focus is on achieving business value and/or on achieving IT

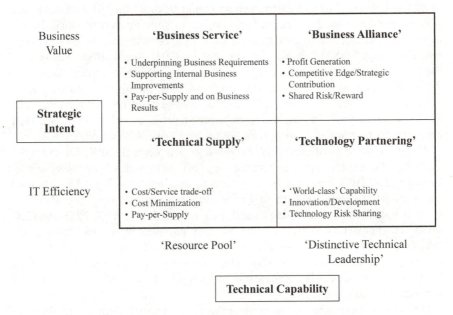

Fig. 9.8. *IT sourcing relationships: intent and capability*

efficiencies. On the horizontal axis, technical capability refers to choosing to externally source to gain a distinctive technical leadership, or to gain access merely to technical resources that form a resource pool not otherwise available to you, in cost per quality terms. The matrix sets up four possible relationships. By far the most common is the 'Technical Supply' relationship where the objective is to achieve IT efficiencies by hiring external resources. In such a relationship the fundamental focus is on cost minimization, and the rendering of IT as a variable cost. The major debates will centre around the cost-service trade-off, and measurement systems will also be constructed around this. The most obvious example in this study is the ESSO-ITNet arrangement. However, large components of the Xerox-EDS, SEMA-BPX and Syncordia-BPX, IR-EDS, and BAe-CSC deals were also of this nature, especially in the telecoms, mainframe processing, base operations, and support areas. One thing we have learned in this study is that even these elements need careful management not just on the contract, but on all the relationship dimensions (Kern 1999).

Another possible relationship we call 'Business Service'. Here the objective is to use an external IT supplier who can improve service to the business by not only delivering more precisely on changing business requirements, but also by, for example, being involved in business process improvement projects. Here the contract will be about both IT efficiency for business impact, and the supplier's contribution to business improvement. Here one would expect additional processes and relationship mechanisms for involving the supplier more closely in business issues. The evaluation debate would be more on business value and suitable metrics, based on the business impact of supplier performance. In this respect it is interesting to note that on some figures business process outsourcing may reach $US14.7 billion in revenues in 2002. Again, BAe, Xerox, and the IR all perceived themselves as having 'business service' components in their deals with their major outsourcing suppliers. One example we noted was at Rolls-Royce in 1997/8, where EDS and its management consulting arm, A.T. Kearney, participated in business re-engineering projects with Rolls-Royce staff and were to be rewarded proportionate to the business improvements.

A third type of relationship is 'Technology Partnering'. BPX, for example, explicitly chose three suppliers because they had 'best-in-class' capability in particular areas. BPX expected future-proofing on the technological front, with the suppliers keeping BPX abreast of leading-edge technology, and also proactively innovating in technologies and their application to BPX. EDS and CSC presented themselves as potential technology partners in the IR, Xerox, and BAe cases also. Here one would expect sharing in technology risks, but also a sharing in the benefits that resulted. Here the supplier takes the lead on many IT issues. The focus is on innovation and supplier proactivity, a premium IT service, and leading-edge IT.

One creative example is the joint venture between FI Group and Bank of Scotland (BoS). In June 1998 they formed First Banking Systems. By 1999 the venture comprised 310 people from the BoS, and 120 people, including project managers, from FI. Both groups remained employees of their respective companies, and both groups kept their own terms, conditions, and pay rates. FBS is jointly owned. The deal committed the bank to underwrite £30 million for five years. FI Group takes a loss on any costs over the fixed price. The joint venture has worked on development projects for the bank, including a new core banking system. In the first year FBS reduced overheads, and brought in new customers from the Bank of Scotland Group.

Finally, all too many large-scale outsourcing arrangements are presented as 'Strategic Alliances'. For us such an alliance assumes a working together to make offerings to the external market place, as for example at Xerox-EDS, and sharing risks and rewards of such endeavours. The focus here is on business expansion, the main debates will be around business goals, mutual contribution, and shared rewards. Lacity and Willcocks (1998) found many so-called strategic alliances in IT outsourcing to be largely fee-for-service contracts; moreover the risk-reward elements were too small a part of the relationship to make a difference in terms of motivation and focus. This was certainly the case in Xerox-EDS. One successful example was that of Philips Electronics, in the early 1990s, when it formed Origin with a Dutch-based software house. Over time Philips' development staff, then its data centre and processing staff went over to the jointly owned Origin, which provided services back to Philips, but also built up an external clientele for its services.

Clarifying these options, and when they are most suitable, is an important precondition for establishing the right relationship mechanisms and evaluation regimes. In practice we have seen all too many organizations contract and manage tightly for cost efficiency, but then also expect the sort of business value-added that could only be got from a 'Business Service' relationship, or the technical innovation and proactivity that could only be provided through 'Technology Partnering'. This partly explains why BPX was disappointed with at least two of its 1993–8 suppliers. In another way, and much to CSC's frustration, BAe managed CSC tightly though the deal ostensibly had 'Business Service' and 'Technology Partnering' components. It was only after several years, and after CSC had made large investments in making the IT function efficient, that BAE managers started being interested in allowing CSC to tap the other possibilities for revenue.

Cultural and financial factors often drive these misconceptions. We saw in BPX how early on traditional cost reduction approaches prevailed in the deals though the deals had been paraded as more about technology partnering. At the same time, for example, a supplier will find it difficult to sustain a 'Business Service' or 'Technology Partnering' orientation if the money is not going to be there. Sometimes it is lack of the right kind of partnering capability, in either or both client and supplier, as we saw in the IR early on, and at ESSO-ITNet. More frequently there is a lack of clarity at the scoping and evaluation phases of IT outsourcing, to identify precisely which components require what metrics and what relationship arrangements.

This is not helped by the fact that for any IT outsourcing deal of any significant size, different parts will be founded on different intents, and need qualitatively different relationship and evaluation arrangements. For example, Xerox clearly applied the notion of a 'strategic relationship' to apply to the vast majority of its deal, when certain parts required a business service orientation, and still others a technical supply or technology partnering one. BPX kept asking where was the value-added, but had put in relationship structures and processes, and had regional cultures that inhibited this value-added coming through. The situation becomes even more confused when there are a number of suppliers because each might require a different set of relationships, given the strategic intent for that part of the deal, yet the pressure may be on to treat them all in the same way—as was the case for example at BPX.

Given these considerations we offer the framework in Figure 9.8 as a way for a client to think through exactly what he/she is trying to achieve with different parts of its IT outsourcing, and what the implications of this analysis might be for relationship arrangements and assessment regimes.

MANAGING THE RELATIONSHIP ADVANTAGE ACROSS SIX PHASES

In complementary work in which both authors participated, we were able to identify six major phases in IT outsourcing arrangements (see Lacity and Willcocks 2000*a*, 2000*b*). A summary of these phases, and what the major focus of each needs to be, is shown in Table 9.1.

The present study corroborates this as a highly useful classification, and confirms the relevance of the objectives and tasks for each phase, as detailed in the table. From its findings in looking at over 100 case histories and carrying out extensive survey research, that previous work also brought attention to bear on why relationships were so difficult to manage, and also clarified the different kinds of relationships that could be found even within the same deal. Thus, that study pointed out the number and complexity of relationships to be found. It identified eight major groups of stakeholders each with their own set of expectations. Within the customer there are invariably senior business managers, senior IT managers, IT staff, and IT users. Within the supplier can be found senior managers, account managers, and IT staff. Invariably, as we found in all our case studies in the present study, there are a number of other contractors and subcontractors also providing IT services. Given that the expectations and goals of these stakeholder groups will frequently not coincide, it can be seen that relationship management in the areas studied by this book—intent, contract, structure, interactions, and behaviour—becomes a significant task.

The present study also corroborates our previous finding that stakeholder relationships are quite dynamic. For example, the same two people can fight one minute, and collaborate the next. Four types of relationships were evident in both studies. The first was *tentative relationships*, when stakeholders had no shared history, and were unsure whether goals were shared, complementary, or conflicting—see for example all our cases at their beginnings. Secondly, we observed *adversarial* relationships when stakeholder goals were felt to be in conflict e.g. over realigning the contract at Xerox, on EDS's asset re-evaluation at the IR. Thirdly, stakeholders often operated *collaboratively*, where goals were shared, for example where supplier senior managers and account managers had the shared goal of negotiating a deal with enough leeway to ensure profit margins. Finally, *cooperative* relationships manifested themselves when goals were complementary. At Esso-ITNet each party needed something from the other party to succeed, thus moving the arrangement from a 'winner's curse' for both supplier and customer, to a more productive relationship.

However, the present study also deepens our understanding of what it is to manage across the six phases in three ways.

1. *The Relationship Dimension.* Our previous study focused a great deal on relationships in IT outsourcing. However, while it provided a great deal of rich evidence on how relationships were conducted, and many guidelines for practice, it focused on many other salient issues, and did not arrive at a comprehensive, codified understanding of the main elements in relationships and how they can be managed. The present study suggests that relationship management is something that deserves fundamental attention at the scoping phase, using for example the thinking embodied in Figure 9.8. Thereafter the construction, staffing, and dynamics of relations require specialized management, across all other subsequent phases. Here the thinking and prescriptions distilled and represented in Figure 9.6 becomes a comprehensive management guide, if relationship advantages are to be gained.

2. *Evaluation and Relationships.* Previous studies, by ourselves and others, have always come back to the importance of measurement/evaluation in IT outsourcing (see also Chapter 1). Dynamic, accurate evaluation is invariably placed by researchers and those involved in IT outsourcing as a 'necessary but insufficient' condition for success. On reflection, the present study actually shows there to be no great gulf between measurement and the relationship dimension; they actually should be mutually supportive. Put more boldly, implicit within Figure 9.8 is the notion of a fully working evaluation and metrics system, supporting the type of relationships being erected. We can see such evaluation regimes at work, though not always functioning optimally, in all our cases, with BPX perhaps being the most mature and consistently successful. Our observation is that the appropriate evaluation regime, arrived at in Phase 2 of Table 9.1, and incorporated in the 'Contract' dimension in Figure 9.6, is fundamental to achieving what we call 'the relationship advantage', with the other components in Figure 9.6 ensuring that the evaluation regime is in the right set of contexts and properly actioned. Let us consider this proposition in more detail, using an example.

Table 9.1. *Six phases of an IT outsourcing arrangement*

Scoping phase	Evaluation phase	Negotiation phase	Transition phase	Middle phase	Mature phase
Activities					
• Identify core IT capabilities	• Measure baseline services	• Conduct due diligence to verify RFP baseline claims	• Distribute contract to IT users	• Benchmark performance to (theoretically) reset prices	• Recalibrate investment criteria to reflect shorter time horizon for recouping investments
• Identify IT activities for potential outsourcing using business, economic, and technical criteria	• Measure baseline costs	• Negotiate service level agreements	• Interpret the contract	• Realign the contract to reflect changes in technology and business	• Determine if the relationship will be terminated or extended
	• Create RFP	• Create responsibility matrixes	• Establish post-contract management infrastructure and processes		
	• Develop evaluation criteria	• Price work units	• Implement consolidation, rationalization, standardization	• Involve the supplier on more value-added areas	
	• Invite external and internal bids	• Negotiate terms for employee transfer			

Table 9.1. *Continued*

Scoping phase	Evaluation phase	Negotiation phase	Transition phase	Middle phase	Mature phase
		• Negotiate mechanisms for contractual change, including benchmarking, open-book accounting, non-exclusivity clauses, and pricing schedules	• Validate service scope, costs, levels, and responsibilities for baseline services • Manage additional service requests • Foster realistic expectations of supplier performance • Publicly promote the contract		
Objective					
Identify flexible IT organization, including IT activities for potential outsourcing	Select best and final offer	Sign contract(s)	Establish operational performance	Achieve value-added above operational performance	No lapses in operational performance during final transition

We have already argued that in IT outsourcing many organizations operate on the mistaken belief that external IT vendors can be experts not only at technology supply, but at their own line of business as well. In practice, of course, expecting even a 'world-class' IT supplier to be similarly skilled in an area not their core business, e.g oil at BPX and ESSO, tax collection at the IR, is unrealistic to say the least. Our cases show that if there is to be business advantage—not just technical efficiencies—to be derived from IT outsourcing, it must be driven from the business side, with the business managers and core in-house team accepting responsibility for key actions.

We can provide an example of the integrated performance measurement regime that could be put in place to support the relationships shown in Figure 9.8 in order to achieve optimal business advantage. The template in Figure 9.9, from Willcocks, Graeser, and Pisanias (1998), was developed for a major international and financial property service company (IFAPS).

The bottom half of the figure represents how outsourcing value can be maximized from the Technology Supply contribution in the 'utilities area' (legacy systems, mainframe, midrange, desktop, communications). Four significant features here are:

- a fully staffed contract management team—BPX, BAe, and the IR were particularly good in this area;
- A focus on developing measures that rewarded/penalized for the business impact of technical efficiency, rather than focusing just on technology performance—few of our case studies were good at this area;
- The stimulation of proactive behaviour through suitable metrics, for example how well suppliers interface with other suppliers, contract dispute, and commissioning new work metrics—again most of our cases were not good at utilizing such metrics;
- Smart contracting using market baselines regularly reviewed—all except ESSO were quite 'smart' on this.

With the utility systems up and running under this evaluation regime, the company would be more satisfied with its IT and suppliers, but would still be looking hard for the elusive added business value from its IT—BPX for example. The approach suggested to IFAPS was to develop an innovation team responsible for identifying additional business opportunities available from IT, for creating new business ideas, business process improvements, and step-change innovation. Business value drivers would also be regularly identified through the strategy-making process; e.g at IFAPS these included prices to external customers, customer service/satisfaction, revenue growth.

All this needs to be converted into a measurement system. The process is shown in the top right of Figure 9.9. The business impactors for any new initiative are worked into a value proposition which can then be tested for alignment against the business value drivers. If this process is managed rigorously and in detail, various usable metrics can be derived. An important separation

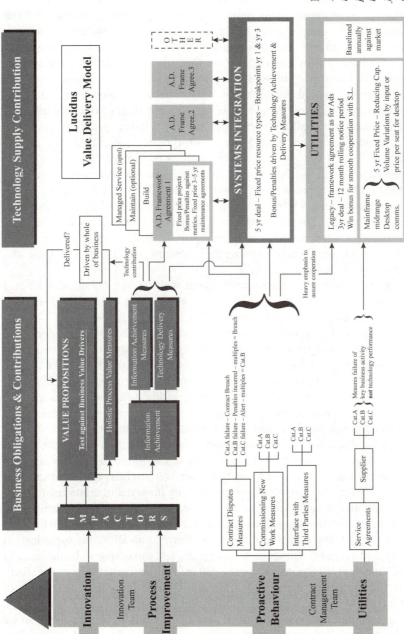

Fig. 9.9.
Example of an integrated performance measurement framework

Source: Robert White and Lucidus.

occurs at this point between information achievement and technology delivery metrics—not once did we witness this in any of our case histories. The latter metrics are concerned with building and application of technology, for example budget milestones delivered to specification, timeliness, and efficiency of systems development. Information achievement is a more profound measure of business impact. For example, at IFAPs a centralized knowledge base was being developed. One information achievement target was the development of a library search engine for key words. One measure was that, using the system, a trained staff member could find a key word in under ten seconds.

The IT supplier would be tracked on the information achievement and technology delivery measures. Where these are fulfilled then payments, including agreed bonuses will result. Where these are not fulfilled, penalties should be raised. In the development area (Figure 9.9 top right-hand corner), if a project is abandoned, then the supplier would return a pre-agreed percentage of the development costs. It should be noted that the 'information achievement' measures feed into the applications development and systems integration components shown in Figure 9.9, rather than the utilities aspect of the technological supply contribution. The latter is much more about cost efficiency, while there is a lot more business value to be gained for the development area if clients know how to set up suitable measurement systems, incentivize suppliers, and link activity with business goals.

Though BPX linked supplier measurement with its own balanced scorecard system, no other client organization in our study came near putting in place such an integrated performance measurement approach. All—even BPX—complained of not achieving much valuable innovation, process improvement, and business value-added from their suppliers. However, we are very clear that unless an integrated performance measurement system—something like the one described here—is put in place to underpin, inform, and guide relationship management, this would continue to be an unsurprising outcome. In this area, as in many others, as we pointed out in Chapter 1, client organizations still expect too much from the supplier, and not enough from themselves.

3. *Supplier Capabilities.* We would like to draw attention to one final area that has received virtually no academic study, and is often in practice assumed to be unproblematic, but in fact emerges from our study as quite critical. It is intuitively obvious that suppliers too are heavily involved in relationship management, but all our cases show examples where they were not necessarily good at these tasks. At the IR it was at the client's insistence that relationship processes and staffing began to happen. At Xerox, and BPX, the organization of supply and account management sometimes left something to be desired. At ESSO, ITNet was as responsible for the collapse of the relationship as the client. At BAe the partnering word was informally banned for a time as a result of disconnects between the supplier's relationship promises and actual behaviours. This suggests that, just as we identified core IT capabilities for the client, so we need also to begin to identify core supplier capabilities that can help to lever-

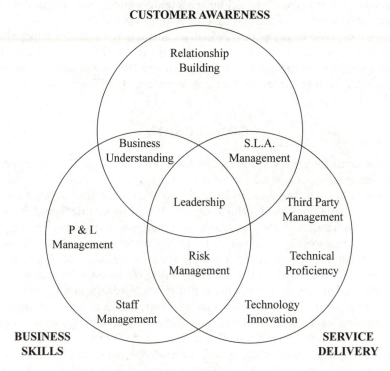

Fig. 9.10. *Supplier capabilities in IT outsourcing*

age the relationship into one of mutual business advantage. A review of the case evidence enables a first view on supplier capabilities needed to support the relationship advantage. These are shown in Figure 9.10.

Our view is that suppliers need to have three core capabilities in the areas of business skills, customer awareness and service delivery. Moreover their capabilities in these areas need to be in sufficient numbers and physically located and organized to fit with the capabilities of the client organization, and of any other suppliers involved. The proactive coordinating and governance skills lie in leadership and risk management—both applied on behalf of the client as well as the supplier. In the service delivery area the supplier needs to be able to also manage service level agreements and third parties well, and also have technology innovation capability. Its business skills, or lack of them, can directly impinge on the relationship with the client organization. These include profit and loss management (including cost control and budget management) and staff management. At the interface between business skills and customer awareness is business understanding, to include business applications knowledge and an understanding of the client's business. Relationship building includes customer interaction skills. The interface roles of SLA management, leadership, risk management, and business understanding are critical for coordination developing and facilitating the relationship.

This is a provisional perspective, which we intend to research much more fully, because the evidence from our study is that the possession and application of these capabilities can make a key difference to how the relationship dimension is conducted, and so to the levels of success experienced in IT outsourcing.

CONCLUSION

Our reflections for practice took us into several further contributions. A review of the many components of the relationship dimension clarified the relative importance of each, but also underlined how interdependent intent, contract, structure, interactions, and behaviour are. We also provided guidelines for planning for relational efficiency and advantageous outcomes. The original analytical framework was found to be highly useful as a guide to the issues needing attention if a relationship advantage is to be achieved. However, we developed the framework in three further ways. We noted, from our research, the additional impact of internal factors of vision, business, and IT strategy on relationships, and also of external market, economic, legislative, competitive, and technological factors. Contract complexity was also highlighted as a significant factor affecting operability. The macro structure of the venture in terms of size, complexity, and stability also engendered risks, and required much greater relationship effort. Structure at the micro level also emerged as an area fraught with difficulty and unintended consequences, as we saw particularly in BPX and Xerox.

Our study has also highlighted the manifold risks in IT outsourcing, and in this chapter we have pointed out the dangers of a 'winner's curse' arising, affecting relationships and outcomes for both supplier and client. We also pointed to the additional importance of clarifying types of relationship and developing suitable relationship arrangements and supporting evaluation regimes across the six phases of any IT outsourcing venture. Finally, a provisional statement was offered for the key supplier capabilities needed to feed into making IT outsourcing arrangements productive.

In all this, it is clear that the relationship dimension, and what supports effective relationships, are critical to IT outsourcing success. Also clear is that, if, as we believe, IT outsourcing can be conceived as achieving a relationship advantage, then this presents profound management challenges for the ways in which IT outsourcing is more typically conducted. We started this study for two reasons: because practitioners told us that relationships were key in IT outsourcing, and because, paradoxically, there were so few studies that took a relationship perspective. The book has thus contributed by showing just how important relationships are, and by providing ways forward for practitioners and researchers alike.

In a piece of deliberate understatement, a manager we interviewed once told us that in IT outsourcing there was no such thing as an instant relationship. IT outsourcing can be understood in many ways but it is certainly well to operate on the assumption that managing it to success involves dealing with a fundamentally high-risk, relationship business.

REFERENCES

Ang, S., and Straub, D. (1998). 'Production and Transaction Economies and IS Outsourcing: A Study of the US Banking Industry'. *MIS Quarterly* (December), 535–42.

Blois, K. J. (1996). 'Relationship Marketing in Organizational Markets: When is it Appropriate?' *Journal of Marketing Management*, 12: 161–73.

Currie, W., and Willcocks, L. (1998). *New Strategies in IT Outsourcing*. Business Intelligence, London.

DiRomualdo, A., and Gurbaxani, V. (1998). 'Strategic Intent for IT Outsourcing'. *Sloan Management Review*, 39/4: 67–80.

Feeny, D., and Willcocks, L. (1998). 'Core IS Capabilities for Exploiting IT'. *Sloan Management Review*, 39/3: 1–26.

Fitzgerald, G., and Willcocks, L. (1994). 'Contracts and Partnerships in the Outsourcing of IT', in *Proceedings of the 15th International Conference on Information Systems*, ICIS, Vancouver, 91–8.

Kern, T. (1999). 'Relationships in Information Technology Outsourcing: An Exploratory Research Study of a Conceptual Framework'. Unpublished D.Phil. thesis, University of Oxford.

—— and Silva, L. (1998). 'Mapping the Areas of Potential Conflict in the Management of Information Technology Outsourcing', in *Proceedings of the European Conference on Information Systems*, Aix-en-Provence.

—— Willcocks, L., and Van Heck, E. (2000). 'Evidence of a Winner's Curse in IT Outsourcing and its Effects on the Outsourcing Relationship', in *Academy of Management Conference*, August 2000, Toronto.

Lacity, M. C., and Hirschheim, R. (1993). *Information Systems Outsourcing: Myths, Metaphors and Realities*. John Wiley & Sons Ltd., Chichester.

—— and Willcocks, L. (1998). 'An Empirical Investigation of Information Technology Sourcing Practices: Lessons from Experience'. *MIS Quarterly*, 22/3: 363–408.

—— —— (2000a). *IT Outsourcing: A State-of-the-Art Report*. Templeton Research Report 1, Templeton College, Oxford.

—— —— (2000b). *Global IT Outsourcing: Search for Business Advantage*. Wiley, Chichester.

Macaulay, S. (1963). 'Non-Contractual Relations in Business: A Preliminary Study'. *American Social Review*, 28/1: 55–67.

Macneil, I. R. (1974a). 'Commentary: Restatement (Second) of Contracts and Presentation'. *Virginia Law Review*, 60/4: 589–610.

—— (1974b). 'The Many Futures of Contracts'. *Southern California Law Review*, 47/3: 691–816.

Uzzi, B. (1997). 'Social Structure and Competition in Interfirm Networks: The Paradox of Embeddedness'. *Administrative Science Quarterly*, 42: 35–67.

Van de Ven, A. H., and Ring, P. S. (1994). 'Developmental Processes of Cooperative Interorganizational Relationships'. *Academy of Management Review*, 19/1: 90–118.

White, R., and James, B. (1996). *The Outsourcing Manual*. Gower Publishing Ltd., Aldershot.

Willcocks, L., Graeser, V., and Pisanias, N. (1998). *Developing the IT Scorecard*. Business Intelligence, London.

—— Lacity, M., and Kern, T. (2000). 'Risk Mitigation in IT Outsourcing Strategy Revisited: Longitudinal Case Research at LISA'. *Journal of Strategic Information Systems* (September).

—— and Sauer, C. (2001). 'The Risks and Hidden Costs in IT Outsourcing'. In *Financial Times Mastering Risk*. Financial Times/Prentice Hall, London.

Appendix 1

Research Methodology

The approach we followed for investigating outsourcing relationships—which in essence was to understand 'what' outsourcing relationships are and 'how' they are managed—was an in-depth longitudinal case research method. Case research in this context has been shown particularly appropriate for exploratory and explanatory research of the type undertaken for this book (Newman and Sabherwal 1990; Pettigrew 1990; Walsham 1993). It allowed us to investigate 'sticky, practice-based problems [such as outsourcing relationship practice] where the experiences of actors are important and the context of action is critical', as Benbasat, Goldstein, and Mead (1987: 371) suggest.

Essentially a case study as Yin (1989: 13) noted and we see it, is defined as:

an empirical inquiry that investigates a contemporary phenomenon within its real-life context, especially when the boundaries between phenomenon and context are not clearly evident. [It] copes with the technically distinctive situation in which there will be many more variables of interest than data points, and as one result relies on multiple sources of evidence, with data needing to converge in a triangulating fashion, and as another result benefits from the prior development of theoretical propositions to guide data collection and analysis.

Research Design

The research design for this book was influenced by four main points. First, to investigate the outsourcing relationship and the potential analytical and explanatory power of the framework in distinctive contexts we selected a range of case studies that are representative of current total, global, selective, public sector, and multiple alliance outsourcing practice. Table A1.1 provides an overview of the case companies involved.

Second, the outsourcing relationship, as with other similar inter-firm relationships, involves multiple stakeholders including users/benefactors of the outsourcing service, client relationship managers, vendor's account management team, and the vendor's technical service groups. Since the focus of this book was to attain an understanding of the relationship from the client's or customer's perspective, we decided early on to concentrate on the client's relationship managers' point-of-view, who essentially act as the client firm's boundary spanners in the interorganizational relationship. Furthermore, we sought to understand individual client managers' tasks and roles in managing the relationship to acquire an appreciation of what will be particularly important in outsourcing relationship management.

Third, since the senior directors play a pivotal role in managing the relationship, especially in terms of resolving conflicts that arise in day-to-day relationship management, this study designated the IT Director as the key contact point through which to access the relationship. As we explain in the section on Data Collection, the views and perceptions of senior IT managers, Finance Director, Operations Managers, as well as other

Table A1.1. *Case study overview*

Organization	Industry	Turnover (1997)	Vendor(s)	Start	Length	Characteristics
British Aerospace Plc	Aerospace	£8bn	Computer Science Corporation (CSC)	1993	10yrs	Total
Xerox Corporation	Electronics & services	$17.6bn	Electronic Data Systems (EDS)	1994	10yrs	Global
British Petroleum	Nuclear fuels	£46bn	SAIC, Sema, EDS, BT Syncordia	1993	5yrs	Multiple alliances
ESSO Plc	Nuclear fuels	£3.6bn	ITNet	1995	5yrs	Selective
Inland Revenue	Public institution	N/A	EDS	1993	10yrs	Public sector

individuals involved in handling the outsourcing deal were also gathered, but our focus was on investigating and understanding relationship practice at the operational level.

Finally, the fourth research issue focused on attaining a comprehensive insight into relational issues in outsourcing, for which it was essential that we also interview and gather data from the supplier's point of view on the individual relationship. In turn, views on and perceptions of the relationship were gathered from Senior Vendor Managers in charge of single and multiple accounts across the globe.

Case Selection

The selection of the cases was informed in essence by three key criteria: (1) they represented well-known IT outsourcing deals with considerable uncertainties due to the nature of the deal or the particular industry of the customer that demanded extensive cooperation; (2) they (excluding ESSO) were negotiated with the specific intention to develop a 'strategic relationship' as the service, technology, and business requirements could not be comprehensively formulated at the time of contracting; and (3) we were able to gain access to major participants and stakeholders over an extended period of years, which combined with existing case materials allowed us to study the relational developments longitudinally.

Moreover, the selection of the cases was informed by our interpretive stance in doing case research (Lee 1991; Walsham 1995). The interpretive tradition does not reflect on how typical or representative a case may be, but rather on its potential explanatory power (Smith 1990). Stake (1994) distinguishes between three purposes for studying specific cases: 'intrinsic', 'instrumental', and 'collective'. The intrinsic case study is undertaken because one wants better understanding of this particular case. The instrumental case study is carried out to provide insight into an issue or refinement of theory.

The case is of secondary interest; it plays a supportive role, facilitating our understanding of something else. The choice of case is made because it is expected to advance our understanding of that other interest. Because we simultaneously have several interests, often changing, there is no line distinguishing intrinsic case study from instrumental; rather, a zone of combined purpose separates them. (Stake 1994: 237)

The third type is a collective case study where researchers study a number of cases jointly in order to inquire into a particular phenomenon, population, or general condition. Our research clearly did not involve merely 'intrinsic' or 'collective' case studies, but rather was a combination of 'intrinsic/instrumental' studies. In fact, our case selection reasoning in many ways is summarized by Stake's (1994) quote above. Moreover, because our case studies have paradigmatic characteristics in terms of their outsourcing undertaking and broad base of relationship practice, we found that extensive studies of the case companies' deals would be of real interest and value to understanding outsourcing relationship management.

Data Collection and Interviewing

Data for the case was collected between February 1992 and June 2000 through interviews and reviews of various documentation. The documentation included internal documents such as bid documentation, transition status reports, infrastructure change requests, memos, contract extracts concerning particular service infrastructures such as

Table A1.2. *Overview of interviewees*

Participants' job position	Number of participants
Senior Manager (CFO, CEO, Purchasing Executive, Controller)	5
Global or Corporate IT Director	5
CIO, IT Director, or IT Manager	26
Outsourcing Relationship Managers	5
IS/IT staff involved in operational management	24
Senior or Global Account Manager	4
Vendor operational account manager or executive	11
Vendor account staff (quality managers, client service managers)	3
Consultants	3
Lawyers	2
Total	88

network maintenance, telecoms, and computing support, annual service reviews, other reports such as strategy documents and change proposals, a number of presentations by senior managers from both the customer and vendor companies, and numerous organizational charts from the initial outset to the various changes over the years. In addition, secondary literature was collected including a DBA thesis by Davis (1996) which covered the Xerox case, a number of journal articles covering the cases outset, process management, and organizational changes, a number of relevant books, existing published case studies by Harvard Business School and the European Case Clearing House, numerous current and backdated newspaper articles were accessed through various CD-ROM databases, and various trade press articles from *Computing*, *InformationWeek*, *ComputerWeekly*, *CIO*, and *Management Today* were collected.

The researchers conducted over eighty interviews, most of which were held at various locations and sites of the case study companies. Table A1.2 summarizes the job titles of the participants. The interviews lasted between 90 and 180 minutes. They were conducted using open-ended questions informed by our understanding of IT outsourcing, interorganizational relationships, and relationship management. The semi-structured interview protocol was designed to elicit data about the outsourcing situation, relationship practice, and the constructs of the relationship framework. All interviewees were assured of anonymity to promote open discussions. Similar to Kirsch's (1997) approach, any one of the questions posed aimed to shed light on a number of issues. For example, the following question posed to the General Manager of Information Management shed light on the importance of the structural issues and information exchanges, and the current state of the outsourcing relationship between the two parties:

What were some of the recent management difficulties you encountered in operationalizing the contract and the relationship?

Throughout the interview process the authors endeavoured to collect data about particular instances or examples in the relationship that supported or could be interpreted to explain the constructs of the framework. For this we used the main dimensions of the framework as a guide to relevant management issues, since these had been derived from an existing understanding of outsourcing relationships and business-to-business relationship practices. With these guiding the investigation, a series of questions were devised that directed discussions towards the issues and elements of what we had categorized under each particular dimension of the framework. For example data concerning some of the exchanges was collected through the following questions:

Does your supplier deliver upon its service requirements? Why? Why not?
How do you handle service change requests?
Do you review on a regular basis these change requests and your supplier's service performance?

These questions were particularly useful in eliciting data from the managers about the exchange processes and whether these were being met or whether there were particular problem areas, for example, a lack of information flowing between the parties managing the relationship. Subsequent questions raised in the interview under one of the main questions like the above then helped in obtaining a better understanding of the issues by asking participants to give specific examples of incidents. To uncover these, we pursued an approach to questioning that Schein[1] (1987: 120) employed to explore organizational cultures: '[respondents were asked] to recall events that caused problems for which the organisation had no ready solution or events that challenged existing norms and solutions [. . .], or anything interpersonal that was unusual or tension provoking and required some kind of response.'

Throughout the interview process, we tried to address in a number of ways issues of construct validity and reliability. Construct validity in essence is concerned with establishing that the correct measures are used, which in qualitative research as Yin (1993) and Kirk and Miller (1986) suggest, can be increased when using multiple sources of data. Indeed in our research, we used multiple sources of data including tape recorded interviews, documents, reports, newspaper articles, and many others (see above). The resulting data was found to converge in various ways. Any inconsistencies were handled in two ways. First, interviews were transcribed and sent to interviewees for verification of correctness. Any issues that were unclear in the interviews were subsequently raised with interviewees in either follow-up interviews or brief telephone discussions with participants. Second, inconsistencies in data about an issue were either addressed in further interviews and/or resolved through scanning the extensive documentation that had been collected by then. For example, on one occasion an interviewee could not remember precisely the transitional stages that their supplier had proposed in their deal for the first six months and in another a participant could not recall the exact monthly base cost, both of which could be determined typically in the documentation collected.

The issue of reliability, as Kirk and Miller (1986) and Yin (1993) explain, is concerned in essence with the consistency of the data. In other words, if the case research were to be repeated, would the researchers arrive at the same results? This tends to be

---

[1] Quoted in Kirsch (1997).

a particularly complex issue to address in qualitative, i.e. interview-based research. However, one of the primary approaches to ensure reliability in some way is to build and provide access to a case study database. This database records and provides access to the data and the material that informed the observations and interpretations of the authors. In addition, a number of other techniques were pursed to increase reliability. First, all interviews were tape recorded and transcribed, which yielded approximately 2,500 pages of single-lined interview data. Second, all interviews were verified for correctness (as noted above), but also for content with each of the interviewees. Third, all sources of the data collected throughout the case study were dated, sorted, and catalogued into a database. Fourthly, existing published case material outlining the early development of the outsourcing arrangements were used to corroborate the data we had gathered. Finally, the write-up of the case study went through numerous iterations and an early version of each case was shown to responsible stakeholders in each case who provided additional clarifying and insightful feedback.

Data Analysis and Case Development

In line with Glaser and Strauss's (1967) and Parkhe's (1993) suggestion, our analysis to elicit key data that explained the case companies' relationship development went through numerous iterations of various data sources, i.e. interviews, reports, and articles which we had accumulated over the years, to then formulate a coherent and consistent story. With each iteration cycle—following the 'hermeneutic circle' principle to case study development (see Klein and Myers 1999)—the story line began to take shape. In addition, we also began to move back and forth between the data and the theoretical constructs of the model, eliciting corroborative data of our framework's main dimensions and elements. The initial draft of the narrative was of course very descriptive in nature, but it provided a mechanism for sorting and categorizing the large volumes of data we had and further enabled us to move towards a more in-depth analysis through subsequent iterations. The initial draft also gave us an opportunity to discuss the version with the managers in the case companies, who often very kindly clarified a number of aspects. This was an important verification of the findings concerning the story line. It was also an essential step of what Yin (1989: 84) suggests as developing a clear 'chain of evidence', which in addition to our case-study database would allow others to 'follow the derivation of any evidence from initial research questions to ultimate case study conclusions'.

To clarify, the iteration process for developing the case studies was essentially split into two parts. First, the analysis followed the approach advocated by Klein and Myers (1999), Newman and Sabherwal (1990), and Parkhe (1993) of moving back and forth between the data from the interviews, reports, and documents, and the case story line identifying corroborative data for the overall relational development. The objective here was to 'arrive at conclusions that found clear support both in the big picture represented by the case description and in the detailed transcripts' (Newman and Sabherwal 1990: 33). Second, the analysis (undertaken in parallel to the first) entailed using open coding labels to identify conceptual labels which in most cases were driven by the conceptual framework, whereas others were suggested by the data. Open coding in essence is a process of analysing the data to place conceptual labels on them (Strauss and Corbin 1990), which according to Kirsch (1997) involves further procedures for then making comparisons and asking specific questions about the phenomenon being investigated.

Most of the conceptual labels were derived from the framework and helped to manage the large amount of interview data gathered. The end result of the coding was the assignment of a conceptual label to each quote in the interviews that corroborated the framework. Together these two data analysis approaches allowed us to sift through the large amounts of case data collected and stored in our case database.

Finally, the end results were the extremely rich and eye-opening case studies as presented in the book on relationship development in outsourcing.

REFERENCES

Benbasat, I., Goldstein, D., and Mead, R. (1987). 'The Case Research Strategy in Studies of Information Systems'. *MIS Quarterly*, 11/3: 369–86.

Davis, K. J. (1996). 'IT Outsourcing Relationships: An Exploratory Study of Inter-organizational Control Mechanisms'. Unpublished DBA Thesis, Graduate School of Business Administration, Harvard University, Boston, 310.

Glaser, B., and Strauss, A. (1967). *The Discovery of Grounded Theory: Strategies of Qualitative Research*. Weidenfeld & Nicolson, London.

Kirk, J., and Miller, M. (1986). *Reliability and Validity in Qualitative Research*. Sage, Beverly Hills, Calif.

Kirsch, L. J. (1997). 'Portfolios of Control Modes and IS Project Management'. *Information Systems Research*, 8/3: 215–39.

Klein, H. K., and Myers, M. (1999). 'A Set of Principles for Conducting and Evaluating Interpretive Field Studies in Information Systems'. *MIS Quarterly*, 23/1: 67–94.

Lee, A. S. (1991). 'Integrating Positivist and Interpretive Approaches to Organizational Research'. *Organization Science*, 2/4: 342–65.

Newman, M., and Sabherwal, R. (1990). 'Determinants of Commitment to Information Systems Development: A Longitudinal Investigation'. *MIS Quarterly*, 20/1: 23–54.

Parkhe, A. (1993). ' "Messy" Research, Methodological Predispositions, and Theory Development in International Joint Ventures'. *Academy of Management*, 18/2: 227–68.

Pettigrew, A. M. (1990). 'Longitudinal Field Research on Change: Theory and Practice'. *Organization Science*, 1/3: 267–92.

Schein, E. H. (1987). *Organizational Culture and Leadership*. Jossey-Bass Publishers, San Francisco.

Smith, N. C. (1990). 'The Case Study: A Useful Research Method for Information Management'. *Journal of Information Technology*, 5/3: 123–33.

Stake, R. E. (1994). 'Case Studies', in N. K. Denzin and Y. S. Lincoln (eds.), *Handbook of Qualitative Research*. Sage Publications, Thousand Oaks, Calif., 236–47.

Strauss, A., and Corbin, J. (1990). *Basics of Qualitative Research: Grounded Theory Procedures and Techniques*. Sage Publications, Newbury Park, Calif.

Walsham, G. (1993). *Interpreting Information Systems in Organizations*. John Wiley & Sons Ltd., Chichester.

Walsham, G. (1995). 'The Emergence of Interpretivism in IS Research'. *Information Systems Research*, 6/4: 376–94.

Yin, R. K. (1989). *Case Study Research: Design and Methods*. 2nd edition, Sage Publications, Newbury Park, Calif.

—— (1993). *Applications of Case Study Research*. Sage Publications, Newbury Park, Calif.

Appendix 2

The Research Process: Founding the Analytical Frameworks

The research to develop the analytical frameworks has been much more extensive than the case studies and Chapter 2 actually suggest. A more accurate overview is provided in Table A2.1. The first stage of our research included a survey and in-depth interviews, which focused primarily on generating a larger picture of outsourcing and the relationship issue. This was purposely undertaken in parallel as few research studies on the relationship dimension in outsourcing were available at the outset of this research project in late 1995. This lack implied that no adequate relationship framework was available for investigating outsourcing relationships holistically, nor was sufficient research available to use as the basis for a framework. Essentially, this early phase comprised an iteration between the empirical research, a review of relevant relationship studies, and theory research. In particular, the preliminary research informed the framework development by helping to determine the core notions that undergird outsourcing, which subsequently prescribed the theoretical foundation of the framework. Secondly, the findings then interactively informed the choice of the dimensions and elements in the conceptual framework. This proved fundamental for bridging the gap between theory and practical reality. Finally, on a different matter, the research strategy also proved invaluable in identifying potential candidates for the in-depth interviews and the case studies (see Appendix 1).

The second stage contextualized the outsourcing relationship in five paradigmatic case studies, thus presenting a setting in which the conceptual framework could be used as a heuristic tool. The individual dimensions of the framework provided a lens through which the multiple perspectives[1] of the interviewees could then be deconstructed to generate an understanding of general relationship practice in the case. A number of interesting findings across the cases emerged, which the cross-case analysis in Chapter 8 addressed in detail. The key question that remains is whether the framework proved consistent in the data it elicited across the cases to allow us to suggest whether the framework is sufficiently comprehensive to characterize and analyse the outsourcing relationship. An underlying objective inherent to the former question is to determine what relationship management commonly entails in outsourcing. This is the theme in our analysis sections in Chapters 3–7 and of Chapter 8 and 9.

---

[1] For this we adapted the underlying notions of Linstone's (1981) multiple perspective analysis of decision making. He propounded that one can expect multiple perspectives on an issue to overlap in certain areas, and it is those areas of commonality that provide the shared understanding and resulting shared commitment to making a decision.

Table A2.1. *Overview table of empirical research*

Research	STAGE ONE—PRELIMINARY RESEARCH		STAGE TWO—MAIN RESEARCH
	Survey	**In-depth interviews**	**Case studies**
Main findings	• Degree of outsourcing • Length • Reasons • Outsourcing strategy • Objectives achieved • Quantifiable benefits • Outsourcing evaluation • Vendor evaluation • Vendor selection • Business environment evaluation • Risk evaluation • Trust • Security & confidentiality	• Contract • Performance monitoring • Costs • Management structure • Expectations • Cultural influences • Conflicts • Trust • Control	Relationships developed between: • Xerox & EDS • BAe & CSC • BPX & SAIC, Sema, Syncordia • ESSO & ITNet • IR & EDS
Outsourcing stages	Prior to outsourcing, vendor selection, and outcomes	Contract & post-contract management	Evolutionary development over a number of years (all stages)
Focus	Broad overview of UK outsourcing practice	Relationship practice in client-vendor firms	Specific case contexts
Framework development	• Underlying theoretical concepts—financial, legal, & relational (i.e. organizational & behavioural) • Informed choice of transaction cost theory, contract theory, and interorganizational relationship theory	• Interactive development of dimensions and elements in theory and practice • Conceptual framework formulated	• Use of the framework to investigate relationships • In parallel validation of its dimensions, elements, and potential as a heuristic tool

386   *Appendix 2*

REFERENCE

Linstone, H. A. (1981). 'The Multiple Perspective Concept: With Application to Technology Assessment and Other Decision Areas'. *Technological Forecasting and Social Change*, 20: 275–325.

Index